First World War
and Army of Occupation
War Diary
France, Belgium and Germany

23 DIVISION
Divisional Troops
104 and 105 Brigade Royal Field Artillery,
Divisional Trench Mortar Batteries
and Divisional Ammunition Column
24 September 1914 - 31 October 1917

WO95/2176

The Naval & Military Press Ltd
www.nmarchive.com
Published in association with The National Archives

Published by

The Naval & Military Press Ltd

Unit 10 Ridgewood Industrial Park,
Uckfield, East Sussex,
TN22 5QE England
Tel: +44 (0) 1825 749494

www.naval-military-press.com
www.nmarchive.com

This diary has been reprinted in facsimile from the original. Any imperfections are inevitably reproduced and the quality may fall short of modern type and cartographic standards.

Contents

Document type	Place/Title	Date From	Date To
Heading	WO95/2176/1		
Heading	23rd Division Divl Artillery 104th Brigade R.F.A. Aug 1915-Dec 1916 To 4 Army		
War Diary		15/02/1916	01/03/1916
Heading	23rd Division 104th Brigade RFA Vol. I Aug No. 1 15 To Dec 16		
War Diary	Bordon	20/08/1915	31/08/1915
Heading	23rd Division 104th Bde. R.f.a Vol 2 Sept 15		
War Diary	Tournehem	01/09/1915	05/09/1915
War Diary	Bandringhem	06/09/1915	06/09/1915
War Diary	Strazeele	07/09/1915	08/09/1915
War Diary	Armentieres	09/09/1915	30/09/1915
Heading	23rd Division 104th Bde. R.f.a. Vol.3 121/7767 Oct & Nov 15		
War Diary	Armentieres	10/10/1915	30/11/1915
Heading	23rd Division 104th Bde R.f.a. Vol.4 121/7911		
War Diary	Armentieres	02/12/1915	31/12/1915
Heading	B&/104 Battery Vol I		
Heading	104 Bde. R.F.A. 23rd Div. Vol.5 In Fus.		
War Diary		01/01/1916	30/04/1916
Heading	H.Q 104 Bde R.F.A.		
War Diary		01/05/1916	11/05/1916
War Diary		04/05/1916	27/05/1916
War Diary	Barlin	14/06/1916	24/06/1916
War Diary		20/06/1916	30/06/1916
Heading	104 R.F.A. Vol 6		
Heading	War Diary 23rd Divisional Artillery. 104th Brigade R.F.A. July 1916		
War Diary		01/07/1916	31/07/1916
Heading	23rd Divisional Artillery.104th Brigade Royal Field Artillery August 1916		
War Diary		01/08/1916	24/08/1916
War Diary		24/08/1916	31/08/1916
War Diary	Ploegsteert	01/09/1916	09/09/1916
War Diary	Meteren	09/09/1916	12/09/1916
War Diary	St Gratien	13/09/1916	19/09/1916
War Diary	Somme Area	20/09/1916	29/09/1916
War Diary	Contalmaison	29/09/1916	16/10/1916
War Diary	High Wood	17/10/1916	31/10/1916
War Diary	St Gratien	01/11/1916	15/11/1916
War Diary	Martinpuich	16/11/1916	17/12/1916
War Diary	Steenvoorde	18/12/1916	31/12/1916
Heading	WO95/2176/2		
Heading	23rd Division Divl Artillery 105th Brigade R.F.A. Aug 1915-sep 1916. Broken Up		
Heading	23rd Division 105th Bde. R.F.A. Vol I August 15 To Sep 16		
War Diary	Bordon	20/08/1915	25/08/1915
War Diary	Havre	26/08/1915	27/08/1915
War Diary	Bonningues Les Ardres	28/08/1915	31/08/1915

Heading	23rd Division 105th Bde. R.f.a. Vol 2 Sep 1 & Oct 15		
War Diary	Bonningues-lez-Ardres	01/09/1915	06/09/1915
War Diary	Bandringhem	07/09/1915	07/09/1915
War Diary	Borre	08/09/1915	08/09/1915
War Diary	Chapelle Armentieres	09/09/1915	25/09/1915
War Diary	La Vesee	26/09/1915	26/09/1915
War Diary	Armentieres	27/09/1915	12/10/1915
Heading	23rd Division 105th Bde. R.f.a. Vol 3 121/7693 Nov.15		
War Diary	Armentieres	13/10/1915	31/10/1915
War Diary		07/10/1915	05/11/1915
War Diary	Armentieres	08/11/1915	30/11/1915
Heading	23rd Div 105th Bde. R.f.a. Vol 4 121/7910		
War Diary	Armentieres	01/12/1915	01/01/1916
Heading	105th Bde. R.F.A. Vol.5 Jan 16		
War Diary	Armentieres	02/01/1916	02/01/1916
War Diary		01/01/1916	09/01/1916
War Diary	Armentieres	09/01/1916	31/01/1916
Heading	105 Bde R.F.A. Vol.6. 23rd Div.		
War Diary	Armentieres	01/02/1916	19/02/1916
War Diary	Blaringhem	20/02/1916	29/02/1916
Heading	105 R.F.A. Vol.7		
War Diary	Bailleul Les. Pernes.	01/03/1916	07/03/1916
War Diary	Carency Sector	08/03/1916	10/03/1916
War Diary	Carency	11/03/1916	21/03/1916
War Diary	Calonne Ricouart	21/03/1916	24/03/1916
War Diary	Hersin	25/03/1916	19/04/1916
War Diary	Divion	20/04/1916	14/05/1916
War Diary	Barlin	15/05/1916	14/06/1916
War Diary	Barlin & Divion	15/06/1916	15/06/1916
War Diary	Divion	16/06/1916	16/06/1916
War Diary	Mametz	17/06/1916	25/06/1916
War Diary	La. Lachaussee	27/06/1916	27/06/1916
War Diary	Cardonnette	30/06/1916	30/06/1916
Heading	War Diary 23rd Divisional Artillery. 105th Brigade R.F.A. July 1916		
War Diary	Cardonnette	01/07/1916	01/07/1916
War Diary	St. Gratien	02/07/1916	05/07/1916
War Diary	Fricourt	06/07/1916	31/07/1916
Heading	23rd Divisional Artillery 105th Brigade Royal Field Artillery August 1916		
Miscellaneous	HQRA Herewith War Diary of 105th Bde Rfa for August 1916	01/09/1916	01/09/1916
War Diary	Bottom Wood X.29.a (Sheet-57-d)	01/08/1916	14/08/1916
War Diary	Querrieux	15/08/1916	17/08/1916
War Diary	Eecke	18/08/1916	19/08/1916
War Diary	B.II.d.3.7. (Sheet.36.)	20/08/1916	31/08/1916
Heading	Officer i/c A.G's Office At The Base.	12/11/1916	12/11/1916
War Diary	B.II.d.3.7 Sheet 36 Ploegsteert	01/09/1916	03/09/1916
War Diary	Ploegsteert	01/09/1916	03/09/1916
Heading	WO95/2176/3		
Heading	23rd Division Divl Artillery 23rd Divl Trench Mortars Oct 1915-1917 Oct To Italy		
Heading	G.H.Q. 21 Trench Hour Batty Oct 15 To Jan 19 Vol IV		
War Diary	Line in front of Armentieres	01/10/1915	31/10/1915
Heading	G.H.Q. 21 Trenches Mortar Battery Nov Vol V 121/7779		

War Diary	Line in front of Armentieres	01/11/1915	30/11/1915
Heading	G.H.Q. 21 Trench Mortar Batty Dec Vol. VI 121/7957		
War Diary	Line in front of Armentieres	01/12/1915	31/01/1916
Heading	23 21 Trench In Bty. Vol VIII		
War Diary	Line in front of Armentieres	01/02/1916	29/02/1916
Heading	Y23 TM Bty. late 21 Vol IX		
War Diary		01/03/1916	11/03/1916
War Diary	Line in Front of Souchey	12/03/1916	19/03/1916
War Diary	Angres Sector	20/03/1916	31/03/1916
Heading	Y23 TM Bty late 21 Bty Vol 10		
War Diary	Angres Sector	01/04/1916	22/04/1916
War Diary	Fosse de La Clarence	23/04/1916	13/05/1916
War Diary	Angres Sector	14/05/1916	15/06/1916
War Diary	Auchon Villers Sector	16/06/1916	25/06/1916
War Diary	Auchon Villers	26/06/1916	18/07/1916
War Diary	Albert	19/07/1916	31/07/1916
Miscellaneous	The Organisation Of The 23rd Divisional Medium Trench Mortar Batteries Will In Future Be As Follows. Tactically.		
Miscellaneous	Administrative.	08/06/1916	08/06/1916
Miscellaneous			
Heading	23rd Divisional Artillery. "Y"/23rd Trench Mortar Battery August 1916		
War Diary	Line in Front of Contalmaison	01/08/1916	25/08/1916
War Diary	Line in Front of Ploegsteert	26/08/1916	31/08/1916
Miscellaneous	23rd Division No. A/802/18	01/08/1916	01/08/1916
Miscellaneous	Head-quarters, Twenty-third Division.	28/07/1917	28/07/1917
War Diary	Line in Front of Ploegsteert.	01/09/1916	23/09/1916
War Diary		24/09/1914	30/09/1914
War Diary		01/10/1916	29/10/1916
War Diary	Ypres Line In Front Of Sanctuary Wood	30/10/1916	09/11/1916
War Diary	Ypres	10/11/1916	30/01/1917
War Diary		01/01/1917	30/01/1917
War Diary	Ypres Salient	11/02/1917	26/02/1917
War Diary		25/02/1917	27/02/1917
War Diary	Ypres Salient (Zillebeke Sector)	00/02/1917	00/02/1917
War Diary	Rumminghem	01/03/1917	10/03/1917
War Diary	Rumminghem	05/03/1917	05/03/1917
War Diary	Franch	06/03/1917	06/03/1917
War Diary	Rumminghem	11/03/1917	19/03/1917
War Diary	Herzeele	20/03/1917	31/03/1917
Heading	Re War Diary Of Y23 Inf Bty. For Nov 1916		
Miscellaneous	R.A. 23rd Division No. SL 37/2	11/07/1917	11/07/1917
Miscellaneous	23rd Division No. A/802/18. R.A. 23rd Division.	10/07/1917	10/07/1917
Miscellaneous	R.A. 23rd Division No. S.L. 37/2	05/07/1917	05/07/1917
Miscellaneous	Headquarters, 23rd. Division.	23/06/1917	23/06/1917
Miscellaneous	23rd Division No. A./802/18	20/06/1917	20/06/1917
Miscellaneous	Headquarters, 23 Division.	15/06/1917	15/06/1917
War Diary		01/04/1917	31/05/1917
War Diary	Eperlecques	01/03/1917	31/03/1917
Heading		28/03/1917	28/03/1917
Heading	War Diary 23rd Divisional Trench Mortars June 7th June 30 1917		
Heading	CPL Pope M.M 54920 RFA		
War Diary	Halifax Camp 28.g.13.d.	07/07/1917	13/07/1917
War Diary	28.g.31.c.	14/07/1917	23/07/1917

War Diary	Rest Billets Near Boeschepe	21/07/1917	30/07/1917
Miscellaneous	Head-quarters 23rd. Divisional (A)	11/07/1917	11/07/1917
War Diary	Rest Billets Near Boeschepe	01/07/1917	04/07/1917
War Diary	Ref. map 1/40,000 Belgium & France Sheet 28 Hallebast Corner 28 N.2.b.48	04/07/1917	08/07/1917
War Diary	Hallebast Corner	09/07/1917	14/07/1917
War Diary	Ref. Map 1/10,000 Zillebeke	14/07/1917	15/07/1917
War Diary	Hallebast Corner	16/07/1917	31/07/1917
Miscellaneous	Operation Orders. By. Capt. V.E. Cotton. R.F.A. D.T.M.O. 23rd Divn. Appendix A.	03/07/1917	03/07/1917
Operation(al) Order(s)	Operation Order No. 2 By Appendix B	15/07/1917	15/07/1917
Operation(al) Order(s)	Operation Orders No. 3 By Capt V.E. Cotton D.T.M.O 23rd Divn. Appendix. C	16/07/1917	16/07/1917
Operation(al) Order(s)	Operation Order No 4 By Capt V.E. Cotton D.T.M.O. 23 Divn. Appendix D	17/07/1917	17/07/1917
Operation(al) Order(s)	Operation Order No. 5 By Capt V.E. Cotton D.T.M.O. 23rd Divn Appendix E	18/07/1917	18/07/1917
Operation(al) Order(s)	Operation Order No. 6 By D.T.M.O. 23rd Divn. Appendix. F	30/07/1917	30/07/1917
War Diary		01/08/1917	31/08/1917
War Diary	Sheet 28 Belgium & France 1/40,000 N2.g.4.8 Hallebast Corner	01/08/1917	15/08/1917
War Diary	Sheet 27 1/40,000 F 24 a.5.5	16/08/1917	31/08/1917
War Diary	Sheet 27 F.24.a.5.5	01/09/1917	06/09/1917
War Diary	Sheet 28 H.34.a.	08/09/1917	25/10/1917
War Diary	Westoutre	26/10/1917	31/10/1917
Heading	WO95/2176/4		
Heading	23rd Division Divl Artillery 23rd Divl Ammn Column Aug 1915-1917 Oct To Italy		
Heading	23rd Division 23rd Divl. A.C. Vol. 1 Aug & Sept. 15		
War Diary	Bordon	20/08/1915	27/08/1915
War Diary	Southampton	27/08/1915	27/08/1915
War Diary	Havre (Fine)	28/08/1915	28/08/1915
War Diary	Andruicq (Showery)	30/08/1917	30/08/1917
War Diary	In Train (Fine)	29/08/1915	29/08/1915
War Diary	Zouafques (Wet)	31/08/1915	31/08/1915
War Diary	Zouafques (Cloudy)	01/09/1915	01/09/1915
War Diary	Zouafques (Dull)	02/09/1915	02/09/1915
War Diary	Zouafques (Rain)	03/09/1915	03/09/1915
War Diary	Zouafques (Still Wet)	04/09/1915	04/09/1915
War Diary	Zouafques (Dull)	05/09/1915	05/09/1915
War Diary	Renescure (Fine)	07/09/1915	07/09/1915
War Diary	Le Tir Anglais (Fine)	08/09/1915	14/09/1915
War Diary	Froid Nid (Fine)	15/09/1915	22/09/1915
War Diary	Froid Nid (Fine during Day Thundershim)	23/09/1915	23/09/1915
War Diary	Froid Nid (Damp Dull Dark Night)	24/09/1915	25/09/1915
War Diary	Froid Nid (Wet Dark Night)	26/09/1915	26/09/1915
War Diary	Froid Nid (Dull All Day)	26/09/1915	27/09/1915
War Diary	Froid Nid (Dull With slight Showers during evening)	27/09/1915	27/09/1915
War Diary	Froid Nid (Dull & Heavy)	28/09/1915	28/09/1915
War Diary	Froid Nid (Wet)	29/09/1915	29/09/1915
War Diary	Froid Nid (Wet All Day)	30/09/1915	30/09/1915
Heading	23rd Division 23rd Divl A.C. Vol.2 Oct 15		
War Diary	Froid Nid (Dry but very Cold)	01/10/1915	01/10/1915
War Diary	Froid Nid (Fine)	02/10/1915	03/10/1915
War Diary	Froid Nid (Dull With Showers)	04/10/1915	04/10/1915

War Diary	Froid Nid (Rain)	05/10/1915	05/10/1915
War Diary	Froid Nid (Morning Dry but Cloudy)	06/10/1915	06/10/1915
War Diary	Froid Nid (Fine)	07/10/1915	10/10/1915
War Diary	Froid Nid (Dull)	11/10/1915	11/10/1915
War Diary	Froid Nid (Fine)	12/10/1915	20/10/1915
War Diary	Froid Nid (Fine Cloudy)	21/10/1916	21/10/1916
War Diary	Froid Nid (Dull)	22/10/1915	22/10/1915
War Diary	Froid Nid (Dull Cold)	22/10/1915	23/10/1915
War Diary	Froid Nid (Fine but ?Misty)	23/10/1915	23/10/1915
War Diary	Froid Nid (Cold having to rain)	24/10/1915	24/10/1915
War Diary	Froid Nid (Very wet all day & night)	25/10/1915	25/10/1915
War Diary	Froid Nid (Bright day)	26/10/1915	26/10/1915
War Diary	Froid Nid (Wet)	27/10/1915	27/10/1915
War Diary	Froid Nid (Rain all day)	28/10/1915	28/10/1915
War Diary	Froid Nid (Dull)	29/10/1915	30/10/1915
War Diary	Froid Nid (Rain)	31/10/1915	31/10/1915
Miscellaneous			
Heading	23rd Division 23rd Divl. A.C. Vol.3 121/7656 Nov 15		
War Diary	Froid Nid (Rain All Day)	01/11/1915	01/11/1915
War Diary	Froid Nid (Dull)	02/11/1915	02/11/1915
War Diary	Froid Nid (Wet)	03/11/1915	03/11/1915
War Diary	Froid Nid (Fine)	04/11/1915	07/11/1915
War Diary	Froid Nid (Dull)	08/11/1915	08/11/1915
War Diary	Froid Nid (Damp)	09/11/1915	09/11/1915
War Diary	Froid Nid (Wet)	10/11/1915	10/11/1915
War Diary	Froid Nid (Showery)	11/11/1915	11/11/1915
War Diary	Froid Nid (Wet)	12/11/1915	12/11/1915
War Diary	Froid Nid (Dump)	13/11/1915	13/11/1915
War Diary	Froid Nid (Cold)	14/11/1915	14/11/1915
War Diary	Froid Nid (Wet)	15/11/1915	15/11/1915
War Diary	Froid Nid (Dull)	16/11/1915	16/11/1915
War Diary	Froid Nid (Fine)	17/11/1915	17/11/1915
War Diary	Froid Nid (Wet)	18/10/1915	18/10/1915
War Diary	Froid Nid (Fine)	19/11/1915	19/11/1915
War Diary	Froid Nid (Dull)	20/11/1915	20/11/1915
War Diary	Froid Nid (Cold)	21/11/1915	21/11/1915
War Diary	Froid Nid (Frost)	22/11/1915	22/11/1915
War Diary	Froid Nid (Wet)	23/11/1915	23/11/1915
War Diary	Froid Nid (Cold & Dull)	24/11/1915	24/11/1915
War Diary	Froid Nid (Wet)	25/11/1915	25/11/1915
War Diary	Froid Nid (Dull)	26/11/1915	26/11/1915
War Diary	Froid Nid (Frost)	27/11/1915	28/11/1915
War Diary	Froid Nid (Wet)	29/11/1915	29/11/1915
War Diary	Froid Nid (Mild During & Rain)	30/11/1915	30/11/1915
Heading	23rd D.A.C. Vol.4 121/7911		
Miscellaneous			
War Diary	Froid Nid (Fine)	01/12/1915	01/12/1915
War Diary	Froid Nid (Wet)	02/12/1915	04/12/1915
War Diary	Froid Nid (Fine Day Wet In Eve.)	05/12/1915	05/12/1915
War Diary	Froid Nid (Dull & Wet)	06/12/1915	06/12/1915
War Diary	Froid Nid (Bright Hangry to Wet.)	07/12/1915	07/12/1915
War Diary	Froid Nid (Bright And Windy)	08/12/1915	08/12/1915
War Diary	Froid Nid (Wet & Very Cold)	09/12/1915	09/12/1915
War Diary	Froid Nid (Wet)	10/12/1915	10/12/1915
War Diary	Froid Nid (Very Wet)	11/12/1915	11/12/1915
War Diary	Froid Nid (Dull, Wet & Cold)	12/12/1915	12/12/1915

War Diary	Froid Nid (Bright, Cold)	13/12/1915	13/12/1915
War Diary	Froid Nid (Fair)	14/12/1915	14/12/1915
War Diary	Froid Nid (Dull Raw Day)	15/12/1915	15/12/1915
War Diary	Froid Nid (Dull & Cold)	16/12/1915	16/12/1915
War Diary	Froid Nid (Fine Cold)	17/12/1915	17/12/1915
War Diary	Froid Nid (Dull)	18/12/1915	18/12/1915
War Diary	Froid Nid (V. Wet)	19/12/1915	19/12/1915
War Diary	Froid Nid (Dull Heavy)	20/12/1915	20/12/1915
War Diary	Froid Nid (Rain)	21/12/1915	21/12/1915
War Diary	Froid Nid (Brighter)	22/12/1915	22/12/1915
War Diary	Froid Nid (V. Wet)	23/12/1915	23/12/1915
War Diary	Froid Nid (Wet-dull)	24/12/1915	24/12/1915
War Diary	Froid Nid (Showery)	25/12/1915	25/12/1915
War Diary	Froid Nid (Bright Day)	26/12/1915	26/12/1915
War Diary	Froid Nid (V. Windy With Showers)	27/12/1915	27/12/1915
War Diary	Froid Nid (Fair)	28/12/1915	28/12/1915
War Diary	Froid Nid (Fine)	29/12/1915	29/12/1915
War Diary	Froid Nid (Dull)	30/12/1915	30/12/1915
War Diary	Froid Nid (Wet)	31/12/1915	31/12/1915
Heading	23rd Div A Column Vol. V		
War Diary	Froid Nid (Fair)	01/01/1916	01/01/1916
War Diary	Froid Nid (Damp)	02/01/1916	02/01/1916
War Diary	Froid Nid (Dry Cold)	03/01/1916	03/01/1916
War Diary	Froid Nid (Fine)	04/01/1916	04/01/1916
War Diary	Froid Nid (Cold)	05/01/1916	05/01/1916
War Diary	Froid Nid (Sunny)	06/01/1916	06/01/1916
War Diary	Froid Nid (Fine)	07/01/1916	07/01/1916
War Diary	Froid Nid (Showery)	08/01/1916	08/01/1916
War Diary	Froid Nid (Wet)	09/01/1916	10/01/1916
War Diary	Froid Nid (Damp)	11/01/1916	11/01/1916
War Diary	Froid Nid (Dry Cold)	12/01/1916	12/01/1916
War Diary	Froid Nid (Cold, Bright)	13/01/1915	13/01/1915
War Diary	Froid Nid (Cold)	14/01/1916	14/01/1916
War Diary	Froid Nid (Dull & Damp)	15/01/1916	15/01/1916
War Diary	Froid Nid (Fine)	16/01/1916	16/01/1916
War Diary	Froid Nid (Dull & Damp)	17/01/1916	17/01/1916
War Diary	Froid Nid (Dull Wet)	18/01/1916	18/01/1916
War Diary	Froid Nid (Fine, Windy at Night)	19/01/1916	19/01/1916
War Diary	Froid Nid (Fair Showery)	20/01/1916	20/01/1916
War Diary	Froid Nid (Dull Windy)	21/01/1916	21/01/1916
War Diary	Froid Nid (Dull Wet & Windy)	22/01/1916	22/01/1916
War Diary	Froid Nid (Fine)	23/01/1916	23/01/1916
War Diary	Froid Nid (Bright)	24/01/1916	24/01/1916
War Diary	Froid Nid (Bright Cold)	25/01/1916	25/01/1916
War Diary	Froid Nid (Fine)	26/01/1916	26/01/1916
War Diary	Froid Nid (Dull With Rain)	27/01/1916	27/01/1916
War Diary	Froid Nid (Fair)	28/01/1916	28/01/1916
War Diary	Froid Nid (Fine)	29/01/1916	29/01/1916
War Diary	Froid Nid (Dull Heavy Mish)	30/01/1916	30/01/1916
War Diary	Froid Nid (Cold)	31/01/1916	31/01/1916
Heading	On His Majesty's Service War Diary Of 23rd Divl. Ammn. Col. R.f.a. From 1.2.16 To 29.2.16		
Heading	23rd D.A.C. Vol. 6		
War Diary	Froid Nid (Bright)	01/02/1916	01/02/1916
War Diary	Froid Nid (Bright many Cloudy To Rain)	02/02/1916	02/02/1916
War Diary	Froid Nid (Fairly Bright but Cold & Windy)	03/02/1916	03/02/1916

War Diary	Froid Nid (V. Windy Dull To Rain)	04/01/1916	04/01/1916
War Diary	Froid Nid (Bright)	05/01/1916	05/01/1916
War Diary	Froid Nid (Fair Rain)	06/02/1916	06/02/1916
War Diary	Froid Nid	06/02/1916	06/02/1916
War Diary	Froid Nid (Fair To Bright Cold Wind)	07/02/1915	07/02/1915
War Diary	Froid Nid (Dull To Rain)	08/02/1916	08/02/1916
War Diary	Froid Nid (Clear Bright)	09/02/1916	09/02/1916
War Diary	Froid Nid (Fine)	10/02/1916	10/02/1916
War Diary	Froid Nid (Wet All Day)	11/01/1916	11/01/1916
War Diary	Froid Nid (Dull And Cold)	12/01/1916	12/01/1916
War Diary	Froid Nid (Fair)	13/01/1916	13/01/1916
War Diary	Froid Nid (Fair & Bright V. Windy)	14/01/1916	14/01/1916
War Diary	Froid Nid (Dull Rain H Wind All Day)	15/01/1916	15/01/1916
War Diary	Froid Nid Dull (Slight Rain V. Windy)	16/01/1916	16/01/1916
War Diary	Froid Nid (V. Windy)	17/01/1916	17/01/1916
War Diary	Froid Nid (V. Wet. H. Wind)	18/02/1916	18/02/1916
War Diary	Froid Nid	18/02/1916	18/02/1916
War Diary	Froid Nid (C. Wind Fair)	19/02/1916	19/02/1916
War Diary	Shawl Berquin (Bright Frost)	20/02/1916	20/02/1916
War Diary	Neuf Berquin Dull & Cold Neuf Berquin	21/02/1916	21/02/1916
War Diary	Neuf Berquin (V. Cold Snow All Day)	22/02/1916	22/02/1916
War Diary	Neuf Berquin (Snow All Day)	23/02/1916	23/02/1916
War Diary	Neuf Berquin (Bright)	24/02/1916	24/02/1916
War Diary	Neuf Berquin (Snow Dull)	25/02/1916	25/02/1916
War Diary	Neuf Berquin (Dull Moon-bright) Than Set in	26/02/1916	26/02/1916
War Diary	Neuf Berquin (Damp Rain Mishy Day)	27/02/1916	27/02/1916
War Diary	Neuf Berquin (Very Damp Mishy)	28/02/1916	28/02/1916
War Diary	Neuf Berquin Bright-dull-With Rain In Afternoon Dull Rain Night Sanchy.	29/02/1916	29/02/1916
Heading	War Diary Of 23rd Divisional Ammn Column From 1.3-16. To 31-3-16 Volume 1		
Heading	23 Div A Col Vol 7		
War Diary	Sachin (Fine)	01/03/1916	02/03/1916
War Diary	Sachin (Dull-Snow)	03/03/1916	03/03/1916
War Diary	Sachin (Snow All Day)	04/03/1916	04/03/1916
War Diary	Sachin (Snow)	04/03/1916	05/03/1916
War Diary	Sachin (Fair)	05/03/1916	05/03/1916
War Diary	Sachin (Snow-All Day)	06/03/1916	07/03/1916
War Diary	Sachin (Fair)	08/03/1916	08/03/1916
War Diary	Caucourt	08/03/1916	08/03/1916
War Diary	Caucourt (Fair-Cloudy-Snow)	09/03/1916	09/03/1916
War Diary	Caucourt (Dull-Cold)	10/03/1916	10/03/1916
War Diary	Caucourt (Dull-Row)	11/03/1916	11/03/1916
War Diary	Caucourt (Fine Fairly Clear)	12/03/1916	13/03/1916
War Diary	Caucourt (Bright Clear)	13/03/1916	14/03/1916
War Diary	Caucourt (Dull-Fine)	15/03/1916	15/03/1916
War Diary	Caucourt (Dull)	16/03/1916	16/03/1916
War Diary	Caucourt (Fair)	17/03/1916	17/03/1916
War Diary	Caucourt (Dull-Bright)	18/03/1916	18/03/1916
War Diary	Caucourt (Fine)	19/03/1916	19/03/1916
War Diary	Caucourt (Fine-Cloudy)	20/03/1916	20/03/1916
War Diary	Bruay (Fine-Cloudy)	20/03/1916	20/03/1916
War Diary	Bruay (Dull Damp)	21/03/1916	21/03/1916
War Diary	Bruay (Wet)	22/03/1916	22/03/1916
War Diary	Bruay (Dull Saw)	23/03/1916	23/03/1916
War Diary	Bruay (Snow All Day)	24/03/1916	24/03/1916

War Diary	Barlin (Fairly Bright Afternoon)	24/03/1916	24/03/1916
War Diary	Barlin (Dull Wet)	25/03/1916	25/03/1916
War Diary	Barlin (Wet Morning Brighter Aftenoon)	26/03/1916	26/03/1916
War Diary	Barlin (Dull Wet)	27/03/1916	27/03/1916
War Diary	Barlin	27/03/1916	27/03/1916
War Diary	Barlin (Fine)	28/03/1916	29/03/1916
War Diary	Barlin (Bright)	30/03/1916	30/03/1916
War Diary	Barlin (Fair)	31/03/1916	31/03/1916
War Diary	Barlin (Bright)	01/04/1916	01/04/1916
War Diary	Barlin (Fine)	02/04/1916	02/04/1916
War Diary	Barlin (Sunny)	03/04/1916	03/04/1916
War Diary	Barlin (Fine)	04/04/1916	04/04/1916
War Diary	Barlin (Cold)	05/04/1916	05/04/1916
War Diary	Barlin (Dull-Rain Night)	06/04/1916	06/04/1916
War Diary	Barlin (Dull-Cold)	07/04/1916	07/04/1916
War Diary	Barlin (Bright)	08/04/1916	08/04/1916
War Diary	Barlin (Fine)	09/04/1916	09/04/1916
War Diary	Barlin (Dull-cold)	10/04/1916	10/04/1916
War Diary	Barlin (Wet)	11/04/1916	11/04/1916
War Diary	Barlin (Dull, Cold, Wet Windy)	12/04/1916	12/04/1916
War Diary	Barlin (Bright Showery)	13/04/1916	13/04/1916
War Diary	Barlin (Windy Snowing)	14/04/1916	14/04/1916
War Diary	Barlin (Bright Windy Snowing)	15/04/1916	15/04/1916
War Diary	Barlin (Fair)	16/04/1916	16/04/1916
War Diary	Barlin (Wet-windy)	17/04/1916	17/04/1916
War Diary	Barlin (wet-cold-windy)	18/04/1916	18/04/1916
War Diary	Barlin (wet, Cold. Windy)	19/04/1916	19/04/1916
War Diary	Barlin (Wet Moon. Fine Day)	20/04/1916	20/04/1916
War Diary	Bruay	20/04/1916	20/04/1916
War Diary	Bruay (Fine-Dull)	21/04/1916	21/04/1916
War Diary	Bruay (Wet)	22/04/1916	22/04/1916
War Diary	Bruay (Bright)	23/04/1916	23/04/1916
War Diary	Bruay (Bright-Dull)	24/04/1916	24/04/1916
War Diary	Bruay (Clear)	25/04/1916	25/04/1916
War Diary	Bruay (Bright)	26/04/1916	28/04/1916
War Diary	Bruay (Fine)	29/04/1916	01/05/1916
War Diary	Bruay. (Fine Cloudy Snowing)	02/05/1916	02/05/1916
War Diary	Bruay (Fine Inf Showing)	03/05/1916	03/05/1916
War Diary	Bruay (Fine)	04/05/1916	04/05/1916
War Diary	Bruay (Dull Sulhy)	05/05/1916	05/05/1916
War Diary	Bruay (Fine-Windy)	06/05/1916	06/05/1916
War Diary	Bruay (Fair)	07/05/1916	07/05/1916
War Diary	Bruay (Dull With Rain)	08/05/1916	08/05/1916
War Diary	Bruay (Rain With Cold Wind)	09/05/1916	09/05/1916
War Diary	Bruay (Cloudy Cold-Bright)	10/04/1916	10/04/1916
War Diary	Bruay (Dull-Cloudy)	11/05/1916	11/05/1916
War Diary	Bruay (Dull)	12/05/1916	12/05/1916
War Diary	Bruay (Dull-Cold)	13/05/1916	13/05/1916
War Diary	Bruay (Dull-Damp)	14/05/1916	14/05/1916
War Diary	Bruay (Wet-Cleared)	15/05/1916	15/05/1916
War Diary	Barlin	15/05/1916	15/05/1916
War Diary	Barlin (Bright)	16/05/1916	16/05/1916
War Diary	Barlin (Fine)	17/05/1916	21/05/1916
War Diary	Barlin (Dull-Rain Cool)	22/05/1916	22/05/1916
War Diary	Barlin (Fine-cloudy)	23/05/1916	23/05/1916
War Diary	Barlin (Dull)	24/05/1916	24/05/1916

War Diary	Barlin (Dull-Snowing)	25/05/1916	25/05/1916
War Diary	Barlin (Fair)	26/05/1916	26/05/1916
War Diary	Barlin (Fine)	27/05/1916	30/05/1916
War Diary	Barlin (Bright)	31/05/1916	31/05/1916
War Diary	Barlin (Fine)	01/06/1916	03/06/1916
War Diary	Barlin (Dull-cold, Windy)	04/06/1916	04/06/1916
War Diary	Barlin (Dull)	05/06/1916	05/06/1916
War Diary	Barlin (Heavy With Showers-Bright)	06/06/1916	06/06/1916
War Diary	Barlin (Dull)	07/06/1916	07/06/1916
War Diary	Barlin (Bright-Dull-Rain)	08/06/1916	08/06/1916
War Diary	Barlin (Dull-Showery)	09/06/1916	09/06/1916
War Diary	Barlin (Dull Thunder Rain)	10/06/1916	10/06/1916
War Diary	Barlin (Dull Thunder Show With Rain)	11/06/1916	11/06/1916
War Diary	Barlin (Dull-cold Wet)	12/06/1916	12/06/1916
War Diary	Barlin (Dull-Cold-wet)	13/06/1916	13/06/1916
War Diary	Barlin (Dull Cold)	14/06/1916	14/06/1916
War Diary	Barlin (Dull Cold)	15/06/1916	15/06/1916
War Diary	Barlin (Fine-cold)	16/06/1916	16/06/1916
War Diary	Tangry	16/06/1916	16/06/1916
War Diary	Tangry (Fair)	17/06/1916	17/06/1916
War Diary	Roquitoire	17/06/1916	17/06/1916
War Diary	Roquitoire (Fine-Cloudy)	18/06/1916	18/06/1916
War Diary	Roquitoire (Dull-Mishy)	19/06/1916	19/06/1916
War Diary	Roquitoire (Rain-Fair)	20/06/1916	20/06/1916
War Diary	Roquitoire (Dull)	21/06/1916	21/06/1916
War Diary	Roquitoire (Sulhy)	22/06/1916	22/06/1916
War Diary	Roquitoire (Sulhy-Thunder-Rain-Fair)	23/06/1916	23/06/1916
War Diary	Roquitoire Sunny With Clouds)	24/06/1916	24/06/1916
War Diary	Roquitoire (Hot Sunny)	25/06/1916	25/06/1916
War Diary	Argoeuves (Showery)	26/06/1916	27/06/1916
War Diary	Argoeuves (Dull)	28/06/1916	28/06/1916
War Diary	Argoeuves (Fair)	29/06/1916	29/06/1916
War Diary	Argoeuves (Sunshine)	30/06/1916	30/06/1916
War Diary	Allonville	30/07/1916	30/07/1916
War Diary	Allonville Fine	01/07/1916	01/07/1916
War Diary	Beaucourt	01/07/1916	01/07/1916
War Diary	Beaucourt Fine	02/07/1916	05/07/1916
War Diary	Albert Dull & Cold	06/07/1916	06/07/1916
War Diary	Dernancourt Dull & Cold.	06/07/1916	06/07/1916
War Diary	Dernancourt Rainy & Dull	07/07/1916	07/07/1916
War Diary	Dernancourt Dry & Cloudy	08/07/1916	09/07/1916
War Diary	Dernancourt Fine One Shower of rain	10/07/1916	10/07/1916
War Diary	Dernancourt Fair	11/07/1916	11/07/1916
War Diary	Dernancourt Cloudy But Dry.	12/07/1916	13/07/1916
War Diary	Dernancourt Fine One Shower in the Morning	14/07/1916	14/07/1916
War Diary	Dernancourt Fine with Clouds.	15/07/1916	15/07/1916
War Diary	Dernancourt. Fine Morn Dull afternoon Wet Evening	16/07/1916	16/07/1916
War Diary	Dernancourt Dull Cloudy Day One Light Showers	17/07/1916	17/07/1916
War Diary	Albert	17/07/1916	17/07/1916
War Diary	Albert. Dull Cold Day Cloud Might	18/07/1916	18/07/1916
War Diary	Albert Bright A Few Clouds	19/07/1916	19/07/1916
War Diary	Albert Bright Day	20/07/1916	20/07/1916
War Diary	Albert Clear-Bright	21/07/1916	21/07/1916
War Diary	Albert Dull Morning Bright Afternoon	22/07/1916	22/07/1916
War Diary	Albert Dull Day	23/07/1916	23/07/1916
War Diary	Albert Bright Day	24/07/1916	29/07/1916

War Diary	Albert Bright Day Hot	30/07/1916	30/07/1916
War Diary	Albert Bright Day Very Hot	31/07/1916	31/07/1916
Heading	23rd Divisional Artillery. 23rd. Divisional Ammunition Column August 1916		
Heading	A 23 Division Herewith War Diary 23 II AC For Month Of August 1916		
War Diary	Albert Bright Day	01/08/1916	02/08/1916
War Diary	Albert Clear Day Hot	03/08/1916	03/08/1916
War Diary	Albert Bright Day	04/08/1916	09/08/1916
War Diary	Albert Dull Day	10/08/1916	10/08/1916
War Diary	Albert Bright Day	11/08/1916	13/08/1916
War Diary	Albert Dull Day	14/08/1916	14/08/1916
War Diary	Beaucourt Dull Day	15/08/1916	15/08/1916
War Diary	Queerie UX	16/08/1916	17/08/1916
War Diary	Godew Aervelde	18/08/1916	19/08/1916
War Diary	Lemena Gatte	20/08/1916	28/08/1916
War Diary	Papot	29/08/1916	04/09/1916
War Diary	Heavy Rail	05/09/1916	05/09/1916
War Diary	Papot	06/09/1916	06/09/1916
War Diary	Papot Bright Day	07/09/1916	09/09/1916
War Diary	Schaexken	10/09/1916	12/09/1916
War Diary	St. Gratien	13/09/1916	19/09/1916
War Diary	Laveville	20/09/1916	23/09/1916
War Diary	Beecourt Wood	24/09/1916	09/10/1916
War Diary	Mirvaux	10/10/1916	14/11/1916
War Diary	Fricourt	15/11/1916	06/12/1916
War Diary	Laveville	07/12/1916	08/12/1916
War Diary	Villers Bocage	09/12/1916	09/12/1916
War Diary	Occoches	10/12/1916	11/12/1916
War Diary	Vacquerie Le-Boucq	12/12/1916	12/12/1916
War Diary	Valuhon	13/12/1916	13/12/1916
War Diary	Ligny-Les-Aire	15/12/1916	15/12/1916
War Diary	Boiseghem	16/12/1916	17/12/1916
War Diary	Reveld	18/12/1916	31/12/1916
War Diary	H.13.c. Sheet 28	01/01/1917	02/01/1917
War Diary	Belgium	03/01/1917	04/01/1917
War Diary	Poperinghe	05/01/1917	25/02/1917
War Diary	Herzeele	26/02/1917	26/02/1917
War Diary	Bolizeele	27/02/1917	28/02/1917
War Diary	Ruminghem	01/03/1917	21/03/1917
War Diary	Lederzeele	22/03/1917	22/03/1917
War Diary	Herzeele	23/03/1917	19/04/1917
War Diary	Poperinghe	20/04/1917	30/04/1917
War Diary	Poperinghe	01/05/1917	02/05/1917
War Diary	Reveld	03/05/1917	11/05/1917
War Diary	Poperinghe	12/05/1917	13/06/1917
War Diary	H.31.c.5.0	14/06/1917	22/06/1917
War Diary	Q.23.c.8.5	23/06/1917	04/07/1917
War Diary	N.3.b.2.9 Sheet 28	05/07/1917	09/07/1917
War Diary	N.3.b.2.9	10/07/1917	10/07/1917
War Diary	N. I Central	11/07/1917	15/08/1917
War Diary	F.24.a.5.5	16/08/1917	22/08/1917
War Diary	A.30.b.9.7	23/08/1917	31/08/1917
War Diary	Sheet 28 A.30.b.9.7	01/09/1917	07/09/1917
War Diary	Hamhoek	08/09/1917	08/09/1917
War Diary	Boeschepe	09/09/1917	31/10/1917

23RD DIVISION
DIVL ARTILLERY

104TH BRIGADE R.F.A.

AUG 1915 - DEC 1916

To 4 ARMY

Army Form C. 2118.

Instructions regarding War Diaries and Intelligence Summaries are contained in F. S. Regs., Part II. and the Staff Manual respectively. Title pages will be prepared in manuscript.

WAR DIARY
or
INTELLIGENCE SUMMARY.

(Erase heading not required.)

Place	Date	Hour	Summary of Events and Information	Remarks and references to Appendices
	15/2/16.	8.0 AM	Attached for duty with BIDDULPH Group, 8th Divisional Artillery. Marched from WITTES to DOULIEU arriving at DOULIEU at 2.0 p.m. 2/LT DOLAN, H.E. and 2/LT PRING, N.G. reported their return from leave in ENGLAND.	FR
	16/2/16.	8.15 AM	Gun detachments and Battery Staff leave DOULIEU and march via ESTAIRES, SAILLY, BAC-ST-MAUR to position near FLEURBAIX (H34.a.6.5. Sheet 36) and take over from A/74 BDE R.F.A.	FR
	17/2/16		Preparations made for moving wagon-line to billet near FLEURBAIX and move commenced, but was forbidden by the General on account of its being too near the front-line and also to Infantry Headquarters.	FR
	18-2-16		Quiet.	FR
	19-2-16	11.15 AM	Wagon-line moved to LA BOUDRELLE. G.10.A.9.8. Sheet 36.	FR
	20-2-16		Quiet.	FR
		9.30 pm	Test S.O.S. received. Battery stood to for 20 mins.	
		10.0	Warning received re probable gas attack.	
	21-2-16		Quiet.	FR
	22-2-16			
	23-2-16			FR
	24-2-16	11.15 pm	Owing to a Divisional mistake a false 'Gas' message was received.	FR
	25-2-16		Quiet.	
	26-2-16			FR
	27-2-16			FR

(Bracketed note, 18-2-16 to 27-2-16:) During this time everything was quiet. There were no operations whatever and all available time was spent in improvement of gun-position, building screenings, emplacements, concealed pathways and in instructional lectures on ammunition etc.

2353 Wt. W2544/1454 700,000 5/15 D. D. & L. A.D.S.S./Forms/C. 2118.

Instructions regarding War Diaries and Intelligence Summaries are contained in F. S. Regs., Part II. and the Staff Manual respectively. Title pages will be prepared in manuscript.

WAR DIARY
or
INTELLIGENCE SUMMARY.
(Erase heading not required.)

Army Form C. 2118.

Place	Date	Hour	Summary of Events and Information	Remarks and references to Appendices
	28/2/16.		Preparations made to move battery to wagon-line. Relief commenced by a section of the 5th Bty R.F.A at 8.0pm. Guns taken and ammunition from pits removed.	FR
		9.30pm.	Relief completed and march to wagon-line commenced.	
	29-2-16.		At wagon-line. Fatigues.	FR
	1/3/16.	7.30AM	Marched away from wagon-line.	FR
		8.30.	Rendez-vous at 102 Bde Am. Col at LA GORGUE. March with BIDDULPH Group to FLORINGHEM via MERVILLE, ST VENANT and LILLERS.	
		4.30pm.	Rejoin 104 BDE R.F.A.	

2353 Wt. W2544/1454 700,000 5/15 D. D. & L. A.D.S.S./Forms/C. 2118.

23rd Division

121 / 6787

104th Brigade R.F.A.

Vol: I

August. 15.

to

Dec 16

9

CONFIDENTIAL

Instructions regarding War Diaries and Intelligence Summaries are contained in F. S. Regs., Part II. and the Staff Manual respectively. Title pages will be prepared in manuscript.

WAR DIARY or ~~INTELLIGENCE SUMMARY~~. 104th Brigade R.F.A.

(Erase heading not required.)

Army Form C. 2118.

Place	Date	Hour	Summary of Events and Information	Remarks and references to Appendices
BORDON	20.8.15		Order to mobilize received. Officers and men recalled from leave	
	21.8.15 to 25.8.15		Drawing Equipment Ammunition Clothing and Stores from Field Stores ALDERSHOT	
	26.8.15		The Brigade entrained at BORDON Station for SOUTHAMPTON and embarked on various steamers	
	27.8.15		Disembarked at HAVRE. Marched to No 5 Rest Camp	
	28.8.15		Entrained at GARE DES MARCHANDISES for Concentration Camp.	
	28.8.15 and 29.8.15		Arrived ST OMER and marched to TOURNEHEM where Brigade was billeted	
	30.8.15		Resting cleaning equipment &c Telephone communication established with R.A. HQrs also between Brigade HQs and all Batteries	
	31.8.15		Battery training proceeded with	

E. Worthy[?]
Colonel
Comdg 104th Brigade R.F.A.

23rd Division

121 / 7595.

104th Bde: R.F.A.

Vol 2

Sept 15

CONFIDENTIAL

Instructions regarding War Diaries and Intelligence Summaries are contained in F. S. Regs., Part II. and the Staff Manual respectively. Title pages will be prepared in manuscript.

WAR DIARY or ~~INTELLIGENCE SUMMARY~~ of 104th BRIGADE R.F.A.

(Erase heading not required.)

Army Form C. 2118.

Place	Date	Hour	Summary of Events and Information	Remarks and references to Appendices
TOURNEHEM	1-9-15		In billets. 23rd DIV. Tactical Exercise	[illegible]
do	2-9-15		do. Divisional R.A. Tactical exercise	[illegible]
do	3-9-15		do. Heavy rain. Battery Training. Very successful concert in Y.M.C.A. Tent in the evening.	[illegible]
do	4-9-15		In billets. Heavy rain. Divisional R A Laying Competition. Battery training.	[illegible]
do.	5-9-15	1.a.m	Order that Divisional moves early on 6-9-15 received	[illegible]
			In billets. Divine service. Settling for billets.	
BANDRINGHEM	6-9-15	6.30am	The Brigade marched with 70th Infantry Brigade group. via NORDAUSQUES – ST MARTIN – South of ST OMER and bivouacked at 5. p.m at BANDRINGHEM. Satisfactory march no casualties	
STRAZEELE	7-9-15	10-a.m	The Brigade marched by itself via ~~[illegible]~~ – BLARINGHEM – SERQUES – HAZEBROUCK to STRAZEELE and occupied billets in and around the village at 6. p.m.	
		7-30pm	Orders received for Brigade less A + C Batteries to proceed tomorrow to be attached to 27th DIV in the firing line for instruction.	
	8-9-15		HQ. B.+D. Batteries move to STEENWERCKE. & Sections from B + D Batteries relieved sections of 99th + 132nd Batteries before ARMENTIERES.	
ARMENTIERES	9-9-15.		B Battery registering D making gun emplacements. A. C + Column still at STRAZEELE.	
	10-9-15 to 15-9-15		Relief of ~~[illegible]~~ 1st BDE R.F.A. continues. Registration + completion of positions. Relief completed + line taken over on 15-9-15.	
	16-9-15 to 20-9-15		Registration improvement + completion of positions, and telephone communications	

Army Form C. 2118.

Instructions regarding War Diaries and Intelligence Summaries are contained in F. S. Regs., Part II. and the Staff Manual respectively. Title pages will be prepared in manuscript.

WAR DIARY of 104th BRIGADE R.F.A

or

~~INTELLIGENCE SUMMARY.~~

(*Erase heading not required.*)

Place	Date	Hour	Summary of Events and Information	Remarks and references to Appendices
ARMENTIERES	21-9-15 to 26-9-15		Bombardment of German Lines in co-operation with attack farther south.	
	27-9-15 to 30-9-15		Nothing to report.	

[signature]
Colonel
Comdg. 104 Brigade. RFA.

2353 Wt. W2544/1454 700,000 5/15 D. D. & L. A.D.S.S./Forms/C. 2118.

23rd Division

104th Bde: R.F.A.
Vol 3

121/7761

Oct & Nov. 15.

CONFIDENTIAL

Instructions regarding War Diaries and Intelligence Summaries are contained in F. S. Regs., Part II. and the Staff Manual respectively. Title pages will be prepared in manuscript.

WAR DIARY
or
INTELLIGENCE SUMMARY.
(Erase heading not required.)

10H^TH BRIGADE R.F.A. Army Form C. 2118.

Place	Date	Hour	Summary of Events and Information	Remarks and references to Appendices
ARMENTIERES	10 Oct 1915		Enemy Artillery slightly active A/10H & B/10H retaliated	
✓	11th		Enemy shelled trenches in I. 21. a & b for about 1½ hrs. B/10H	
✓	12th		B/10H registered with aeroplane observation	
✓	14th		Shelled ESTAMINET DE LA BARRIERE I. 22 b. slightly. This building is apparently strongly fortified	
✓	15th		C/10H returned to old position at H. 12. b. 6. H.	
✓	19th		B/10H D/11H registered on support trenches in I 21. A. with aeroplane observation.	
✓	26th		Germans shelled position of B/10H & farm in front in I 13. b. One man killed	
			The month passed very quietly without any particular incidents	
			The telephone system was overhauled & improved.	

[signature]
Colonel

104TH BRIGADE - ROYAL FIELD ARTILLERY - No. .... Date. ....

2353 Wt. W2544/1454 700,000 5/15 D. D. & L. A.D.S.S./Forms/C. 2118.

CONFIDENTIAL

Instructions regarding War Diaries and Intelligence Summaries are contained in F. S. Regs., Part II. and the Staff Manual respectively. Title pages will be prepared in manuscript.

WAR DIARY
or
~~INTELLIGENCE SUMMARY.~~
(Erase heading not required.)

10th BRIGADE. R.F.A

Army Form C. 2118.

Place	Date	Hour	Summary of Events and Information	Remarks and references to Appendices
ARMENTIERES	1.11.15		Weather bad. Work on Alternative Gun Positions. Laying of Brick standings for horses at wagon lines. Building of shelters etc. bathing resorting of brush wood & timber from forest at LA MOTTE continued daily throughout the month	
do	2nd 3rd		Weather bad	
do	5th		Neighbourhood of D/104 in I 13 c. shelled one man wounded. 2/Lt E.E. Bowley joined from D.A.C. posted to Amm. Column. Repair of damage to Gun Positions & dug outs caused by wet weather. These repairs continued throughout the month; the damage was due to (1) Gun pits made in the summer having been dug in below winter water level. (2) In building Gun pits & dug outs heavy iron beams supporting roofs had been laid on the sandbag walls with little or no other support, instead of being also supported with strong uprights. Results being when the wet weather came the sandbags burst & the walls gave way causing collapse of pit	
do	9th		Enemy Artillery more active. Number of good flash observations taken at night. Very clear day & night.	
do	10th		Very clear day.	
do	11th		New work in Enemy's Salient I. 21 b. & breastwork at I. 22 c. shelled. Enemy did not retaliate. Very clear day wet evening.	
do	12th		Some night firing by Germans. Useful flash observations were made from night observation Stations.	
do	13th		A/104 fired 8 rds on new breastwork I. 22 c during the night with gun in detached position in the open. Mist & rain all day.	
do	14th		During the night A/104 fired 40 rds with detached gun on breastwork which effectively prevented repairs. Major REINIGER. B/104 sent to Convalescent Home at Steenwerck.	
do	17th		Very wet & misty	
do	18th		Enemy Artillery very active. ARMENTIERES heavily shelled. A/104 fired 230 rounds in retaliation. During night 18th–19th A/104 fired 45 rounds on breastwork I. 22. c with detached gun in open	
do	19th		Very quiet.	
do	20th		A/104 fired on screen at I. 22 c during night	E. A. Hobday Comd.

2353 Wt. W2544/1454 700,000 5/15 D. D. & L. A.D.S.S./Forms/C. 2118.

CONFIDENTIAL.

Instructions regarding War Diaries and Intelligence Summaries are contained in F. S. Regs., Part II. and the Staff Manual respectively. Title pages will be prepared in manuscript.

WAR DIARY or INTELLIGENCE SUMMARY.

(Erase heading not required.)

Army Form C. 2118.

104TH BRIGADE RFA.

Place	Date 1915.	Hour	Summary of Events and Information	Remarks and references to Appendices
ARMENTIERES	Nov. 21st		Some registration of new zone. Registration of trenches opposite I 26.5 and I 20.1.	
do	22nd		Zone extended to right to cover trenches I 26.5 and I. 20.1. Very quiet day.	
do	23rd		Very misty quiet day	
do	24th		Artillery slightly more active. 2/Lt F.S. MATEER posted to C/104 2/Lt S.R. THORP posted to B/104. Lieut J. BOTSFORD. attached to A/104 for instruction.	
do	29th		Slight bombardment of communication trenches in conjunction with Heavies (6" Hows) who bombarded Distillerie at I 27.d	
do	30th		Good light and considerable movement reported in German Lines. D/104 fired 60 rounds on one of our aeroplanes which was brought down in the German Lines at I 22. d. 9.1 but did not succeed in setting it on fire.	

[signature] Colonel

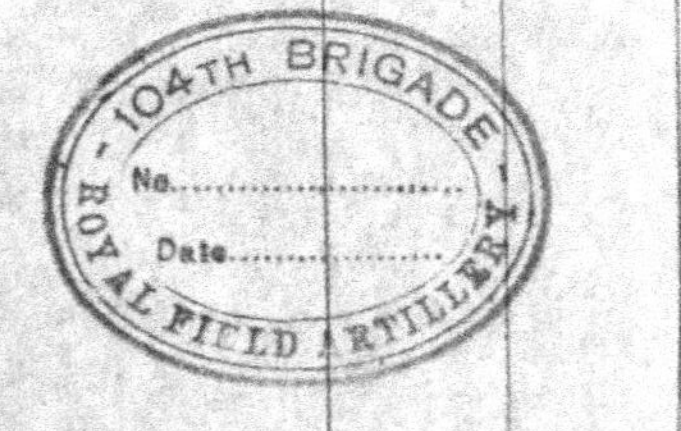

23rd Division

104th Bde. R[?]s.

Vol 4

121/7911

CONFIDENTIAL

Instructions regarding War Diaries and Intelligence Summaries are contained in F. S. Regs., Part II. and the Staff Manual respectively. Title pages will be prepared in manuscript.

WAR DIARY or INTELLIGENCE SUMMARY. 104th Bde RFA.

(Erase heading not required.)

Army Form C. 2118.

Place	Date	Hour	Summary of Events and Information	Remarks and references to Appendices
ARMENTIERES	2.12.15		Very quiet day. Misty. Enemy shelled ARMENTIERES and H.3.d. & I.1.c during the night 2nd & 3rd	
	3.12.15		Wet very thick	
	4.12.15		A/104 & B/104 had to evacuate mens dugouts owing to floods move to buildings near	
	5.12.15		D/104 completed building of new gun pit to replace pit flooded out.	
	6.12.15		Bombardment of fire trench I.22.a 3.6½ – I.22.a 6.9 and 1st support and communication trenches in rear, in conjunction with 105th Bde Hows. 300 rds fired. Produced very little retaliation	
	7.12.15		Bombardment of enemy salient at I 26 d. under Divisional orders in conjunction with Artillery Group on our right, & Heavies. Wire cut on front of 20 yds on that salient by D/104. D/104 fired 40 rounds on wire during night.	
	9.12.15		Wire cuts at I.16.d ½ 2 and I 22 a. 0.4. 150 rounds expended in each case. ARMENTIERES shelled by Germans in the afternoon. Heavy retaliation by 21st DIV. Our Howitzers also retaliated & we fired 200 rounds on same account. 104th Bde HQ Stables in ARMENTIERES hit & set on fire. 3 horses killed. Bom Wainwright did good service. Foggy wet day	
	10.12.15		Enemy shelled trenches I 26.5 and I 20.1 heavily in the morning. We retaliated with about 600 rounds. During the night A/104 fired 40 rounds with detached gun on damaged enemy parapet at I.22.a.5.7.	
	11.12.15		Wire cut on front of 30 yds at I.21.d.1.9 Slight bombardment of adjacent trenches. Wooden repairs on breach at I 22 a 3.6½ broken up & further damage to parapet by A/104. B/104 fired 50 rounds into trench I.21.d. 4½ 4 to I.21.d.7.3.	
	12.12.15		Damaged parapet at I.22.a 3.6½ bombarded by A/104 & C/104 200 rounds fired. A/104 fired on this point during the night	
	13.12.15		B/104 commenced wire cut at I.21.d.3.4½ which was stopped by O.C. Bde after about 40 rounds had been fired as fuzes No 85 were burning very irregularly. C/104 fired during the night on parapet at I.22 a 3.6½.	
	14.12.15		In conjunction with 4.5 How Battery Trenches in GERMAN HOUSE Salient in I.21.d were bombarded for 1½ hours. Fire appeared very effective. Ammn expended 350 rounds. No night firing as the 63rd Inf Bde were being relieved by the 24th Bde in the trenches.	
	15.12.15		Assisted with 12 Batteries in operations by 21st DIV on our left, searching for 3 periods German trenches in I 21 d & I.17 a. Ammn expended 400 rds. During night 15/16th A/104 fired on breach at I.22 a 3.6½.	

2353 Wt. W2544/1454 700,000 5/15 D. D. & L. A.D.S.S./Forms/C. 2118.

CONFIDENTIAL

WAR DIARY or INTELLIGENCE SUMMARY.

(*Erase heading not required.*)

Army Form C. 2118.

Instructions regarding War Diaries and Intelligence Summaries are contained in F. S. Regs., Part II. and the Staff Manual respectively. Title pages will be prepared in manuscript.

104th BRIGADE, RFA

Place	Date	Hour	Summary of Events and Information	Remarks and references to Appendices
ARMENTIERES	16.12.15		Operations in conjunction with 21st DIV continued at 3.18 am. 400 rounds fired on same objective for one hour during which time infantry occupied German trench in I.21. for 20 mins. Operations entirely successful. Divisional Artillery scheme postponed. Observation impossible	
	17.12.15		Very misty. nothing to report	
	18.12.15		At 6.30 am Enemy blew up a mine in 21st DIV. area. in I.11.c0 Heavy shelling followed and our batteries stood by but were not called upon.	
	19.12.15		Enemy shelled 21st DIV area & LA CHAPELLE D'ARMENTIERES heavily from 6.30 am to 11.30 am 3 direct hits on Observation Station of A/104 at I.9.c.2½.5. We retaliated with about 300 rounds for shelling on our area at request of 21st DIV. ARTY.	
	20.12.15		B/104 carried out wire cut at I 21.d 3 5. Wire not very thoroughly cut	
	21.12.15		A/104. commenced wire cut at I 22 a. 3. 6½. Did not complete as observation became impossible through mist.	
	22.12.15		Divisional Artillery Scheme postponed Observation bad. B/104 commenced wire cut at I 21. d 3 5 but stopped on account of mist.	
	23.12.15		A/104 cut wire at I 22.a. 3 6½ & bombarded parapet doing considerable damage.	
	24.12.15		Barrage Scheme on GERMAN HOUSE Salient I 21.d practised with satisfactory results. Shelled GRAND MARAIS house I.23.c 7 5 supposed store depot. Enemy retaliated on batteries shelling B/104 I.13.a with 4.2 Hows. No casualties to personnel or materiel. they also shelled C/102 in I 8 a very heavily. we retaliated vigorously.	
	25.12.15		Bombardment of German parapet in I 22 a & trenches in rear. Considerable damage to parapet. A/104 shelled by 4.2 for half an hour, but range inaccurate & no casualties.	
	26.12.15		Bombardment of parapet at I. 21.c.1 0	
	27.12.15		Quiet day. Enemy slightly shelled CHAPELLE D'ARMENTIERES.	
	28.12.15		Wire cutting scheme by C/104 & A/103. Trenches I 21 d and I.15.2 heavily shelled in retaliation. No. 11 Target registered by Aeroplane (D/105)	
	29.12.15		Scheme cancelled owing to mist in morning, and Infy relief in afternoon. Aeroplane Registration carried out.	
	30.12.15 31.12.15		Very quiet	

[illegible signature], Lieut. Col. R. A. Comdg 104th Bde

B D/104 Bakery
Vol. I

104 Bde.

R. F. A.

23rd Div

Vol 5.

Jan Feb.

CONFIDENTIAL

Instructions regarding War Diaries and Intelligence Summaries are contained in F. S. Regs., Part II. and the Staff Manual respectively. Title pages will be prepared in manuscript.

WAR DIARY
or
~~INTELLIGENCE SUMMARY.~~
(Erase heading not required.)

104TH BRIGADE. R.F.A.

Army Form C. 2118.

Place	Date	Hour	Summary of Events and Information	Remarks and references to Appendices
	1.1.16	1.30 am	Infy raid on Salient in I 21. d. supported by Barrage of Artillery fire, the latter being very successful. Telephone system worked excellently.	
	2.1.16		Rain & mist – Quiet day.	
	3.1.16		Quiet Day.	
	4.1.16		Bombardment of TRAMWAY HOUSE, GRAND MARAIS (I.28.c) DISTILLERIE (I.27.b) LARGE FARM and BREWERY (I 22.c) in conjunction with Hows. Shooting good.	
	5.1.16		nothing to report.	
	6.1.16		Machine Gun emplacements reported were engaged with good results.	
	7.1.16		Quiet day Rainy but clear intervals.	
	8.1.16		do	
	12.1.16		Slight bombardment of parapet in I 22 a in conjunction with Howitzers.	
	14.1.16	11.15am	Slight bombardment of hostile parapet in I 21.b in conjunction with Trench Mortars & Machine Guns	
		12 noon to 12.15pm	Part of 3rd Corps Retaliation Scheme. Each gun fired 10 rounds on German trenches.	
		4.10pm	A/104 joined in bombardment of enemy parapet followed by smoke demonstration. Enemy manned their parapet strongly who were then subjected to searching fire.	
	17.1.16		D/104 wire cut at I 21.c	
	19.1.16		Enemy Artillery more active GRIS POT & L'ARMÉE shelled in the morning with 4.2 Hows Trench I 21.1 heavily shelled between 12.30 & 2.30 pm We retaliated vigorously on their trenches & supposed Bttn HQ.	
	21.1.16		Quiet. Much movement observed behind enemy lines in I.36. 2nd Lt Hagen posted to Bde A.C.	
	22.1.16		A/104 did wire cut on salient in I 21. d. 1½. 9½	
	23.1.16		Some aeroplane registration by B/104 & D/104 Quiet day	
	25.1.16		Officers from 175 Bde. A/104 did wire cuts at I. 21.b and I 16.d.	
	26.1.16		B/104 wire cut at I 26.b. Increased enemy artillery activity induced vigorous retaliation from us. Officers NCOs & men of 34th DIV ARTY attached to HQ. Batteries & Am Col for instruction preparatory to taking over	
	27.1.16		Kaisers Birthday Hostile Artillery showed more activity. We retaliated vigorously. Wire cut at I. 22. a 2¼. 6½.	
			At 11.30 pm the enemy commenced shelling trench in I 21. c. heavily. We retaliated with effect obtaining superiority.	
	28.1.16		Enemy Artillery active all day commencing with bombardment of trenches at 4.30 am. Our parapet in I. 21. was knocked down on a length of 50 yds. We retaliated vigorously.	[illegible] Colonel Cmdg 104 Bde [illegible]
	29.1.16		Quiet.	

CONFIDENTIAL

Instructions regarding War Diaries and Intelligence Summaries are contained in F. S. Regs., Part II. and the Staff Manual respectively. Title pages will be prepared in manuscript.

WAR DIARY
or
~~INTELLIGENCE~~ SUMMARY.

(*Erase heading not required.*)

Army Form C. 2118.

10TH BRIGADE, R.F.A.

Place	Date	Hour	Summary of Events and Information	Remarks and references to Appendices
	30.1.16	[illegible]	Very quiet thick mist all day. On night 30/31st an Infantry raid was arranged against trenches in I 22 a, with barrage of Artillery fire, but owing to presence of hostile patrols was abandoned. Batteries stood to from 9.30 pm to 1.30 am.	
	31.1.16	[illegible]	No activity.	
			During the month direct telephone communication between Batteries & Companies in front line trenches which they covered was established. Company Commanders having the right to call on Batteries for retaliation. These lines are maintained by Batteries.	

E. J. Hopley[?]
Colonel Cmdg
10th Bde RFA

2353 Wt. W2544/1454 700,000 5/15 D. D. & L. A.D.S.S./Forms/C. 2118.

CONFIDENTIAL

Instructions regarding War Diaries and Intelligence Summaries are contained in F. S. Regs., Part II. and the Staff Manual respectively. Title pages will be prepared in manuscript.

WAR DIARY
or
~~INTELLIGENCE SUMMARY.~~
(Erase heading not required.)

Army Form C. 2118.

104TH BRIGADE. R.F.A.

Place	Date	Hour	Summary of Events and Information	Remarks and references to Appendices
	1.2.16 to 5.2.16		Quiet	
	6.2.16		Divisional Test Gas Alarm	
	7.2.16 to 9.2.16		Quiet	
	10.2.16		One section A/104 relieved by A/175 Bde RFA. One section B/104 relieved by B/175 Bde RFA. One section C/104 relieved by C/175 Bde RFA. One section D/104 relieved by D/160 Bde RFA. Reliefs completed by 8.0 pm. Guns being exchanged with relieving Batteries. Hostile Artillery shelled trenches. We retaliated.	
	11.2.16		One section each Battery marched at 7.45 am STEENWERCK. VIEUX-BERQUIN. LA MOTTE. PAPOTE MORBECQUE. BOESINGHEM to WITTES to Reserve. Headquarters Staff 175 Bde RFA arrived to take over at 6.0 pm. Hostile Artillery fairly active. We retaliated.	
	12.2.16		Hostile Artillery active. Engaged in retaliation. Remaining sections of batteries relieved and returned to Wagon lines.	
	13.2.16		Relieved sections of batteries marched at 7.45 am to WITTES under command of MAJOR PEINIGER. Amm Col relieved marched to WITTES. Bde HQ remained in charge of Artillery Group. Hostile Artillery very active shelling trenches & billet area. Heavy retaliation.	
	14.2.16		Quiet. Orders received for D/Battery to march on 15th to DOULIEU (Sheet 36 A.F. 29. d. 6 0.) to be attached to 8th Div Arty.	
	15.2.16		D. Battery marched from WITTES to join 8th Div Arty.	
	16.2.16 17.2.16 18.2.16		A B & C Batteries & Amm. Col in rest at WITTES.	
	19.2.16		Bde HQ relieved marched to WITTES via MERVEILLES – FORET DE NIEPPE & to rest billets.	
	20.2.16 21.2.16 22.2.16		In rest billets less D/104	
	23.2.16	11 am 6 pm	Received orders that Div Arty would march on the following day. Necessary orders issued. ~~6pm~~ Received order that move was postponed.	
	24.2.16 to 28.2.16		In rest billets. Training proceeded with	
	28.2.16	12.15 pm 6.30 pm	Intimation that Div would probably move tomorrow. Intimation that move would probably be at 7.0 am.	[illegible]

2353 Wt. W2544/1454 700,000 5/15 D. D. & L. A.D.S.S./Forms/C. 2118.

CONFIDENTIAL

WAR DIARY
or
~~INTELLIGENCE SUMMARY.~~

(*Erase heading not required.*)

10TH BRIGADE. R.F.A.

Army Form C. 2118.

Instructions regarding War Diaries and Intelligence Summaries are contained in F. S. Regs., Part II. and the Staff Manual respectively. Title pages will be prepared in manuscript.

Place	Date	Hour	Summary of Events and Information	Remarks and references to Appendices
	29.2.16.	4 am.	Orders received for Bde to march today to PERNES via AIRE. - ST HILAIRE - FERFAY. Head of Column to pass starting point. Level Crossing on WITTES - AIRE road at 8.0 am. HQ. A. B + C Batteries + Amn Col marched accordingly.	
		12.45pm	Arrived at PERNES and halted to water + feed. Received instructions that Bde would be billeted at FLORINGHEM 3/4 miles back + returned there. Bde in billets at FLORINGHEM by 4.30 pm. March discipline very good. Horses arrived in excellent condition. No casualties	

E.A. ...
Lt Col Cmdg
10th Bde RFA

2353 Wt. W2544/1454 700,000 5/15 D. D. & L. A.D.S.S./Forms/C. 2118.

Instructions regarding War Diaries and Intelligence Summaries are contained in F. S. Regs., Part II. and the Staff Manual respectively. Title pages will be prepared in manuscript.

10TH BRIGADE, R.F.A. **WAR DIARY** *or* ~~**INTELLIGENCE SUMMARY.**~~ CONFIDENTIAL Army Form C. 2118.

(Erase heading not required.)

Place	Date	Hour	Summary of Events and Information	Remarks and references to Appendices
	1.3.16		Received orders that D Battery would rejoin and be billeted in FLORINGHEM today. D. Battery arrived at 4.0pm & went into billets	
	2.3.16		In billets FLORINGHEM	
	3.3.16		— do. —	
	4.3.16	6.0am.	Officers Commanding A.B. & C Batteries went forward to reconnoitre position near CARENCY which they were to take over from the French	
	5.3.16	9.0am	One Section & Battery Staff of A.B.&C Batteries moved to wagon lines in forward area at ESTREE-CAUCHIE Sheet 36B. W.2 to relieve section of French Batteries, & became detached from the Brigade passing to command of O.C. A Group both tactically & administratively	
	7.3.16	10.30am	Remaining sections of A.B.&C Batteries & the Bde Amm. Column marched to ESTREE CAUCHIE and passed to command of O.C. A Group. Colonel Hobday took command of Reserve Group comprising Headquarters, 10th Bde RFA, D/102 Bde, D/103 Bde, D/104 Bde, C/105 Bde. D/102 moved into billets at FLORINGHEM reporting at 11.30am. D/103 moved into billets at FLORINGHEM reporting at 4.30am.	
	8.3.16	9.0am	Reserve Bde marched via DIVION, HOUDAIN & REBREUVE to billets. HQ 10th Bde. D/102 Bde and D/104 at OHLAIN. D/103 Bde & C/105 Bde at BARRAFFLES (Sheet 36B. P.24 & P.17 respectively) Billeting was very difficult as the former village was full of French troops.	
	9.3.16		Billets at OHLAIN re arranged on French Infantry marching out.	
	10.3.16	11.30am	Reserve Brigade marched to Reserve Billets at FREVILLIERS. Part of village occupied by French Artillery	
	11.3.16		Rearrangement of billets on French Artillery marching out. Plenty of good cover for all horses.	
	12.3.16		Orders received that Major HARTLAND-MAHON would take over command of Reserve Group and 10th Bde RFA	
		7.30pm	Major HARTLAND-MAHON arrived & command handed over to him	
		~~9pm~~	~~Orders received that Batteries of Reserve Group would relieve batteries of 2nd Division by sections on the nights of 14th/15th & 15th/16th March respectively.~~	
	~~15.3.16~~		~~O.C. Group & Battery Commanders went forward to make reconnaissance~~	
				E A Hobday Colonel Comdg 10th Bde RFA

2353 Wt. W2544/1454 700,000 5/15 D. D. & L. A.D.S.S./Forms/C. 2118.

CONFIDENTIAL

WAR DIARY
or
INTELLIGENCE SUMMARY.
(Erase heading not required.)

10TH BRIGADE, R.F.A.

Army Form C. 2118.

Instructions regarding War Diaries and Intelligence Summaries are contained in F. S. Regs., Part II. and the Staff Manual respectively. Title pages will be prepared in manuscript.

Place	Date	Hour	Summary of Events and Information	Remarks and references to Appendices
	12.3.16	9.0am	Orders received that Batteries of Reserve Group would relieve Batteries of 2nd Division by sections on the nights 14th/15th March respectively	
	13.3.16		O.C. Group & Battery Commanders went forward to make reconnaissance	
	14.3.16		One section each Battery Reserve Group marched to Wagon lines in 2nd Divisional Area to go into action on night 14th/15th March	
			Orders received for H.Q. to march to HERSIN & take over billets of 5th LONDON BDE. at K.35.d.9.3 (Sheet 36B) on 15th	
	15.3.16		Remaining sections Reserve Group marched to 2nd Div. Area to go into action on night 15th/16th	
		10.30am	10th Bde H.Q. marched to billets at HERSIN.	
		2.0pm	Arrived at HERSIN.	
		7.0pm	Major R.G. MATURIN, D.S.O, R.F.A, arrived on posting to command 10th Brigade, R.F.A. Command handed over to him.	

[signature] Major R.F.A.
Comdg 10th Brigade R.F.A.

CONFIDENTIAL

Instructions regarding War Diaries and Intelligence Summaries are contained in F. S. Regs., Part II. and the Staff Manual respectively. Title pages will be prepared in manuscript.

WAR DIARY
or
INTELLIGENCE SUMMARY.
(Erase heading not required.)

10th Brigade R.F.A.

Army Form C. 2118.

Place	Date	Hour	Summary of Events and Information	Remarks and references to Appendices
	16.3.16 to 22.3.16		HQ. 10th Brigade RFA in billets at HERSIN.	
	22.3.16 to 24.3.16		On the nights of 22nd/23rd and 23rd/24th A. B & C Batteries relieved 40th, 50th & 16th Batteries, 34th Bde RFA respectively. One section each night on relief of 2nd Div by 23rd Div.	
	24.3.16		All Batteries & Bde Amn Col come under command of Bde HQ.	
		10. am	Bde HQ relieved HQ 34th Bde RFA at BULLY GRENAY. Sheet 36B R.5.d.	
			All units 10th Bde & C/105 Bde (4.5 Hows) form CALONNE Group, covering front from M.9.d.8.0 to M.20.c.5.3 (Sheet 36c)	
	24.3.16 to 31.3.16		Batteries in action. Engaged in Registration & Retaliation. Quiet	

R J [signature] Lt Col
Commanding 10th Brigade RFA

2353 Wt. W2544/1454 700,000 5/15 D. D. & L. A.D.S.S./Forms/C. 2118.

CONFIDENTIAL

Instructions regarding War Diaries and Intelligence Summaries are contained in F. S. Regs., Part II. and the Staff Manual respectively. Title pages will be prepared in manuscript.

WAR DIARY
or
INTELLIGENCE SUMMARY.

(Erase heading not required.)

XX 1[illegible]

104 Brigade R.F.A.

Army Form C. 2118.

Vol. 7

Place	Date	Hour	Summary of Events and Information	Remarks and references to Appendices
	1-4-16		Some hostile shelling of our trenches to which we retaliated.	
	2-4-16 - 6-4-16		Quiet. Slight hostile shelling & retaliation by us.	
	8-4-16		Wire cut at M.15.b.6.2 by A/104 & at M.21.a.9½.6½ & M.15.d.3.0 by B/104 preparatory to a feint attack	
	9-4-16		2nd Lt A.S. MASON wounded & evacuated to Field Ambulance.	
	10.4.16		In conjunction with infantry & group on our right a feint attack was carried out with the object of causing material damage & killing Germans.	
		1.30pm to 4.29pm	A steady bombardment of hostile front line, support & communication trenches carried out.	
		4.29pm	An intense bombardment of front line trench for 1 minute; the infantry lighting smoke candles.	
		4.30pm	All guns lifted to support line & maintained and intense fire thereon for 5 minutes.	
		4.35	All guns dropped again & bombarded front line heavily with shrapnel for 1 minute.	
		4.36	Operations finished. Enemy did not retaliate very much. During deliberate bombardment they placed slight barrage over our support trench and during intense bombardment they placed barrage in front of our fire trench. They ceased fire when our operations ceased.	
	11-4-16 to 16-4-16		Nothing to report.	
	17-4-16		Orders for relief by 2nd Div on night of 19/20th received. S.A.A. section of Amm Col relieved by S.A.A. Section 41st Bde & marched to billets at CAMBLAIN CHATELAIN (Sheet 36B I.15)	
	18-4-16		Orders for relief issued	
	19.4.16		Night of 19/20th Batteries relieved by Batteries of 2nd Div as follows:- A/104 by 70th Batt[illegible]; B/104 by 50th Batty; C/104 by one section 50 Batty & one section 70 Batty. D/104 by one section 15th Batty & one section 48 Batt[illegible]. Bde Amm Col relieved by 41st Bde Amm Col. All reliefs were completed by 10 pm guns being left in pits & handed over stripped. Guns of 2nd Div taken over in lieu. Ammunition in gun lines also handed over. All Batts & Amm Col (including S.A.A. section) marched to billets at LA THIEULOYE (Sheet 36B O.30 & N.25).	

8353 Wt. W2544/1454 700,000 5/15 D. D. & L. A.D.S.S./Forms/C. 2118.

Instructions regarding War Diaries and Intelligence Summaries are contained in F. S. Regs., Part II. and the Staff Manual respectively. Title pages will be prepared in manuscript.

CONFIDENTIAL

WAR DIARY or ~~INTELLIGENCE~~ SUMMARY.

(Erase heading not required.)

104 Brigade RFA

Army Form C. 2118.

Place	Date	Hour	Summary of Events and Information	Remarks and references to Appendices
	20.4.16	10am	Command of CALONNE Group handed over to O.C. 34th Bde RFA on completion of relief Bde H.Q. marched to rest billets at LA THIEULOYE	
	21.4.16		Spent by Units overhauling & cleaning up generally.	
	22.4.16		Holiday	
	23.4.16	9.30am	Church Parade Holiday	
	24-4-16		Training programme begun with section training.	
	24-4-16 to 30.4.16		Section Training carried out daily Bde Signalling class under Bde Signalling Officer.	

R J [illegible]
Lt Col RFA
COMMANDING 104th BRIGADE R.F.A.

8353 Wt. W2544/1454 700,000 5/15 D. D. & L. A.D.S.S./Forms/C. 2118.

SECRET

H. Q.
104 Bde R.F.A.

To:—

D.A.G.
3rd Echelon

Herewith War Diary for the month of May 1916 of 104 Bde R.F.A.

104TH BRIGADE
No. ....
Date ....
ROYAL FIELD ARTILLERY

Reginald Hurd
Lt. & Adjt
for Lt-Colonel
COMMANDING 104th BRIGADE R.F.A.

CONFIDENTIAL

Instructions regarding War Diaries and Intelligence Summaries are contained in F. S. Regs., Part II. and the Staff Manual respectively. Title Pages will be prepared in manuscript.

WAR DIARY
or
~~INTELLIGENCE SUMMARY~~
(Erase heading not required.)

XXIII
104 Bde R F A
Vol 8

Army Form C. 2118

Place	Date	Hour	Summary of Events and Information	Remarks and references to Appendices
	1-5-16 to 11-5-16		Brigade in Rest billets Battery Training & Brigade Signalling class continued	
	4-5-16		Capt J T Richards proceeded to ENGLAND under orders & struck off strength	
	5-5-16		Command of Bde Amm Col taken over by Lieut Coulter	
	10-5-16		Orders for relief of 2nd Div Arty by 23rd Div Arty in SOUCHEZ & ANGRES Sections received. Brigade HQrs to remain at LA THIEULOYE in command of composite Brigade in rest. A/104 Brigade to remain at LA THIEULOYE as Divisional Training Battery. Remainder of Brigade in rest composed of Amm. Col 104 Bde R F A; C/103 Bde and C/105 Bde.	
	12-5-16		One section B/104 marched to relieve section of 16 Btty at X.28.b.4.5 (Sheet 36b 1/40,000) & came under orders of O.C. SOUCHEZ Group. D/104 marched to relieve sections of 15th & 71st Batteries at R.11.c.8.2 (Sheet 36b 1/40,000) and came under orders of O.C. ANGRES Group.	
	13-5-16		C/104 marched to take up gun position at R.34.d.9.6. and came under orders of O.C. SOUCHEZ Group.	
	14-5-16		B/104 less 1 section marched to wagon lines at K.34.a.5.4 C/103 arrived at LA THIEULOYE & came under orders of O.C. Bde Under re-organisation of Divisional artillery the Brigade Amm. Col. was abolished and transferred to No 1 Section 23rd Div. Amm. Col with all personel horses equipment etc. 2/Lt EASTWOOD reported arrival & posted to D/104.	
	16-5-16		2/Lt HOGARTH reported arrival & posted to A/104	
	14-5-16		Reorganisation of Div Arty: D/104 transferred to 105 Bde R F A & become C/105 Bde. C/105 Bde R F A (4.5" How Batty) transferred to 104 Bde R F A & become D/104 Bde R F A	
	21-5-16	11.30pm	Orders received that all units of Reserve Bde to be ready to march on one hours notice.	

R [illegible] Major
COMMANDING 104th BRIGADE R.F.A.

1875 Wt. W593/826 1,000,000 4/15 J.B.C. & A. A.D.S.S./Forms/C. 2118.

Army Form C. 2118

CONFIDENTIAL

Instructions regarding War Diaries and Intelligence Summaries are contained in F. S. Regs., Part II. and the Staff Manual respectively. Title Pages will be prepared in manuscript.

WAR DIARY
or
~~INTELLIGENCE SUMMARY~~
(Erase heading not required.)

104 Bde RFA

Place	Date	Hour	Summary of Events and Information	Remarks and references to Appendices
	22-5-16	6.30am	D/104 Bde marched under orders to CAUCOURT to report to O.C. 34th Bde R.F.A. there.	
		2.0pm	Bde H.Q & A/104 Bde marched to billets in forward area at BARLIN. C/103 Bde marched to billets in forward area at HERSIN. A/104 came under command of O.C. SOUCHEZ Group. Bde H.Q remained at BARLIN in administrative command only of Bde.	
	27-5-16		A/104 moved to position at R.12. a 8.3 (Sheet 36B) & came under command of IV Corps Counter Battery Group.	
			D/104 moved to position at M. 8 a.7.8 (Sheet 36b) & came under command of IV Corps Counter Battery Group.	

R. J. Wal[illegible] Major
COMMANDING 104th BRIGADE R.F.A.

1875 Wt. W593/826 1,000,000 4/15 J.B.C. & A. A.D.S.S./Forms/C. 2118.

104TH BRIGADE, R.F.A.

Instructions regarding War Diaries and Intelligence Summaries are contained in F. S. Regs., Part II. and the Staff Manual respectively. Title Pages will be prepared in manuscript.

WAR DIARY or INTELLIGENCE SUMMARY

(Erase heading not required.)

XXIII

CONFIDENTIAL

Army Form C. 2118

104 RFA Vol 9

Place	Date	Hour	Summary of Events and Information	Remarks and references to Appendices
BARLIN	14.6.16		Sections of each battery relieved by 47th Div Arty on night of 14th/15th	
	15.6.16		Bde HQ and relieved Sections of Batteries marched to billets at CALONNE RICOUART.	
			Remaining sections of batteries relieved on night of 15th/16th.	
	16.6.16		Bde HQ and one Section each Battery marched from CALONNE RICOUART to billets in manoeuvre area at THEROUANNE. Remaining sections each battery marched to billets at CALONNE RICOUART. Division in GHQ Reserve from 6 pm.	
	17.6.16		Remaining sections each battery marched to THEROUANNE.	
	18.6.16 to 24.6.16		In billets. Training for open warfare on 1st Army Special manoeuvre area	
	20.6.16		Orders received to prepare to entrain on 24th/25th.	
	21.6.16		Billeting Party ½ Lt Skinner proceeded to new area.	
	25.6.16		Brigade entrained at BERGUETTE Station moved by rail to LONGUEAU (Map AMIENS) via St POL and DOULLENS. Detrained marched to billets at LA CHAUSSÉE. Division in GHQ Reserve.	
	30.6.16		Brigade marched to billets at CARDONNETTE with remainder of 23rd Div. Arty.	

R J Watson[?] Lt Col RFA
COMMANDING ... R.F.A.

1875 Wt. W593/826 1,000,000 4/15 J.B.C. & A. A.D.S.S./Forms/C. 2118.

WAR DIARY

23rd Divisional Artillery.

104th BRIGADE R. F.A.

JULY 1916

Sheet 1

10th BRIGADE. R.F.A

Instructions regarding War Diaries and Intelligence Summaries are contained in F. S. Regs., Part II. and the Staff Manual respectively. Title Pages will be prepared in manuscript.

WAR DIARY
or
INTELLIGENCE SUMMARY
(Erase heading not required.)

CONFIDENTIAL 23 Army Form C. 2118. July

104 RFA Vol 10

Place	Date	Hour	Summary of Events and Information	Remarks and references to Appendices
	1.7.16		Orders received that Division was at 6 hours notice to move from 12 noon today	
		10pm	Moved to ST GRATIEN (Sheet 62D) and bivouaced in open field.	
	2.7.16		In bivouac. Orders received that Divnl Artillery would stand fast tonight	
	3.7.16		~~Orders received that Division would move to FRESHENCOURT on the 4th inst. Reinforcements to 8th Division. Later cancelled~~	
	4.7.16		Brigade Commander reconnoitred battery positions near FRICOURT (Sheet 62D)	
	5.7.16	4 pm	Orders for Brigade to march at once to positions in F.2.b & d (Sheet 62D)	
			Brigade Commander, Battery Commanders & Staffs left at once.	
		6 15pm	Brigade marched & took up covered positions in the open on the night 5th/6th	
			Wagon lines at E.10.c. (Sheet 62D)	
	6.7.16		Concealment of batteries registration	
	7.7.16	4 20am to noon	Barrage fire in support of 24th & 68th Inf Bde's attack on CONTALMAISON and line E & W. Ground gained but attack on CONTALMAISON unsuccessful. The Brigade supplied FOO with 68th Inf Bde but communication with him was never established. Barrage fire throughout day. 2/Lt G.DELAMAIN posted to A/104	
	8.7.16		2/Lt H. HALL wounded. Maintaining barrages. Barrage fire during night	
	9.7.16		2/Lt HUTCHINSON reported on transfer from DAC and posted to B/104	
			2/Lt MACKENZIE reported on transfer from DAC and posted to D/104	
			2/Lt A.M. HOGARTH wounded and died of wounds.	
			Registration by batteries	
		6pm to 6.30pm	Barrage to repel enemy infantry attack E of BAILIFF WOOD X.16 a (Sheet 57D) Attack repulsed	
		6.35pm	Barrage fire to support Infantry attack on BALIFF WOOD.	
			Barrage fire during night	
	10.7.16	4 pm to 6.30pm	Brigade opened fire in support of attack by 69th Inf Bde on CONTALMAISON at 4.30pm Attack successful & CONTALMAISON occupied.	
		6.30pm	Barrage fire to cover consolidation opened.	

Sheet (2.)

10TH BRIGADE, RFA

WAR DIARY
or
INTELLIGENCE SUMMARY
(Erase heading not required.)

CONFIDENTIAL.

Army Form C. 2118

Instructions regarding War Diaries and Intelligence Summaries are contained in F. S. Regs., Part II. and the Staff Manual respectively. Title Pages will be prepared in manuscript.

Place	Date	Hour	Summary of Events and Information	Remarks and references to Appendices
	10.7.16	9.5pm	Counter attack on CONTALMAISON reported. Barrage increased.	
			Counter attack repulsed.	
		10.55pm	All batteries on night barrage	
	11.7.16		23rd Divnl Arty support 1st Division on relief of 23rd Division Infantry.	
			Barrage fire during day N.E of CONTALMAISON.	
		8pm	Night barrage by one section each battery	
			Evening of 11th one section each battery moved forward to covered positions in the open in X.27.c and d and F.3.b. N of FRICOURT	
	12.7.16		Intermittent barrage fire during day & night.	
			Remaining sections of batteries moved to new positions.	
			Bde HQ moved to dugout in F.3.b.3.5 (Sheet 62D)	
			Capt F.J. RICHARDS C/10th wounded.	
	13.7.16		Intermittent barrage fire during day & night to 3.0am	
	14.7.16	3.am to 6.30am	All Batteries barrage trenches in X.12.a (Sheet 57D) to support attack on German 2nd line from LONGUEVAL to BAZENTIN LE PETIT WOOD	
		6.30am to 2.0pm	Barrage continued at slow rate	
		2.0pm to 2.50pm	Barrage to support attack by 21st & 1st Divisions N.E of BAZENTIN LE PETIT WOOD. Attack postponed at 2.50pm	
		9.0pm	Night barrage opened	
	15.7.16	8.55am	Barrage fire opened in support of attack by 3rd Inf Bde on German 2nd line trenches X.12.a.5.7 to X.5.b.3.1 throughout day. Attack unsuccessful.	
			Defensive barrage at night. Guns in action at noon A Battery 3 guns B. Battery 2. C. Battery 3. D Battery 4.	
	16.7.16		D Battery bombarded steadily front trench of German 2nd line in X.5.d (Sheet 57D.SE)	
			Continuous shrapnel fire on new German trenches in S.1 and 2 (Sheet 57C SW)	
		11.50pm	Barrage fire in support of successful attack by 3rd Bde at midnight on	

Sheet (3)

104TH BRIGADE RFA

Instructions regarding War Diaries and Intelligence Summaries are contained in F. S. Regs., Part II. and the Staff Manual respectively. Title Pages will be prepared in manuscript.

WAR DIARY
or
INTELLIGENCE SUMMARY
(Erase heading not required.)

CONFIDENTIAL

Army Form C. 2118

Place	Date	Hour	Summary of Events and Information	Remarks and references to Appendices
	16.7.16 Contd		Front & support trenches of 2nd Line in X.12 a to X.5 d inclusive	
			Guns in Action A Batty 3. B Batty 2. C Batty 4. D Batty 4.	
	17.7.16	12.50am onwards	Slow defensive barrage by 18 pdr batteries over newly gained trenches.	
		2.30pm	Orders for Brigade to move forward to new positions in X.23 (Sheet 57 d. S.E)	
			Batteries move forward to near CONTALMAISON & brought into action in positions as follows:- (Sheet 57d S.E) A/104 X.22 d 0.9. B/104 X.23 c 9.9. C/104 X.23 a 8.0 D/104 X.23.d 2.7	
	18.7.16	12.15am to 5.0am	D/104 shelled trench junction X.6 a 5.8	
			All Batteries registering during day.	
		2 pm	Bde H.Q. moved forward to X.23. c 8.2	
		9 pm	All batteries on night barrage.	
			Guns in Action A/104 4. B/104 2. C/104 3. D/104 4.	
	19.7.16	5.0am	Batteries ceased firing on night barrage. Registration on new German front line trench in X.6.a & S.1.b & d (Sheets 57D & 57C) by all Batteries	
	20.7.16	5.0am	Night barrage stopped. Increased hostile artillery activity in neighbourhood of battery positions which in present operations, up to now, had been practically nil.	
			Guns in action. A/104 4. B/104 3 C/104 4 D/104 4.	
	21.7.16		Quiet day. 2/Lt W. CRANSHAW posted to D/104.	
		9 pm	Night barrage opened	
	22.7.16	4.0am to 6.0am	Barrage fire in support of attack by 2nd Inf Bde on new German Line in X.6.a & S.1.d. (Sheet 57d & 57c). Attack unsuccessful.	
	23.7.16		Defensive barrage	
		6.45pm	Bombardment by D/104 of MUNSTER ALLEY	
			Night barrage	

1875 Wt. W593/826 1,000,000 4/15 J.B.C. & A. A.D.S.S./Forms/C. 2118.

Sheet (4) 104TH BRIGADE, RFA

WAR DIARY
or
INTELLIGENCE SUMMARY
(Erase heading not required.)

CONFIDENTIAL

Army Form C. 2118

Instructions regarding War Diaries and Intelligence Summaries are contained in F. S. Regs., Part II. and the Staff Manual respectively. Title Pages will be prepared in manuscript.

Place	Date	Hour	Summary of Events and Information	Remarks and references to Appendices
	24.7.16		Defensive barrage only.	
	25.7.16	2.0am to 6.30am	Firing in support of unsuccessful attack by 3rd Inf Bde in conjunction with 1st Australian Divn on trenches S.E of POZIERES. Subsequent Defensive barrage.	
		4.45pm	Barrage fire against counter attack from direction of BAPAUME road which was driven back. Continuous defensive fire throughout night	
	26.7.16		Intermittent defensive fire. Lt H.E. DOLAN wounded slightly at duty.	
	27.7.16	6.0am to 8.0am	Fire in support of Infy attack on our right	
			Quiet day. Defensive barrage at night. 2/Lt L.G. LOCK posted to A/104	
	28.7.16		Quiet day	
		1.0pm to 3.0pm	Bombardment of trench by D/104.	
		9.0pm to 5.0am	Night barrage. Slow rate.	
	29.7.16	1.30pm to 2.30pm	Bombardment of MUNSTER ALLEY (X.6.a) by D/104	
		3.0pm to 3.30pm	Slight bombardment of Communications by 18 pdr Batteries	
		9.40pm to 11pm	Barrage fire by all Batteries in support of Infy attack on MUNSTER ALLEY.	
		11pm onwards	Night barrage on Communications to MARTINPUICH.	
	30.7.16	2.0am to 4.40am	Barrage moved to cover MUNSTER ALLEY where Infy had made some progress.	
		4.40am to 5.10am	Searching communications to MARTIN PUICH at increased rate of fire.	
		6.10pm to 7.10pm	Searching communications to MARTINPUICH in support of operations by 19th Division on our right.	
		9pm to 3.0am	Night barrage on communications to MARTINPUICH.	

1875 Wt. W593/826 1,000,000 4/15 J.B.C. & A. A.D.S.S./Forms/C. 2118.

Sheet (5)

104th BRIGADE, R.F.A.

Instructions regarding War Diaries and Intelligence Summaries are contained in F. S. Regs., Part II. and the Staff Manual respectively. Title Pages will be prepared in manuscript.

WAR DIARY
or
INTELLIGENCE SUMMARY
(Erase heading not required.)

CONFIDENTIAL

Army Form C. 2118

Place	Date	Hour	Summary of Events and Information	Remarks and references to Appendices
	31.7.16		Quiet day	
		9 pm to 5 am	Night barrage on Communications to MARTINPUICH.	
			Ammunition Expended during month:–	
			Shrap. / H.E.	
			18 pdr. 29048 rds. 9771 rds. Total 50,935 rds.	
			4.5 55 rds. 12051 rds.	

R. G. Maturin [?] Lt Col RFA
Comd 104th Bde RFA

1875 Wt. W593/826 1,000,000 4/15 J.B.C. & A. A.D.S.S./Forms/C. 2118.

23rd Divisional Artillery.

104th BRIGADE

ROYAL FIELD ARTILLERY

AUGUST 1 9 1 6

Army Form C. 2118

Instructions regarding War Diaries and Intelligence Summaries are contained in F. S. Regs., Part II. and the Staff Manual respectively. Title Pages will be prepared in manuscript.

104th BRIGADE R.F.A.

WAR DIARY
or
INTELLIGENCE SUMMARY

(Erase heading not required.)

CONFIDENTIAL

Place	Date	Hour	Summary of Events and Information	Remarks and references to Appendices
	1.8.16	8.30am to 5.0am	Defensive Night Barrage between SWITCH LINE & MARTIN PUICH	
	2.8.16	3.0pm to 3.30pm	Slight Bombardment of SWITCH LINE searching back to MARTIN PUICH	
		8.30pm	Night barrage commenced	
		10.5pm	Five minutes gun fire on false S.O.S alarm	
	3.8.16	5.0am	Night Barrage ceased	
		2.0 to 4.0pm	D/104 bombarded MUNSTER ALLEY in conjunction with other How batteries	
		8.30pm	Night Barrage commenced	
	4.8.16	5.0am	Night barrage ceased	
		2 to 4pm	D/104 bombarded MUNSTER ALLEY in conjunction with other How batteries	
		9.15pm	Barrage fire in support of infantry attack on MUNSTER ALLEY maintained at varying rates till	
	5.8.16	10.30am	Barrage ceased.	
		11.0pm	Night barrage commenced	
	6.8.16	5.0am	Night Barrage ceased.	
		4.0pm to 9.20pm	Barrage at varying rates in support of Infantry operations on SWITCH LINE	
		9.20pm	Night barrage commenced	
	7.8.16	3.0am	Increased rate of fire	
		4.0am	Normal Rate	
		5.0am	Ceased fire.	
	8.8.16	8.30pm to midnight	Night barrage.	

1875 Wt. W593/826 1,000,000 4/15 J.B.C. & A. A.D.S.S./Forms/C. 2118.

Army Form C. 2118

104 BRIGADE R.F.A

WAR DIARY
or
INTELLIGENCE SUMMARY

(Erase heading not required.)

CONFIDENTIAL.

Instructions regarding War Diaries and Intelligence Summaries are contained in F. S. Regs., Part II. and the Staff Manual respectively. Title Pages will be prepared in manuscript.

Place	Date	Hour	Summary of Events and Information	Remarks and references to Appendices
	9.8.16	8.30 pm	Night Barrage commenced	
	10.8.16	5.0 am	Night barrage ceased	
		2.0 pm	Continuous Barrage fire for purpose of isolating German line between S.1 d 9½ 9 and X 6 a 4 7 commenced and maintained continuously in conjunction with remainder of Div Arty until 10.15 pm 12.8.16.	
	12.8.16	10.15 pm	Barrage fire in support of attack by 2 Brigades 15th Div Arty on SWITCH LINE which had been isolated maintained until 11.30 am on 13th August. Attack of left Bde only successful. SWITCH LINE from X 6 a 4 6 to S 8 d 2 9 taken.	
	13.8.16		Relief of 23rd Div Arty by 47th Div Artd commenced. 1st Sections of all batteries relieved by 8 pm & marched to wagon lines. Relief by Batteries as follows:— A/104 by A/235 Bde, B/104 by B/235 Bde; C/104 by C/235 Bde D/104 by D/235 Bde	
	14.8.16	8.0 pm to 6.0 am	Night Defensive Barrage	
		9.30 am	1st Sections of Batteries marched to billets at BEHENCOURT (Sheet 62 D) 2nd Sections of batteries relieved by 6.0 pm & marched to wagon lines.	
		6.0 pm	Bde H.Q relieved by H.Q. 235 Bde & marched to billets at BEHENCOURT. Total Ammunition expended during operations in IV Army Area — 13 pdr Shr 45,972 HE 14,558 rds; 4.5 How: 5.5 rds 18,991 rds 4.3 common. Total 79,571 rounds	
	15.8.16		2nd Sections of Batteries marched to camp at QUERRIEUX (Sheet 62 D) Bde H Q & 1st sections marched from BEHENCOURT to camp at QUERRIEUX.	
	16.8.16	4.0 pm	A Battery marched to AMIENS & entrained at SALEUX Station (Sheet 27) detraining at GODEWAERSVELDE and marching to billets at EECKE Remaining batteries of Bde H.Q followed at 3 hour intervals.	
	17.8.16		All Brigade arrived in billets at EECKE. Orders for relief of 41st Div Artd by 23rd Div Art received	

1875 Wt. W593/826 1,000,000 4/15 J.B.C. & A. A.D.S.S./Forms/C. 2118.

104 BDE R F A

WAR DIARY
or
~~INTELLIGENCE SUMMARY.~~
(Erase heading not required.)

CONFIDENTIAL

Army Form C. 2118.

104 RFA

Vol 11

Instructions regarding War Diaries and Intelligence Summaries are contained in F. S. Regs., Part II. and the Staff Manual respectively. Title pages will be prepared in manuscript.

Place	Date	Hour	Summary of Events and Information	Remarks and references to Appendices
	18.8.16		Bde Commander & Orderly Officer proceeded to Rt Group HQ 41st Div B.12 Central (Sheet 36 NW)	
	19.8.16		Battery Commanders proceeded to Battery positions which they were to take over A/104 to A/184 at C.13 d 1 3; B/104 to B/184 C 2 a 5 5; C/104 to C/184 at C 13 a 9 8; D/104 to D/184 at C.1 d 1 4.	
		9.30am	One section each battery marched to wagon lines in forward area. – A/104 at B 14 a 5 8 B/104 at D 8 c 2 3. C/104 at B.14. a 3.8 D/104 at B 11 c 6 5 sections relieved sections of outgoing batteries on night 19th/20th	
	20.8.16		HQ & remaining sections marched to forward area. Remaining sections relieved outgoing sections in evening. Reliefs completed by 8 30 pm. All guns were exchanged. Stripped Bde HQ relieved HQ 184 Bde at B.12 Central (on completion of relief of batteries) taking over command of Right Group consisting of 104 Bde & A/102 Bde in position at C14 c 8 9. Front covered by Group from C.16 b 7 4 to V.28 a 1½ ½. Trenches 90 to 106 inclusive held by 68th Infy Bde.	
	21.8.16 to 26.8.16		Quiet. Registration proceeded with.	
	24.8.16	noon	Re-arrangement of Groups. Divisional front to be covered by two Groups instead of three. Right group consisting of H.Q. 104 Bde, A/104; B/104; C/104; D/104; A/102 Bde; A/103 Bde; D/105 Bde.	
	25.8.16 to 29.8.16		Quiet. Registration of batteries carried out also instruction of young officers	
	30.8.16	1.30am	On night of 29th/30th the Right Group bombarded trenches from 1.30am to 2.5am in conjunction with liberation of gas by 68th Infy Bde.	
		2.20am	Rt Group formed evening barrage for small raid by 68th Infy Bde	
	31.8.16		Quiet day.	

R [signature]
Lieut Colonel

SECRET

Instructions regarding War Diaries and Intelligence Summaries are contained in F. S. Regs., Part II. and the Staff Manual respectively. Title pages will be prepared in manuscript.

WAR DIARY
~~or~~
~~INTELLIGENCE SUMMARY.~~
(Erase heading not required.)

10TH BDE R.F.A.

Army Form C. 2118.

Vol 12

Place	Date	Hour	Summary of Events and Information	Remarks and references to Appendices
PLOEGSTEERT	SEPT 1, 2		Quiet day.	
	3		The Brigade was reorganized in to 2 6-gun 18-pounder batteries and 2, 4-gun 4.5" Howitzer Batteries. C/104 was split up, one section going to make up A/104 and the other to B/104. D/105, became F/45th L-Col. W. A. NICHOLSON took over command of the Brigade at 6 P.M. 2Lt J. C. S. DAVIES became Adjutant, Lt R. KUSEL going to 102 Bde R.F.A.	
	4, 5, 6, 7		Quiet day. Instruction of young officers carried on.	
	8		One section of A/104, B/104 and C/104 was relieved by section of the 88th Bde R.F.A.	
	9th		Sections relieved the day before marched back to billets north of BAILLEUL. Remaining sections of A, B, C. 104 Bde were relieved, the relief being completed by 7. P.M. C/104 withdrew its guns from the pits after dark.	
METEREN	10th		The remaining sections of Batteries and the Brigade Headquarters marched back to billets north of BAILLEUL.	
	11th		In billets.	
	12th		The Brigade entrained by batteries at BAILLEUL WEST for the SOMME area. Bde Hdqrs travelled with D/104. Entraining was accomplished easily under schedule time. Detraining took place at LONGEAU. Batteries marched independently to bivouacs near St GRATIEN.	

2353 Wt. W2544/1454 700,000 5/15 D. D. & L. A.D.S.S./Forms/C. 2118.

SECRET

Instructions regarding War Diaries and Intelligence Summaries are contained in F. S. Regs., Part II. and the Staff Manual respectively. Title pages will be prepared in manuscript.

WAR DIARY ~~or~~ ~~INTELLIGENCE SUMMARY.~~

(*Erase heading not required.*)

104TH BDE RFA.

Army Form C. 2118.

Place	Date	Hour	Summary of Events and Information	Remarks and references to Appendices
ST GRATIEN	SEPT 13th 14th 15th 16th 17th 18th		In bivouac.	
	19th		The Brigade marched to wagon lines of 72 Bde near ALBERT. First sections of batteries went in to action that night, relieving batteries at the 72nd Bde. D/104 went in to a new position.	
SOMME AREA	20th		Remaining personnel took over from 72nd Bde. Col NICHOLSON took over command at 1 P.M. Night barrage.	
	21st		2nd Lt. F. G. DELAMAIN, A/104 was killed. Quiet day. Usual night barrage.	
	22nd		Quiet day. Usual night barrage.	
	23rd		The Brigade fired in support of a minor infantry attack in the afternoon. Usual night barrage.	
	24th		B/104 fired during the morning at snipers in trees along the ALBERT-BAPAUME road.	
	25th		The Brigade fired in support of infantry attack between 12.30 P.M. and 4.0 P.M.	
	26th		C/104 and D/104 bombarded trench in M.26 central with about 750 rounds, O.C. D/104 observing.	
	27th		A/104 and B/104 D/104 fired at an M.G in M.26.b.2.7½. Quiet day.	
	28th		Quiet day. All batteries spent the day registering various points on the FLERS LINE and support trench also on DESTREMONT FARM.	
	29th		At 5.15 AM A and B batteries barraged round DESTREMONT FARM and C/104 bombarded the farm itself. Firing ceased at 6 AM and the infantry assaulted it.	

2353 Wt. W2544/1454 700,000 5/15 D. D. & L. A.D.S.S./Forms/C. 2118.

SECRET

Instructions regarding War Diaries and Intelligence Summaries are contained in F. S. Regs., Part II. and the Staff Manual respectively. Title pages will be prepared in manuscript.

WAR DIARY ~~or~~ ~~INTELLIGENCE SUMMARY~~

(*Erase heading not required.*)

104TH BDE RFA.

Army Form C. 2118.

Place	Date	Hour	Summary of Events and Information	Remarks and references to Appendices
CONTALMAISON	Sept 29th		A/104 put forward a single gun to cut wire ~~[illegible]~~ on the FLERS LINE. In the afternoon a bombardment of LE SARS was carried out. Usual night barrage.	
	30th		B/104 went back to rest in the Wagon Line. Brigade Hdqrs moved from BOTTOM WOOD to CONTALMAISON VILLA. Quiet day.	

[illegible signature]
Lt Colonel
Commdg 104 Bde R.F.A.

2353 Wt. W2544/1454 700,000 5/15 D. D. & L. A.D.S.S./Forms/C. 2118.

23 104 Bde RFA Vol 13

Army Form C. 2118.

Instructions regarding War Diaries and Intelligence Summaries are contained in F. S. Regs., Part II. and the Staff Manual respectively. Title pages will be prepared in manuscript.

WAR DIARY
or
~~INTELLIGENCE SUMMARY~~.

(Erase heading not required.)

Place	Date Oct	Hour	Summary of Events and Information	Remarks and references to Appendices
CONTALMAISON	1st		The Brigade fired during the afternoon in support of a successful attack by the 70th Infantry Brigade on the trenches in front of LE SARS. A night barrage was maintained on the left flank	
	2nd		C/104 and D/104 bombarded the FLERS LINE and SUPPORT from M.15.c.9½.9 and M.15.c.7:8½ respectively for 100 yds to the North. A night barrage was maintained.	
	3rd 4th		Quiet. Night barrages as usual.	
	5th		Registration, preparatory to further operations was carried out.	
	6th		Quiet day. Registration continued.	
	7th		The Brigade fired in support of an attack on LE SARS by the 68th & 69th Infantry Brigades. Results very satisfactory. A warning order for the relief of the Brigade was received in the evening.	
	8th		The Personnel of C/104 relieved that of D/252 and the personnel of D/104 relieved that of D/251 preparatory to going out of the line the next day. Cancellation of relief received in the evening.	
	9th		Quiet day. The Brigade came under the command of the 15th D.A at 9 AM.	
	10th		A certain amount of registration was carried out. D/104 registered points in WARLENCOURT. A night barrage was maintained.	
	11th		A daily bombardment of GALWITZ TRENCH was commenced. Task of B/104 to cut wire at long range at about M.10.d.5:4.	
	12th		Above programme continued.	
	13th 14th 15th 16th		Above programme continued.	

Instructions regarding War Diaries and Intelligence Summaries are contained in F. S. Regs., Part II. and the Staff Manual respectively. Title Pages will be prepared in manuscript.

WAR DIARY
or
~~INTELLIGENCE SUMMARY~~
(Erase heading not required.)

Army Form C. 2118

Place	Date	Hour	Summary of Events and Information	Remarks and references to Appendices
HIGH WOOD	17th		Hqrs 104 Bde moved to a spot, previously prepared, about 400 yds south of HIGH WOOD. Usual daily programme of shooting was carried out.	
	18 19 20		Quiet. Usual programme ie bombardment of GALWITZ TRENCH continued.	
	21		Fresh programme for day and night shooting received. By day B/104 cut wire as before and C and D/104 bombard GALWITZ TRENCH and SUPPORT in M.14.a. By night B/104 searched the road running South of WARLENCOURT through M.10.d. and the howitzer batteries searched the roads running E & W through M.10.a and b and N & S through M.5.a and d. and M.11.a.	
	22 23		Above programme continued.	
	24		Orders received for special bombardment in support of attack on GALWITZ LINE. Battery Commanders met at H.Q. 104 Bde to discuss programme with Brigade Commander who had previously been to a conference with G.O.C.R.A. 15th Div.	
	25		Special lines were laid out for communication with two special F.O.O's who were to go over with the Infantry. Programme postponed till 28th.	
	26 27		Usual bombardment continued. Orders received on 27th postponing attack till 30th.	
	28th		Warning order for relief of 104 Bde by 103 Bde received. Usual bombardment continued.	
	29th		Usual bombardment continued. O.C. and Adjt 103 Bde arrived at H.Q. 104 Bde. 1 section of A. B and D batteries relieved by sections of A. C. and D/103 respectively. C/104 to remain in position.	
	30th		Section relieved on night of 29/30th marched to St GRATIEN. Remaining section relieved. O.C. 103 Bde took over command in the evening.	
	31st		Remaining section marched to billets in St GRATIEN.	

[illegible] Major RA
Comg 104 Bde R.F.A.

1875 Wt. W593/826 1,000,000 4/15 J.B.C. & A. A.D.S.S./Forms/C. 2118.

SECRET

Instructions regarding War Diaries and Intelligence Summaries are contained in F. S. Regs., Part II. and the Staff Manual respectively. Title Pages will be prepared in manuscript.

WAR DIARY ~~or~~ ~~INTELLIGENCE SUMMARY~~

(Erase heading not required.)

Army Form C. 2118.

23

104th BRIGADE. RFA

Vol 14

Place	Date 1916 Nov	Hour	Summary of Events and Information	Remarks and references to Appendices
St GRATIEN	1st 2nd 3rd 4th 5th		In billets. Leave granted to men to go in to AMIENS daily. One officer per battery granted short leave to PARIS.	
	6th		Inspection of personnel of batteries (dismounted) by G.O.C.R.A. 23rd Div. at 3PM.	
	7th 8th 9th 10th		In billets.	
	11th		'C' Battery 104th Bde. R.F.A. arrived in billets.	
	12th		In billets.	
	13th		G.O.C.R.A. 23rd Div inspected 'C' battery 104th Bde. and presented the Military Medal to Gr NEWBURY B/104 and Gr SELL C/104.	
	14th		Warning order for relief of 102nd Brigade received.	
	15th		First Sections of 'A' 'B' and 'D' Batteries 104th Bde, moved up to the line, under command of MAJOR GROSE D/104, starting at 6.AM. Col. NICHOLSON went up to H.Q. 102 Bde at 10.30.AM.	
MARTINPUICH	16th		H.Qrs 104 Bde and remaining portions of 'A', 'B' and 'D' Batteries went up. O.C. 104 Bde took over the command from O.C. 102 Bde. at 3PM. A/102 came under the tactical command of O.C. 104 Bde. R.F.A.	
	17th		Quiet day.	

2449 Wt. W14957/M90 750,000 1/16 J.B.C. & A. Forms/C.2118/12.

Instructions regarding War Diaries and Intelligence Summaries are contained in F. S. Regs., Part II. and the Staff Manual respectively. Title Pages will be prepared in manuscript.

WAR DIARY

~~or~~

INTELLIGENCE ~~SUMMARY~~

(Erase heading not required.)

Army Form C. 2118.

Place	Date NOV	Hour	Summary of Events and Information	Remarks and references to Appendices
MARTINPUICH	18th		A/104; B/104 and A/102 put up a barrage to assist a successful attack by the 2nd Corps at 6.10. A.M.	
			A/104 barraged from M.8.d.0:3 to M.9.c.1:2. A/102 " " M.9.c.1:2 to M.9.c.6:3½. B/104 " " M.8.d.0:3 to M.8.d.3:0. } { SECRET MAP 1/10,000 LE SARS to LOUPART WOOD and LE BARQUE.	
	19th 20th 21st		Quiet days. Firing at night on roads and tracks.	
	22nd		D/104 commenced a daily bombardment of GAMP TRENCH.	
	23rd		A small bombardment was carried out in the afternoon at 3.PM. D/104 bombarded the BUTTE TRENCH from BAPAUME ROAD to M.10.d.8:½, and the 18 Pdrs bombarded the GALWITZ LINE from M.10.d.9:2 to M.10.d.6:4.	
	24th 25th 26th 27th 28th		Quiet. Firing at night in bursts at irregular intervals on tracks and roads in M.9 and M.3. Daily bombardment of GAMP TRENCH by D/104. Foggy.	
	29th		Very foggy. Firing was kept up on roads and tracks all day. At 5.PM, in consequence of a prisoners statement that a relief was expected that night, the rate of fire was increased to 100 rounds per hour for 18 Pdr batteries and 60 rds per hour for D/104. At 5.15 PM; 6.45 P.M.; 9.0 P.M; and 10.55 P.M. a special bombardment of LITTLE WOOD (M.10.c.0:8) took place. A/104 and A/102 put shrapnel round the wood while B/104 and D/104 searched the wood with H.E.	
	30th		Quiet day.	

W. A. [illegible] Lieut Col
Comdg 104 Bde R.F.A.

2449 Wt. W14957/M90 750,000 1/16 J.B.C. & A. Forms/C.2118/12.

104 Bde. R.F.A.

Instructions regarding War Diaries and Intelligence Summaries are contained in F. S. Regs., Part II. and the Staff Manual respectively. Title pages will be prepared in manuscript.

WAR DIARY
~~or~~
~~INTELLIGENCE SUMMARY.~~
(Erase heading not required.)

Army Form C. 2118.

Vol 15

Place	Date	Hour	Summary of Events and Information	Remarks and references to Appendices
MARTINPUICH	December 1st 2nd 3rd		Quiet days. Night firing was carried out as usual.	
	4th		First sections of A, B and D batteries were relieved by Sections of A, B and D Batteries 241st Brigade R.F.A. after dark.	
	5th		Remaining sections were relieved. Lt Col NICHOLSON handed over the command to Lt Col COLVILLE at 8 PM. First sections marched to billets at MOLLIENS-AU-BOIS.	
	6th		Remaining Sections and C/104 marched to billets at MOLLIENS-AU-BOIS.	
	7th 8th		In billets. Cleaning up and preparing for the march.	
	9th		The Brigade marched to billets at BARLY, starting at 7.15 A.M. Route via BEAUVAL GEZAINCOURT - HEM.	
	10th		Resting in billets.	
	11th		March to billets at BOUBERS-SUR-CANCHE (H.Q. C+D Batts) and LIGNY-SUR-CANCHE (A+B Batts), via BONNIÈRES.	
	12th		The Brigade marched to HUCLIER (H.Q. A+B Batts) and TROISVAUX (C+D Batts) via St POL. Very bad weather with snow and driving wind.	
	13th		In Billets at HUCLIER and TROISVAUX	
	14th		The Brigade marched to billets at AUCHY-AU-BOIS via PERNES, starting at 9.15 am	
	15th		The Brigade marched to billets at THIENNES via AIRE.	
	16th		In billets at THIENNES.	
	17th		The Brigade marched to billets at STEENVOORDE	

104 Bde. R.F.A.

Instructions regarding War Diaries and Intelligence Summaries are contained in F. S. Regs., Part II. and the Staff Manual respectively. Title pages will be prepared in manuscript.

WAR DIARY

~~or~~

~~INTELLIGENCE SUMMARY.~~

(Erase heading not required.)

Army Form C. 2118.

Place	Date	Hour	Summary of Events and Information	Remarks and references to Appendices
STEENVOORDE	18th 19th 20th 21st 22nd 23rd		In billets at STEENVOORDE. Time spent in cleaning up harness, vehicles etc. Parties went to the baths daily.	
	24th		The N.C.O's & men of the Brigade had their Christmas dinners, owing to the Brigade being ordered to march to the CALAIS training area on the 26th	
	25th		Christmas Day. Preparations for the march were made. A concert was given to the men in the evening.	
	26th		The Brigade marched to billets at LEDERZEELE and WULVERDINGE.	
	27th		The march was continued to billets at NORDAUSQUES.	
	28th		The Batteries, starting at half hour intervals, marched to billets at FRAMEZELLE (HQ & D Bty) AUDINGHEN (B Bty) and TARDINGHEN (A & C Btys). A Battery started at 6.30 AM C at 7 AM D at 7.30 AM and B at 7.55 AM. The Baggage Train started at 8 AM.	
	29th		The day was spent in cleaning harness and vehicles.	
	30th		Training commenced. Riding drill was carried out during the morning. In the afternoon orders were received to move in to the ESCALLES area.	
	31st		The Brigade marched to billets at ESCALLES and PEUPLINGUES. Great difficulty was experienced in finding sufficient room as all the barns were full of unthrashed grain.	

[signature] Lieut-Col
COMMANDING 104th BRIGADE R.F.A.

2353 Wt. W2544/1454 700,000 5/15 D. D. & L. A.D.S.S./Forms/C. 2118.

23RD DIVISION
DIVL ARTILLERY

105TH BRIGADE R.F.A.

AUG 1915-SEP 1916.

BROKEN UP

23rd Division

121/7595.

105th Bde: R.F.A.

Vol I

August / 15

to

Sep '16

Confidential

Headquarters
105 Bde RFA

Army Form C. 2118.

Instructions regarding War Diaries and Intelligence Summaries are contained in F. S. Regs., Part II. and the Staff Manual respectively. Title pages will be prepared in manuscript.

WAR DIARY
or
~~INTELLIGENCE SUMMARY.~~

(Erase heading not required.)

Place	Date	Hour	Summary of Events and Information	Remarks and references to Appendices
Bordon	20/8/15	5 pm	Order to Mobilize received, Officers, N C O's and men recalled from leave.	
	20/8/15		Drawing Equipment, Ammunition, Clothing etc from Field Stores Aldershot	
	to 24/8/15			
	25/8/15		Amm Col. B. C. D. A Batteries, (Hdqrs with A) entrained for Southampton and on arrival embarked on various boats for Havre. No casualties on voyage, very smooth voyage.	
Havre	26/8/15		Brigade went into No 5 Rest Camp and moved on by rail to a Concentration camp at various times of that and following day.	
	27/8/15		A & B Batteries detraining at Audruicq and C & D Batteries and Ammun Column at St Omer.	
Louringues lez-Ardres	28/8/15		All units had arrived and occupied their billets by 6 pm, the brigade being quartered at various farm houses in the village. No other troops being near. The 23rd Division concentrated on either side of St Omer – Calais Road from NIELLES-lez ARDRES to TILQUES.	
	29/8/15		Resting, cleaning equipment etc. Divine Service.	
"	30/8/15		Rest and making bivouacs etc habitable.	
	31/8/15		Brigade Parade, registering zones on northern bank of St Louis River	

[signature] Lieut. R.F.A. Adjutant 105 Brigade R.F.A.

2353 Wt. W2544/1454 700,000 5/15 D. D. & L. A.D.S.S./Forms/C. 2118.

121/7430

23rd Division

105th Bde: R.F.A.

Vol 2

Sept & Oct 15

2

Confidential

Instructions regarding War Diaries and Intelligence Summaries are contained in F. S. Regs., Part II. and the Staff Manual respectively. Title pages will be prepared in manuscript.

WAR DIARY or INTELLIGENCE SUMMARY.

(Erase heading not required.)

Headquarters 105th Bde. R.F.A.

Army Form C. 2118.

Place	Date	Hour	Summary of Events and Information	Remarks and references to Appendices
Tonninques-lez-Ardres	1/9/15 to 5/9/15		Training Continued, registering Fire Zones, route march for the Division. Weather extremely wet.	
– " –	6/9/15		23rd Divisional Artillery marched to BANDRINGHEM and CAMPAGNE, 105th Brigade bivouacked at BANDRINGHEM.	
BANDRINGHEM.	7/9/15		Continued the march to BORRE and STRAZEELE, 105th Brigade at BORRE in billets.	
BORRE	8/9/15		March continued to STEENWERCK where batteries bivouacked for 2 hours, afterwards going on to CHAPELLE ARMENTIERES, one section of each battery going into action same night. "C" Battery was detached from brigade and attached to 20th DIVISION for instruction. Brigade Ammunition Column split up and sent one sub-section to each battery; a few details remaining at BORRE. A, B & D Batteries were attached to units of 27th DIVISION for instruction and eventually occupying the positions of the batteries to which they were attached.	
CHAPELLE ARMENTIERES	9/9/15	8 pm	Remaining sections moved up from Wagon line into action. Batteries opened fire with one section of Guns prior to the other section being brought up.	

T. C. George
Lieut. R.F.A.
Adjutant 105 Brigade R.F.A.

2353 Wt. W2544/1454 700,000 5/15 D. D. & L. A.D.S.S./Forms/C. 2118.

3

105th Bde. R.F.A.

Army Form C. 2118.

Instructions regarding War Diaries and Intelligence Summaries are contained in F. S. Regs., Part II. and the Staff Manual respectively. Title pages will be prepared in manuscript.

WAR DIARY

or

~~INTELLIGENCE SUMMARY.~~

(Erase heading not required.)

Confidential

Place	Date	Hour	Summary of Events and Information	Remarks and references to Appendices
CHAPELLE ARMENTIERES	9/9/15 to 13/9/15		Registering Targets within the Zones allotted to batteries. Bde. Zone, Front of Trenches 52-66. Batteries in action at:- "A" H.7.b.4.4. "B" H.8.a.7.4. "D" H.13.b.4.9. 1/20,000 36 N.W. Zones extending from WEZ MACQUART to FARM HOUSSAIN. Bde. Hdqrs at I.1.c.1.6.	
"	14/9/15		Brigade attached to 8th Division. Batteries moved to positions as follow:- "A" LA VESEE. "B" GRIS POT. "D" Le COROMBALOT.	
	22/9/15		Batteries bombarded enemy's trenches in accordance with 8th Division Arty. Operation Order No 5. 30 rounds H.E. per gun being fired.	
	23/9/15 to 24/9/15		Bombardment of enemy's trenches continued.	
	25/9/15	4-25 A.M.	Bombardment of enemy's trenches resumed, preparatory to the assault by Infantry.	
"		4-30 A.M.	Assault by Infantry on hostile trenches between CORNER FORT N.6.8.6 and BRIDOUX FORT I.31.d. Fire lifted during assault. 50 rounds H.E. per gun being fired.	
"		3.15 p.m.	"A" Battery had a direct hit on one ~~of~~ Gun Emplacement which exploded the ammunition (lyddite) in the emplacement and killed the detachment, 1 Sgt. and 6 Others. A second hit on the telephone dugout killed a telephonist and wounded 2 others. Nature of projectile believed to be 4·2" Howitzer.	

[signature] Lieut. R.F.A.
Adjutant 105 Brigade R.F.A.

2353 Wt. W2544/1454 700,000 5/15 D. D. & L. A.D.S.S./Forms/C. 2118.

4

105th Bde R.F.A. **WAR DIARY** ~~or INTELLIGENCE SUMMARY.~~ Confidential

Army Form C. 2118.

Instructions regarding War Diaries and Intelligence Summaries are contained in F. S. Regs., Part II. and the Staff Manual respectively. Title pages will be prepared in manuscript.

(Erase heading not required.)

Place	Date	Hour	Summary of Events and Information	Remarks and references to Appendices
~~26/9/15~~ LA VESEE	26/9/15		"A" Battery was moved to new position of Gris Pot - la Vesee Road I.13.C.4.4. 1/20,000 N.W. but owing to its proximity to an 18 Pdr. Battery immediately in rear and a counter battery being required it was moved after 4 or 5 days to le CROMBALOT.	
ARMENTIERES	Night of 27-28		Brigade rejoined 23rd Division for tactical purposes, ceasing to be attached to 8th Division. D/105 moving to I.8.a.5.5. A/105 + B/105 remaining in their present positions.	Operation Order No 4 23rd Divn Arty.
	Night of 28-29		C/105 rejoined from 20th Division and occupied a position at I.1.d.5.2. The Brigade is now complete and is placed under the direct orders of G.O.C. R.A. and considered to be a separate group.	Operation Order No 5
	30/9 to 10/10/15		Practically no firing on either side except for registration purposes	
	11/10/15		Germans ~~attack~~ bombarded our Trench 61, C/105 ordered to fire 12 rounds on German trench opposite 61 and D/105 to do same. Enemy's fire not having ceased D/105 continued to bombard his parapet, firing 41 rounds in all. During the firing 2 small field guns obtained direct hits on gun emplacements of C/105 but practically no damage was done. No casualties occurred.	
	12/10/15		C/105 moved to new position at I.1.d.1.9., an excellent position in kitchen garden, this position is so well concealed that it cannot be located from the air. (Aeroplane reconnaissance report of 26/10/15)	[signature] Lieut. R.F.A. Adjutant 105 Brigade R.F.A.

2353 Wt. W2544/1454 700,000 5/15 D. D. & L. A.D.S.S./Forms/C. 2118.

23rd Division

105th Bde: R.F.A.

Vol: 3

121/7693

Nov. 15

5/

Instructions regarding War Diaries and Intelligence Summaries are contained in F. S. Regs., Part II. and the Staff Manual respectively. Title pages will be prepared in manuscript.

WAR DIARY 105 Bde. R.F.A.
~~or INTELLIGENCE SUMMARY.~~

(Erase heading not required.)

Army Form C. 2118.

Place	Date	Hour	Summary of Events and Information	Remarks and references to Appendices
ARMENTIERES	13/10/15 to 31/10/15		Defence Orders issued to batteries to form a barrage of fire on 23rd Divn. front in case of an attack. A/105, fire distributed over Support Trenches I. 31. d. 8. 6½. to I. 31. d. 10. 4. (inclusive) B/105, Support trenches I. 31. d. 10. 4. (exclusive) to I. 32. c. 4. 7 (inclusive). Rate, section fire 30 secs. The dividing line of 8th and 23rd Divn. fronts are trenches 51 - 52. Trenches 52 to 66 being held by 23rd Divn. Registration by aeroplane and F.O.O. carried out daily, weather permitting and some hostile Artillery being replied to by retaliation on 1st Line and Support trenches.	Lieut. R.F.A. Adjutant 105 Brigade R.F.A. F George
	7/10/15		Trenches on 23rd Divn. Front Nos. 52 to 66 re-numbered as follows:- I. 32. I. 26. 1. I. 26. 2. I. 26. 3. I. 26. 4. I. 26. 5. I. 20. 1. I. 20. 2. I. 21. 1. I. 21. 2. I. 21. 3. I. 21. 4. I. 15. 1. I. 15. 2. I. 16. New numbers did not become universal until end of Octr.	
	2/11/15		2 Hostile batteries engaged, effect not known; some retaliation carried out.	
	4/11/15		12 Rounds fired on Hostile battery at I 30. c. 2. 6. in retaliation	
	5/11/15		Enemy fired some 130 rounds on this front, various types	

2353 Wt. W2544/1454 700,000 5/15 D. D. & L. A.D.S.S./Forms/C. 2118.

6

WAR DIARY 105 Bde. R.F.A.

or

~~INTELLIGENCE SUMMARY~~.

(Erase heading not required.)

Army Form C. 2118.

Instructions regarding War Diaries and Intelligence Summaries are contained in F. S. Regs., Part II. and the Staff Manual respectively. Title pages will be prepared in manuscript.

Place	Date	Hour	Summary of Events and Information	Remarks and references to Appendices
ARMENTIERES			of gun being used, e.g. 15 C.M. How. 10·5 C.M. How. and Gun. 4·65 in. Gun (believed to have been captured from the French) and 7·7 cm Field Gun. Retaliation ordered on ENNETIERES.	
	8/11/15		A party of Munition workers visited various units of the Divn and B/105 fired 6 rounds at an hostile battery, O.3.d.9.1. for their edification. The party was then taken to the trenches and a few more rounds fired over their heads.	
	9/11/15		Enemy fired about 90 rounds from 15 C.M. How. 10·5 C.M. How 4·65 in. and 7·7 C.M. Field guns, round about GRIS POT X roads and ARMENTIERES. We replied with 50 into LA VALLEE, ENNETIERES and BLANC COULON. B.S.M. Keeley A/105 awarded the D.C.M. for gallantry on 25/9/15. Presented with medal by Major Genl. Babington.	George Lieut. R.F.A. Adjutant 105 Brigade R.F.A.
	10/11/15		About 250 rounds fired by the enemy, chiefly into CHAPELLE d'ARMENTIERES and ARMENTIERES. We fired 94 into the enemy's trenches and suspected billets in rear.	
	11/11/15		More than 100 rounds fired by the enemy, some 60 odd	

2353 Wt. W2544/1454 700,000 5/15 D. D. & L. A.D.S.S./Forms/C. 2118.

7

WAR DIARY ~~or~~ ~~INTELLIGENCE SUMMARY~~.

105 Bde. R.F.A.

Army Form C. 2118.

Instructions regarding War Diaries and Intelligence Summaries are contained in F. S. Regs., Part II. and the Staff Manual respectively. Title pages will be prepared in manuscript.

(Erase heading not required.)

Place	Date	Hour	Summary of Events and Information	Remarks and references to Appendices
			being fired into CROMBALOT and vicinity.	
ARMENTIERES	11/11/15		We fired by means of aeroplane ~~239~~ observation, 237 rounds into German trenches and billets and about 40 more at working parties and battery positions.	
	12/11/15		A hostile battery near SATTE RUE fired 30 rounds 10.5 cm. at LA TOULETTE, about 50% were blinds. We fired at screens I.22.c., some 55 rounds.	
	15/11/15		The enemy fired about 12 rounds into GRIS POT. During the day we fired 15 rounds into LA VALLEE, 15 into TROIS FETUS and 50 into ENNETIERES.	
	18/11/15		Enemy fired about 400 rounds into GRIS POT ARMENTIERES and CHAPELLE d'ARMENTIERES. We replied with 350 rounds into LA VALLE, HALTE x ROADS, RADINGHEM, ENNETIERES, PREMESQUES and road junctions, in addition to trenches.	
	21/11/15		The 23rd Divn. front was extended to the right, taking over trenches I.31.1. I.31.2. I.31.3. I.31.4. and I.31.5. from 8th Divn. the front now being from I.31.0.0.0. to I.16.C.7.9.	

H. George
Lieut. R.F.A.
Adjutant [illegible] Brigade R.F.A.

2353 Wt. W2544/1454 700,000 5/15 D. D. & L. A.D.S.S./Forms/C. 2118.

8

WAR DIARY or ~~INTELLIGENCE SUMMARY~~.

105 Bde. R.F.A.

Army Form C. 2118.

Instructions regarding War Diaries and Intelligence Summaries are contained in F. S. Regs., Part II. and the Staff Manual respectively. Title pages will be prepared in manuscript.

(Erase heading not required.)

Place	Date	Hour	Summary of Events and Information	Remarks and references to Appendices
ARMENTIERES	23/11/15		Points registered, about 23 rounds fired. Enemy fired about 5 into LA VESEE 7.7 cm.	
	25/11/15		Points on trenches registered, enemy fired very little.	
	26/11/15		D/105 fired on a hostile battery at I.29.c.7.8. (15 rounds) and B/105 at billets. Enemy fired about 20 into CHAPELLE d'ARMENTIERES. 40 into LA VESEE, and vicinity	
	27/11/15		SNIPERS HOUSE registered. Enemy fired 80 odd, chiefly into LA VESEE and ARMENTIERES	
	28/11/15		Enemy fired 100 rounds all along the front. We did not reply	
	29/11/15		Bombardment of the Distilleries I.27.b.5.5. and the Hostile Salient at I.26.c.8.1. was carried out in accordance with a pre-arranged scheme. B/105 fired 40 rounds, C/105 20 rounds and D/105 25 rounds. In addition D/105 fired 20 rounds at a supposed battery position at I.29.a.2.2. and A/105 fired 23 rounds at hostile battery at O.13.b.7.0. the flashes of this btty being seen. A direct hit was obtained, a separate explosion	[signature] Lieut. R.F.A. Adjutant 105 Brigade R.F.A.

2353 Wt. W2544/1454 700,000 5/15 D. D. & L. A.D.S.S./Forms/C. 2118.

9

WAR DIARY or ~~INTELLIGENCE SUMMARY~~. 105 Bde. RFA. Army Form C. 2118.

(*Erase heading not required.*)

Instructions regarding War Diaries and Intelligence Summaries are contained in F. S. Regs., Part II. and the Staff Manual respectively. Title pages will be prepared in manuscript.

Place	Date	Hour	Summary of Events and Information	Remarks and references to Appendices
			being heard after shell had burst. The 23rd Divl. Arty. and 2	
ARMENTIERES	29/11/15		Siege Batteries, 24 - 30, 8" How. and 6" How. were all engaged	
			on this scheme.	
	30/11/15		C/105 engaged hostile battery at I.35. b. 6½. 9½ and although it failed to obtain a hit several shell fell near the gun emplacements and in the hedge near the battery. 30 rounds fired. The enemy fired 162 at CROMBALOT and L'ARMEE B/105 fired 10 rounds at supposed battery position at O.3. b. 6.0.	

H. George
Lieut., R.F.A.
Adjutant 105 Brigade R.F.A.

2353 Wt. W2544/1454 700,000 5/15 D. D. & L. A.D.S.S./Forms/C. 2118.

23rd Divn

105th Bde: R.F.A.
Vol: 4

121/7910

10/

Instructions regarding War Diaries and Intelligence Summaries are contained in F. S. Regs., Part II. and the Staff Manual respectively. Title pages will be prepared in manuscript.

WAR DIARY
or
INTELLIGENCE SUMMARY.
(Erase heading not required.)

Army Form C. 2118.

Place	Date	Hour	Summary of Events and Information	Remarks and references to Appendices
ARMENTIE RES.	1 12/15		Enemy shelled BOIS GRENIER and CHAPELLE D'ARMENTIERES with 10.5 Cm. and 4.65 in. (69 rounds). We retaliated on Observation Stations and road junctions near WEZ MACQUART 65 rounds.	
	2 12/15		Enemy fired 15 rounds into Chapelle d'Armentieres between 9.30 AM. and 11 A.M. and at 8.30 p.m. some 5 or 6 rounds from the 4.65" battery along the Road H.6.d. to I.1.d., we fired 10 rounds into PREMESQUES at 8.35 pm. During the night of 2/3 the enemy fired a single gun at intervals of 10 or 15 minutes along the roads RUE MARLE, L'ARMEE and CHAPELLE d'ARMENTIERES.	
	3 12/15		Practically no shelling on either side. Very wet and misty all day.	
	4 12/15	3.30pm.	A/105 fired at 77 m.m. battery in O.14.b. (one round). B/105 fired 10 into HALTE in retaliation for enemy shelling on observing station at I.19.c.9.6. At 4.20 pm. the enemy shelled ARMENTIERES STATION and vicinity with 5.9" How. about 20 rounds. Casualties reported amongst troops on roads, 4 killed, several wounded, believed to be Durham Light Infantry.	[signature] Lieut. R.F.A. Adjutant 105 Brigade R.F.A.

2353 Wt. W2544/1454 700,000 5/15 D. D. & L. A.D.S.S./Forms/C. 2118.

11

WAR DIARY 105th Bde, R.F.A.

~~or~~

~~INTELLIGENCE SUMMARY~~.

(Erase heading not required.)

Army Form C. 2118.

Instructions regarding War Diaries and Intelligence Summaries are contained in F. S. Regs., Part II. and the Staff Manual respectively. Title pages will be prepared in manuscript.

Place	Date	Hour	Summary of Events and Information	Remarks and references to Appendices
ARMENTIERES	5/12/15	11.30 am.	C/105 fired 15 rounds at Salient in I.26.b. (fire trench) 2 hits on parapet, 4 in trench. About 20 yards of wire entanglement destroyed. D/105 fired at a supposed hostile battery at I.23.c.3.½. (2 rounds) battery ceased firing after 1st round. B/105 registered on parapet I.26.b.8.2.	
	6/12/15	1.30 pm to 3.45 pm	Enemy shelled reserve trenches and searched roads CHAPELLE-D'ARMENTIERES to ARMENTIERES, about 80 rounds (4.2" and 4.7" shells.) "B" Group carried out a scheme, Cutting wire and breaching the enemy's parapet in I.22.a. 184 rounds of Lyddite fired by this brigade and 2 breaches being made in parapet and wire considerably damaged. Explosions with No 100 + 44 fuzes were very poor.	
	7/12/15		"A" Group carried out a scheme, B/105 bombarded parapet at I.26.b.8.2. to I.26.b.7½.5 and fired 70 rounds H.E. doing considerable damage to parapet, fuze No 100 delay action used, 4 blinds. C/105 also bombarded parapet at I.26.b.7½.5. to I.26.b.8½.8½. and probably hit dug outs in trenches as wood etc, was seen to fly up now and again, there were 3 blinds. C/105 also fired 30 rounds into enemy support trench at I.27.a.2.4. to I.27.a.3.6. (2 blinds). D/105 fired 6 rounds at WEZ MACQUART (Tuileries) supposed Observing station in retaliation for shelling of LILLE POST, (our O.P.) The enemy fired about 60	
		11 A.M.	heavy shell into H.29.a. probably 5.9" and about 30 into H.29.b. (4.2") at 3 pm. also 12 (4.2") into I.1.d. and 12 (77 m/m) into I.9.d. about 2.30 pm. The shell fired into I.1.d. were believed to be French shell as they were fitted with French pattern fuzes.	

W.A. Nicholson
LIEUT. COLONEL, R.F.A.
COMMANDING 105TH BRIGADE, R.F.A.

2353 Wt. W2544/1454 700,000 5/15 D. D. & L. A.D.S.S./Forms/C. 2118.

Instructions regarding War Diaries and Intelligence Summaries are contained in F. S. Regs., Part II. and the Staff Manual respectively. Title pages will be prepared in manuscript.

12

WAR DIARY ~~or~~ ~~INTELLIGENCE SUMMARY~~. 105th Bde. R.F.A.

(*Erase heading not required.*)

Army Form C. 2118.

Place	Date	Hour	Summary of Events and Information	Remarks and references to Appendices
ARMENTIERES	8/12/15	11.30 AM to 4 pm.	Enemy fired about 125 rounds, principally 4.2" How. into CHAPELLE D' ARMENTIERES and I.9.c. also H18.a. where they appeared to be searching for one of our heavy batteries. Bearings of flashes were taken. D/105 retaliated on WEZ MACQUART and GRAND MARAIS for hostile shelling of CHAPELLE D' ARMENTIERES.	
		2.30 pm.	B/105 fired 40 rounds with one gun on front trench I.26.C.8.1. to I.32.a.8¼.8½. and was very effective, many shots seen to rake the fire trench and parapet. The Right Section of this battery made 3 breaches in the parapet of enemy's front trench, at I.32.a.6.6½. to I.32.a.8¼.8½., the breaches were 2 ft. deep and from 12 to 15 yards long. Some shots entered trench and threw up boards and material. Considerable damage done to wire. 3 Enemy aeroplanes over GRIS POT after this battery started firing, they were not driven off by our anti-aircraft Guns or planes and eventually crossed their lines near point where their parapet was being damaged.	
	9/12/15	11.35 AM	B/105 fired 20 rounds at parapet I.32.a.4½.3. at request of Infantry in order that a quantity of water which was dammed by the parapet could be released and allowed to flow into the enemy's trench through the breach thus made. This was not successful as the parapet was found to be very thick and it was estimated that 200 rounds would be required to make the breach.	
		1.30 pm.	Enemy shelled RUE MARLE and Railway Crossing, causing several Casualties, 15 to 20 5.9 Howitzer, and during the next 2 hours some rounds fell into ARMENTIERES, apparently from the same battery.	

[signature]
LIEUT. COLONEL, R.F.A.
COMMANDING 105TH BRIGADE, R.F.A.

2353 Wt. W2544/1454 700,000 5/15 D. D. & L. A.D.S.S./Forms/C. 2118.

13

WAR DIARY ~~INTELLIGENCE SUMMARY~~.

105th Bde. R.F.A

Army Form C. 2118.

Instructions regarding War Diaries and Intelligence Summaries are contained in F. S. Regs., Part II. and the Staff Manual respectively. Title pages will be prepared in manuscript.

(Erase heading not required.)

Place	Date	Hour	Summary of Events and Information	Remarks and references to Appendices
	9/12/15	1 p.m. to 3 p.m.	Enemy shelled Cross Roads I.1.d.9.1 and vicinity, also H.18.C. about 53 rounds into latter area, all 4.2". We replied by shelling ENNETIERES, RADINGHEM, BEAUCAMPS, LA VALLEE and a Battery position at I.36.a.0.2.	
	10/12/15	9-15 to 4 pm	Enemy distributed his fire over the 23rd Div. area firing about 250 rounds, we replied with 300 rounds on his support trenches chiefly, and also fired at 2 batteries, one in action at O.8.b.4½.0. which could be seen, and a supposed battery position at I.36.a.1.4. B/105 observed flashes and identified 4 gun emplacements at O.8.b.4½.0. and ranged on battery; after getting the short bracket the detachments could be seen running into a copse near the position. A deliberate rate of fire was then opened and two hits were obtained on the emplacements. It is believed that some ammunition was destroyed as a separate explosion followed the burst of one of our shell.	
	11/12/15	2.15 to 3 pm	D/105 bombarded Trench at I.21.b.7.3 to I.21.b.5.0 doing considerable damage, with 100 rounds Lyddite. We also fired at LE MAISNIL obtaining 8 hits on the WHITE HOUSE, suspected O.P. A/105 C/105 fired at Hostile battery at I.36.a.1.3 which was seen firing. Enemy fired very little, only 50 rounds being reported.	

A. a. Nicholson

LIEUT. COLONEL. R.F.A.
COMMANDING 105TH BRIGADE. R.F.A.

Instructions regarding War Diaries and Intelligence Summaries are contained in F. S. Regs., Part II. and the Staff Manual respectively. Title pages will be prepared in manuscript.

WAR DIARY
~~or~~
~~INTELLIGENCE SUMMARY.~~
(Erase heading not required.)

14

105th Bde R.F.A.

Army Form C. 2118.

Place	Date	Hour	Summary of Events and Information	Remarks and references to Appendices
	12/12/15	11.30 a.m.	C/105 fired on trenches I.26.b.7.5. & I.26.b.8.6. in "B" Group scheme, 40 rds. but the rounds were not observed. Enemy did not fire today.	
	13/12/15	12 Noon to 2-15 p.m.	"A" Group scheme. A & C Batteries bombarded parapet at I.26.c.9.2 to I.26.c.7¾.1. and I.32.a.8.8. to I.26.c.7¾.1. doing considerable damage and throwing timber and other material into the air. D/105 retaliated on hostile parapet at I.22.b.3.7. opposite trench I.15.2. for shelling of our support trenches. Enemy fired at the Cross roads I.1.d. 5 rounds 7.7 c.m. and also 2 rounds with 5.9 How at I.1.a. 3.45 p.m., and some into our support trenches.	
	14/12/15	1.30 p.m.	C/105 bombarded front trench at I.21.d.2.9 in B Group scheme. 50 rds AE. Material being thrown into the air, amongst which was a wheel barrow, the parapet was not breached however. Burst being poor T.N.T. gave 4 blinds out of 9. Mark V Gaine, fuze 100 gave better results but detonations often poor. Telephone wire cut by shrapnel during the series, cutting off communication with F.O.O. D/105 at same time bombarded parapet at point of Salient I.21.b.4½.3½. doing a good deal of damage to parapet 30% hits. The "shorts" broke up wire and chevaux de frise, the "overs" sent up debris of planks, footboards and wire revetments. Enemy fired very few rounds only is reported.	

W. A. Nicholson
LIEUT. COLONEL, R.F.A.
COMMANDING 105TH BRIGADE, R.F.A.

W. W. [illegible] 454 [illegible] D. D. & L. A.D.S.S./Forms/C. 2118.

15

WAR DIARY 105th Bde. R.F.A.

or

~~INTELLIGENCE SUMMARY~~.

(*Erase heading not required.*)

Army Form C. 2118.

Instructions regarding War Diaries and Intelligence Summaries are contained in F. S. Regs., Part II. and the Staff Manual respectively. Title pages will be prepared in manuscript.

Place	Date	Hour	Summary of Events and Information	Remarks and references to Appendices
	15/12/15	2.45 to 3.15 pm	Enemy shelled Chapelle d'Armentieres with 4.2", flashes seen and bearings taken, about 40 shell. We retaliated by firing at 2 battery positions at I 24. d. 5. 7. and I. 29. c. 7. 6.	
	16/12/15	2.30 to 4 pm	Enemy shelled BOIS GRENIER with 7.7 cm and 10.5 cm about 100 rds. We retaliated on front trench, support trench and LE BAS HAU Road.	
	17/12/15		No firing on either side.	
	18/12/15		A party of Recruiting Committee under Lord Derby's scheme of Voluntary service, visited the Divisional Area and B/105 fired one round at RADINGHEM for their edification. About 20 rounds fired by hostile batteries at H. 36. d. and vicinity, 3 were blinds.	
	19/12/15	8.45 am	Enemy commenced shelling Cross roads at I. 1. d. and from then until 11 am shelled I. 9. a., this being part of an attack on the Division on our left, 21st Division.	
		11.5 am	We retaliated on the enemy front trenches at I. 16. d. (67 rds.) to assist 21st Divn.	
		12.15 pm	C/105 fired 45 rounds on front trench at I. 32. a. 4. ¼ to I. 32. a. 4½. ½. "A" Group scheme. Wire to F.O.O. badly cut by shrapnel.	

N. A. Thicknesse
LIEUT. COLONEL, R.F.A.
COMMANDING 105TH BRIGADE, R.F.A.

2353 Wt. W2544/1454 700,000 5/15 D. D. & L. A.D.S.S./Forms/C. 2118.

Instructions regarding War Diaries and Intelligence Summaries are contained in F. S. Regs., Part II. and the Staff Manual respectively. Title pages will be prepared in manuscript.

16

WAR DIARY ~~or~~ ~~INTELLIGENCE~~ ~~SUMMARY.~~

(Erase heading not required.)

105th Bde R.F.A.

Army Form C. 2118.

Place	Date	Hour	Summary of Events and Information	Remarks and references to Appendices
	19/12/15	1 pm	A/105 also fired at parapet I.32.c.3.9¾ to I.32.a.4.¼, 15 rounds. "A" Group scheme.	
			B/105 shelled houses at I.32.c.4.7. & I.32.c.5.8. (15 rds.) obtaining 10 hits.	
	20/12/15	12-15 to 1 pm.	D/105 bombarded German House I.21.c.1½.1. (15 hits) shooting consistent. Almost 50% blind and 20% explosions poor. Ground very soft. (50 rds.)	
		12-15	Enemy retaliated on our trenches at I.21.a.9.4 to I.21.a.9.7 30 rounds 7.7 cm.	
		3.30 to 4 pm	About 30 rounds fired into I.8.a. by a 4.2 battery believed to be behind LE BLANC COULON.	
	21/12/15	1-45 pm	"B" Group scheme. D/105 bombarded parapet at I.22.a.3.6½. (30 rds.) 12 hits. 2 blinds. small breach in parapet. No reply from enemy.	
	22/12/15	11 am.	A 7.7 cm. battery fired 4 rounds at A/105 position, obtained hit on Barn, no damage.	
		12 Noon 12-45 pm	D/105 put 15 rounds into CAPINGHEM, Infantry billets of 179th Regt.	
			—"—	
			The information regarding disposition of German troops and their billets obtained from prisoners taken by 21st Division is being used	

W. A. [illegible]
LIEUT. COLONEL, R.F.A.
COMMANDING 105TH BRIGADE, R.F.A.

2353 Wt. W2544/1454 700,000 5/15 D. D. & L. A.D.S.S./Forms/C. 2118.

Instructions regarding War Diaries and Intelligence Summaries are contained in F. S. Regs., Part II. and the Staff Manual respectively. Title pages will be prepared in manuscript.

17

WAR DIARY 105th Bde R.F.A

~~or~~

~~INTELLIGENCE~~ SUMMARY.

(Erase heading not required.)

Army Form C. 2118.

Place	Date	Hour	Summary of Events and Information	Remarks and references to Appendices
	22/12/15	1-15 pm to 1-40 pm	A machine gun emplacement located at I 22. a. 3. 6½. was now shot at and believed to have been knocked out.	
	23/12/15		We fired about 80 rounds at various points; 2 battery positions; and front trenches. Some registration carried out. Enemy fired over 300 rounds during the day, from 5.9", 4.2" and 7.7 cm. distributed over the Divisional area.	
	24/12/15		"B" Group carried out a scheme, D/105 firing 84 rounds on "German House," "Grand Marais" and Parapet at I. 21. b. ½. 3. A/105 practised barrage at I. 22. a. 8. 8½, 30 rds. effect good. The enemy fired about 200 rounds at BOIS GRENIER, CHAPELLE D' ARMENTIERES and other points in the Divl. area.	
	25/12/15	11 am.	Christmas Day. "B" Group carried out a scheme, D/105 bombarding parapet at I. 22. a. 3. 6½ to I. 22. a. 6. 9. and Communication trench in rear. "Large Farm" was also shelled. No. 33 German Battery at I. 24. a. 5. 7½ was firing and after 20 rounds had been directed at it by D/105 it ceased to fire.	
		2pm.	Artillery Officers billet at FME. DE L'EPERONNERIE was shelled	

W.A. Nicholson
LIEUT. COLONEL, R.F.A.
COMMANDING 105th BRIGADE, R.F.A.

2353 Wt. W2544/1454 700,000 5/15 D. D. & L. A.D.S.S./Forms/C. 2118.

18 **WAR DIARY** ~~or~~ 105th Bde. R.F.A. Army Form C. 2118.

~~INTELLIGENCE SUMMARY.~~

(Erase heading not required.)

Instructions regarding War Diaries and Intelligence Summaries are contained in F. S. Regs., Part II. and the Staff Manual respectively. Title pages will be prepared in manuscript.

Place	Date	Hour	Summary of Events and Information	Remarks and references to Appendices
	25/12/15		in the hope that the occupants might be disturbed whilst at Dinner. Altogether, this brigade fired 221 rounds at various targets during the day and although the Hun must have been frightfully annoyed, he did not respond to any great extent.	
	26/12/15	12.30 p.m	Hostile 5.9 battery shelled H.17.d.5.3. (8 rds.) and 3.15 p.m to 3.45 p.m. a 4.2" battery shelled H.24.a.1.3 and vicinity, 20 rounds.	
		3 pm to 3.50 pm	A/105 was heavily shelled by 5.9" battery, 25 rounds falling in or near the position. 2 hits on Gun Emplacements. One Gun had muzzle blown off. The battery was shooting at 12 noon and had a premature with No 100 fuze, which may have given the position away. The shell burst about 15 ft. from the muzzle and is believed to have been caused by the shell being left in the bore for four minutes after the gun had become heated through firing. The shell probably became heated to the same extent as the gun during the four minutes, with the result that it burst prematurely.	
		12 to 12.50 p.m.	"A" Group carried out a scheme of annoyance by bombarding likely billets in RADINGHEM and along LE BAS HAU Road. B/105 firing 36 rounds, effect very good.	
		12 Noon	A/105 shelled battery position at O.13.b.5.4. (41 rounds) obtaining several hits on houses	

W. A. Nicholson
LIEUT-COLONEL, R.F.A.
COMMANDING 105th BRIGADE, R.F.A.

2353 Wt. W2544/1454 700,000 5/15 D. D. & L. A.D.S.S./Forms/C. 2118.

19

Instructions regarding War Diaries and Intelligence Summaries are contained in F. S. Regs., Part II. and the Staff Manual respectively. Title pages will be prepared in manuscript.

WAR DIARY or ~~INTELLIGENCE SUMMARY.~~

(Erase heading not required.)

105th Bde. R.F.A.

Army Form C. 2118.

Place	Date	Hour	Summary of Events and Information	Remarks and references to Appendices
			behind the battery. A small explosion followed after one of our shell had burst; probably ammunition in gun pit.	
		12.45 pm.	C/105 bombarded parapet at I.21.c.1.0. to I.21.c.3.1. with 80 rds. of Lyddite, the effect was good, a fair amount of timber being thrown up. 5 blinds with No 100 fuze. "B" Group scheme.	
		2pm	D/105 retaliated on ENNETIERES with 20 rounds of H.E. hitting several houses.	
	27/12/15	2pm	Hostile battery in I.36.a.1.4. fired about 40 rounds in vicinity of I.8.b. C/105 engaged this battery and silenced it after 20 rounds. Enemy fired about 150 rounds at various points, chiefly into Chapelle d' Armentieres.	
	28/12/15	1p.m.	B/105 registered with aeroplane on trench at I.26.d.1½.1½. and D/105 on I.21.d.3.7. also with aeroplane.	
		4pm	D/105 retaliated on trench opposite I.21.4. for shelling of our trench I.31.4. by a 4.2" How. The enemy fired about 230 rounds during the day.	
	29/12/15	2.15 pm	A/105 having moved to a new position about 300x EAST of their former position registered on the enemy's parapet at I.32.a.8.8½. with 3 guns, the fourth being returned to Ordnance for exchange, the gun and carriage having been condemned.	

[illegible signature]
LIEUT-COLONEL, R.F.A.
COMMANDING 105th BRIGADE, R.F.A.

Instructions regarding War Diaries and Intelligence Summaries are contained in F. S. Regs., Part II. and the Staff Manual respectively. Title pages will be prepared in manuscript.

20

WAR DIARY ~~or~~ ~~INTELLIGENCE SUMMARY.~~

105th Bde. R.F.A.

Army Form C. 2118.

(Erase heading not required.)

Place	Date	Hour	Summary of Events and Information	Remarks and references to Appendices
			The effect was good, direct hits being obtained with each gun. 6 bombs with No 100 Fuze. (23 rds.)	
	29/12/15	12.30 pm	B/105 completed registration with aeroplane of the point at I.26.d.12.1½. (4 rds.) A report having been received that Chapelle d' Armentieres was being shelled, C/105 fired at PREMESQUES CHURCH, a supposed observing station, 15 rds. H.E. too hazy to observe effect. The enemy fired about 55 rds. only today.	
	30/12/15		The enemy fired about 40 rounds on our front today, all 77 c.m. apparently. We did not fire.	
	31/12/15		A F.O.O. located 4 machine guns which fired at night from houses at LARGE FARM, I.22.c.6.9, House at I.29.a.12.3., Houses at I.16.a.7.0. and I.22.b.9.5½., D/105 fired 20 rounds at each target and obtained about 35 hits, no sign of guns at either place. A/105 registered by aeroplane on N.30.a.9.2½ and O.25.b.1.8. The Division attacked German trenches in accordance with pre-arranged scheme. The right attacking party failing to reach the hostile trenches owing to the enemy turning on a searchlight just before the attempt was made. A/105 + B/105 fired 5 rds. & 12 rds. only owing to this failure.	

LIEUT. COLONEL, R.F.A.
COMMANDING 105TH BRIGADE, R.F.A.

2353 Wt. W2544/1454 700,000 5/15 D. D. & L. A.D.S.S./Forms/C. 2118.

21

WAR DIARY 105th Bde. R.F.A.

Army Form C. 2118.

~~or~~

~~INTELLIGENCE SUMMARY~~.

(*Erase heading not required.*)

Instructions regarding War Diaries and Intelligence Summaries are contained in F. S. Regs., Part II. and the Staff Manual respectively. Title pages will be prepared in manuscript.

Place	Date	Hour	Summary of Events and Information	Remarks and references to Appendices
	Night 31/12/15 – 1/1/16	1-33 to 2-20 am	C/105 fired 140 rds. H.E. at trenches I. 21. b. 10. 3. during the attack of ~~[illegible]~~ left party and D/105 149 rounds on "German House". The party entered the trenches and found one sentry only; he was disposed of and as the enemy had not been surprised and nothing further could be gained, the party returned. Our casualties were few, due to machine gun fire; 9th Yorks and 10th Northumberland Fusiliers were the attacking units.	No. 3. G. 139/2.

N. A. Nicholson
LIEUT. COLONEL, R.F.A.
COMMANDING 105TH BRIGADE, R.F.A.

2353 Wt. W2544/1454 700,000 5/15 D. D. & L. A.D.S.S./Forms/C. 2118.

105th Bgde R.F.A.

Vol. 5

Jan '16

23

Instructions regarding War Diaries and Intelligence Summaries are contained in F. S. Regs., Part II. and the Staff Manual respectively. Title pages will be prepared in manuscript.

Confidential.

22

WAR DIARY ~~or INTELLIGENCE SUMMARY.~~

105th Bde. R.F.A.

(*Erase heading not required.*)

Army Form C. 2118.

Place	Date	Hour	Summary of Events and Information	Remarks and references to Appendices
ARMENTIERES	2/1/16	11.45 a.m.	C. B/105 fired 35 rounds at a machine gun emplacement at I.26.d.3½.7. obtaining 8 hits on parapet, several blinds were noticed, detonation poor as a rule. C/105 retaliated on Trenches I.26-5. and I.20.1. for shelling of our fire trenches. A/105 retaliated on Houses near X roads O.2.d.1.7. 10 H.E. B/105 also retaliated on LE GRAND MAISNIL FME. 15 H.E. both for shelling of Left Bn. Hdqrs. Right Sector.	
			D/105 carried out an experiment with Chilworth Smoke Powder to obtain ballistics of C.S.P. Cartridge, firing 24 rounds H.E. at a wall I.22.b.2.1. The experiment proved that the range obtained with C.S.P. was equal to that of ordinary ballistite, that a certain amount of smoke was given off and very little flash. 2 rounds were fired at night and it was noticed that the flash was reduced considerably.	[signature illegible] Lieut. R.F.A. Adjutant 105 Brigade R.F.A.
	1/1/16		During the day the enemy fired 45 rounds at various points on our front, following upon the raid made by the Division as reported on sheet 21.	
	2/1/16	9 A.M.	A 4.2 hostile battery shelled X roads in I.1.d. with H.E. intermittently until 3 p.m. and during the day about 200 rounds were fired by the enemy, RUE FLEURIE being particularly heavily shelled.	

2353 Wt. W2544/1454 700,000 5/15 D. D. & L. A.D.S.S./Forms/C. 2118.

Instructions regarding War Diaries and Intelligence Summaries are contained in F. S. Regs., Part II. and the Staff Manual respectively. Title pages will be prepared in manuscript.

23

WAR DIARY ~~or INTELLIGENCE SUMMARY.~~

(Erase heading not required.)

105th Bde. R.F.A.

Army Form C. 2118.

Place	Date	Hour	Summary of Events and Information	Remarks and references to Appendices
	3/1/16.	8.45 A.M. to 11.30 A.M.	A 5.9" battery from direction of FORT ENGLOS fired 100 rounds at a battery of 21st Division in I 9 C. knocking the battery out, some casualties resulting. The gun emplacements were badly damaged and the battery withdrawn from the position. C/105 at a supposed battery position at I.29. d. 5. 8. in support of 21st Division. Enemy's batteries at I 30. C. 3. 8. and behind houses at LE PARADIS were also engaged. We also fired on CHATEAU D' HESPEL and other points, 128 rounds being fired in all. The enemy fired 70 odd rounds at other points in Chapelle d' Armentieres and our trenches.	W R [signature] Lieut. R.F.A. Adjutant 105 Brigade R.F.A.
	4/1/16		Enemy fired about 68 rounds today on trenches and vicinity of Chapelle d' Armentieres. D Group carried out a scheme, bombarding GRAND MARAIS FARM and TRAMWAY HOUSE, 100 rds H.E. and 18 pdrs firing Shrapnel, about 20 hits were obtained and a good deal of damage done. B. C. D. being engaged on this. A/105 registered on FME HOUSSAIN. B/105 also fired on Reserve trenches I 32. and I 26. 2. for shelling of our trenches.	
	5/1/16.		A/105 registered on Zero Line, and BRIDOUX FORT and also engaged a battery at N.24 b. 8. 8. by aeroplane observation.	

2353 Wt. W2544/1454 700,000 5/15 D. D. & L. A.D.S.S./Forms/C. 2118.

Instructions regarding War Diaries and Intelligence Summaries are contained in F. S. Regs., Part II. and the Staff Manual respectively. Title pages will be prepared in manuscript.

23

WAR DIARY ~~or~~ ~~INTELLIGENCE SUMMARY.~~

105th Bde. R.F.A.

(Erase heading not required.)

Army Form C. 2118.

Place	Date	Hour	Summary of Events and Information	Remarks and references to Appendices
	5/1/16	9.30 to 2.40 pm	Hostile 5.9 battery on sound bearing from H.30.b.7½.3. of 150° TRUE. fired 67 rds. on D/102 at H.24.C.3.2. getting hits on one gun, no casualties. and 4.2" + 77 m/m batteries firing about 40 rounds at various points	
		10.30 AM. 1.30 pm	B/105 retaliated on LE BAS HAU ROAD, 15 H.E. and later registered single gun on point I ~~[illegible]~~ 33.a.7.10. LE QUESNE ROAD.	
		11.45 pm to	B/105 fired 5 rounds at I. ~~[illegible]~~ 33.a.7.10. in conjunction with 6"	
	6/1/16	1.30 AM	Heavy Battery.	
	"		During the day the enemy fired over 200 rds. at various points on our front, chiefly at Trenches and Roads. B/105 located at I.30.a.9.1. a 4.2" battery which was active, flashes being seen and 3 gun emplacements being noticed. 3 rounds were fired, and the battery was bracketed. Information was then sent to "Heavies" who however did not shoot at it.	
	7/1/16	10.30 A.M.	A report received from B/103 observing station that a heavy gun could be seen at the cross roads at I.36.C.1.4. which appeared to have been struck. Heavy Siege Batteries were put on to it	[signature] Lieut. R.F.A. Adjutant 105 Brigade R.F.A.

2353 Wt. W2544/1454 700,000 5/15 D. D. & L. A.D.S.S./Forms/C. 2118.

Instructions regarding War Diaries and Intelligence Summaries are contained in F. S. Regs., Part II. and the Staff Manual respectively. Title pages will be prepared in manuscript.

2B4

WAR DIARY ~~or INTELLIGENCE SUMMARY.~~ 105th Bde. R.F.A

(Erase heading not required.)

Army Form C. 2118.

Place	Date	Hour	Summary of Events and Information	Remarks and references to Appendices
1	7/1/16	1.30 p.m.	but did not hit it. D/105 was then put on to it but owing to rain coming on observation became very bad and only 8 rounds out of 14 fired could be observed, the effect of the 8 rounds not being known. A Group carried out a scheme: bombarding a battery at D.14 b.1.7. A/105 fired 50 rounds and obtained 12 hits. The enemy fired about 80 rounds, chiefly in Chapelle d'Armentieres vicinity.	
O	8/1/16		During the night of 7th/8th D/105 fired 57 rounds of Shrapnel at the Cross Roads I.36.C.1½.4. but the gun was removed before it became light. A/105 registered points on trenches I 31.1. I 31.2. I 31.3. from new position, and retaliated on a 5.9" Battery at N.30.b.3.5. (10 Rds.) B/105 registered PERISCOPE HOUSE, O.2.d.7¼.4. C/105 registered a House I.29.a.1½.7½. Chapelle d'Armentieres was shelled, about 50 rds.	
	9/1/16		C. & D. Batteries registered on GRAND MARAIS FME. I.28.C.2.4 and TRAMWAY HOUSE, I.28.C.6½.4½. A/105 spotted a 77mm battery at N.23.b.8.2. and engaged it, firing 12 pdr. H.E. Several shells burst in the hedge from which the flashes came.	[signature] Lieut. R.F.A. Adjutant 106 Brigade R.F.A.

2353 Wt. W2544/1454 700,000 5/15 D. D. & L. A.D.S.S./Forms/C. 2118.

25

WAR DIARY
or
~~INTELLIGENCE SUMMARY.~~
(Erase heading not required.)

Army Form C. 2118.

105 Bde RFA

Instructions regarding War Diaries and Intelligence Summaries are contained in F. S. Regs., Part II. and the Staff Manual respectively. Title pages will be prepared in manuscript.

Place	Date	Hour	Summary of Events and Information	Remarks and references to Appendices
ARMENTIERES	9/1/16		~~About~~ About 90 rounds fell in Chapelle d'Armentieres, near the BREWERY at BOIS GRENIER & trenches in front of BRIDOUX FORT.	[signature] Lieut. R.F.A. Adjutant 106 Brigade R.F.A.
	10/1/16		105th Brigade Scheme was carried out; C/105 bombarded WEZ MACQUART and D/105 WEZ MACQUART and the TUILLERIES 100 rounds being fired. The enemy fired very little about 45 rounds being reported.	
	11/1/16		The brigade was ordered to take on counter battery work and at 10 A.M. a battery position at I.29.b.5.1. was shelled effect not known.	
		11.50 A.M.	B/105 spotted a battery at I 30.a.8½.1. 2 gun pits could be seen. 20 rounds were fired at this target and two hits on No 3 gun emplacement obtained.	
		1 pm.	Flashes of a battery at I.23.b.8½.6½. seen from aeroplane; C/105 fired 20 rounds at it but could not observe effect. A battery of 21st Division was heavily shelled by 5.9" and 8" 110 rounds being fired and practically no damage done.	

Instructions regarding War Diaries and Intelligence Summaries are contained in F. S. Regs., Part II. and the Staff Manual respectively. Title pages will be prepared in manuscript.

96.

WAR DIARY
or
~~INTELLIGENCE SUMMARY.~~
(Erase heading not required.)

105 Bde RFA

Army Form C. 2118.

Place	Date	Hour	Summary of Events and Information	Remarks and references to Appendices
ARMENTIERES	12/1/16		Scheme for "B" Group was carried out. D/105 bombarding ESTAMINET DE LA BARRIERE (I 22 b 5.0) and C/105 the BREWERY (I 22 c 8.4) with 15 rounds apiece. Good results were obtained. Very little hostile shelling took place.	
	13/1/16		Quiet day. Hostile 77 mm battery fired 50 rounds into CHAPELLE D'ARMENTIERES (I 9 c 1.D).	
	14/1/16	11.15 am	Scheme for "B" Group carried out. C/105 bombarded LARGE FARM. 25 rds.	
		12.0	Corps retaliation Scheme "CD" practised. Enemy retaliated firing 50 rds on SHAFTSBURY AVENUE.	
		4.0	Scheme with infantry took place. C/105 & D/105 bombarded enemy parapet at I 22 a. Infantry sent up smoke. Enemy fired about 100 rds of 77 mm into CHAPELLE D'ARMENTIERES.	
	15/1/16	11.30 am	Scheme for "B" Group. C/105 bombarded LARGE FARM	
		12 noon	Corps retaliation Scheme "CD" practised. Only half number of rounds fired. A/105 retaliated on battery at O 9 c 2.3 which ceased fire.	
			During day, enemy shelled our salient (R I 21 & I 21 c) with 4.2's & 77's.	

B. R. [signature]
Lieut. R.F.A.
Adjutant 105 Brigade R.F.A.

2353 Wt. W2544/1454 700,000 5/15 D. D. & L. A.D.S.S./Forms/C. 2118.

Instructions regarding War Diaries and Intelligence Summaries are contained in F. S. Regs., Part II. and the Staff Manual respectively. Title pages will be prepared in manuscript.

27.

WAR DIARY
or
~~INTELLIGENCE SUMMARY.~~

(Erase heading not required.)

105 Bde RFA

Army Form C. 2118.

Place	Date	Hour	Summary of Events and Information	Remarks and references to Appendices
ARMENTIERES	15/1/16		Enemy put 12 rounds of 77mm into LILLE POST (I 15 b 6½ 9½) D/105 OP). D/105 retaliated successfully on BEZ MACQUART.	
	16/1/16		Enemy shelled Trenches I 31.1 I 32 & I 26.1 during early afternoon. B/105 retaliated on trenches opposite, & A/105 on 2 hostile gun positions – O 14 b 8.7 & O 13 c 3.0.	
	17/1/16		A/105 Registered 4 points by aeroplane in support trenches in I 31 & O 1. They also retaliated on 2 battery positions. Enemy artillery very quiet.	
	18/1/16		In a scheme for "A" group A/105 breached parapet at I 31 c 7.0 – 9 in conjunction with some heavies & 18 prs. D/105 shelled hostile battery at I 21 d 2.2 with 40 rds. D/105 also fired 50 rounds at a steel cupola in enemy parapet at I 16 d 1½.4½ – & scored 4 direct hits rendering cupola useless – Enemy artillery was ~~very~~ quiet all day	
	19/1/16		The Howitzer brigade scheme. Brigade salvos on LAVALLEE at 8 am followed by one of Shrapnel. This stirred the enemy up and	[signature] Lieut. R.F.A. Adjutant 105 Brigade R.F.A.

2353 Wt. W2544/1454 700,000 5/15 D. D. & L. A.D.S.S./Forms/C. 2118.

Instructions regarding War Diaries and Intelligence Summaries are contained in F. S. Regs., Part II. and the Staff Manual respectively. Title pages will be prepared in manuscript.

98.

WAR DIARY
or
~~INTELLIGENCE SUMMARY~~.
(Erase heading not required.)

105 Bde RFA

Army Form C. 2118.

Place	Date	Hour	Summary of Events and Information	Remarks and references to Appendices
ARMENTIERES	19/1/16 Contd		He shelled the following points I 1 d 0.8, I 15 B 8½.9½, H 30 b 7.3. H 18 c fairly heavily. As part of the scheme B/105 fired 16 rds at enemy trench at I 32 c 0.8½ and 30 rds a Enemy trench I 26 B 9½.4. He also fired 30 rounds on trenches I 32 & I 26.1 in retaliation. C/105 fired 80 rds a supports opposite I 21.1 by way of retaliation.	A.R.P. [illegible] Lieut. R.F.A. Adjutant 106 Brigade R.F.A.
	20/1/16		~~Quiet day~~ D/105 shelled ~~an~~ the steel cupola at I 16 d ½ 2½ with 17 rds but did not hit it owing to very gusty wind. The enemy shelled the Fme de la HALLERIE & supports in I 9 c during the day with 4.2's & 77s, but did no damage.	
	21/1/16		In a scheme for "A" group B/105 bombarded parapet I 32 a 9.10 with good results. A/105 bombarded battery at O 14 b 2.6½ fire reported effective. Enemy shelled trenches I 15 1 & 2, for which D/105 retaliated effectively on the trenches opposite. The enemy also put a few 77's into BOIS GRENIER.	

2353 Wt. W2544/1454 700,000 5/15 D. D. & L. A.D.S.S./Forms/C. 2118.

Instructions regarding War Diaries and Intelligence Summaries are contained in F. S. Regs., Part II. and the Staff Manual respectively. Title pages will be prepared in manuscript.

29.

WAR DIARY
or
~~INTELLIGENCE~~ SUMMARY.
(*Erase heading not required.*)

105 Bde RFA

Army Form C. 2118.

Place	Date	Hour	Summary of Events and Information	Remarks and references to Appendices
ARMENTIERES	22/1/16		D/105 fired again a steel cupola at I 16 d ½. 2½ & obtained a direct hit on the 12th round which entirely demolished it. Enemy arty was very quiet. At 10.30 pm. Enemy shelled LAVESEE. We replied with a Bde salvo on ENNETIERES which effectively silenced it.	[signature] Lieut. R.F.A. Adjutant 106 Brigade R.F.A.
	23/1/16		At 8.30 am the Germans started putting a few 4.2's into ARMENTIERES – D/105 retaliated with 10 rds on CAPINGHEM and A/105 on BEAUCAMPS – during afternoon the enemy shelled RUE D'HANCARDRIE in H 29 & H 30 with 4.2's.	
	24/1/16		Brigade stood by for counter battery work for 21st division at 11.30 – batteries at I 29 a 3.6 & I 30 a 8½.1 were successfully engaged – Very little enemy shelling in the divisional area – a few rounds into BOIS GRENIER & CHAPELLE D'ARMENTIERES.	
	25/1/16		Scheme for "B" group carried out – C & D/105 bombarding parapet where wire had been cut in 2 places, small breaches being made. Our O.P. at LILLE POST was slightly shelled – D/105 retaliated	

2353 Wt. W2544/1454 700,000 5/15 D. D. & L. A.D.S.S./Forms/C. 2118.

Instructions regarding War Diaries and Intelligence Summaries are contained in F. S. Regs., Part II. and the Staff Manual respectively. Title pages will be prepared in manuscript.

30.

WAR DIARY
or
~~INTELLIGENCE SUMMARY.~~
(*Erase heading not required.*)

105 Bde RFA

Army Form C. 2118.

Place	Date	Hour	Summary of Events and Information	Remarks and references to Appendices
ARMENTIERES	25/1/16 Contd		Successfully in WEL MACQUARTS. The enemy also shelled the BOIS GRENIER GRIS POT ROAD with 77s.	[illegible] Lieut. R.F.A. Adjutant 105 Brigade R.F.A.
	26/1/16		About 10.30 am the enemy started shelling Bn HQ in I 15 c. For this we retaliated on FLEUR D'ECOSSE, PETIT MARAIS and the front & support trenches opposite I 15.1 & I.21.4. About mid-day they started shelling LA VESEE so we put 2 brigade salvoes into LA VALLEE, with good effect. Later in the day they put a few rounds near RUE MARLE, so we retaliated on CAPINGHEM & stopped it. We fired about 160 rounds in all.	
	27/1/16		Kaiser's Birthday. The Germans commenced by shelling the Bn HQ in I 15 c, also the support trenches in I 9 c & I 14 d fairly heavily. We retaliated heavily for this on the supports of I 21.1 & 2 & I.15.2 & I.16 – firing in all about 120 rounds. 35 of these were fired by C/105 at a gun reported to be in LARGE FARM	

2353 Wt. W2544/1454 700,000 5/15 D. D. & L. A.D.S.S./Forms/C. 2118.

31.

WAR DIARY
or
~~INTELLIGENCE SUMMARY.~~
(*Erase heading not required.*)

105 Bde R.F.A.

Army Form C. 2118.

Instructions regarding War Diaries and Intelligence Summaries are contained in F. S. Regs., Part II. and the Staff Manual respectively. Title pages will be prepared in manuscript.

Place	Date	Hour	Summary of Events and Information	Remarks and references to Appendices
ARMENTIERES	27/1/16 cont^d		The gun was reported to have been knocked out, having received 3 direct hits. At about 11.30 am. the enemy commenced shelling our front line trenches I.31.1 to I.31.5 very heavily, with 5.9s, 4.2s, & 77s – the parapet was damaged & wire cut. We retaliated very heavily with B, C & D batteries, firing nearly 300 rounds at the front & support trenches opposite. Hostile fire ceased about 1.30 pm. Later in the day C/105 put a few rounds in a suspected battery at I 29 a 4.4 by request of 91st division. The enemy were quiet during afternoon. About 11.0 pm at night, however, they commenced bombarding the trenches of the left batt^n of the left sector very heavily. We replied at once with C & D batteries on the trenches opposite, & the fire ceased about midnight – about 200 rds being fired by us.	
	28/1/16		The enemy started another bombardment of the trenches of the right Bn. of left sector at 4.15 am. We turned B C & D batteries on the trenches opposite, & the fire subsided about 4.45 am. having fired about 100 rounds.	[signature] Lieut. R.F.A. Adjutant 105 Brigade R.F.A.

2353 Wt. W2544/1454 700,000 5/15 D. D. & L. A.D.S.S./Forms/C. 2118.

Instructions regarding War Diaries and Intelligence Summaries are contained in F. S. Regs., Part II. and the Staff Manual respectively. Title pages will be prepared in manuscript.

32.

WAR DIARY

or

~~INTELLIGENCE SUMMARY.~~

(Erase heading not required.)

105 Bde RFA

Army Form C. 2118.

Place	Date	Hour	Summary of Events and Information	Remarks and references to Appendices
ARMENTIERES	28/1/16 contd		At about 10.0 am the enemy commenced bombarding the front & support lines & Bn HQ of the left Bn left sector - C & D batteries retaliated on the trenches opposite, & later on B also. The enemy stopped firing at about 1.0 pm, but reopened at 3.15 pm on the salient. I 21.1 & I 21.2 also I 21.3 & Bn HQ, cutting wire & damaging parapet - We retaliated on trenches opposite also I 20.1, I 26.2 & I 26.3 & I 26.5 - The enemy eventually ceased fire about 4.30 pm. The brigade fired during the day 850 rounds in addition to those fired at 4.30 am.	Lieut. R.F.A. Adjutant 106 Brigade R.F.A.
	29/1/16		It was very quiet during the morning - but at 1.20 pm the enemy opened a heavy fire of 4.2's & 77's on front & support trenches I 21.2 & I 21.3 & I 21.4. C & D batteries retaliated on a point in their front parapet I 21 B 44 with 50 rounds apiece - and the enemy ceased fire at about 2.0 pm. The afternoon was also quiet. Raid on enemy trenches in left sector arranged for 10.0 pm did not take place.	

3353 Wt. W2544/1454 700,000 5/15 D. D. & L. A.D.S.S./Forms/C. 2118.

Instructions regarding War Diaries and Intelligence Summaries are contained in F. S. Regs., Part II. and the Staff Manual respectively. Title pages will be prepared in manuscript.

33.

WAR DIARY
or
~~INTELLIGENCE SUMMARY.~~
(Erase heading not required.)

105 Bde R.F.A.

Army Form C. 2118.

Place	Date	Hour	Summary of Events and Information	Remarks and references to Appendices
ARMENTIERES	30/1/16		Very quiet all day - hardly a shot fired - too misty for observation. Raid which had been prepared, on Right Sector did not come off during night	
	31/1/16		Another very quiet day - very misty - practically no firing.	

W. A. Nicholson
LIEUT. COLONEL, R.F.A.
COMMANDING 105th BRIGADE, R.F.A.

Lieut. R.F.A.
Adjutant 105 Brigade R.F.A.

2353 Wt. W2544/1454 700,000 5/15 D. D. & L. A.D.S.S./Forms/C. 2118.

105 Bde R.F.A.

Vol. 6.

23rd Dn

Confidential

Instructions regarding War Diaries and Intelligence Summaries are contained in F. S. Regs., Part II. and the Staff Manual respectively. Title pages will be prepared in manuscript.

34.

WAR DIARY
or
~~INTELLIGENCE SUMMARY~~.

(*Erase heading not required.*)

105. Bde R.F.A.

Army Form C. 2118.

Place	Date	Hour	Summary of Events and Information	Remarks and references to Appendices
ARMENTIERES	1/2/16 to 6/2/16		6 very quiet days - very little activity on either side - a few trench junctions registered by aeroplane -	
	7/2/16		German artillery was active against BOIS GRENIER during morning - firing about 100 rounds - no damage was done. A/105 fired 30 rds at a large working party which kept on reappearing -	
	8/2/16		Enemy again active against BOIS GRENIER & vicinity - B/105 fired 21 rds at an M.G. Emplacement - by request of infantry	
	9/2/16		Quiet morning - Bde salvo on Bosch ~~[illegible]~~ front parapet at I 26 b 7.5 at about 1.0 pm. Reported very effective - all rounds falling on parapet. Enemy retaliated on BOIS GRENIER	Sheet 36.
	10/2/16		Enemy shelled WINE avenue during morning doing no damage. Very little other firing -	
	11/2/16		Enemy artillery fairly active against our trenches - also LA VESEE - We retaliated on the trenches opposite & LA VALLEE	
	12/2/16		At about 9 am the Germans started a systematic strafe ~~of~~ on trenches & billets on our front - also O.P.s - BOIS GRENIER, LILLE POST, RUE MARLE, L'ARMEE, LA VESEE, GRIS POT & CHAPELLE D'ARMENTIERES were paid most attention.	

[signature] Lieut. R.F.A.
Adjutant 105 Brigade R.F.A.

2353 Wt. W2544/1454 700,000 5/15 D. D. & L. A.D.S.S./Forms/C. 2118.

Army Form C. 2118.

Instructions regarding War Diaries and Intelligence Summaries are contained in F. S. Regs., Part II. and the Staff Manual respectively. Title pages will be prepared in manuscript.

35

WAR DIARY
or
~~INTELLIGENCE SUMMARY~~.
(Erase heading not required.)

Place	Date	Hour	Summary of Events and Information	Remarks and references to Appendices
ARMENTIERES	12/2/16 Contd.		We replied vigorously, firing nearly 400 rounds in all, at Billets, firing mostly brigade salvoes – also at trenches. About 1.30 pm most of the firing ceased – only a little desultory shelling taking place.	
	13/2/16		Very similar to the 12th, except that the firing continued all day, & was perhaps more intense. We expended about 600 rounds during the day.	
	14/2/16		Very quiet except for a 4.2" battery firing on CHAPELLE D'ARMENTIERES. No damage was done, only 50 rounds being fired	
	15/2/16		Very quiet – hardly any shooting at all.	
	16/2/16		Another very quiet day – C & D batteries were relieved by sections of C/176 – 34th Div. & 1 section of A/105 & B/105 were relieved by 1 section of A/176 & D/176. The relief was of personnel only, the guns being handed over in the pits, except for the remaining sections of C/105 & D/105, which C/105 took over. D/105 took over guns of C/176. ~~D/105~~ At 12 midnight C/105 was placed at disposal of GOCRA 8th Div.	[illegible signature] Lieut. R.F.A. Adjutant 105 Brigade R.F.A.

2353 Wt. W2544/1454 700,000 5/15 D. D. & L. A.D.S.S./Forms/C. 2118.

Instructions regarding War Diaries and Intelligence Summaries are contained in F. S. Regs., Part II. and the Staff Manual respectively. Title pages will be prepared in manuscript.

36.

WAR DIARY
or
INTELLIGENCE SUMMARY.

(Erase heading not required.)

Army Form C. 2118.

Place	Date	Hour	Summary of Events and Information	Remarks and references to Appendices
ARMENTIERES	17/2/16		At 7am D/105, & the sections of A & B/105 which had bee relieved marched back into rest at BLARINGHEM, arriving in their billets by 4.0 pm. Very little artillery activity took place on either side.	Lieut, R.F.A. Adjutant 105 Brigade R.F.A.
	18/2/16		Amm. Col. marched into reserve area. Am. Col. of 176 Bde marched up & relieved it. HQ 176 Bde arrived ~~during~~ in the evening. Very little activity on either side during the day.	
	19/2/16		HQ, & the remaining sections of A & B/105 marched to reserve area.	
BLARINGHEM	20/2/16 to 28/2/16		This period was spent at BLARINGHEM, & section training was carried out daily in spite of the snow etc.	
	29/2/16		The brigade marched to BAILLEUL-LES-PERNES & went into billets there that evening.	
	~~7/3/16~~			

W. A. [illegible]

LIEUT. COLONEL, R.F.A.
COMMANDING [illegible] BRIGADE, R.F.A.

2353 Wt. W2544/1454 700,000 5/15 D. D. & L. A.D.S.S./Forms/C. 2118.

105 RFA

Vol 7

23

Confidential

WAR DIARY
or
~~INTELLIGENCE SUMMARY~~.
(Erase heading not required.)

Instructions regarding War Diaries and Intelligence Summaries are contained in F. S. Regs., Part II. and the Staff Manual respectively. Title pages will be prepared in manuscript.

3.7

HQ 105th Bde RFA

Army Form C. 2118.

Place	Date	Hour	Summary of Events and Information	Remarks and references to Appendices
BAILLEUL LES. PERNES.	1/3/16		C/105 & 1st Sec of Amm Col. returned from St Dw.	
	3/3/16		Major Fife sent forward to CHATEAU DE LA HAIE (W12 c 7.8 36B) to reconnoitre positions for how batteries in CARENCY Sector.	
	6/3/16		B/105 sent large working party up to work on their new position at X9B 5.2.	
	7/3/16		HQ staff of 105th Bde (less Col Nicholson who remained behind sick) proceeded to forward area - CARENCY sector. to HQ "A" group at MOULIN TOPART (X8d 3 0.) & took over that evening from the French group HQ. Batteries in "A" group were A/104, B/104, C/104 B/105, also the columns of 104 & 105. A/105 was in "B" group, D/105 in "C" group & C/105 in Reserve group. The 104 batteries in A group took over at 3 am on the night 7th–8th.	[signature] Lieut. R.F.A. Adjutant 105 Brigade R.F.A.
CARENCY Sector	8/3/16		Registering proceeds - otherwise quiet.	
	9/3/16 10/3/16		B/105 got its guns up on 9th & 10th & got registered	

Confidential

Army Form C. 2118.

WAR DIARY
or
~~INTELLIGENCE SUMMARY~~.
(*Erase heading not required.*)

Instructions regarding War Diaries and Intelligence Summaries are contained in F. S. Regs., Part II. and the Staff Manual respectively. Title pages will be prepared in manuscript.

38

Headquarters
105th Bde RFA

Place	Date	Hour	Summary of Events and Information	Remarks and references to Appendices
CARENCY	11/3/16 to 17/3/16		No operations of any importance took place. The enemy was not very aggressive, except in shelling CARENCY with 5.9s which he did frequently, once causing some casualties in A/105.	
	18/3/16 & 20/3/16		Relief of RA. 23rd Div. by RA 47th Div. took place on these 2 dates. The sections of the 47th Div. coming up & taking over on the evenings of 17th/18th & 19th/20th. Sections of 23rd D.A. marched to reserve area — CALONNE RICOUART — on 18th & 20th. Groups & RA HQrs marched on 20th. The Brigade, less C/105, which was still in reserve group, arrived in billets on the afternoon of the 20th.	
CALONNE RICOUART	21/3/16		Spent in cleaning up.	
	22/3/16 to 24/3/16		Relief of RA. 2nd Div. by RA 23rd Div. in the AIX-NOULETTE Sector. 1 section per battery coming up on 22nd/23rd & ~~the other~~ on 23rd/24th. HQ 105 came up on 23rd, to HERSIN.	[signature] Lieut. R.F.A. Adjutant 105 Brigade R.F.A.

2353 Wt. W2544/1454 700,000 5/15 D. D. & L. A.D.S.S./Forms/C. 2118.

Confidential

Instructions regarding War Diaries and Intelligence Summaries are contained in F. S. Regs., Part II. and the Staff Manual respectively. Title pages will be prepared in manuscript.

39.

WAR DIARY

or

~~INTELLIGENCE SUMMARY.~~

(Erase heading not required.)

HQ. 105th Bde RFA

Army Form C. 2118.

Place	Date	Hour	Summary of Events and Information	Remarks and references to Appendices
HERSIN	25/3/16 to 31/3/16		RA 23rd Divn was divided into 3 groups. ~~[illegible]~~ SOUCHEZ Group ANGRES Group & CALONNE Group. A/105 was in Souchez group, B/105 in ANGRES group & D/105 in Calonne group. C/105 which had come into action in this sector with reserve groups 10 days previously, was detailed for counter battery. HQ 105 remained in administrative control of 105th Bde, being ~~[illegible]~~ in reserve.	[signature] Lieut. R.F.A. Adjutant 105 Brigade R.F.A.
			1. 4. 16. [signature] LIEUT. COLONEL, R.F.A. COMMANDING 105TH BRIGADE, R.F.A.	

2353 Wt. W2544/1454 700,000 5/15 D. D. & L. A.D.S.S./Forms/C. 2118.

Confidential

XXIII

Army Form C. 2118.

Instructions regarding War Diaries and Intelligence Summaries are contained in F. S. Regs., Part II. and the Staff Manual respectively. Title pages will be prepared in manuscript.

40/

WAR DIARY or ~~INTELLIGENCE SUMMARY~~. HQ 105th Bde RFA Vol 8

(Erase heading not required.)

Place	Date	Hour	Summary of Events and Information	Remarks and references to Appendices
HERSIN	1/4/16 to 18/4/16		HQ 105th Bde remained in administrative control of 105th Bde being in reserve at HERSIN, the batteries being distributed as follows. A/105 in SOUCHEZ group – B/105 in ANGRES group & D/105 in CALONNE group – C/105 was counter-battery. During that period Fosse 4, near HERSIN station was shelled one day with over 100 8" How shell & for about a week a few 4" gun shell used to fall near the mine every evening to hinder repairs –	W R Pusten Lieut, R.F.A. Adjutant 105 Brigade R.F.A.
	19/4/16 – 20/4/16		The RA 23rd Divn was relieved by RA 2nd Divn on the night of 19th/20th, & marched direct to Billets on relief.	
DIVION.	20/4/16		Billets of 105th Bde at DIVION. All batteries & Column close together except C/105 which remained in the line as counter battery.	
	21/4/16 – 22/4/16		Spent in settling down & cleaning up. The lines taken over were in filthy condition – with tons of manure left all over the place.	

2353 Wt. W2544/1454 700,000 5/15 D. D. & L. A.D.S.S./Forms/C. 2118.

Confidential –

Instructions regarding War Diaries and Intelligence Summaries are contained in F. S. Regs., Part II. and the Staff Manual respectively. Title pages will be prepared in manuscript.

A1.

WAR DIARY
or
~~INTELLIGENCE SUMMARY.~~
(Erase heading not required.)

Army Form C. 2118.

HQ 105th Bde RFA

Place	Date	Hour	Summary of Events and Information	Remarks and references to Appendices
DIVION	23/4/16		Easter Sunday. Holiday. Divine Service. &c –	W R Paston Lieut, R.F.A. Adjutant 105 Brigade R. F. A.
	24/4/16 to 29/4/16		Section training was carried out – Section Gun drill, riding drill for NCOs & battery staff, redrilling, hooking & unhooking casualties on the move, driving drill – section turn-outs.	
	30/4/16		Sunday – Divine Service –	
	[illegible]			

W R Paston for adjt

for LIEUT. COLONEL, R.F.A.
COMMANDING 105TH BRIGADE, R.F.A.

2353 Wt. W2544/1454 700,000 5/15 D. D. & L. A.D.S.S./Forms/C. 2118.

Confidential

WAR DIARY
or
~~INTELLIGENCE SUMMARY.~~
(Erase heading not required.)

Instructions regarding War Diaries and Intelligence Summaries are contained in F. S. Regs., Part II. and the Staff Manual respectively. Title pages will be prepared in manuscript.

42. XXIII HQ 105th Bde RFA. Vol 9

Army Form C. 2118.

Place	Date	Hour	Summary of Events and Information	Remarks and references to Appendices
DIVION	1/5/16 to 13/5/16		Battery Training – Weather was on the whole fine, & much useful work in regaining mobility was accomplished – Divisional Artillery Sports were held on May 11th, on 103rd Bde ground. The 105th Bde won 2 open events out of 3 – namely Officers driving & casualty race.	
	14/5/16		RA 23rd Divn relieved RA 2nd Divn in ANGRES & SOUCHEZ sectors – D/105 which was previously in CALONNE SECTOR had to make new position at R22 c 8½.5. Sheet 36B. A & B/105 went back to their old positions in the AIX-NOULETTE Wood & BULLY-GRENAY respectively – C/105 went into reserve area (to LA THEULOYE) & joined reserve group under O.C. 104th Bde – HQ 105 was in reserve at BARLIN & remained in administrative control of 105th Bde	
BARLIN	15/5/16 to 18/5/16		Nothing of importance occurred. D/105 made good headway with their position –	

H. R. Peel [?] Lieut. R.F.A. Adjutant 105 Brigade R.F.A.

2353 Wt. W2544/1454 700,000 5/15 D. D. & L. A.D.S.S./Forms/C. 2118.

Instructions regarding War Diaries and Intelligence Summaries are contained in F. S. Regs., Part II. and the Staff Manual respectively. Title pages will be prepared in manuscript.

43.

Confidential

WAR DIARY
or
~~INTELLIGENCE SUMMARY~~.
(*Erase heading not required.*)

HQ 105th Bde. R.F.A.

Army Form C. 2118.

Place	Date	Hour	Summary of Events and Information	Remarks and references to Appendices
BARLIN	19/5/16		Complete reorganisation of divisional artillery took place. 4 "mixed" brigades formed instead of 3-18 prs & 1-How Bde. The following changes took place. A/105 became D/102 & vice versa B/105 " D/103 " " C/105 " D/104 " " D/105 remained unchanged. Each Bde now consists of 3-18 pr Batteries & 1 How. Battery. The B.A.C.'s were amalgamated with D.A.C. 103/B.A.C becoming No 1 section 104/BAC becoming No. 2 section, & 105 BAC becoming No. 3 Section 102/BAC became No. 4 Section.	[signature] Lieut, R.F.A. Adjutant 105 Brigade R.F.A.
	20/5/16		Nothing of importance. Hostile artillery fairly active	
	21/5/16 } 22/5/16 }		Attack on Vimy ridge took place during the night. All our batteries fired barrage fire most of the night & following day. Much ammunition was expended. On evening of 22nd 150 gunners from the Div. Arty were sent to 47th Div. Arty temporarily.	

Confidential

WAR DIARY

or

~~INTELLIGENCE SUMMARY~~

(Erase heading not required.)

Army Form C. 2118

44.

HQ 105th Bde R.F.A.

Instructions regarding War Diaries and Intelligence Summaries are contained in F. S. Regs., Part II. and the Staff Manual respectively. Title Pages will be prepared in manuscript.

Place	Date	Hour	Summary of Events and Information	Remarks and references to Appendices
BARLIN	22/5/16 cont^d		The reserve groups came up – ~~[illegible]~~ (N.A.) Capt. Black, comdg A/105 was killed in action – several minor casualties –	
	23/5/16		Our Counter attack on Vimy Ridge took place during the night – Our batteries again assisted with barrage or counter-battery fire.	
	24/5/16		Hostile Artillery very active.	
	25/5/16 to 31/5/16		Things gradually became quieter & more settled.	

[signature] Lieut. Colonel, R.F.A. Commanding 105th Brigade, R.F.A.

[signature] Lieut. R.F.A. Adjutant 105 Brigade R.F.A.

1875 Wt. W593/826 1,000,000 4/15 J.B.C. & A. A.D.S.S./Forms/C. 2118.

Confidential

Instructions regarding War Diaries and Intelligence Summaries are contained in F. S. Regs., Part II. and the Staff Manual respectively. Title Pages will be prepared in manuscript.

45

WAR DIARY
or
~~INTELLIGENCE SUMMARY~~
(Erase heading not required.)

XXIII

Army Form C. 2118

Hq. 105th Bde. R.F.A.

June

Vol 10

Place	Date	Hour	Summary of Events and Information	Remarks and references to Appendices
BARLIN	1/6/16 to 14/6/16		Hqtrs remained in reserve at BARLIN. Batteries in the line as before Nothing of importance occurred – On evening of the 14th 1 section of each Battery was relieved by 47th Div. Arty.	
BARLIN & DIVION	15/6/16		Hqtrs & 1 section per battery which has been relieved marched to DIVION went into billets – On the evening of 15th the remaining sections were relieved by 47th Div. Arty.	
DIVION	16/6/16		Hqtrs and forward sections marched to MAMETZ (near AIRE) The rear sections marched to DIVION	
MAMETZ	17/6/16		Rear sections marched to MAMETZ. The Brigade was completely installed in Billets by 5pm in the afternoon.	
MAMETZ	18/6/16		Sunday – Cleaning up – Divine Service – etc.	
	19/6/16		Divisional day in Special Manoeuvre area. Each Bde. Hqtrs. had a wireless Stn. which worked very well indeed.	W R [illegible] Lt Col. 105 Bde R.F.A.

Confidential

Instructions regarding War Diaries and Intelligence Summaries are contained in F. S. Regs., Part II. and the Staff Manual respectively. Title Pages will be prepared in manuscript.

46.

WAR DIARY
or
~~INTELLIGENCE SUMMARY~~
(Erase heading not required.)

Army Form C. 2118

Hq. 105th Bde R.F.A.

Place	Date	Hour	Summary of Events and Information	Remarks and references to Appendices
MAMETZ	20/6/16		Brigade day — practised taking guns and wagons over trenches	
	21/6/16		Brigade Day	
	22/6/16		Div. Arty. day — practised advance	
	23/6/16		Brigade day	
	24/6/16		Preparation for move by rail	
	25/6/16 to		Entrained at LILLERS STN — batteries at 3 hours interval — starting 8.53 am detrained LONGEAU (Nr AMIENS) marched to billets at LA CHAUSSEE	
LA CHAUSSEE	27.6.16		(12 kilometres N.W. of AMIENS	
			Remained at LA CHAUSSEE — practised signalling, laying, etc.	
CARDONNETTE	30/6/16		Marched to CARDONNETTE (billets)	[signature] Colour [?] to Bde R.F.A.

[signature] Lt Col R.F.A.
Cmdg 105 Bde R.F.A.

1875 Wt. W593/826 1,000,000 4/15 J.B.C. & A. A.D.S.S./Forms/C. 2118.

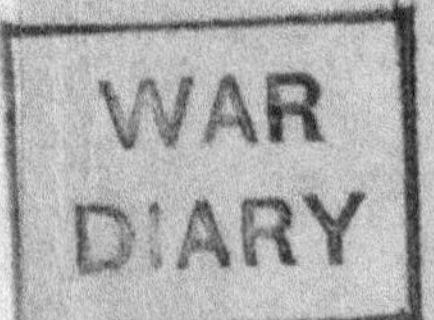

23rd Divisional Artillery.

105th BRIGADE R. F. A.

July 1916

Army Form C. 2118

July

Confidential

WAR DIARY
or
~~INTELLIGENCE SUMMARY~~
(Erase heading not required.)

105th BRIGADE R.F.A

VOL. 11

Instructions regarding War Diaries and Intelligence Summaries are contained in F. S. Regs., Part II. and the Staff Manual respectively. Title Pages will be prepared in manuscript.

Place	Date	Hour	Summary of Events and Information	Remarks and references to Appendices
CARDONNETTE	July 1st	9pm	Marched to Bivouacs at ST. GRATIEN. Bde installed shortly after midnight.	
ST. GRATIEN	2nd to 4th		Remained at St. Gratien. – no events of importance – A certain amount of training in visual and commutator work given to the telephonists.	
– " –	5th	4pm	Orders received to march into action near FRICOURT (F.2. Sheet 62.D.) at once. Bde & Battery Commanders with Battery Staffs trotted forward to reconnoitre – remainder of Bde under Adjutant followed behind 104th Bde. Bde was in action by 3am and digging-in was commenced	
FRICOURT	6th		Digging in – registering etc. – Lt. M.D MOTT – B/105 wounded.	
– " –	7th		24th & 69th Bdes attacked CONTALMAISON & BAILIFF WOOD. Artillery co-operated with barrages etc. – the fire of 105th Bde being mostly directed against BAILIFF WOOD and to the north of it. – The attack was not successful.	
– " –	– " –	9pm	Night barrage on roads & trenches N. of CONTALMAISON & BAILIFF WOOD	

1875 Wt. W593/826 1,000,000 4/15 J.B.C. & A. A.D.S.S./Forms/C. 2118.

Army Form C. 2118

Instructions regarding War Diaries and Intelligence Summaries are contained in F. S. Regs., Part II. and the Staff Manual respectively. Title Pages will be prepared in manuscript.

WAR DIARY
or
~~INTELLIGENCE SUMMARY~~
(Erase heading not required.)

Confidential.

105th Brigade R.F.A.

Place	Date	Hour	Summary of Events and Information	Remarks and references to Appendices
FRICOURT	July 8th	5.0am	Night barrage slowed down to desultory fire to be kept up during day. One battery on BAILIFF WOOD during morning at request of G.O.C. 68th Inf. Bde. During the afternoon a post was established in BAILIFF WOOD	
–"–	–"–	9.0pm	Night barrage opened – Same as previous night.	
–"–	9th	5.0am	Night barrage slowed down. – Day spent in patrol work in the region of BAILIFF WOOD and trench at X.16.a.7.4.	
–"–	–"–	9pm	Night barrage opened as before	
–"–	10th	5.0am	Night barrage lifted.	
		12 noon & onwards	69th Bde attacked CONTALMAISON from West. 105th Bde, co-operating, kept up continuous	
–"–	–"–		barrage in front of infantry, lifting at stated times according to programme. attack was great success – our barrages stated by infantry to have been very effective – The number of dead Germans testified to this	
–"–	–"–	9pm	Night barrage opened.	

1875 Wt. W593/826 1.000,000 4/15 J.B.C. & A. A.D.S.S./Forms/C. 2118.

Instructions regarding War Diaries and Intelligence Summaries are contained in F. S. Regs., Part II. and the Staff Manual respectively. Title Pages will be prepared in manuscript.

WAR DIARY
or
INTELLIGENCE SUMMARY
(Erase heading not required.)

Confidential

Army Form C. 2118.

105th Brigade R.F.A.

Place	Date	Hour	Summary of Events and Information	Remarks and references to Appendices
FRICOURT	July 11		1st Bde (1st Divn.) relieved 69th Bde in front line, and sent out patrols in direction of CONTALMAISON VILLA – established post in PEARL WOOD. During the day a slow barrage was put up on CONTALMAISON VILLA and on German 2nd line for short periods	
–"–	–"–	9 pm.	Night barrage near CONTALMAISON VILLA opened	
–"–	12th	6.0 am	Night barrage lifted.	
	–"–	12 noon	Bde & Battery commanders reconnoitred positions in X.27.	
	–"–	6. pm	One section per battery moved to the new positions selected.	
	–"–	9 pm.	Remaining sections put up night barrage on German 2nd line	
	13th	5.30 am	Night barrage lifted. Morning spent in registering from new positions. about 2 pm remaining sections & Bde HQ moved up.	
		9 pm.	Night lines laid out on German 2nd line. – CONTALMAISON VILLA seized by our infantry	
	14th	3 am to 6.30 am	Bombarded enemy's 2nd line whilst XIII & XV Corps attacked on right	

1875 Wt. W593/826 1,000,000 4/15 J.B.C. & A. A.D.S.S./Forms/C. 2118.

Instructions regarding War Diaries and Intelligence Summaries are contained in F. S. Regs., Part II. and the Staff Manual respectively. Title Pages will be prepared in manuscript.

WAR DIARY
or
INTELLIGENCE SUMMARY
(Erase heading not required.)

Confidential

105th Brigade. R.F.A.

Army Form C. 2118

Place	Date	Hour	Summary of Events and Information	Remarks and references to Appendices
	July 14th	6.30am onwards	Rate of fire slackened – attack reported complete success.	
	– " –	2.0pm to 3pm.	BAZENTIN-LE-PETIT village & wood being captured. – Barraged enemy's 2nd line lifting periodically according to programme, while our infantry tried to bomb up it.	
	– " –	3pm onwards	Rate of fire was gradually slackened off and it was reported that the attack had not been a success; as the trenches were almost obliterated by the heavies.	
		9.0pm.	Night barrage opened	
	15th	5.0am.	Night barrage lifted. – Two more unsuccessful attempts to bomb up the trench were made, during the day, artillery co-operating each time according to programme.	
	– " –	11.0pm.	Night barrage opened on trenches in X.5.a & B.	
	16th	5.0am to 10am.	Barrage lifted. – New german trench running through X.6.a. S.1.D. S.2.a & B reported to have been dug. – called SWITCH LINE – All batteries ordered to register it. This proved impossible as no view was obtainable of it – During afternoon a short bombardment of enemy's trenches & M.G. emplacements in X.5.D was carried out by Hows.	

1875 Wt. W593/826 1,000,000 4/15 J.B.C. & A. A.D.S.S./Forms/C. 2118.

Instructions regarding War Diaries and Intelligence Summaries are contained in F. S. Regs., Part II. and the Staff Manual respectively. Title Pages will be prepared in manuscript.

WAR DIARY
or
~~INTELLIGENCE SUMMARY~~
(Erase heading not required.)

Confidential

Army Form C. 2118

105th Brigade RFA

Place	Date	Hour	Summary of Events and Information	Remarks and references to Appendices
	July 16th	11.50 pm	Our infantry who had under cover of night taken up positions in X.5.C, X.11.B & D & X.12.C assaulted the German 2nd Line from X.5. central southwards. – Attack was completely successful – no opposition being encountered. This attack was supported by artillery barrage which lifted at time of assault on to SWITCH LINE where it remained till 5.0 am.	
	17th	8.45 am to 11.15 pm	The Bde was on slow barrages on SWITCH LINE and German 2nd Line in X.5. a & b.	
		11.20 pm	Registration of 'Switch Line' was rendered possible by capture of the trenches last night, but owing to wire trouble, none was done Night barrage from 9 pm to 5 am on SWITCH LINE	
	18th		Registration of SWITCH LINE was carried out by all batteries before 7 pm. During the afternoon we barraged O.G.1. & main BAPAUME RD at a slow rate.	
		7.20 pm	Barrage was shifted on to O.G.1 in X 5 for 1 hour	
		9.0 pm	Night barrage opened on roads & trenches in R.35 & 36 & M.31	
	19th	8.0 am	Night barrage stopped.	

1875 Wt. W593/826 1,000,000 4/15 J.B.C. & A. A.D.S.S./Forms/C. 2118.

Army Form C. 2118

Instructions regarding War Diaries and Intelligence Summaries are contained in F. S. Regs., Part II. and the Staff Manual respectively. Title Pages will be prepared in manuscript.

WAR DIARY
or
~~INTELLIGENCE~~ SUMMARY
(Erase heading not required.)

Confidential

105th Brigade R.F.A.

Place	Date	Hour	Summary of Events and Information	Remarks and references to Appendices
	July 19th	3pm.	Bde & Battery Commanders reconnoitred new positions in X.17 & 23. One gun per battery moved up in the evening. Position of new HQ will be BOTTOM WOOD	
		9pm	Night barrage opened	
	20th	1.0am to 3.0am	Night barrage lifted back on to main BAPAUME Rd & rate of fire reduced while patrols went out.	
		3am to 5am	Normal night barrage.	
		5am	Barrage stopped.	
		9.30am	Message from HQ.R.A received to cut wire (from new positions) on SWITCH LINE in S.1.D & X.6.a. A 2nd gun per battery moved up at once. ~~Although~~ observation was difficult – wire-cutting was carried out as ordered – but as the reported wire was entirely hidden by long grass, results could not be observed. Remaining sections & Bde HQ were moved up in the evening to the new positions.	
	21st		Wire-cutting on SWITCH LINE continued. – Night barrage – 9pm to 5am	
	22nd		SWITCH LINE re-registered and wire-cutting continued.	

1875 Wt. W593/826 1,000,000 4/15 J.B.C. & A. A.D.S.S./Forms/C. 2118.

Instructions regarding War Diaries and Intelligence Summaries are contained in F. S. Regs., Part II. and the Staff Manual respectively. Title Pages will be prepared in manuscript.

WAR DIARY
or
INTELLIGENCE SUMMARY
(Erase heading not required.)

Confidential

Army Form C. 2118

105th Brigade R.F.A.

Place	Date	Hour	Summary of Events and Information	Remarks and references to Appendices
	July 22nd	4 pm to 6.30 p	~~S~~ Howitzers bombarded SWITCH LINE & MUNSTER ALLEY at a moderate rate.	
	—"—	6.30pm to midnight	Fired on SWITCH LINE at a slow rate	
	23rd	12.25am to 12.30 am	All batteries bombarded SWITCH LINE intensely – 12.30 infantry assaulted it, and barrage lifted a short distance till 12.35, when it was lifted again on to Railway in X.5.a. & fire continued till 2.5 am, when the rate was slackened off till 6 am	
	—"—	6.0am	News received that attack had failed & firing was stopped	
	—"—	9.0am	Ordered to register MUNSTER ALLEY carefully. – this was carried out during morning.	
	—"—	3. pm	Ordered to continue wire-cutting in S.1.D. – which was done up to 7. pm	
	—"—	6pm to 7pm	D/105 bombarded part of MUNSTER ALLEY.	
	—"—	9pm to 5.am	Night barrage on SWITCH LINE	
	24th		D/105 registered junction of MUNSTER ALLEY & O.G.2. during afternoon & bombarded it from 6 to 7.15 pm with good effect	
	—"—	8.50pm	S.O.S signal on our front. – Barrage fire was opened & kept up until 10.30pm. When normal night barrage rate was resumed.	

1875 Wt. W593/826 1,000,000 4/15 J.B.C. & A. A.D.S.S./Forms/C. 2118.

Instructions regarding War Diaries and Intelligence Summaries are contained in F. S. Regs., Part II. and the Staff Manual respectively. Title Pages will be prepared in manuscript.

WAR DIARY
or
~~INTELLIGENCE SUMMARY~~

(Erase heading not required.)

Confidential.

105th Brigade. RFA

Army Form C. 2118

Place	Date	Hour	Summary of Events and Information	Remarks and references to Appendices
	July. 25th	12:30am	Infantry attacked MUNSTER ALLEY - artillery firing according to programme until 4:50am. When	
	-"-	4:50am	attack not having succeeded, 18 pdrs were put on the N.E. half of MUNSTER ALLEY and the Hows. on the junction with SWITCH LINE. - Fire was gradually slowed down till 6:30am when it	
	-"-	6:30am	ceased altogether.	
	-"-	8:30am	Fire was re-opened on same targets & kept up at slow rate all day.	
	-"-	6.0pm	D/105 bombarded junction of MUNSTER ALLEY & SWITCH LINE till 6:45 pm.	
	26th	3:0am	Infantry again attacked MUNSTER ALLEY - artillery firing according to programme from 3.5am to 4:30am - A certain amount of bombing took place in MUNSTER ALLEY during the day.	
		9.pm	Night barrage opened.	
		9.2pm	S.O.S. signal on our front - Barrage opened according to instructions - Dropped back to normal	
		10.pm	rate at 10pm.	
	27th	5.am	Night barrage lifted.	
		10:am	D/105 retaliated on SWITCH LINE for ½ hour for shelling of our trenches - otherwise a quiet day.	
		9pm.	Night barrage opened.	
	28th		12 midnight to 2 am we lifted night barrage 200 yds while patrols went out.	

1875 Wt. W593/826 1,000,000 4/15 J.B.C. & A. A.D.S.S./Forms/C. 2118.

Army Form C. 2118

Instructions regarding War Diaries and Intelligence Summaries are contained in F. S. Regs., Part II. and the Staff Manual respectively. Title Pages will be prepared in manuscript.

WAR DIARY
or
~~INTELLIGENCE SUMMARY~~
(Erase heading not required.)

Confidential.

103rd Brigade RFA

Place	Date	Hour	Summary of Events and Information	Remarks and references to Appendices
	July 28th	5.0am	Night barrage ceased	
		11.0am	D/105 bombarded junction of MUNSTER ALLEY & SWITCH LINE while bombing was in progress in MUNSTER ALLEY – This fire was continued most of the afternoon.	
	" "	9 pm	Night barrage commenced – 10.30 pm to 1 am fire lifted 250 yds while patrols went out.	
	29th	5 am	Night barrage lifted	
		1.30pm to 2.30pm	D/105 bombarded junction of SWITCH LINE & MUNSTER ALLEY heavily.	
		3 to 3.30pm	Rehearsed barrage on SWITCH LINE, lifting gradually to MARTIN PUICH.	
		9 pm	Night barrage commenced	
		10- to 12.30pm	Lifted 250 yds for patrols to go out	
	30th	2.0am	It was reported that 69th Bde had captured a further portion of MUNSTER ALLEY also part of the SWITCH LINE near GLOSTER ALLEY. – accordingly our night barrage was lifted 200 yds	
		4.40am	A feint was made the artillery bombardment lasting till 5.10am, when we ceased fire. It was reported later in the day that we no longer held the SWITCH LINE but held all GLOSTER ALLEY.	
		6.10pm	Put up a barrage on left flank of 19th Divn while they attacked until 7.10 pm. – D/105 then bombarded junction of SWITCH & MUNSTER ALLEY till 8 pm also from 10 pm till daylight	

1875 Wt. W593/826 1,000,000 4/15 J.B.C. & A. A.D.S.S./Forms/C. 2118.

Army Form C. 2118

Instructions regarding War Diaries and Intelligence Summaries are contained in F. S. Regs., Part II. and the Staff Manual respectively. Title Pages will be prepared in manuscript.

WAR DIARY
or
~~INTELLIGENCE SUMMARY~~
(Erase heading not required.)

Confidential

105th Brigade RFA

Place	Date	Hour	Summary of Events and Information	Remarks and references to Appendices
	July 31st		Quiet day — re-registration of junction of SWITCH & MUNSTER ALLEY	
		9pm.	Night barrage opened - fire lifted 100 yds from 10 to 12.30 am for patrols.	
			31/7/16.	
			[illegible signature] LIEUT. COLONEL, R.F.A. COMMANDING 105TH BRIGADE, R.F.A.	

1875 Wt. W593/826 1,000,000 4/15 J.B.C. & A. A.D.S.S./Forms/C. 2118.

23rd Divisional Artillery.

105th BRIGADE

ROYAL FIELD ARTILLERY

AUGUST 1 9 1 6

HQRA -

Herewith War Diary of 105th Bde RFA for August - 1916.

W. R. Pastern, Adjt
105th Bde RFA.

1/9/16.

"A"

23 DIVISION

Forwarded please

[illegible] Lt
a/Staff Capt
A G RA 23 Div
1/9/16

Confidential

56

Army Form C. 2118.

WAR DIARY
or
~~INTELLIGENCE~~ SUMMARY.

(Erase heading not required.)

HQ 105th Bde. RFA

Vol 12

Instructions regarding War Diaries and Intelligence Summaries are contained in F. S. Regs., Part II. and the Staff Manual respectively. Title pages will be prepared in manuscript.

Place	Date	Hour	Summary of Events and Information	Remarks and references to Appendices
BOTTOM WOOD X.29.a (Sheet 57.D)	August 1st		Quiet day.	
		8.30 pm	Night barrage opened.	
	2/8/16.	5.0 am	Night barrage ceased	
	"	3.0 pm to 3.30 pm	Bombardment of SWITCH LINE with field guns, according to programme.	
"	"	5.0 pm to 6.0 pm	D/105 bombarded junction of SWITCH LINE and MUNSTER ALLEY with good results.	
	"	8.30 pm to	} Night Barrage.	
	3/8/16.	5.0 am		
	"	5.0 am	Repeated bombardment of 3 pm yesterday on SWITCH LINE.	
	"	2.0 pm to 4.0 pm	D/105, in conjunction with other Howitzers, bombarded TORR TRENCH with good results	
	"	8.30 pm to	} Night Barrage.	
	4/8/16.	5.0 am		
	"		Registration of SWITCH LINE N.W. of MUNSTER ALLEY carried out by all Batteries	
	"	2.0 pm to 4.0 pm	D/105 repeated yesterdays bombardment.	
	"	9.15 pm to 10.30 pm	} Barrage opened to support bombing attack at MUNSTER ALLEY.	

2353 Wt. W2544/1454 700,000 5/15 D. D. & L. A.D.S.S./Forms/C. 2118.

Instructions regarding War Diaries and Intelligence Summaries are contained in F. S. Regs., Part II. and the Staff Manual respectively. Title pages will be prepared in manuscript.

57

Confidential.

WAR DIARY
or
~~INTELLIGENCE SUMMARY~~.

(Erase heading not required.)

HQ. 105th Bde R.F.A.

Army Form C. 2118.

Place	Date	Hour	Summary of Events and Information	Remarks and references to Appendices
BOTTOM WOOD X.29.a. Sheet 57.D.	4/8/16. to 5/8/16.	11 pm to 5.0am	Night Barrage.	
	– " –		Registration etc.	
	– " – to 6/8/16	8.30pm to 5.0am	Night Barrage.	
	– " –	9.0am to 11.0am	D/105, in conjunction with other Howitzers, bombarded SWITCH LINE	
	– " –	3.0pm to 4.0pm	Barrage as from 9.0am to 11.0am repeated.	
	– " –	4.0pm	18 pdr. Barrage opened in support of further attack on MUNSTER ALLEY, which was captured up to point X.6.a.0.4, where a block was made. Capt. F.J. Richards wounded. Barrages etc, were kept up till about 9.30pm when night barrage was opened. Rate was increased from 3.0am to 4.0am, as a counter-attack was feared.	
	7/8/16 – " –	5.0am	Night barrage ceased.	
	– " –		Quiet day.	
	– " – to 8/8/16	8.30pm to 5.0am	Night barrage	
	– " –		Quiet days – Night Barrages as usual. Lieut. T.J. Craig posted to C/105 from 104th Bde and 2nd Lt. H.C. Campbell posted to D/105	

Confidential

Instructions regarding War Diaries and Intelligence Summaries are contained in F. S. Regs., Part II. and the Staff Manual respectively. Title pages will be prepared in manuscript.

58

WAR DIARY
or
~~INTELLIGENCE~~ SUMMARY.

(Erase heading not required.)

HQ. 105th Brigade. RFA

Army Form C. 2118.

Place	Date	Hour	Summary of Events and Information	Remarks and references to Appendices
BOTTOM WOOD X.29.a Sheet 57.D	9/8/16.		Quiet day. Night barrage as usual	
	10/8/16 & 11/8/16.		Barrage commenced at 2 pm to isolate that portion of SWITCH LINE from X.6.a.4.7 to S.1.D.9½.9.	
			This barrage was kept up in reliefs until 10.15 pm	
			Lieut. T. J. Craig wounded. 11/8/16.	
	12/8/16.		At 10.15 pm a slow barrage was opened on SWITCH LINE, which at 10.30 pm became intense and infantry assaulted SWITCH TRENCH. After a succession of lifts a barrage was maintained until 11.20am on 13th. The left Bde was ~~[illegible]~~ successful but the right failed to capture the "elbow."	
	13/8/16.		Reliefs of 23rd D.A. by 47th D.A.	
			One section per battery, as under, was relieved at 6.0 pm & marched to Wagon Lines	
			A/105 by A/236 B/105 " B/236 C/105 " C/236 D/105 " D/236.	
	14/8/16		These sections marched to billets at FRECHENCOURT.	
			Remaining sections and Bde HQ being relieved at 6 pm and marched to Wagon Lines	
QUERRIEUX	15/8/16		2nd Sections and HQ marched to camp near QUERRIEUX and were joined by 1st Sections.	
"	16/8/16.		Cleaning up.	
	17/8/16.		Bde entrained at LONGEAU ~~and~~ & SALEUX in the morning and detrained at BAILLEUL & GODEWAERSVELDE the same evening and marched to billets near EECKE. Orders for relief of 41st Div. Arty. by 23rd Divn Arty. received.	

2353 Wt. W2544/1454 700,000 5/15 D. D. & L. A.D.S.S./Forms/C. 2118.

Confidential

Instructions regarding War Diaries and Intelligence Summaries are contained in F. S. Regs., Part II. and the Staff Manual respectively. Title pages will be prepared in manuscript.

59.

WAR DIARY
or
~~INTELLIGENCE SUMMARY.~~
(Erase heading not required.)

H.Q. 105th Bde R.F.A.

Army Form C. 2118.

Place	Date	Hour	Summary of Events and Information	Remarks and references to Appendices
EECKE.	18/8/16		Brigade Commander, Orderly Officer, and telephonists went to Centre Group. H.Q. of 41st Divn. Arty. at B.11.D.3.7. (Sheet 36).	
– " –	19/8/16		Battery Commanders and telephonists rode to Group HQ and on to their Batteries. One section per battery moved up and relieved one section of 187 Bde. R.F.A. in the evening at 8 pm. as under:- A/105 relieved A/187 at B.6.D.7.0. B/105 " B/187 " U.25.A.6.4. C/105 " C/187 " B.6.B.2.7 D/105 " D/187 " U.20.D.2.2.	
B.11.D.3.7 (Sheet 36)	20/8/16		HQ & 2nd Sections moved up and relieved HQ & 2nd Sections of 187 Bde at 8 pm. The Div. Arty. was divided into 3 groups - Right - Centre - Left. 105th HQ ran Centre Group - consisting of A.B.C. & D/105 and B/102. Front covered by Group - U.28.C.8.8 to U.15.D.8½.5.	
– " –	21/8/16 to 24/8/16		Quiet days - Practically no hostile fire. Lieut. L.R.P. Sanderson & 2/Lt. G.D. Gale posted to 41st Divn. Arty on 22.8.16. Registration was carried out by all Batteries. ~~At~~ noon on 24th. the artillery was re-grouped into 2 groups Right Group under OC 104th Bde & Left Group under OC 103rd Bde. A & D/105 went to Right Group. B & C/105 & B/102 to Left Group.	
– " –	25/8/16 to 31/8/16		HQ. 105 Bde. remained in Administrative control of 105 Bde. — work on Wagon Lines etc.	

1/9/16.

[signature]
LIEUT. COLONEL, R.F.A.
COMMANDING 105TH BRIGADE, R.F.A.

2353 Wt. W2544/1454 700,000 5/15 D. D. & L. A.D.S.S./Forms/C. 2118.

CONFIDENTIAL.

Officer i/c

A.G's Office at the Base.

Herewith War Diary, 105th Brigade R.F.A. for period 1st-3rd September, 1916.

The Brigade was finally disbanded on 3rd Septr: 1916.

[illegible signature]

Captain,

12. 11. 1916. Staff Captain R.A. 23rd Division.

Instructions regarding War Diaries and Intelligence Summaries are contained in F. S. Regs., Part II. and the Staff Manual respectively. Title Pages will be prepared in manuscript.

60

WAR DIARY
or
~~INTELLIGENCE SUMMARY~~
(Erase heading not required.)

HQ 105th Bde RFA

Army Form C. 2118.

Place	Date	Hour	Summary of Events and Information	Remarks and references to Appendices
B11 D 3.7 Sheet 36 PLOEGSTEERT	1st 2nd		Reorganisation of Div Arty – completed by 6pm Sept. 3rd inst.	
	3rd		102 } 103 } to consist of 3 – 6 gun 18 pr. & 1 – 4 gun How –	
			104 " " 2 – 6 gun " – 2 – 4 gun "	
			HQ 105 – Disbanded – personnel sent to other units –	
			A/105 sends 1 Section to A/102 & 1 to B/102	
			B/105 " " " B/103 " – C/103	
			C/105 " " " C/102 " – A/103	
			D/105 Becomes C/104.	
			Lt Col Nicholson went to command 104 Bde via Col Mathews – to command A/102 –	
			Lt Davies goes to be adjt 104 –	
			Lt Pasteur went to C/104	

2449 Wt. W14957/M90 750,000 1/16 J.B.C. & A. Forms/C.2118/12.

Instructions regarding War Diaries and Intelligence Summaries are contained in F. S. Regs., Part II. and the Staff Manual respectively. Title Pages will be prepared in manuscript.

61

WAR DIARY
or
~~INTELLIGENCE SUMMARY~~
(Erase heading not required.)

HQ 105 Bde RFA

Army Form C. 2118.

Place	Date	Hour	Summary of Events and Information	Remarks and references to Appendices
PLOEGSTEERT	1st 2nd 3rd	Contd	Battery officers disposed of as follows.	
			Capt Willcocks H.F. to command C/104	
			" Young D.R. " " C/102	
			Lieut Andrews A., 2/Lt McLachlan B., 2/Lt Hamer F.H., 2/Lt Watson N.J., 2/Lt Brown N.C., 2/Lt Blyth L.B. – to 102	
			2/Lt Bucknall W.D., 2/Lt Higlett A.S., Lieut Warden V. – to 103	
			2/Lt Seale T.E., 2/Lt Mills W.R.G., 2/Lt Eastwood H., 2/Lt Farr E.T.C., 2/Lt Dent J.	
			2/Lt L.S. Campbell, all officers of D/105 – to 104.	
			4/9/16	
			N.A. Thompson[?] Lt. Col. Cmdg 105th Bde RFA	

23RD DIVISION
DIVL ARTILLERY

23RD DIVL TRENCH MORTARS

OCT 1915 - ~~JAN 1919~~
1917 OCT

TO ITALY

L

G.H.Q.

att.d 23 Div

121/7470

21 French How.r Batty.

V

Oct., 15

to

Jan '19

Vol IV

Ref

Ch.

Army Form C. 2118.

WAR DIARY
or
~~INTELLIGENCE SUMMARY~~
(Erase heading not required.)

Instructions regarding War Diaries and Intelligence Summaries are contained in F. S. Regs., Part II. and the Staff Manual respectively. Title pages will be prepared in manuscript.

21st Trench Battery — Attached 23rd Division.

Hour, Date, Place	Summary of Events and Information	Remarks and references to Appendices
Line in front of ARMENTIERES	No firing Work at concrete dug out I 21 a 55.0.	Armed with 40. mm (1½") Vickers Trench Howitzer.
1st October 1915.		
2nd " "	" "	Map reference to Sheet 36. B. Series.
3rd " "	" "	
4th " "	" "	Map references to Emplacements RUE du BOIS.
5th " "	" "	
6th " "	" "	'A' Trench 60 I 21 c 8.8.
7th " "	" "	B " 61 I 21 c 85.05
8th " "	" "	C " 61 I 21 a 8.0.
	Fired to register E. Emplacement RUE du BOIS at 4.1 p.m. Enemy replied with 2 heavy trench mortars ~~& one~~ sausage machine. Fighting continued till 5.30 p.m.	D " 61 I 21 a 9.1
9th " "		E " S60 I 21 a 55.0.
10th " "	No firing	F " S61 I 21 a 6.05
	" "	G " S61 I 21 a 7.1.
11th " "		H " 61 I 21 a 8.3.
	Enemy opened fire at 9.30 a.m. with field guns, howitzers & a number of trench mortars. Fired till 11 a.m. in reply from 'C' 'F' & 'G' emplacements. Amm^n expended. Battery withdrawn to billets to await a fresh supply	I " 62 I 21 a 9.6.

[signature] Capt R.F.A.
Comdg 21st Trench Battery

1247 W 3299 200,000 (E) 8/14 J.B.C. & A. Forms/C. 2118/11.

Instructions regarding War Diaries and Intelligence Summaries are contained in F. S. Regs., Part II. and the Staff Manual respectively. Title pages will be prepared in manuscript.

Army Form C. 2118.

WAR DIARY
or
~~INTELLIGENCE SUMMARY~~

(Erase heading not required.)

21st Trench Battery — Attached 23rd Division.

Hour, Date, Place	Summary of Events and Information	Remarks and references to Appendices
Line in front of Armentières 12th October 1915	Battery in Billets. Work on concrete dug-out. I.21.a.55.0.	Armed with 1½" Vickers Howitzer.
13th " "	" " " " "	
14th " "	" " " " "	Map References to Sheet 36 B. Series
15th " "	" " " " "	
16th " "	" " " " "	
17th " "	" " " "	
18th " "	" " " "	
19th " "	" " " "	
20th " "	" " " "	
21st " "	" " " 2/Lt Coles posted to command 21st Trench Battery. 2/Lt Egerton attached for instruction.	
22nd " "	Work on concrete dug-out.	
23rd " "	Arrival of consignment of 53 rounds light. " "	J.F.P. Coles 2/Lt 3/2 York R
24th " "	Gunner Chalk killed. Work on concrete dug-out	
25th " "	Arrival of consignment of 100 rounds heavy. " "	Comdg 21st Trench Battery
26th " "	Front detachment + 2 guns went into Trenches	
27th " "	no firing. Work on dug-out	
28th " "	" " " " 'G' Emplacement. I.21.a.7.1.	
29th " "	2/Lt G. C. Gaiden attached for further instruction. " 'H' (I.21.a.8.3) + I (I.21.a.9.6) Emplacements.	
30th " "	no firing. Rear detachment + 2 guns went into trenches	
31st " "	" " Work on dug-out roof.	

1247 W 3299 200,000 (E) 8/14 J.B.C. & A. Forms/C. 2118/11.

23

G H G.

21 Trench Mortar Batty

Nov

Vol V

121
4779

2d

Cw

Instructions regarding War Diaries and Intelligence Summaries are contained in F. S. Regs., Part II. and the Staff Manual respectively. Title pages will be prepared in manuscript.

WAR DIARY
or
INTELLIGENCE SUMMARY

Army Form C. 2118.

(Erase heading not required.)

21st Trench Battery attached 23rd Division

Hour, Date, Place	Summary of Events and Information	Remarks and references to Appendices
Line in front of Armentieres		Armed with 40 m/m (1½") Vickers Trench Howitzer.
1st Nov. 1915	No firing. Work on dug out roof I 21 a 55.0	
2nd " "	" " . Weather too bad for work	Map references to sheet 36
3rd " "	" " . Work at dug-outs I.21.a 65.05	B. Series
4th " "	" " . 'D' 'H' + 'I' Emplacements abandoned, new emplacement made at 'A' 10 yds nearer parapet. Work at dug-out + trench to same revetted with wire netting + stakes.	Map references to Emplacements RUE DU BOIS.
5th " "	— " —	'A' Trench 60 I 21 c/a 8.8
6th " "	no firing. Revetting on trench to dug-out finished	'B' " 61 I 21 c/a 85.95
7th " "	" " . Work on sides of trench to concrete dug-out (I.21.a.55.0)	'C' " 61 I 21 a 8.0
8th " "	— " —	'D' " 61 I 21 a 9.1
9th " "	" " . Finished revetting trench to dug-out. Fired from 'B' Emplacement I 21.c 85.95 3.20 pm in reply to Enemy's retaliation to our catapult	'E' " S60 I 21 a 55.0
10th " "	no firing.	'F' " S61 I 21 a 6.5
11th " "	— " —	'G' " S61 I 21 a 7.1
12th " "	— " —	'H' " 61 I 21 a 8.3
13th " "	— " —	'I' " 61 I 21 a 9.6
14th " "	— " —	
15th " "	" " . Work on bomb shelters at 'F' Empl. I.21.a.6.05	O.R. Coles 2/Lt 3/E. York. R.
	" . Work on bomb shelters at 'F' + 'G' Empl. I.21.a.6.05 and I.21.a.7.1.	Comdg 21st Trench Battery

1247 W 3299 200,000 (E) 8/14 J.B.C. & A. Forms/C. 2118/11.

Instructions regarding War Diaries and Intelligence Summaries are contained in F. S. Regs., Part II. and the Staff Manual respectively. Title pages will be prepared in manuscript.

WAR DIARY
or
~~INTELLIGENCE SUMMARY~~

(Erase heading not required.)

Army Form C. 2118.

21st Trench Battery attached 23rd Division.

Hour, Date, Place	Summary of Events and Information	Remarks and references to Appendices
Line in front of ARMENTIERES		Armed with 1½" Vickers Trench Howitzer
16th November 1915	no firing. O.C to St Venant (1st Army School of Trench Howitzers)	
	—— " ——	
17th " "	" " .	Map References to Sheet 36 B. Series
	—— " ——	
18th " "	" " . Erecting new Bomb shelter at 'F' I 21.a. 6.05	
	—— " ——	
19th " "	" " . Repairing Bomb shelter at 'G' I 21.a. 7.1.	
	—— " ——	
20th " "	" " .	
	—— " ——	
21st " "	" " . 2 N.C.O's and 14 gunners sent back to 1st ARMY SCHOOL as ordered. arrival of 5 privates from 69th I.B.	
	—— " ——	
22nd " "	no firing.	
	—— " ——	
23rd " "	" " . Work on trench leading to O.C.'s dug-out	
	—— " ——	
24th " "	" " . 69th I.B. relieved by 68th I.B.	
	—— " ——	
25th " "	" " . 2/Lieut GADEN rejoined SCHOOL OF MORTARS	D.F.P. Coles 2/Lt 3/E. York. R
	—— " ——	
26th " "	" " .	Comdg 21st Trench Battery
27th " "	—— " ——	
28th " "	" " . Put new roof on front detachment Dug-out.	
29th " "	—— " ——	
	" " .	
	—— " ——	
	—— " ——	
30th " "	" " . Draining work at E Empl.t (I 21 a 55.0) + also at new dug-out.	

1247 W 3299 200,000 (E) 8/14 J.B.C. & A. Forms/C. 2118/11.

23

GSG

21 Trench Mortar Batty

Dec

Vol. VI

121/7957

Instructions regarding War Diaries and Intelligence Summaries are contained in F. S. Regs., Part II. and the Staff Manual respectively. Title pages will be prepared in manuscript.

WAR DIARY
or
~~INTELLIGENCE SUMMARY~~

(*Erase heading not required.*)

Army Form C. 2118.

21st Trench Battery attached 23rd Division

Hour, Date, Place	Summary of Events and Information	Remarks and references to Appendices
Line in front of ARMENTIERES		Armed with 40 mm (1½") Vickers Trench Howitzer.
1st December 1915	No firing. Work on O.C.'s dug-out	
2nd "	" " . Work as above + at 'E' Emplt. I 21. a. 55.0	Map references to Sheet 36 B. Series
3rd " "	" " . Work at 'E' Emplt. Borrowed 2 ptes from front line	
4th " "	" " "	Map references to Emplacements
5th " "	" " . Cleared earth away from O.C.'s dug-out and began new trench to dug-out at E Emplacement. Borrowed 5 men from front line. Carrying party of 1 N.C.O + 10 men from 68th I.B. moved ammunition from billet (I 1 c 2 6) to Brasserie (I 1 d 45.40.)	RUE DU BOIS. 'A' Trench 60 I 21 c 8.8. 'B' " 61 I 21 c 85.9[illegible] 'C' " 61 I 21 a 8.0 'E' " S 60 I 21 a 55.0
6th " "	No firing. Rear detachment came out of action. Work on new Trench to dug-out at E Emplacement. 'E' I 21 a 55.0 + 'F' Emplacements abandoned.	'F' " S 61 I 21 a 6.0[illegible] 'G' " S 61 I 21 a 7.[illegible]
7th " "	No firing. Work at 'B' Emplacement I 21 c 85.95.	
8th " "	" " . Work on new trench + at Concrete dug-out.	
9th " "	" " . Work as usual "	
10th " "	Fired from 'A' I 21 c 88 and 'C' I 21 a 8.0 Emplacements, 45 rounds in all, in reply to Enemy's Trench mortars, Howitzers + field guns. Order from 3rd Corps received - not to fire again until consignment of fuzes (No 121) arrives.	D.P. Coles 2/Lt 3/E. York R. Comdg 21st Trench Battery

1247 W 3299 200,000 (E) 8/14 J.B.C. & A. Forms/C. 2118/11.

Instructions regarding War Diaries and Intelligence Summaries are contained in F. S. Regs., Part II. and the Staff Manual respectively. Title pages will be prepared in manuscript.

WAR DIARY
or
INTELLIGENCE SUMMARY

(Erase heading not required.)

Army Form C. 2118.

21st Trench Battery attached 23rd Division.

Hour, Date, Place	Summary of Events and Information	Remarks and references to Appendices
Line in front of ARMENTIERES		Armed with 1½" Vickers Trench Howitzer.
11th December 1915.	No firing. Work in Front detachment dug-out + on Trench to concrete dug-out	"
12th " "	" " Ditto	Map References to Sheet 36 B. Series
13th " "	" " "	"
14th " "	" " 68th I.B relieved by 24th I.B. Work as above	
15th " "	" " Work as usual	
16th " "	" " Trench to concrete dug-out finished	
17th " "	" " Started new Emplacements at I 21 a 55.05	
18th " "	" " Work at Emplacement	D.H. Coles 2/Lt 3/E. York R
19th " "	" " Work at Emplacement	
20th " "	" " 2/Lieut Cowbrough attached to the Battery for instruction	Comdg 21st Trench Batty

1247 W 3299 200,000 (E) 8/14 J.B.C. & A. Forms/C. 2118/11.

Instructions regarding War Diaries and Intelligence Summaries are contained in F. S. Regs., Part II. and the Staff Manual respectively. Title pages will be prepared in manuscript.

WAR DIARY
or
~~INTELLIGENCE SUMMARY~~

(Erase heading not required.)

Army Form C. 2118.

21st Trench Battery attached 23rd Division

Hour, Date, Place	Summary of Events and Information	Remarks and references to Appendices
Line in front of ARMENTIERES		Armed with 1½" Vickers Trench Howitzer.
21st December 1915	No firing. B (I 21 c 85.95) and C (I 21 a 8.0.) Emplacements abandoned. Work at new Emplacement. 2/Lieut Egerton ordered to St. VENANT and posted to command No. 69 Trench Battery attached 23rd Division. 1st Army order. Battery permanently attached 24th I.B.	— " —
		Map References to Sheet 36. B, Series
		— " —
22nd " "	" " Work on new Emplacement	
23rd " "	Arrival of consignment of 136 fuzes No. 121	
24th " "	Two guns in action. New Emplacement finished	
25th " "	No firing. New Emplacement made at I 21 a 60.05	
26th " "	" "	
27th " "	Bombardment of German front line opposite T. 60 + 61 by our heavy guns opened at 10 am. Infantry ordered to move from the above named trenches. Fired five rounds heavy from 'A' Emplacement to ~~try~~ re-register + to try new fuze (121). Great success. 50% Tubes friction T bad. New Emplacement I 21 a 55.05 destroyed by Whizz bangs	D. F. Pholes 2/Lt 8/E. York R Comdg 21st Trench Battery

1247 W 3299 200,000 (E) 8/14 J.B.C. & A. Forms/C. 2118/11.

Army Form C. 2118.

Instructions regarding War Diaries and Intelligence Summaries are contained in F. S. Regs., Part II. and the Staff Manual respectively. Title pages will be prepared in manuscript.

WAR DIARY
or
INTELLIGENCE SUMMARY

(Erase heading not required.)

21st Trench Battery attached 23rd Division

Hour, Date, Place	Summary of Events and Information	Remarks and references to Appendices
Line in front of ARMENTIERES		armed with 1½" Vickers Trench Howitzer
27th December (Cont.)	arrival of consignment of 90 Bombs light.	
	— " —	— " —
28th "	NO Firing.	Map References to Sheet 36 B. Series
	— " —	
29th "	" " 24th I.B relieved by 69th I.B.	
	— " —	— " —
30th "	"	
	— " —	
31st "	" " made four new emplacement	
	No 1 at I 21 c 8.3. } No 2 " I 21 c 85.85 } No 3 " I 21 a 60.05 } No 4 " I 21 a 85.45 } all trained on German House; No 4 also covering trenches S.W. of "	D H Coles 2/Lt 3/E. York R.
	Put up new dug-out at I 21 a 7.1	
	Carrying party 50 " West Riding Regt. Brought up 50 rounds ammunition.	Comdg 21st Trench Battery
	— " —	

1247 W 3299 200,000 (E) 8/14 J.B.C. & A. Forms/C. 2118/11.

Instructions regarding War Diaries and Intelligence Summaries are contained in F. S. Regs., Part II. and the Staff Manual respectively. Title pages will be prepared in manuscript.

WAR DIARY
or
INTELLIGENCE SUMMARY

(Erase heading not required.)

Army Form C. 2118.

21st Trench Battery attached 23rd Division

Hour, Date, Place	Summary of Events and Information	Remarks and references to Appendices
Line in front of ARMENTIERES		Armed with 1½"
1st January 1916	Fired from Nos 1. 2. 3 & 4 Emplacements (RUE DU BOIS) at 1.33 am till 1.48 am at German House & Trenches S.W of same during bombardment by our Artillery. Raiding party of 9th Yorkshire Regt went out from T. 62. Retaliation fairly heavy, very few casualties.	Vickers Trench Howitzer — " — Map References to Sheet 36 B. Series — " — Map References to Emplacements RUE DU BOIS
2nd " "	No firing. Work at all Emplacements.	No 1 Trench 60 I 21 c 8 8.
3rd "	— " — [illegible] of consignment of 40 rounds heavy (long-tail) & 40 rounds light.	No 2 " 60 I 21 c 35. 85
4th " "	— " —	No 3 " S.61 I 21 a 6.05
	No firing.	No 4 " 62 I 21 a 85. 45
5th " "	" " — " —	— " —
6th " "	Fired from Nos 1 & 2 Emplacements at 10 am to destroy sap & annoy Hun generally. (45 rounds) retaliated with 'sausages' & whizz bangs. — " —	D.H. Coles 2/Lt 3/E. York R. Comdg 21st Trench Battery
7th " "	No Firing. Infantry carrying parties brought up 64 light & 12 heavy. Removed guns from Salient to cond line. — " —	
8th "	No firing. — " —	

1247 W 3299 200,000 (E) 8/14 J.B.C. & A. Forms/C. 2118/11.

Army Form C. 2118.

WAR DIARY
or
~~INTELLIGENCE SUMMARY~~

Instructions regarding War Diaries and Intelligence Summaries are contained in F. S. Regs., Part II. and the Staff Manual respectively. Title pages will be prepared in manuscript.

21st Trench Battery (*Erase heading not required.*) attached 23rd Division

Hour, Date, Place	Summary of Events and Information	Remarks and references to Appendices
Line in part of ARMENTIERES		Armed with 1½" Vickers Trench Howitzer
9th January 1916	No firing. guns replaced in Salient	— " —
10th " "	" " . Work on Dug-out in Cord line	Map References to sheet 36
11th " "	— " —	B Series
12th "	" " Ditto	— " —
13th " "	— " —	
	Fired from No 1 gun at 2 p.m in retaliation & also for registration (16 rounds) Gunner Woodward slightly wounded	
14th " "	— " —	
	Fired from Nos 2 & 4 guns in conjunction with Artillery at 11.25 am (28 rounds) Targets German House & trenches N.E of same. Enemy fired about 40 [illegible] in return.	
15th " "	— " —	
	No firing. 68th I.B. relieved 69th I.B.	D.F. Coles 2/Lt 3/? York R.
16th	— " —	
	" " . Work on dug-out in cord line	Comdg 21st Trench Battery
17th " "	— " —	
	ditto Bombardment by our Artillery	
18th " "	— " —	
	" " . Work on dug-out	
19th " "	— " —	
	" . ditto	
	— " —	

1247 W 3299 200,000 (E) 8/14 J.B.C. & A. Forms/C. 2118/11.

Army Form C. 2118.

WAR DIARY
or
~~INTELLIGENCE SUMMARY~~
(Erase heading not required.)

Instructions regarding War Diaries and Intelligence Summaries are contained in F. S. Regs., Part II. and the Staff Manual respectively. Title pages will be prepared in manuscript.

21st Trench Battery attached 23rd Division

Hour, Date, Place	Summary of Events and Information	Remarks and references to Appendices
Line in front of ARMENTIERES		Armed with 1½" Vickers Trench Howitzer
20th January 1916	no firing.	— " —
21st " "	" " .	Map references to sheet 36. B. Series
22nd " "	Fired from No 4 at 2·30 p.m. to destroy hostile machine gun emplacement & to damage parapet etc. for D.L.I. Fired from No 2 gun to silence hostile Trench Mortars, had to stop after 10 rounds owing to faulty charges.	— " —
23rd " "	no firing. Work on dug-out in cord line	
24th " "	" " . ditto	
25th " "	" " . "	
26th " "	" " . "	
27th " "	Fired from No 2 gun at 11.30 p.m. during period of hostile frightfulness. Silenced their Mortars.	D.F.P. Coles 2/Lt 3/E. York. R.
28th " "	NO firing. Hostile frightfulness all day. Minenwerfer active	Comdg 21st Trench Battery
~~29th~~		

1247 W 3299 200,000 (E) 8/14 J.B.C. & A. Forms/C. 2118/11.

Army Form C. 2118.

WAR DIARY

or

~~INTELLIGENCE SUMMARY~~

(Erase heading not required.)

Instructions regarding War Diaries and Intelligence Summaries are contained in F. S. Regs., Part II. and the Staff Manual respectively. Title pages will be prepared in manuscript.

21st Trench Battery attached 28th Division

Hour, Date, Place	Summary of Events and Information	Remarks and references to Appendices
Line in front of ARMENTIERES		armed with 1½"
29th January 1916	Fired from No 2 gun at p.m. 18 rounds to quiet hostile Mortars. Gunner Ray wounded.	Vickers Trench Howitzer
	— " —	— " —
30th " "	No firing. 2 N.C.O's + 10 gunners arrived from S VENANT to replace Infantry personnel.	Map references to Sheet 36 B. Series
	— " —	— " —
31st " "	No firing. 68th I.B relieved by 24th I.B	
	— " —	

D.H.P. Coles. 2/Lt
3/E. York. R.
Comdg 21st Trench Battery

1247 W 3299 200,000 (E) 8/14 J.B.C. & A. Forms/C. 2118/11.

23

21 Trench M Bty

Vol VIII

Army Form C. 2118.

WAR DIARY
or
~~INTELLIGENCE SUMMARY~~

(Erase heading not required.)

Instructions regarding War Diaries and Intelligence Summaries are contained in F. S. Regs., Part II. and the Staff Manual respectively. Title pages will be prepared in manuscript.

21st Trench Battery attached 23rd Division

Hour, Date, Place	Summary of Events and Information	Remarks and references to Appendices
Line in front of ARMENTIERES		Armed with 1½" Vickers Trench Howitzer
1st February 1916	No firing. Infantry personnel sent away to rejoin units	
2nd " "	" " — " —	Map references to Sheet 36 B. Series
3rd " "	" " — " —	— " —
4th " "	" " — " —	Map references to Emplacements RUE DU BOIS
5th " "	" " Dug out in Cord lane finished.	No 1 Trench I21 c 33
6th " "	" " — " —	No 2 " I21 c 35.36
7th " "	" " — " —	No 3 " I21 a 6.03
8th " "	" " — " —	No 4 " I21 a 35.45
9th "	" " — " —	— " —
10th "	" — " —	
	three R.A. officers attached for instruction for four days	
11th "	— " —	
	1 Officer 11 other Ranks No 61 Trench Battery 34th Division attached for instruction previous to taking over.	

D H P Coles 2/Lt
3/E York R.
Comdg 21st Trench Battery

1247 W 3299 200,000 (E) 8/14 J.B.C. & A. Forms/C. 2118/11.

Army Form C. 2118.

Instructions regarding War Diaries and Intelligence Summaries are contained in F. S. Regs., Part II. and the Staff Manual respectively. Title pages will be prepared in manuscript.

WAR DIARY

or

~~INTELLIGENCE SUMMARY~~

21st Trench Battery *(Erase heading not required.)* attached 24th I.B 23rd Division

Hour, Date, Place	Summary of Events and Information	Remarks and references to Appendices
Line in front of ARMENTIERES		Armed with 1½"
12th February 1916	Fired from Nos 1 + 2 at 3.15 pm in response to general frightfulness (25 rounds)	Vickers Trench Howitzer
	— " —	— " —
13th " "	Fired from Nos 1 + 2 at 3.30 pm during hostile strafe	Map References to
	— " —	Sheet 36 B. Series
14th " "	24th I.B 23rd Division relieved by 103rd I.B. 34th Div. 21st Trench Battery attached 103rd I.B till further Orders.	— " —
	— " —	
15th " "	no firing. Removed gun from No 1 to No 3.	
	— " —	
16th " "	" " . Made new emplacement - Cord line	
	— " —	
17th " "	" "	
	— " —	
18th " "	Handed over guns + ammunition to 61st Trench Battery Left RUE MARLE for ERQUINGHEM	D H P Coles 2/Lt 3/E York R
	— " —	
19th " "	Handed over handcarts by order 23rd Division	Cmdg 21st Trench Bty
	— " —	
20th " "	Left ERQUINGHEM 2.30 pm via STEINBWERK arrived VIEUX BERQUIN 6.15 pm.	
	— " —	
21st "	Left VIEUX BERQUIN at 8.30 am arrived STEINBECK 12.30 pm	
	— " —	

1247 W 3299 200,000 (E) 8/14 J.B.C. & A. Forms/C. 2118/11.

Instructions regarding War Diaries and Intelligence Summaries are contained in F. S. Regs., Part II. and the Staff Manual respectively. Title pages will be prepared in manuscript.

WAR DIARY

or

~~INTELLIGENCE SUMMARY~~

(Erase heading not required.)

Army Form C. 2118.

21st Trench Battery attached 23rd Division

Hour, Date, Place	Summary of Events and Information	Remarks and references to Appendices
22nd February 1916	Rest	
23rd " "	— " —	
24th " "	— " —	
25th " "	— " —	
26 " "	— " —	
27th " "	— " —	
28th " "	— " —	
29th " "	Marched at 10.30am to THIENNES. Entrained 12.30pm arrived at CALONNE RICOUART at 2pm. Marched to BRUAY. Division attached IV Corps.	
	— " —	

O.H.P. Coles 2/Lt
3/E. York. R
Comdg 21st Trench Bty

1247 W 3299 200,000 (E) 8/14 J.B.C. & A. Forms/C. 2118/11.

Y 23 T M Bty
late 21

Vol IX

Instructions regarding War Diaries and Intelligence Summaries are contained in F. S. Regs., Part II. and the Staff Manual respectively. Title pages will be prepared in manuscript.

WAR DIARY

or

~~INTELLIGENCE SUMMARY~~

(Erase heading not required.)

Army Form C. 2118.

21st Trench Battery Attached 23rd Division

Hour, Date, Place	Summary of Events and Information	Remarks and references to Appendices
1st March 1916	no work.	Armed with 2" M.L. Howitzer
2nd " "	Battery with 24th I.B. inspected by IV Corps Commander	— " —
3rd " "	— " — Four 2" guns & stores arrived.	
4th " "	— " — no work.	
5th " "	— " — "	
6th " "	— " — Drew 8 handcarts from Ordnance. Left BRUAY (under 69th I.B. orders) at 10.45 am marched via BARLIN – HERSIN – GRAND SERVIN to PETIT SERVIN arrived 3 pm. found billets.	
7th " "	— " — Started behind 8th Yorks at 6.15 pm with two guns complete in limber, unloaded at Com Trench. Carried one gun complete to centre Battn HQ. Returned to Billets at 7 am 8th March.	
8th	— " — Re-arranged Billets	
9th	— " — Started for Trenches at 5.30 pm. Carried both guns up to French Trench Battery dug-outs in 3rd line. Returned 1 am 10th March	
10th	Work – Billets. ~~Transport~~ 69th I.B. relieved by 24th I.B.	D F P Coles 2/Lt 3/ E. York R. Comdg 21st Trench Battery
11th	Started with 6 men 1 NCO & S.M. for Trenches at 4 am. Dug in two beds returned 1 pm.	

Army Form C. 2118.

WAR DIARY
or
~~INTELLIGENCE SUMMARY~~

Instructions regarding War Diaries and Intelligence Summaries are contained in F. S. Regs., Part II. and the Staff Manual respectively. Title pages will be prepared in manuscript.

21st Trench Battery (Erase heading not required.) Attached 23rd Division

Hour, Date, Place	Summary of Events and Information	Remarks and references to Appendices
Line in part of SOUCHEY		Arrived with 2" M. L. Howitzer
12th of March 1916	no work.	—"—
	—"—	
13th " "	Arrival of 140 rounds for X/47 Battery placed in dug-outs on CARENCY road by R.A.M.C station.	
	—"—	
14th " "	Handed over guns + equipment and 5 hand carts to X/47 Battery. ~~the Arrival of~~ 140 Rounds, also handed over	
	—"—	
15th " "	Designation of Battery changed from 21st Trench Battery to Y/23 Trench Mortar Battery R.A.	
	—"—	
16th " "	Moved from PETIT SERVINS to BRUAY	
	—"—	
17th " "	O.C. to Trenches (ANGRES Sector) with officers 69th I.B.	
	—"—	
18th " "	Moved from BRUAY to HERSIN	
	—"—	
19th " "	Moved from HERSIN to billets in PETIT SAINS. Took over billets + 2 guns in Trenches + 10 rounds in Trenches + 300 rounds in Bomb store from X/2 Trench Battery (late 69th)	J.H.P. Coles 2/Lt 3/E. York R. Comdg Y/23 Trench Bty
	—"—	

1247 W 3299 200,000 (E) 8/14 J.B.C. & A. Forms/C. 2118/11.

Army Form C. 2118.

WAR DIARY
or
~~INTELLIGENCE SUMMARY~~
(Erase heading not required.)

Instructions regarding War Diaries and Intelligence Summaries are contained in F. S. Regs., Part II. and the Staff Manual respectively. Title pages will be prepared in manuscript.

Y/23 Trench Battery Attached 23rd Division

Hour, Date, Place	Summary of Events and Information	Remarks and references to Appendices
ANGRES Sector 20th March 1916	Fired from left hand gun ten rounds at 3 p.m. by request C.O. 8th Yorks to silence hostile Rifle grenades + whizz-bangs – obtained silence. Carrying parties lent by Infantry brought up 55 rounds. Took up one of the new Howitzers from billet to detachment's dug-out in GUM BOOT trench. From 7 p.m. to 7.30 p.m. German strafed our trenches with light stuff, possibly in retaliation for our afternoon shoot.	Armed with 2" M.L. Trench Howitzer — " — Map reference to Sheet 36 c S.W — " — Map references to Emplacements. ANGRES Sector
21st " "	— " — Fired from L.H. gun five rounds at 12 midday by request C.O. 8th YORKS to shut up rifle grenades also to annoy Hun. Started emplacement for third gun in GUMBOOT trench. Fired from L.H. gun (M.19.d.9.4.) 1 round at 3.30 p.m. silencing hostile grenades and catapult bombs. Fired from R.H. gun (M.25.d.8.7) 2 rounds at 4 p.m. to register on Bosche trenches opposite supposed mine	No 1 gun M.19.d.9.7. No 2 " M.19.d.9.4. No 3 " M.25.d.8.7. — Officers dug-out M.19.d.9.4 Left detachment " M.19.d.9.7 Right " " M.25.b.6.6 Reserve Bomb Store R.24.c.8.7
22nd	— " — No firing. Finished emplacement in GUM BOOT Trench (M.19.d.9.7.) Telephones laid from M.19.d.9.7 and M.25.d.8.7 to M.19.d.9.4.	O H Coles 2/Lt 3/E. York R Comdg Y/23 Trench Bty

1247 W 3299 200,000 (E) 8/14 J.B.C. & A. Forms/C. 2118/11.

Instructions regarding War Diaries and Intelligence Summaries are contained in F. S. Regs., Part II. and the Staff Manual respectively. Title pages will be prepared in manuscript.

WAR DIARY

or

~~INTELLIGENCE SUMMARY~~

(Erase heading not required.)

Army Form C. 2118.

Y/23 Trench Battery — Attached 23rd Division

Hour, Date, Place	Summary of Events and Information	Remarks and references to Appendices
ANGRES SECTOR 23rd MARCH 1916	Fired from No 3 gun (M.25.d.8.7) 9 Rounds at 4.30 pm by request of 10th WEST RIDING Regiment in retaliation for rifle grenades etc. Excellent shooting. Blew up dug-out, made large breach in parapet. — " —	Armed with 2" M.L. Howitzer — " — Map Reference to Sheet 36c S.W. — " —
24th " "	No firing. Arrival of more ammunition — " —	
25th " "	" " Arranged with C.O. Artn Battn for Am: Store at R.24.c.8.7 in MOROCCO SOUTH. — " —	
26th " "	" " Arrival of 200 rounds ammunition	
27th " "	" " Made up rounds to 25 per 1 & 2 guns, 35 per 3 gun — " —	
28th " "	Fired 9 rounds (3 per gun) at 3.25 pm in conjunction with Artillery. Brought up 4th gun. — " —	
29th " "	Took up ~~up~~ 30 rounds to Bomb Store in MOROCCO S. (R.24.c.8.7) Dug in 4th gun (No 3) at M.25.b.6.6. Fired 2 rounds retaliation at 4pm from No 1 gun. Mended telephone wires. — " —	D.F.P. Coles 2/Lt 3/E. York R. Comdg Y/23 Trench Bty RA

1247 W 3299 200,000 (E) 8/14 J.B.C. & A. Forms/C. 2118/11.

Instructions regarding War Diaries and Intelligence Summaries are contained in F. S. Regs., Part II. and the Staff Manual respectively. Title pages will be prepared in manuscript.

WAR DIARY
or
~~INTELLIGENCE SUMMARY~~
(Erase heading not required.)

Army Form C. 2118.

Y/23 Trench Battery 23rd Division (Att'd 69th I. B.)

Hour, Date, Place	Summary of Events and Information	Remarks and references to Appendices
ANGRES SECTOR		
30th March 1916	Fired 2 rounds from No. 3 gun at 12.5 pm Retaliation	Armed with 2" M. L. Howitzer.
	" 4 rounds from No. 1 gun " 12.30 pm "	— " —
	" 2 rounds from No. 3 gun " 5 pm Registration	Map References to Sheet 36c S. W.
	— " —	
31st " "	Fired 9 rounds (3 per Nos 1, 2 + 3 guns) at 5.10 am in accordance with Infantry Scheme to intimidate Fritz + quell early morning frightfulness. Ammunition brought up from MOROCCO to establishment of 25 rounds per gun.	— " — Map References to Emplacements No 1 gun M 19. d. 9. 7. No 2 gun M 19. d. 9. 4. No 3 gun M 25. b 6. 6. No 4 gun M 25. a 8. 7.
	— " —	
28th March	Gunner C. Sherman 50370 posted to Battery	
30th March	" A. E. Simpson 57056 " " "	

D. P. Coles 2/Lt
3/E. York. R.
Comdg Y/23 T. M. Bty

Y 2 3 T M Bty
late 21 Bty

Vol 10

Army Form C. 2118.

Instructions regarding War Diaries and Intelligence Summaries are contained in F. S. Regs., Part II. and the Staff Manual respectively. Title pages will be prepared in manuscript.

WAR DIARY
or
~~INTELLIGENCE SUMMARY~~

(Erase heading not required.)

Y/23 Trench Battery 23rd Division

Hour, Date, Place	Summary of Events and Information	Remarks and references to Appendices
ANGRES SECTOR		Armed with 2" M. L. Howitzer
1st April 1916	No firing.	— " —
2nd " "	Fired 2 rounds from No 3 at 6 pm retaliation	Map references to
	— " —	Sheet 36c S. W.
3rd " "	no firing.	— " —
	— " —	
4th " "	90 rounds brought up to "advanced bomb store in MOROCCO SOUTH R. 24. c 8. 7.	Map references to gun Emplacements.
5th " "	Fired from No 2 gun at 2.45 pm registration wire cutting	No 1 gun M 19 d 9. 7.
	Fired from No 3 " " 4.30 pm	No 2 gun M 19 d 9. 4.
	" " No 4 " " 5.45 pm 7 rounds retaliation by request 9th Yorkshire Regt. Made bomb Store by No 3 gun	No 3 gun M 25 b 6. 6.
	— " —	No 4 gun M 25 d 2. 7.
6th " "	Fired from Nos 1 + 2 gun 2 rounds each at 7.57 am on M. 20. c. 5. 1 (Orders 69th I. B.)	— " —
		Reserve bomb Store R. 24. c. 8. 7
7th "	Fired from Nos 1 + 2 guns ~~2 rounds~~ rounds each at 12.50 pm on M. 20. a. 7. 1 (Orders 69th I. B)	
	Fired No 4 gun 3 rounds at 5.15 pm (request 9th Yorks)	D. H. P. Coles 2/Lt. 3/E. York R
	" No 1 2 + 3 guns 2 rounds apiece at 7 pm — retaliation to Bosch Mortar (12 lb) located at M 26 a. 4 8.	Comdg Y/23 Trench Bty RA
	— " —	—

1247 W 3299 200,000 (E) 8/14 J.B.C. & A. Forms/C. 2118/11.

Instructions regarding War Diaries and Intelligence Summaries are contained in F. S. Regs., Part II. and the Staff Manual respectively. Title pages will be prepared in manuscript.

WAR DIARY

or

~~INTELLIGENCE SUMMARY~~

(Erase heading not required.)

Army Form C. 2118.

Y/23 Trench Battery 23rd Division

Hour, Date, Place	Summary of Events and Information	Remarks and references to Appendices
ANGRES SECTOR 7th April 1916	Fired from No 4 gun 5 rounds at 4.45 pm in conjunction with Strafe engineered by 9th Yorkshire Regt. Fired from No 1 gun 1 round at 5 pm retaliation Broken bed at No 3 gun replaced by spare one Telephonic com: arranged between selves & 9th Yorkshire H.Q. — " —	Armed with 2" M.L. Howitzer. — " — Map references to Sheet 36c S.W. — " —
8th " "	NO firing — " —	
9th " "	Fired from No 1 gun 4 rounds at 10 am retaliation for Hun grenades by request 8th York R. ~~Fired~~ guns renumbered from Right by order of our NEW Trench Mortar officer. Fired ~~from~~ No 3 gun 10 rounds at 12.15 pm to cut wire at M.20.c.4.3 to put wind up Fritz Fired from No 2 gun 14 rounds at 1 pm to cut wire at M.26.a.2.7. Results excellent parapet breached behind wire. Fritz's shrapnel missed gun by 50 yds. — " —	D H P Coles 2/Lt 3/E. York R. Comdg Y/23 Trench Bty R.A.

1247 W 3299 200,000 (E) 8/14 J.B.C. & A. Forms/C. 2118/11.

Army Form C. 2118.

Instructions regarding War Diaries and Intelligence Summaries are contained in F. S. Regs., Part II. and the Staff Manual respectively. Title pages will be prepared in manuscript.

WAR DIARY
or
~~INTELLIGENCE SUMMARY~~

Y/23 Trench Battery R.A. (Erase heading not required.) 23rd Division.

Hour, Date, Place		Summary of Events and Information	Remarks and references to Appendices
	ANGRES SECTOR		armed with 2" M. L Howitzer
10th	April 1916	No firing.	
		— " —	— " —
11th	" "	Fired at 5.30 pm from No 4 gun 3 rounds retaliation. Two spare beds drawn from R.A. H.Q. & taken to trenches	Map references to Sheet 36c S.W.
		— " —	— " —
12th	" "	No firing.	
		— " —	
13th	" "	No firing. Two spare positions made at	
		— " —	
14th	" "	Fired at 11.30 am from No 4 gun 4 rounds by request O.C. 8th York. R	Map reference to spare positions.
		Fired at 4 pm from No 2 gun 3 rounds } to silence their mortar; No 4 gun 2 rounds } Succeeded.	2 A 3 A
		Fired at 4.45 pm from No 4 gun 2 rounds to put a stop to Fritz's 12 lb mortar which had reopened	
		Fired at 6.10 pm from No 1 gun 3 rounds on M 26 c.5.2 silenced rifle grenades.	
		— " —	
15th	" "	Fired 4.30 am No 3 gun 5 rounds on M 20.c.4½.3.	
		" 4.50 am No 2 " 5 " to stop retaliating mortar	
		" 11 am No 2 " 3 " (request West Riding)	
		" 2.45 am No 1 5" 3 " retaliation	
		" 4.15 pm No 2 A " 1 " registration	

D.F. Coles 2/Lt
3/E. York. R.
Comdg Y/23 Trench Bty R.A.

1247 W 3299 200,000 (E) 8/14 J.B.C. & A. Forms/C. 2118/11.

Army Form C. 2118.

WAR DIARY
or
~~INTELLIGENCE SUMMARY~~

Instructions regarding War Diaries and Intelligence Summaries are contained in F. S. Regs., Part II. and the Staff Manual respectively. Title pages will be prepared in manuscript.

Y/23 Trench Battery R.A *(Erase heading not required.)* 23rd Division.

Hour, Date, Place	Summary of Events and Information	Remarks and references to Appendices
ANGRES SECTOR		
16th April 1916	Fired 5.30 pm. No 4 gun 3 rounds request H.L.I.	armed with 2" M.L. Howitzer.
	Major Dodgson D.S.O. inspected positions of Battery for the first time.	— " —
	69th I.B 23rd Div. relieved by 5th I.B. 2nd Div.	Map references to Sheet 36c S.W.
	— " —	— " —
17th " "	No firing.	
	— " —	
18th " "	Fired 10.30 am. No 4 gun 6 rounds retaliation for mortars + grenades requested by H.L.I.	
	— " —	
19th " "	Fired 3 pm. No 3 gun 5 rounds } No 4 gun 4 rounds } retaliation to hostile mortars + grenades.	
	Handed over guns etc to X/2 Battery at 3.30 pm.	
	— " —	
20th	Moved into peace + quiet at FOSSE DE LA CLARENCE.	D.H.P. Coles 2/Lt 3/E. York. R.
	— " —	
21st	Drew 4 guns.	Comdg Y/23 Trench Bty R.A
	— " —	
22nd	Bathing parade to BRUAY.	
	— " —	

1247 W 3299 200,000 (E) 8/14 J.B.C. & A. Forms/C. 2118/11.

6

Instructions regarding War Diaries and Intelligence Summaries are contained in F. S. Regs., Part II. and the Staff Manual respectively. Title pages will be prepared in manuscript.

WAR DIARY
or
~~INTELLIGENCE SUMMARY~~

(Erase heading not required.)

Army Form C. 2118.

Y/23 Trench Battery R.A 23rd Division

Hour, Date, Place	Summary of Events and Information	Remarks and references to Appendices
FOSSE DE LA CLARENCE		Armed with 2" M. L. Howitzer. — " —
23rd April 1916	10.30 am inspected by G.O.C R.A. 3 pm CHURCH PARADE!	
	— " —	
24th " "	Usual parades. Pay.	
	— " —	
25th " "	Inspected by G.O.C 23rd Div.	
	— " —	
26th " "	Test gas R.A.H.Q	
	— " —	
27th " "	Usual parades	
	— " —	
28th " "	" "	
	— " —	
29th " "	Inoculation	
	— " —	
30th " "	Usual parades	
	— " —	

D.F.P. Coles[?] Lt
3/E. York R
Cmdg Y/23 Trench Bty R.A.

1247 W 3299 200,000 (E) 8/14 J.B.C. & A. Forms/C. 2118/11.

XXIII

Y23 TM Bty

Army Form C. 2118.

Vol XI

WAR DIARY

or

~~INTELLIGENCE SUMMARY~~

(Erase heading not required.)

Instructions regarding War Diaries and Intelligence Summaries are contained in F. S. Regs., Part II. and the Staff Manual respectively. Title pages will be prepared in manuscript.

Y/23 Trench Battery RA 23rd Division

Hour, Date, Place	Summary of Events and Information	Remarks and references to Appendices
FOSSE DE LA CLARENCE		Armed with 2" M.L. Howitzer
May 1st 1916	Usual parades.	—"—
2nd "	" "	
3rd "	" " 2nd Lieut COUBROUGH posted as 2nd in Command to Z/23 Trench Battery 2nd Lieut BROCK R.F.A posted as 2nd in command to Y/23 Trench Battery.	
4th "	Firing on range	
5th "	Usual parades	
6th "	" —"— "	
7th "	" —"— "	
8th "	" —"— "	
9th "	" —"— "	
10th "	" —"— "	
11th "	" —"— "	
12th "	" "	
13th "	Fired on the range for G.O.C. R.A.	[signature] 2/Lt 3/E. York. R. Comdg Y/23 Trench Bty R.A

1247 W 3299 200,000 (E) 8/14 J.B.C. & A. Forms/C. 2118/11.

Army Form C. 2118.

Instructions regarding War Diaries and Intelligence Summaries are contained in F. S. Regs., Part II. and the Staff Manual respectively. Title pages will be prepared in manuscript.

WAR DIARY
or
~~INTELLIGENCE SUMMARY~~

Y/23 Trench Battery R.A. (Erase heading not required.) 23rd Division

Hour, Date, Place	Summary of Events and Information	Remarks and references to Appendices
ANGRES SECTOR		
14th May 1916	moved to PETIT SAINS (FOSSE 10) took over billets + guns etc from X/2 Trench Battery 2nd Division.	Armed with 2" M.L. Howitzer.
15th " "	NO firing	— " —
16th " "	Fired at 7.30pm — 2 rounds from No 2 gun } 3 rounds from No 3 gun } by request 9th YORKS in retaliation for sausages + rifle grenades. Succeeded in restoring peace + quiet.	— " —
17th " "	No firing. Work on new Emplacement in GUM BOOT Trench. Put up telephone wires	— " —
18th " "	Fired at 1.30pm. 4 rounds at R.30.b 8.5. from No 3 gun by request Infantry. Enemy at once stopped rifle grenades. Fired at 4pm. 2 rounds as above. Fired at 9.30pm. 2 rounds from No 2 gun silencing hostile rifle grenades. — " —	G.H.P. Coles 2/Lt 3/E. York. R. Cmdg Y/23 Trench Bty R.A

Instructions regarding War Diaries and Intelligence Summaries are contained in F. S. Regs., Part II. and the Staff Manual respectively. Title pages will be prepared in manuscript.

Army Form C. 2118.

WAR DIARY

or

~~INTELLIGENCE SUMMARY~~

(Erase heading not required.)

Y/23 Trench Battery R.A. 23rd Division

Hour, Date, Place	Summary of Events and Information	Remarks and references to Appendices
ANGRES SECTOR		Armed with 2" M.L. Howitzer — " —
19th May 1916	Fired at 6.1 am 4 rounds each from Nos 3 + 4 guns on M.20.c.7.7 and M.20.c.6.4 by order 69th I.B. in conjunction with mine + Artillery. Excellent result. Fired at 4.30 pm 3 rounds from No 4 gun new position Registration on NEW CRATER. — " —	21.5.16 After a four days bombardment + a period of 12 hours interval the Germans attacked on our Left, VIMY RIDGE.
20th " "	Fired from No 3 gun 3 rounds retaliation on NEW CRATER + beyond. (request D Coy 9th Yorks) Fired at 10.30 am from No 4 gun 3 rounds retaliation on ~~NB~~ Enemy Mortar M.20.c.7.4 Fired at 4.45 pm from No 3 gun 5 rounds at M.20.c.9.2 Hun Coy Commanders dug-out direct hit with 3rd round. 4 bodies seen in air! Fired at 5 pm from No 2 gun 6 rounds retaliation by request. Shelled by Fritz for 45 minutes who was evidently much annoyed.	D.H.P. Coles [illegible]Lt 8/E. York. R. Comdg Y/23 Trench Bty RA
21st " "	Fired from No 4 gun 5 rounds retaliation for rifle grenades which ceased. Fired at 5.15 pm from No 3 gun at machine Gun Emplacement M.26.a.3.8.	

1247 W 3299 200,000 (E) 8/14 J.B.C. & A. Forms/C. 2118/11.

Army Form C. 2118.

WAR [DIARY]
or
~~INTELLIGENCE SUMMARY~~
(Erase heading not required.)

Instructions regarding War Diaries and Intelligence Summaries are contained in F. S. Regs., Part II. and the Staff Manual respectively. Title pages will be prepared in manuscript.

Y/23 Trench Battery R.A. 23rd Division

Hour, Date, Place	Summary of Events and Information	Remarks and references to Appendices
ANGRES SECTOR		Armed with 2" M.L. Howitzer
22nd May 1916	~~Fired at~~ No firing. VIMY RIDGE Battle on our right	— " —
23rd " "	Fired at 2.25 pm 2 rounds each from Nos 3 + 4 guns at NEW CRATER + machine gun emplacement. Machine gun has not fired since from that spot.	
	— " —	
24th " "	Fired at a.m. from No 4 gun 1 round on hostile working party – NEW CRATER.	
	Fired at 2.20 pm from No 2 gun 4 rounds at M.26.a.27 knocking out machine gun emplt + snipers post.	
	Fired at 1 pm from No 4 gun 2 rounds at NEW CRATER	
	Fired at 4 pm 1 round each from Nos 3 + 4 at "	
	Fired at 4.45 pm from No 2 gun 3 rounds retaliation by request C.O. 9th Yorks on German front line	
	Fired at 5 pm from No 3 gun 1 round at NEW CRATER	
	Fired at 5.40 pm from No 1 gun 3 rounds retaliation	
	— " —	
25th " "	Fired at 7 am from No 3 gun 2 rounds at NEW CRATER	D.H.P. Coles 2/Lt 3/E. York. R.
	Fired at 9.35 am from No 1 gun 2 " retaliation for Hostile Comdg	Y/23 Trench Bty R.A.
	We blew a mine on our left at 12 pm	
	— " —	

Instructions regarding War Diaries and Intelligence Summaries are contained in F. S. Regs., Part II. and the Staff Manual respectively. Title pages will be prepared in manuscript.

WAR DIARY

or

~~INTELLIGENCE SUMMARY~~

(Erase heading not required.)

Army Form C. 2118.

Y/23 Trench Battery R.A 23rd Division

Hour, Date, Place	Summary of Events and Information	Remarks and references to Appendices
ANGRES SECTOR		
26th May 1916	No firing	Armed with 2" M.L Howitzer
27th " "	Fired from Nos 1.2.3 + 4 guns 30 rounds in retaliation for Enemy's strafe	— " —
28th " "	Fired from all guns 29 rounds in retaliation severely damaged hostile front line + blew up one dug-out. Successfully annoyed Fritz.	
29th " "	No firing	
30th " "	" "	
31st " "	Fired from Nos 3 + 4 guns at 3.30 pm in retaliation for rifle grenades which ceased firing.	

D.H.P. Coles 2/Lt
3/E. York. R
Comdg Y/23 Trench Battery RA

1247 W 3299 200,000 (E) 8/14 J.B.C. & A. Forms/C. 2118/11.

Army Form C. 2118.

Vol 12.

WAR DIARY
or
~~INTELLIGENCE SUMMARY~~
(Erase heading not required.)

Instructions regarding War Diaries and Intelligence Summaries are contained in F. S. Regs., Part II. and the Staff Manual respectively. Title pages will be prepared in manuscript.

Y/23 Trench Battery R. A. 23rd Division

Hour, Date, Place	Summary of Events and Information	Remarks and references to Appendices
ANGRES SECTOR 1st JUNE 1916	Fired at 11 am from Nos 1 + 2 guns at targets M.26.a.2.7, a.2.6, a.5.5, c.2.6 } Fired from No 2 gun at 7.5 pm 3 rounds registration. — " —	Armed with 2" M L Howitzer — " —
2nd " "	Fired at 2.25 pm to 3.30 pm from Nos 2, 3 + 4 13 rounds, retaliation for hostile mortars which ceased firing. — " —	
3rd " "	Fired at 11.30 am from Nos 3 + 4 guns at THOMSON'S crater 3 blinds owing to new fuze 31. C. Fired at 1.40 pm from Nos 2 + 3 guns retaliation again several blinds all new fuze. — " —	
4th " "	Fired 4 rounds from Nos 3 + 4 guns retaliation for rum-jars at request of Infantry. Three Blinds owing to new fuze No 31 C. — " —	D H P Coles 2/Lt 3/E. York R Comdg Y/23 Trench Bty RA
5th " "	Fired 8 rounds (4 Blind) – retaliation — " —	

Army Form C. 2118.

WAR DIARY
or
~~INTELLIGENCE SUMMARY~~

(Erase heading not required.)

Instructions regarding War Diaries and Intelligence Summaries are contained in F. S. Regs., Part II. and the Staff Manual respectively. Title pages will be prepared in manuscript.

Y/23 Trench Battery R.A. 23rd Division

Hour, Date, Place	Summary of Events and Information	Remarks and references to Appendices
ANGRES SECTOR 6th June	Fired 11 rounds retaliation by request Infantry also tested alteration in fuze 31 C. Results unsatisfactory 3 Blinds and one premature.	Armed with 2" M.L Howitzers.
	— " —	— " —
7th "	Fired 12 rounds into THOMSON'S crater to stop Fritz working mine. 2 Blinds. Fired 10 rounds retaliation. 2 Blinds.	X 2" beds found to be very poor. 3 broken in one week
8th "	Fired 1 round to try Newton instantaneous fuze excellent result.	Rifle mechanism never strong enough 4 broken in 2 days.
	— " —	— " —
	Fired 11 rounds retaliation for Rum-jars 4 blinds.	
	— " —	
9th "	Fired at 12.45 pm. from Nos 2.3.4 guns 9 rounds with old fuzes 31 A + B, all burst well. Stopped hostile frightfulness. Fired two rounds at 8.25 pm from Nos 3 + 4 guns	
	— " —	
10th "	Fired at 2.15 pm 14 rounds from Nos 2, 3 + 4 retaliation, breached parapet in two places + enemy ceased fire. At 5.30 pm fired Six rounds retaliation one blind.	D.H.P. Coles ?/Lt 3/E. York R. Comdg Y/23 TMB RA.
	— " —	

Instructions regarding War Diaries and Intelligence Summaries are contained in F. S. Regs., Part II. and the Staff Manual respectively. Title pages will be prepared in manuscript.

WAR DIARY
or
~~INTELLIGENCE SUMMARY~~

Army Form C. 2118.

Y/23 Trench Battery R.A (Erase heading not required.) 23rd Division

Hour, Date, Place	Summary of Events and Information	Remarks and references to Appendices
ANGRES SECTOR		Armed with 2" M.L Howitzers.
11th June 1916	Fired 6 rounds retaliation	— " —
12th " "	no firing	
13th " "	no firing	
14th " "	Fired 21 rounds retaliation + then handed over guns + ammunition in trenches to X/47 Battery. Drew 4 guns from X/47 in billets at FOSSE 10.	
15th " "	Left FOSSE 10 at 9 am. in Motor buses + Lorries + went via BRUAY. St POL; DOULENS to 8th Corps H.Q. from where we went to MAILLY + erected tents for the night	
AUCHON VILLERS Sector		
16th 17th 18th 19th 20th 21st 22nd	Selected two positions in front of WHITE CITY + carried up many rounds, dug in guns in left section + right section. (BLOOMFIELD AVENUE.)	
23rd	Battery went to trenches. Bombardment started	
24th	no firing	
25th	no firing 9 S.M. BALL accidentally wounded	D.F.P. Coles 2/Lt 3/E. York. R. Cmdg Y/23 T.M.B.

1247 W 3299 200,000 (E) 8/14 J.B.C. & A. Forms/C. 2118/11.

Army Form C. 2118.

[WAR DI]ARY or ~~INTELLIGENCE SUMMARY~~

Instructions regarding War Diaries and Intelligence Summaries are contained in F. S. Regs., Part II. and the Staff Manual respectively. Title pages will be prepared in manuscript.

Y/23 Trench Battery R.A (Erase heading not required.) 23rd Division attached 29th Div

Hour, Date, Place	Summary of Events and Information	Remarks and references to Appendices
AUCHONVILLERS		Armed with 2" M.L Howitzers
26th June 1916	Fired 200 rounds on Hun wire using new time fuse	— " —
27th " "	Fired 200 rounds ditto — " —	
28th " "	Fired 200 rounds ditto. All wire reported cut — " —	
29th " "	Fired 130 rounds — " —	
30th " "	Fired 92 rounds. Came out of action & went back to MAILLY. Infantry attacked early next morning on a 16 mile front. Held up opposite BEAUMONT-HAMEL — " —	.
?		

D.A.P. Coles 2/Lt
3/E. York. R
Cmdg Y/23 T.M.B.

Instructions regarding War Diaries and Intelligence Summaries are contained in F. S. Regs., Part II. and the Staff Manual respectively. Title pages will be prepared in manuscript.

WAR DIARY
or
~~INTELLIGENCE SUMMARY~~
(Erase heading not required.)

Army Form C. 2118. 99

appx to Vol I

Y/23 Trench Battery R.A. 23rd Division attached 29th Div

Hour, Date, Place	Summary of Events and Information	Remarks and references to Appendices
AUCHON VILLERS		
1st JULY 1916	Rest at MAILLY-MAILLET	armed with 2" M.L. Howitzer
2nd " "	— " — ditto STURDY wounded	— " —
3rd " "	— " — One gun in action left section	
4th " "	— " — No firing owing to lack of S.A.A. cartridges detachment came out of trenches	2/Lieut Coubrough awarded the MILITARY CROSS
5th " "	— " — Orders received to withdraw guns from trenches. Withdrew guns from right section	Corpl BARTLETT awarded the D.C.M for FEB 1916
6th " "	— " — Withdrew guns from left section	
7th " "	Rest ditto MAILLY-MAILLET (billets)	
8th " "	"	
9th " "	"	
10th " "	"	
11th " "	"	
12th " "	"	
13th " "	"	
14th " "	"	
15th " "	"	
16th " "	"	
17th " "	O.C. to ALBERT via VIII Corps H.Q.	
18th	Battery moved to billets in ALBERT + rejoined 23rd Division III Corps. Left guns at MAILLY Took over guns from Y/38 T.M.B.	

D. H. Coles Lieut 3/E. York. R
Comdg Y/23 Trench Bty R.A.

1247 W 3299 200,000 (E) 8/14 J.B.C. & A. Forms/C. 2118/11.

Instructions regarding War Diaries and Intelligence Summaries are contained in F. S. Regs., Part II. and the Staff Manual respectively. Title pages will be prepared in manuscript.

WAR DIARY
or
~~INTELLIGENCE SUMMARY~~

(Erase heading not required.)

Y/23 Trench Battery R.A. 23rd Division

Army Form C. 2118.

Hour, Date, Place	Summary of Events and Information	Remarks and references to Appendices
ALBERT		Armed with 2" M.L. Howitzer
19th JULY 1916	Rest in ALBERT	
20th " "	—"—	—"—
21st " "	—"—	
22nd " "	—"—	
	2/Lieut BROCK temporarily attached 102 Brigade R.F.A. 18 men + NCO's detailed for work with D.A.C. 6 hours on + 12 hours off. 1st shift 2pm. - 8pm.	
23rd " "	—"— Work at D.A.C.	
24th "	—"— Work at D.A.C.	
25th "	—"— Corporal BURNS sent to 4th Army School of Mortars VALHEUREUX as instructor. N.C.O. and 4 men detailed to keep line between HQRA + Brigades (103 + 104).	
26th " "	—"— Work at D.A.C. and telephone wire patrol	
27th " "	ditto —"—	
28th " "	—"— Work at DAC + wire patrols knocked off. Work repairing dug-outs + erecting tents.	D P Coles Lieut 3/E. York R. Comdg Y/23 Trench Bty RFA

1247 W 3299 200,000 (E) 8/14 J.B.C. & A. Forms/C. 2118/11.

Army Form C. 2118.

WAR DIARY
or
~~INTELLIGENCE SUMMARY~~

Instructions regarding War Diaries and Intelligence Summaries are contained in F. S. Regs., Part II. and the Staff Manual respectively. Title pages will be prepared in manuscript.

Y/23 Trench Battery R.A. (Erase heading not required.) 23rd Division

Hour, Date, Place	Summary of Events and Information	Remarks and references to Appendices
ALBERT		Armed with 2" M.L. Howitzers
29th JULY 1916	Work at D.A.C.	— " —
	— " —	
30th " "	Battery moved in G.S. waggons to billets in SCOTCH REDOUBT trench where ~~the~~ 2nd Lieut de SAUMAREZ BROCK rejoined.	
	— " —	
31st " "	Work on new positions in line in front of CONTALMAISON	
	— " —	

D.H.P. Coles Lieut.
3/2. York R.

Comdg Y/23 Trench Battery R.A.

1247 W 3299 200,000 (E) 8/14 J.B.C. & A. Forms/C. 2118/11.

The Organisation of the 23rd Divisional Medium Trench Mortar Batteries will in future be as follows.

TACTICALLY.

When in the line, the Medium Trench Mortar Batteries will form part of the R.F.A. Group covering the Sector in which they are.

They will, however, be at the immediate call of the Infantry Brigadier Commanding the Sector, or of the Battalion and Company Commanders, as he may direct, both for offensive action and retaliation.

The selection of positions will always be referred to the Infantry Brigadior for approval.

Officers Commanding Groups, besides using the Trench Mortar Batteries for retaliation, will arrange combined Trench Mortar and Field Artillery Shoots for offensive purposes, the concurrence of Infantry Brigadier concerned being obtained.

Telephone communication will be established between Medium Trench Mortar Batteries and their Group H.Q. also with Battalion H.Q. where necessary.

ADMINISTRATIVELY.

One Trench Mortar Battery will be attached to, and administered by each Field Artillery Brigade (vide attached Table).

All R.F.A. Personnel in a Trench Mortar Battery will be posted to Batteries of its F.A.Brigade, being shown on their Field Returns, as surplus to establishment and Detached with Trench Mortar Battery.

All R.G.A. and Infantry Personnel in a Trench Mortar Battery will be shown by its F.A. Brigade as Attached and at duty with T.M.Battery.

The surplus trained personnel now available in the Divisional Artillery, will be divided up among the F.A. Brigades and from it casualties in T.M.Batteries will be replaced till the supply is exhausted, after which casualties in T.M.Batteries will be replaced from the D.A.C. - the men as required being posted from the D.A.C. to Brigades.

To maintain a supply of trained men, the D.A.C. will, each Saturday until further orders, send one Gunner to each T.M.Battery for a week's attachment and training. Every other week, one Corporal or Bombardier, will be sent instead of one Gunner.

When in the line, Medium Trench Mortar Batteries will be rationed by the Infantry Brigades, at all other times, by their F.A. Brigade.

Major,
General Staff 23rd Division.

8/6/16.
S.G.176/2.

SECRET.

Medium T.M.Bty.	Officers.	Headquarters.	Billet.	Front Covered	Guns	Trench Headquarters	Administered by	Under Tactical Control of.
X/23	Lieut. KYLE ※ Lieut. PRIEG.	M.32.c.5.6.	R.22.a.7.5	SOUCHEZ Section.	4 - 2" 2 French	"THE STRAIGHT" M.32.c.5.5.	102nd F.A. Brigade.	Infantry Brigade SOUCHEZ Sector. F.A.Group SOUCHEZ Section.
Y/23	Lieut. COLES ※ 2/Lt. BROCK.	M.19.d.9.6.	R.2.b.5.7.	ANGRES Section Left Battn.	4 - 2"	"GUMBOOT TRENCH" M.19.d.8.5.	103rd F.A. Brigade.	Infantry Brigade ANGRES SECTOR. F.A.Group, ANGRES Sector.
Z/23	Lieut. GEORGE ※ 2/Lt. COWBROUGH.	M.31.b.9.1.	R.2.b.5.7.	ANGRES Section Right Battn.	4 French	TURNING OFF COOKER ALLEY M.31.b.9.3.	104th F.A. Brigade.	Infantry Brigade ANGRES Sector. F.A.Group, ANGRES Section
A/23	2/Lt. CHAMPION ※ 2/Lt. THORP.			In reserve in BAJOLLE LINE.	4 - 2"	HEADQUARTERS TRENCH S.2.a.1.8.	105th F.A. Brigade.	Infantry Brigade SOUCHEZ Sector. F.A.Group SOUCHEZ Sector

※ Commands.

23rd Divisional Artillery.

"Y"/23rd TRENCH MORTAR BATTERY

AUGUST 1 9 1 6

23
Vol 14

Army Form C. 2118.

Instructions regarding War Diaries and Intelligence Summaries are contained in F. S. Regs., Part II. and the Staff Manual respectively. Title pages will be prepared in manuscript.

WAR DIARY
or
~~INTELLIGENCE SUMMARY~~

(Erase heading not required.)

Y/23 Trench Battery R.A 23rd Division

Hour, Date, Place	Summary of Events and Information	Remarks and references to Appendices
Line – part of CONTALMAISON		
1st August 1916	Work in the trenches	Armed with 2" M.L Howitzers
	— " —	— " —
2nd " "	Fired from Nos 1 + 2 guns at 9.15 pm – in conjunction with Infantry attack on MUNSTER ALLEY by 13th D.L.I 69th I.B. — " —	
3rd " "	Work in trenches	
	— " —	
4th " "	Ditto. 69th I.B relieved by 68th I.B.	
	— " —	
5th " "	No firing	
	— " —	
6th " "	" " — " —	
7th " "	" " — " —	
8th " "	" " 68th I.B — relieved by 45th I.B 15th DIV.	
9th " "	" " — " —	
10th " "	" " — " —	
11th " "	" " — " —	
12th " "	— " —	
13th " "	SWITCH LINE taken by R.S.F's	
	— " —	
14th " "	Relieved by 47th Div: Mortars who took over guns in the line. Moved by Lorry to BEAUCOURT	

D.F.P. Coles Lieut
3/E. York. R.
Comdg Y/23 Trench Battery R.A

Instructions regarding War Diaries and Intelligence Summaries are contained in F. S. Regs., Part II. and the Staff Manual respectively. Title pages will be prepared in manuscript.

Army Form C. 2118.

WAR DIARY
or
~~INTELLIGENCE SUMMARY~~
(Erase heading not required.)

Y/23 Trench Battery RA 23rd Division

Hour, Date, Place	Summary of Events and Information	Remarks and references to Appendices
15th August 1916	Rest at BEUUCOURT	Armed with 2" ML Howitzers.
16th " "	— " — Moved by Lorry + hand carts to QUERRIEU	— " —
17th " "	— " — Left QUERRIEU 5 am. Entrained at SALEUX arrived EECKE 6 am. 18th.	
18th " "	— " — Rest	
19th " "	— " — Ditto	
20th " "	Moved by Lorries to billets in PONTE DU NIEPPE took over billets + guns in line from Y/41 TMB	
21st " "	— " — No firing.	
22nd " "	Fired two rounds registration on Hun front line from No 1 gun.	
23rd " "	— " — NO firing.	
24th " "	— " — NO firing. Left Section 69th I.B. 8th YORKS } Right " 68th I.B. 11th NFs }	
25th " "	— " — No firing. Started New offensive position in front of left Section.	[illegible] Cobb Lieut 2/E. York R. Comdg Y/23 Trench Bty RA.

1247 W 3299 200,000 (E) 8/14 J.B.C. & A. Forms/C. 2118/11.

Army Form C. 2118.

Instructions regarding War Diaries and Intelligence Summaries are contained in F. S. Regs., Part II, and the Staff Manual respectively. Title pages will be prepared in manuscript.

WAR DIARY
or
~~INTELLIGENCE SUMMARY~~

1/23 Trench Battery R A *(Erase heading not required.)* 23rd Division IXth Corps

Hour, Date, Place	Summary of Events and Information	Remarks and references to Appendices
L iii – part of PLOEGSTEERT		Armed with 2" ML Howitzer
26th August 1916	No firing — " —	— " —
27th " "	" " — " —	
28th " "	" " — " —	
29th " "	" " telephone communication with Bat HQ — " —	
30th " "	" " — " —	
31st " "	" " — " —	
		D.H.P. Coles Lieut 3/E. York R Comdg 1/23 Trench Bty RA

1247 W 3299 200,000 (E) 8/14 J.B.C. & A. Forms/C. 2118/11.

23rd Division No.A/802/18.

D.A.G., Base.

Please see this office No.A/802/18 dated 11th July 1917, submitting War Diaries of T.M.Batteries, 23rd Division, for period June 7th to 30th.

Your C.R. No.140/2122 dated 7.7.17 gave authority for the diary of the D.T.M.O. to be written up for as long a period as possible, as owing to the changes and deaths of two of our D.T.M.O's., the diaries were missing.

The diary for the period 7th to 30th June was the only one which could be compiled as there were no further back records.

H. C. Owen Capt
DAAG
for Major General,

1st August 1917. Commanding 23rd Division.

W.D.

Head-quarters,
Twenty-third Division.

War Diaries, & Records.
C.R. No.140/2122.

Reference to the attached copy of War Office letter, please cause the undermentioned War Diaries to be forwarded without delay:-

Y.23 Trench Mortar Batteries.........November ,1916.

(Sgnd.) H. Yates,
Captain,
D. A. A. G.,
for D. A. G

G. H. Qrs.,
3rd. Echelon.
28th. July, 1917.

24th June

HEADQUARTERS,
23rd DIVISION.
A802/18
7/8/17.

Head-quarters,
Twenty-third Division.

Reference above copy of correspondence. Can you now please give a reply?

H. Yates
Captain,
D. A. A. G.,
for D. A. G.

G. H. Qrs.,
3rd. Echelon.
28th. July, 1917.

War Diaries & Records.
DATE
C.R. 140/2122.

Army Form C. 2118.

WAR DIARY
or
~~INTELLIGENCE SUMMARY~~
(Erase heading not required.)

Instructions regarding War Diaries and Intelligence Summaries are contained in F. S. Regs., Part II. and the Staff Manual respectively. Title pages will be prepared in manuscript.

Y/23 Trench Battery R.A. 23rd Division

Vol 15

Hour, Date, Place	Summary of Events and Information	Remarks and references to Appendices
Line in part of PLOEGSTEERT.		Armed with 2" M.L. Howitzer.
1st September 1916	Work on new Emplacement at U.27 b 90.95	
2nd " "	no firing. Work continued	Map references to Emplacements etc — Trench Map ST YVES Part of sheet 28.
3rd " "	Firing postponed Work continued	
4th " "	Fired ten rounds registration from No 1 gun at 3 pm. 2 Blind. German retaliated with rifle grenades + small aerial darts.	**Left Section** Offensive dug-out U21 d 15
5th " "	Fired five rounds from No 1 gun at 4 pm. 3 blind owing to damp exploders. Work continued at New Emplacement.	No 1 gun / No 2 gun } Defensive U21 d 20.25; Offensive U27 b 90.95
		Right Section No 1 gun / No 2 gun } Defensive U27 b 7.1; Offensive U27 b 9.1.
6th " "	Fired eight rounds from U.27 b 9.1 no retaliation (4.30 pm)	**Billets:** B 23 d 44
7th " "	Fired at 4.30 pm ten rounds from U 27 b 90.95 registration + ten rounds from No 1 gun. Retaliation with aerial darts + rifle grenades one dart hit No 2 gun no damage	D.R.P. Coles Lieut. 3/E. York R. Cmdg Y/23 Trench Bty RA

1247 W 3299 200,000 (E) 8/14 J.B.C. & A. Forms/C. 2118/11.

Army Form C. 2118.

WAR DIARY
or
~~INTELLIGENCE SUMMARY~~
(Erase heading not required.)

Instructions regarding War Diaries and Intelligence Summaries are contained in F. S. Regs., Part II. and the Staff Manual respectively. Title pages will be prepared in manuscript.

Y/23 Trench Battery R.A. 23rd Division

Hour, Date, Place	Summary of Events and Information	Remarks and references to Appendices
Line in front of PLOEGSTEERT		
8th September 1916	Fired 30 rounds from Nos 1 + 2 guns. Hun trenches considerably damaged. Two hours retaliation with small missiles. Chose new offensive position behind E GAP. + started work on same	Armed with 2" M.C. Howitzer
9th September 1916	Fired 50 rounds. Strafing 40. Retaliation at request Infantry 10. No. 1 gun 35 rounds; No. 2 gun 15 " }	— " —
	Work on new position continued	During last three days firing (108 rds) there were 10 blinds
10th " "	No firing on either side. Relieved in the evening by X/19 Battery. Battery proceeded same night by lorry via BAILLEUILLE + St. JAN CAPPEL to DAC camp. Bivouacked there for night	— " —
11th " "	Took over 4 new guns etc from Ordnance	
12th " "	Proceeded by Lorry to GODDWAERSWELDT + entrained for SALEUX	
13th " "	Arrived SALEUX 12 noon, after considerable delay as usual, proceeded by Lorry to billets at St. GRATTIENS	D.H. Coles Lieut. 3/E. York. R. Comdg Y/23 Trench Bty R.A.

1247 W 3299 200,000 (E) 8/14 J.B.C. & A. Forms/C. 2118/11.

Instructions regarding War Diaries and Intelligence Summaries are contained in F. S. Regs., Part II. and the Staff Manual respectively. Title pages will be prepared in manuscript.

WAR DIARY
or
~~INTELLIGENCE SUMMARY~~
(Erase heading not required.)

Army Form C. 2118.

Y/23 Trench Battery R. A 23rd Division

Hour, Date, Place	Summary of Events and Information	Remarks and references to Appendices
14th September 1916	Inspections of kit + equipment. —"—	Armed with 2" M.L Howitzer —"—
15th " "	Rest —"—	
16th " "	Received orders to be ready to move at two hours notice	
17th " "	Rest. Telephone class started 3½ hrs per diem	Sergt (B.S.M.) BALL now evacuated to England, has been awarded the Military Medal. —"—
18th " "	Rest. Telephone etc. —"—	
19th " "	Battery moved by Lorry to LAVIÉVILLE. Spent the night in tents —"—	
20th " "	Provided guard 1 NCO + 2 gunners for 9 guns complete on ALBERT – BECORDEL road at E 12 a 9.8. Remainder of Battery taken from tents + billeted in barns in village	
21st " "	Telephone class continued also guard on guns. —"—	
22nd " "	Rest —"—	
23rd " "	16 of the Battery detailed to assist bringing back German Whiz-bang guns from beyond MARTINPUICH. Personal message of thanks received from C.R.A for this work. —"—	D.H.P. Coles Lieut 2/E. York. R Comdg Y/23 Trench Bty R.A

Instructions regarding War Diaries and Intelligence Summaries are contained in F. S. Regs., Part II. and the Staff Manual respectively. Title pages will be prepared in manuscript.

WAR DIARY

or

~~INTELLIGENCE SUMMARY~~

(Erase heading not required.)

Army Form C. 2118.

Y/23 Trench Battery R.A 23rd Division

Hour, Date, Place	Summary of Events and Information	Remarks and references to Appendices
24th September 1914	Battery moved to D.A.C Camp at BECOURT WOOD. Party detailed to collect german ammunition – front of CONTALMAISON for WHIZ BANGS. Guard withdrawn from guns on ALBERT–BECORDEL Road + guns brought to BECOURT WOOD.	Armed with 2" M.L Howitzers
	— " —	— " —
25th " "	Voluntary assistance given to DAC at Ammunition Dump.	
	— " —	
26th " "	Ditto...	
	— " —	
27th " "	Work in Dump	
	— " —	
28th " "	Ditto 2/Lieut Brock to COURCELETTE in search of ammunition for german Whizz-bang.	
	— " —	
29th " "	Work on Dump	
	— " —	
30th " "	Ditto	
	— " —	

D.H.P. Coles Lieut. 3/E. York. Reg.

Comdg Y/23 T.M.B'S R.A.

1247 W 3299 200,000 (E) 8/14 J.B.C. & A. Forms/C. 2118/11.

Army Form C. 2118.

23 — Vol 16

WAR DIARY
or
~~INTELLIGENCE SUMMARY~~

(Erase heading not required.)

Instructions regarding War Diaries and Intelligence Summaries are contained in F. S. Regs., Part II. and the Staff Manual respectively. Title pages will be prepared in manuscript.

Y/23 Trench Battery R A — 23rd Division

Hour, Date, Place	Summary of Events and Information	Remarks and references to Appendices
1st October 1916	Work on Dump	Armed with 2" M.L Howitzer
2nd " "	— " —	
	Work on Dump. N.C.O + 4 men to COURCELETTE to bring back German Minnenwerfer	— " —
3rd " "	— " —	
	Orders received to stand by.	
4th " "	— " —	
	Stood by	
5th " "	— " —	
	2 officers 3 N.C.O's + 15 men proceeded to trenches + took over 3 guns in LE SARS Sector, 2 guns taken up with great difficulty to second line. Party returned + took up New HQ in Old O.G.1.	
6th " "	— " —	
	Two positions chosen + guns put into action	
7th " "	— " —	
	Strenuous attempts made to collect parties to carry ammunition to guns but without avail. LE SARS taken in afternoon.	
8th " "	— " —	
	Arrangements made for handing over guns etc to 15th DIV T.M's. One gun brought out.	
9th " "	— " —	
	Handed over to 15th DIV, moved back to BECOURT WOOD, thence by lorries to St GRATIEN.	
10th " "	— " —	
	Rest	
	— " —	

D H P Gibs Lieut 3/E York R
Comdg Y/23 Trench Battery R A

1247 W 3299 200,000 (E) 8/14 J.B.C. & A. Forms/C. 2118/11.

Army Form C. 2118.

WAR DIARY
or
~~INTELLIGENCE SUMMARY~~
(Erase heading not required.)

Instructions regarding War Diaries and Intelligence Summaries are contained in F. S. Regs., Part II. and the Staff Manual respectively. Title pages will be prepared in manuscript.

Y/23 Trench Battery R.A. 23rd Division

Hour, Date, Place	Summary of Events and Information	Remarks and references to Appendices
11th October 1916	Rest	Armed with 2" M.L. Howitzers.
12th " "	"	
13th " "	"	
14th " "	"	
15th " "	"	
16th " "	"	
17th " "	"	
18th " "	"	
19th " "	"	
20th " "	"	
21st " "	"	
22nd " "	"	
23rd " "	Entrained at FRECHENCOURT	
24th " "	} Train journey.	
25th " "		
26th " "	Detrained at RENNENHELST + proceeded to billets at H. 14. 0 ½. 4.	
27th " "	O.C. to trenches in front of SANCTUARY WOOD.	
28th " "	Took over 3 guns etc in line from Y/47. No firing	
29th " "	No firing. No 3 gun out of action	D.H. Blake Lieut 3/E. York Regt Comdg Y/23 Trench Bty RA

1247 W 3299 200,000 (E) 8/14 J.B.C. & A. Forms/C. 2118/11.

Army Form C. 2118.

WAR DIARY

or

~~INTELLIGENCE SUMMARY~~

Instructions regarding War Diaries and Intelligence Summaries are contained in F. S. Regs., Part II, and the Staff Manual respectively. Title pages will be prepared in manuscript.

Y/23 Trench Battery R.A (*Erase heading not required.*) 23rd Division

Hour, Date, Place	Summary of Events and Information	Remarks and references to Appendices
YPRES Line in front of SANCTUARY WOOD		Armed with 2" M.L. Howitzers.
October 30th 1916	~~No firing~~. Fired 11 rounds at 2.30 pm on German 1st + 2nd line in retaliation for 'minnies'. Fritz ceased firing.	
31st 1916	No firing. Work on pits	
		D.H.P. Coles Lieut 3/E. York. Reg Comdg Y/23 Trench Bty R.A

1247 W 3299 200,000 (E) 8/14 J.B.C. & A. Forms/C. 2118/11.

Army Form C. 2118.

Instructions regarding War Diaries and Intelligence Summaries are contained in F. S. Regs., Part II. and the Staff Manual respectively. Title pages will be prepared in manuscript.

WAR DIARY
or
~~INTELLIGENCE SUMMARY~~

(Erase heading not required.)

Y/23 Trench Battery R.A. 23rd Division

Vol

Hour, Date, Place		Summary of Events and Information	Remarks and references to Appendices
YPRES Line in front of SANCTUARY WOOD	1916 Nov: 1st	No firing — " —	Armed with 2" M.L. Howitzer — " —
"	2nd	" " — " —	
"	3rd	Fired 2 rounds registration – no retaliation — " —	
"	4th	Fired 32 rounds at 3.30 p.m. – retaliation to German mortars of all shapes & sizes, mostly large. Stokes fired 98 rounds in our area — " —	
"	5th	Fired till both guns out of action with broken rifle mechanisms (13 rounds) Retaliation. — " —	
"	6th	No firing. Work on positions which owing to rain are almost unfireable. — " —	
"	7th	Ditto — " —	
"	8th	Ditto — " —	
"	9th	Ditto — " —	D F P Coles Lieut/ 3/E. York Regt. Comdg Y/23 T.M.B. R.A.

1247 W 3299 200,000 (E) 8/14 J.B.C. & A. Forms/C. 2118/11.

Army Form C. 2118.

WAR DIARY
or
~~INTELLIGENCE SUMMARY~~

(*Erase heading not required.*)

Instructions regarding War Diaries and Intelligence Summaries are contained in F. S. Regs., Part II. and the Staff Manual respectively. Title pages will be prepared in manuscript.

Y/23 Trench Battery R.A. 23rd Division

Hour, Date, Place	Summary of Events and Information	Remarks and references to Appendices
YPRES November 10th 1916	No firing. Work in old + new emplacements	Armed with 2" M.L. Howitzers
	—"—	—"—
" 11th "	Ditto	
	—"—	
" 12th "	Fired at 3.30 pm 8 rounds from only available gun in retaliation for RUM-JARS	
	—"—	
" 13th "	Guns out of action for the day. Work on pits	
	—"—	
" 14th "	No firing on either side again much work	
	—"—	
" 15th "	" " more work	
	—"—	
" 16th "	" "	
	—"—	
" 17th "	" "	
	—"—	
" 18th "	" "	
	—"—	
" 19th "	Fired 2 rounds registration from new position I 24 d 25.15. + 2 rounds retaliation	
	—"—	
" 20th "	~~No firing~~ Fired 10 rounds at 11.35 pm in conjunction with	
" 21st "	small raid opposite CRAB CRAWL	
	—"—	
	No firing	

D H P Cobs Lieut 3/E York Reg
Cmds Y/23 T.M.Bty R.A.

Army Form C. 2118.

WAR DIARY
or
~~INTELLIGENCE SUMMARY~~

Instructions regarding War Diaries and Intelligence Summaries are contained in F. S. Regs., Part II. and the Staff Manual respectively. Title pages will be prepared in manuscript. Y/23 Trench Battery R.A. *(Erase heading not required.)* 23rd Division

Hour, Date, Place	Summary of Events and Information	Remarks and references to Appendices
YPRES		Armed with 2" M.L. Howitzers
November 22nd 1916	No firing — Work on positions	— " —
23rd	— " — Ditto	
24th	Fired 30 rounds from No. 3 gun in retaliation artillery co-operated & Fritz ceased firing.	Map References of Gun positions
	— " —	No. 1 gun } I.30 b. 75.25
25th	No firing — " —	No. 2 gun }
26th	No firing — " —	No. 3 gun I 24 d 25.15
27th	No firing	
28th	"	
29th	"	
30th	Fired 22 rounds in retaliation 2/LIEUT KENEDY wounded. He was attached for duty with Y Battery for four days	
	— " —	D.H.P. Coles Lieut 3/E. York. R. Comdg Y/23 TMBty R.A.

1247 W 3299 200,000 (E) 8/14 J.B.C. & A. Forms/C. 2118/11.

Army Form C. 2118.

Instructions regarding War Diaries and Intelligence Summaries are contained in F. S. Regs., Part II. and the ~~Staff~~ Manual respectively. Title pages will be prepared in manuscript.

WAR DIARY

or

~~INTELLIGENCE SUMMARY~~

(Erase heading not required.)

Y/23 Trench Bty RA — 23rd Division — Vol 18

Hour, Date, Place	Summary of Events and Information	Remarks and references to Appendices
YPRES		
1st December 1916	No firing	Armed with 2" M.L. Howitzers.
2nd " "	~~Fired~~ " ——"——	——"——
3rd	Bty properly done in. Great strafe by 23rd Divisional mortars. We fired 26 Rounds.	
4th "	No firing. Bty spent day in building new second line.	For the past three weeks only one gun in action. Hence small number of rounds fired.
5th "	Fired 36 rounds in retaliation No. 3 gun	
6th "	Fired 32 rounds ditto	
7th "	Fired 20 rounds. Ceased firing owing to 'dud' S.A.A. cartridges (16 - no. fires!!)	
8th "	No firing. 2nd LIEUT THORP doing duty for Y Battery in addition to his own.	
9th "	no firing	
10th ..	no firing	
11th ..	no firing	
12th ..	no firing	D. F. Coles Lieut 3/C. York R. Cmdg Y/23 TMBty RA

1247 W 3299 200,000 (E) 8/14 J.B.C. & A. Forms/C. 2118/11.

Instructions regarding War Diaries and Intelligence Summaries are contained in F. S. Regs., Part II. and the Staff Manual respectively. Title pages will be prepared in manuscript.

WAR DIARY
or
~~INTELLIGENCE SUMMARY~~
(Erase heading not required.)

Army Form C. 2118.

Y/23 Trench Battery R.A. 23rd Division

Hour, Date, Place	Summary of Events and Information	Remarks and references to Appendices
YPRES		Armed with 2" M. L. Howitzers
13th December 1916	Fired 20 rounds from No 3 gun. Fritz shelled with 5·9 + 4·2	
	— " —	— " —
14th " "	No firing	
15th " "	" "	
16th " "	" "	
17th " "	" "	
18th " "	" "	
19th " "	" "	
20th " "	Fired 27 rounds in the morning retaliation the last 8 after Fritz had stopped shooting. Fired 11 rounds between 3·30 + 4 pm in conjunction with Artillery. Moved in new dug-out (Hedge St) made by CANADIAN Tunnellers + started putting 2 guns in tunnels	
	— " —	
21st " "	No firing.	
22nd " "	No firing.	
23rd " "	" " Gunner Davis wounded + Gunner Collis who remained at Duty.	

D H P [illegible] Lieut 3/E. York R
Comdg Y/23 T.M. Bty RA

1247 W 3299 200,000 (E) 8/14 J.B.C. & A. Forms/C. 2118/11.

Army Form C. 2118.

WAR DIARY
or
~~INTELLIGENCE SUMMARY~~
(Erase heading not required.)

Instructions regarding War Diaries and Intelligence Summaries are contained in F. S. Regs., Part II. and the Staff Manual respectively. Title pages will be prepared in manuscript.

Y/23 Trench Battery R.A. 23rd Division

Hour, Date, Place	Summary of Events and Information	Remarks and references to Appendices
YPRES. 24th December 1916	Premature at No 1 gun Hedge Street, supposed cause, tail going through bank. Capt Davis seriously wounded & 2 others slightly wounded.	Armed with 2" T. M. L. Hornby's
25. December	No firing at all. Fritz heard singing in his trenches.	
26 December	Capt Davis died of wounds at No 18 General Hospital. Fired 15 rounds retaliation from No 2 gun Davidson Street	
27. December	Lieut. Coles proceeded on leave to England.	
28. December	No firing	
29. December	No mortar activity, but considerable unpleasantness caused by shelling in trenches.	R. S. de Saumarez Brock. 2/Lt. R.F.A. Comdg. Y/23 T.M.Bty. R.A.

1247 W 3299 200,000 (E) 8/14 J.B.C. & A. Forms/C. 2118/11.

Instructions regarding War Diaries and Intelligence Summaries are contained in F. S. Regs., Part II. and the Staff Manual respectively. Title pages will be prepared in manuscript.

WAR DIARY

or

~~INTELLIGENCE~~ SUMMARY

(*Erase heading not required.*)

Army Form C. 2118.

V/23 Trench Battery R.A. 23rd Division

Hour, Date, Place	Summary of Events and Information	Remarks and references to Appendices
YPRES 30 December.	Fired 21 rounds in retaliation to Fritz: guns in Hedge Street used for first time since they were moved into pits.	Armed with 2" M.L. Howitzers
31 December	Fired 10 Rounds in retaliation: firing curtailed owing to damaged rifle mechanisms.	

R. S. de S. Brock
2/Lt. R.F.A.
Comdg. V/23 Trench Hy. RA

1247 W 3299 200,000 (E) 8/14 J.B.C. & A. Forms/C. 2118/11.

Instructions regarding War Diaries and Intelligence Summaries are contained in F. S. Regs., Part II. and the Staff Manual respectively. Title pages will be prepared in manuscript.

WAR DIARY
or
INTELLIGENCE SUMMARY.
(*Erase heading not required.*)

Army Form C. 2118.

4 T M Bty
Vol 19

Place	Date	Hour	Summary of Events and Information	Remarks and references to Appendices
	1917			
	Jan 1st		In Right Sector, 145 rounds fired on to enemy front & support lines with good effect.	
	Jan 2nd		Eight rounds fired for registration purposes.	
	Jan 3rd		Everything very quiet, no firing done by us.	
	Jan 4th		Six rounds fired in retaliation for 3 rifle grenades, enemy firing ceased.	
	Jan 5th		Ninety four rounds fired in retaliation for enemy T. M.; observers reported firing very accurate and effective.	
	Jan 6th		Enemy fired a few rifle grenades which we retaliated to with 14 rounds, after which the enemy ceased firing.	
	Jan 7th		Seventy one rounds fired in retaliation to enemy T. M.	
	Jan 8th		One hundred & ninety eight rounds fired in retaliation, reported very accurate & effective. Relieved by 70th L. T. M. B, after which we went to Eric Camp.	
	~~Jan 9th~~ Jan 9th to 15th		Carried out training at Eric Camp.	
	Jan 16th		Took over Left Sector T. Ms from 68th L. T. M. B.	
	Jan 17th to 23rd		No firing took place, 2 new emplacements built during the period	

2353 Wt. W2544/1454 700,000 5/15 D. D. & L. A.D.S.S. Forms/C. 2118.

Instructions regarding War Diaries and Intelligence Summaries are contained in F. S. Regs., Part II. and the Staff Manual respectively. Title pages will be prepared in manuscript.

WAR DIARY
or
INTELLIGENCE SUMMARY.
(Erase heading not required.)

Army Form C. 2118.

Place	Date	Hour	Summary of Events and Information	Remarks and references to Appendices
	Jan 24th		Twenty rounds fired on to enemy front line, enemy did not retaliate	
	Jan 25th to 30th		No firing, enemy very quiet, further work done on defensive emplacements, also new offensive position built in 60 Street	
			H Clarkson Lieut O.C. 69th L.T.M.B.	

Vol

Army Form C. 2118.

Instructions regarding War Diaries and Intelligence Summaries are contained in F. S. Regs., Part II. and the Staff Manual respectively. Title pages will be prepared in manuscript.

WAR DIARY
or
~~INTELLIGENCE SUMMARY~~

(Erase heading not required.)

1/23 Trench Battery, R.A. 23rd Division.

Hour, Date, Place	Summary of Events and Information	Remarks and references to Appendices
Jan. 1. 1917.	Considerable shelling in evening but no mortar activity. Gallery leading to pits in Hedge Street damaged, putting guns temporarily out of action.	Armed with 2" M.L. Howitzers
Jan. 2.	No firing. Lieut Coles mentioned in despatches	
Jan 3.	No firing	
Jan 4th	23 rounds retaliation fired from Nos 1 and 2 guns Davidson.	
Jan 5th	10 rounds fired from No 1 gun Davidson.	
Jan 6th	No firing	
Jan 7	20 rounds retaliation fired. Most of it with silencer.	
Jan 8th	Fired 20 rounds retaliation during firing [illegible] of No 1 Davidson [illegible] & 3 [illegible] mechanisms went wrong [illegible] thereby [illegible] the retaliation	R. [illegible] 2/Lt R.F.A. Comdg 1/23 Trench Bty RA

Instructions regarding War Diaries and Intelligence Summaries are contained in F. S. Regs., Part II. and the Staff Manual respectively. Title pages will be prepared in manuscript.

WAR DIARY
or
~~INTELLIGENCE~~ SUMMARY

Army Form C. 2118.

(*Erase heading not required.*) Y/23 Trench Batty R.A. 23rd Division

Hour, Date, Place	Summary of Events and Information	Remarks and references to Appendices
Jan 9th	fired 4 rounds ~~registration~~ on Fritz wire, but didnt hit it, so turned gun round to try again next day.	armed with 2" M.L. Howitzers.
Jan 10th	fired 4 rounds registration on Fritz wire & hit it this time. Fritz ignored this registration.	
Jan 11th	Lieut. D.F.P. Coles returned from leave.	
Febr 30th	Under the present arrangement, the two batteries in the line are under the control of one officer. This officer is alternately taken from Y & Z Batteries. It is therefore obviously impossible to keep an accurate chronicle of the doings of [illegible] under these circumstances and it has therefore been decided to close this diary until such times, as it can be kept in a proper manner.	D.F.P. Coles Lieut 31.8.16 [illegible] Cmdg Y/23 T.M.B.

1247 W 3299 200,000 (E) 8/14 J.B.C.&A. Forms/C. 2118/11.

Instructions regarding War Diaries and Intelligence Summaries are contained in F. S. Regs., Part II. and the Staff Manual respectively. Title Pages will be prepared in manuscript.

WAR DIARY 23rd DIVnl Trench Mortar Batteries

~~or INTELLIGENCE SUMMARY~~

(Erase heading not required.)

Army Form C. 2118

2131.

Vol 20

Place	Date	Hour	Summary of Events and Information	Remarks and references to Appendices
YPRES SALIENT	February 1917.		In action with three 9.45 inch Heavy Trench Mortars and six 2-inch Medium Trench Mortars in the Zillebeke Sector. Very cold, but fine, weather with a hard frost for first half of month; ground became very hard, and many places, hitherto impassable, owing to mud, were easily visited; digging was very difficult owing to frost making ground like iron for a depth of two feet.	Armed with 9.45 inch + 2 inch M.T. Trench Howitzers.
			Work was continued on no. 1 heavy T.M position in Sanctuary Wood near REDAN, but progress very slow. A concrete platform was laid for mortar and reinforced with angle irons and woven wire. A large amount of material including cement, sand and broken brick (for aggregate), and several hundred concrete slabs (2'0" x 1'0" x 3 in), was taken up the tramway to this position.	Work carried out under supervision of 128th Field Coy R.E. (Capt. Podmore) (Lt. Christie R.E.)
			C.R.A. (Brig-Gen Sir D. Arbuthnot) and Commandant T.M School (2nd Army) (Sir J. Keane) visited all the medium and heavy emplacements and also front line O.P. They were both of the opinion that the concrete emplacement mentioned above was not satisfactory owing to the large amount of labour and material required, and owing to fact that concrete has not proved to be a suitable material for gun-or mortar-platforms.	
			A certain amount of Firing by Medium and Heavy Mortars was carried out	

R. L. Johnson. Capt. R.A. D.T.M.O. 23 DIV

1875 Wt. W593/826 1,000,000 4/15 J.B.C. & A. A.D.S.S./Forms/C. 2118.

Instructions regarding War Diaries and Intelligence Summaries are contained in F. S. Regs., Part II. and the Staff Manual respectively. Title Pages will be prepared in manuscript.

WAR DIARY
or
INTELLIGENCE SUMMARY
(Erase heading not required.)

23rd Divnl Trench Mortar Batteries

Army Form C. 2118 p. 2

Place	Date	Hour	Summary of Events and Information	Remarks and references to Appendices
YPRES SALIENT	FEBRUARY 1917		chiefly in retaliation for hostile Trench Mortaring. Heavy T.M.'s fired 20 rounds one day.	Armed with 9.45 inch and 2 inch M.L. Trench Howitzers
		11/2/17	Capt C. W. Britten left for England to proceed on a Battery Commanders' Course before assuming command of C Battery 102nd Bde R.F.A. Lieut Johnson took over duties of D.T.M.O.	
		13/2/17	2/Lt. A.D. Smith posted to V/23 H.T.M.B. from B/102.	
			Lt. J.S. Kyle M.C. ~~posted~~ assumed command of V/23 and became Captain.	
			2/Lt. S.R. Thorp assumed command of Z/23 ~~and~~ (vice Lt. Hawkins evac to England) and ~~became~~ became Lieut.	
		26/2/17	2/Lt. V. Smyth (Z/23) went to Hospital.	
			Towards the end of the month the Medium Mortars were ordered to assist 18prs in cutting Wire for a small raid. Attempts were made chiefly on Lt. R.L. Johnson on four separate days, but not successfully. Some wire was cut opposite Stewart Street (G. Sap End) on last day, but in the end a Bangalore Torpedoe, prepared and fired by R.E. was used for the raid; a German Trench was entered and found unoccupied.	Lt Christie R.E.
		25/2/17	A Trench Mortar Officers' Mess was formed; 2/Lt. A.D. Smith began an energetic Mess-Secretaryship on 26th.	
		27/2/17	Relief by 39th Div., proceeded to rest billets at RUMINGHEM, Lt. A. Goodfellow, billeting Officer. Officers at end of month as follows V/23 Capt. J.S. Kyle M.C. 3rd East Yorks, 2/Lt. B. McLachlan R.F.A., 2/Lt. A.D. Smith R.F.A.; X/23 Lt. A. Goodfellow. Y/23 2/Lt. D.F.P. Coles 3rd East Yorks, 2/Lt. R.S. de S. Brock; Z/23 Lt. S.R. Thorp	R L Johnson Lt. D.T.M.O. 23 DIV

Instructions regarding War Diaries and Intelligence Summaries are contained in F. S. Regs., Part II. and the Staff Manual respectively. Title Pages will be prepared in manuscript.

WAR DIARY

~~or~~

~~INTELLIGENCE SUMMARY~~

(Erase heading not required.)

23rd Divl. Trench Mortar Batteries

Army Form C. 2118

7 h. 3

Place	Date	Hour	Summary of Events and Information	Remarks and references to Appendices
YPRES SALIENT (ZILLEBEKE SECTOR)	February 1917		S. M. H. A. Ball V/23 H.T.M. Battery received a permanent Commn., and was posted to 58th Divnl. Artillery, where he at once received command of a Trench Mortar Battery. Corporal A. Yates Z/23 was awarded the Military Medal for gallant conduct in removing Ammunition under shell fire from a Bomb Store which had caught fire. His recommendation for an award was strongly supported by Col. Walker 13th D.L.I. (who saw Cpl. Yates at the time) R. L. Johnson Captn. R.A. D.T.M.O. 23rd Div.	Armed with 9.45 inch + 2 inch M.L. Trench Howitzers.

1875 Wt. W593/826 1,000,000 4/15 J.B.C. & A. A.D.S.S./Forms/C. 2118.

Instructions regarding War Diaries and Intelligence Summaries are contained in F. S. Regs., Part II. and the Staff Manual respectively. Title pages will be prepared in manuscript.

WAR DIARY
Y/23 Trench ~~or~~ Battery, R.A.
~~INTELLIGENCE SUMMARY.~~
(Erase heading not required.)

23rd Division

Vol 21

Army Form C. 2118.

23

Place	Date	Hour	Summary of Events and Information	Remarks and references to Appendices
Rumminghem	March 1st to 3rd (inclusive)		The Medium Mortars of the 23rd Division, came out of action in the YPRES SALIENT on the morning of the 27th of February, and the batteries once more came under direct control of the Battery commander. On the evening of the 27th Y Battery arrived at Rumminghem, having travelled there by Motor Lorry via CASSELL and WATTEN, and were billeted in a farm house on the Banks of the VAA Canal. The Battery being now in rest, attention is given to the smartening up of personnel and Equipment, during the morning, and to sport in the afternoon.	Armed with 2" M.L. Howitzers.
	March 4th		Guns, hand carts, tool-boxes etc all thoroughly cleaned. A gun park is made, and suitable places for stacking of rifles and Equipment. In the afternoon the medium mortars under the Captaincy of Cpl Rands of Y Battery played No 3 Section at football, and were beaten with the score of 1 nil.	

[illegible] Lieut. 3/E. York R.
Comdg Y/23 Trench Bty R.A.

2353 Wt. W2544/1454 700,000 5/15 D. D. & L. A.D.S.S./Forms/C. 2118.

Army Form C. 2118.

Instructions regarding War Diaries and Intelligence Summaries are contained in F. S. Regs., Part II. and the Staff Manual respectively. Title pages will be prepared in manuscript.

WAR DIARY or ~~INTELLIGENCE SUMMARY.~~

V/23 ~~Trench~~ Battery R. A. 23rd Division.

(Erase heading not required.)

Place	Date	Hour	Summary of Events and Information	Remarks and references to Appendices
Rumminghem	March 8th		Weather so cold that parades were impossible. The medium Batteries therefore paraded together except for a short Route march. In the afternoon the men played football among themselves.	Armed with 2" T/L Howitzer
	9th		Gun Parades, [illegible]; 2" position dug. In the afternoon the medium mortars under the Captaincy of Cpl Rands defeated V/23 by 3 goals to nil at football. Snow fell at intervals during the day.	
	10th		Parades as usual. ~~X/23~~ had a shoot in the morning ~~at~~ which all N.C.O's & men of the mortars attended for purposes of instruction in observation. Only two bombs were fired however owing to the absence of S.A.A. Cartridges. In the evening the combined talent of the Mortars and D.A.C. gave the first of a series of performances in the village concert hall. The C.R.A. inspected the [illegible], [illegible], and rifles of the battery at 12 noon, and found them to be in a satisfactory condition.	E R Coles Lieut. R. Y. Regt. Comdg V/23 Trench Bty R.A.

2353 Wt. W2544/1454 700,000 5/15 D. D. & L. A.D.S.S./Forms/C. 2118.

Instructions regarding War Diaries and Intelligence Summaries are contained in F. S. Regs., Part II. and the Staff Manual respectively. Title pages will be prepared in manuscript.

WAR DIARY
or
INTELLIGENCE SUMMARY.
(Erase heading not required.)

4/23 Trench Battery, R.A.

23rd Division

Army Form C. 2118.

Place	Date	Hour	Summary of Events and Information	Remarks and references to Appendices
Rumminghem March 19	5th		Parades as usual in the morning. Snow fell during the previous night making the ground slippery and the air cold, so parades were of a vigorous nature. In the afternoon the Medium played the Heavies at football defeating them 4-1; Y Battery was well represented in the team, and played a noble part in the game.	Armed with 2" M. Howitzers
March 6th	6th		Parades as usual in the morning. Unusually fine weather but cold wind. Afternoon spent in kicking a foot-ball about.	
	7th		Weather cold and dull. Battery went for a short route march in the morning. On their return they had their photograph taken with two of the guns, the officers were present for this event. In the afternoon the Mediums under Cpl Rands played football against 2nd Section DAC the result of the match being a draw with the score of one all.	

D H Coles Lieut.
Reg:
3/E 4/23 Trench Bty RA
Comdg

2353 Wt. W2544/1454 700,000 5/15 D. D. & L. A.D.S.S./Forms/C. 2118.

Instructions regarding War Diaries and Intelligence Summaries are contained in F. S. Regs., Part II. and the Staff Manual respectively. Title pages will be prepared in manuscript.

WAR DIARY
or
INTELLIGENCE SUMMARY.

7/23 Trench Battery R.A.

23rd Division.

(Erase heading not required.)

Army Form C. 2118.

Place	Date	Hour	Summary of Events and Information	Remarks and references to Appendices
Rommingham	March 11th		Sunday. parade at 9.50 instead of usual time. Inspection of personnel and billets by D.T.M.O at 10 a.m. D.T.M.O expressed satisfaction. In the afternoon the mediums played a football match against the R.E's (I.W.T.) and defeated them one nil, the victory was considerable as the opposing team had 4 professionals playing for them.	Armed with 2" M.L. Howitzers
	12th		Battery dug trenches as targets for practice shoot in the morning and in the afternoon. There was a second performance at the theatre in the evening, which was well attended and well received	
	13th		Two N.C.O's went on a day's course of instruction in the art of bomb throwing. In the afternoon the Battery shot off eight rounds; the shoot was a failure, as for reasons unknown, the bombs fell all over the place, and seldom in the right place.	
	14th		Parades as usual. weather bad so it wasn't possible to do very much	
	15th		The whole Battery together with the other trench mortar Btys of the division	

D. F. [illegible] Lieut. [illegible] 3/2 York. Regt. Commdg 7/23 Trench Battery R.A.

2353 Wt. W2544/1454 700,000 5/15 D. D. & L. A.D.S.S./Forms/C. 2118.

Instructions regarding War Diaries and Intelligence Summaries are contained in F. S. Regs., Part II. and the Staff Manual respectively. Title pages will be prepared in manuscript.

WAR DIARY
or
~~INTELLIGENCE~~ SUMMARY.

Army Form C. 2118.

23rd Division.

Y/23 TRENCH BATTERY, R.A. (Erase heading not required.)

Place	Date	Hour	Summary of Events and Information	Remarks and references to Appendices
ROMINGHEM.	March 15th		marched to Esperlecques to go through a gas test. They were put through the ordinary helmet drill, and then took their places in the trench while gas was discharged at them. Two 2" guns were taken with the Bty in order that they might practise the gun drill with their helmets on, and while gas was actually being discharged.	Arnesworth? 2" T.M. Battery?
	16th.		Parades as usual. Lectures on Mills Bombs, and the art of throwing them, were given by the N.C.O's who had attended the course at the Bomb School. The men then practised throwing the bombs, a keen competition ensued.	
	17th.		Parades as usual. Subsections competed in carrying their guns over the open ground & placing them in action, laying them on a given target. In the afternoon Y played Z at football, the result being a draw with the score of one all.	
	18th.		Inspection of billets and equipment by O.C. and D.T.M.O. In the afternoon the mediums played No 2 Section D.A.C., result of match a draw with the score of nil.	D F P Coles Lieut 3/E. York. Regt Comdg Y/23 Trench Battery R.A.

2353 Wt. W2544/1454 700,000 5/15 D. D. & L. A.D.S.S./Forms/C. 2118.

Instructions regarding War Diaries and Intelligence Summaries are contained in F. S. Regs., Part II. and the Staff Manual respectively. Title pages will be prepared in manuscript.

WAR DIARY
or
~~INTELLIGENCE SUMMARY.~~
(*Erase heading not required.*) Y/23 Trench Mortar Battery.

Army Form C. 2118.

23rd Division.

Place	Date	Hour	Summary of Events and Information	Remarks and references to Appendices
Rumingham	March	19th	Battery filled in trenches dug a few days ago for targets. Preparations made for moving. Cpl Bartlett went in charge of the advance party for billeting, & after drawing tents & erecting a camp. The [illegible] are to be attached to No 3/D.A.C. for the move & until further orders.	armed with 2" M.C. [illegible]
HERZEEL		20th	Short parade in the morning, after which battery had orders to pack up everything that could be packed, and get things ready generally for departure.	
		21st	Btty: moved at 9 am from Rumingham by motor lorry to Borseel, where they arrived at midday. Fairly comfortable quarters were found for all ranks, but nothing was unpacked as orders were given to be ready to move on at 8.00 am in the morning.	
		22nd	Moved on to Herzeel, where the battery arrived at about eleven o'clock. The N.C.O's and men were accomodated in tents, and the officers in billets in the village.	[illegible] Lieut. 3/E. York. Reg. Cmds Y/23 Trench Battery R.A.

2353 Wt. W2544/1454 700,000 5/15 D. D. & L. A.D.S.S./Forms/C. 2118.

Instructions regarding War Diaries and Intelligence Summaries are contained in F. S. Regs., Part II. and the Staff Manual respectively. Title pages will be prepared in manuscript.

WAR DIARY or INTELLIGENCE SUMMARY.

Y/23 Trench Battery. R.A. 23rd Division.

(Erase heading not required.)

Army Form C. 2118.

Place	Date	Hour	Summary of Events and Information	Remarks and references to Appendices
HERZEEL.	March	23rd	Parades as usual in morning. In afternoon Bty played Soccer against Sigs of 8th Yorks & Lancs, and defeated them 4-2.	armed with 2" M.L. Howitzers
		24th	Parades again as usual, with the exception of a bombing Competition between Batteries, which, after a tie with V, Y Battery easily won, carrying off a prize of 25 francs. In the afternoon the Mediums once more defeated the Heavies at football, with the score of 7-2.	
		25th	Sunday. Voluntary church parade in the morning.	
		26th	2/Lt R. S. de Saumarez-Brock second in command for the past year of Y/23 Trench Battery posted to command 2/23 Trench Battery, & entitled to wear the badges of Lieutenant while so in command.	
		27th	2/Lt Oclam W.H. posted as second in command to Y/23 Trench Battery. News was received that 2/Lt O.C.M. Carlough M.C. a former second in command of this battery & subsequently O.C. of 2/23 T.M.B., has been appointed acting Major, and has received command of an 8" How Battery.	

[Signature] Capt. Lieut. 3/2 Yorks. R. Cmdg Y/23 Trench Battery R.A.

2353 Wt. W2544/1454 700,000 5/15 D. D. & L. A.D.S.S./Forms/C. 2118.

Instructions regarding War Diaries and Intelligence Summaries are contained in F. S. Regs., Part II. and the Staff Manual respectively. Title pages will be prepared in manuscript.

WAR DIARY
or
~~INTELLIGENCE SUMMARY~~ Y/23 Trench Batty. R.A. 23rd Division

(Erase heading not required.)

Army Form C. 2118.

Place	Date	Hour	Summary of Events and Information	Remarks and references to Appendices
HERZEELE	28th		Parades as usual in morning. In the afternoon, the representative team of all the mortars played against D 104, and were defeated 1, nil after an excellent game. The men who were not playing were marched to Oudezeel, where the game was, and afterwards were marched back.	arrived [?] 2nd Lt H. L. Hankin [?]
	29th		Parades as usual.	
	30th		Parades as usual.	
	31st		Parade as usual weather bad.	
			As the postings and casualties of the battery have not always been entered into the diary during the past 18 months, here follows a complete list of the same - which may be taken as an appendix to the events so far recorded.	
			18.10.15 Gr Chalk. Killed in action.	
			20.11.15. Bdr Davis, G. Bdr Coles. C. a/Bdr Rogerson. A. a/Bdr Blew J. Grs Alker, S. Bales, D. Bentley. W. Clarke W. Elvenworth [?] [illegible]	D H Coles Lieut 3/E. York R. Comdg Y/23 Trench Bty R.A.

Instructions regarding War Diaries and Intelligence Summaries are contained in F. S. Regs., Part II. and the Staff Manual respectively. Title pages will be prepared in manuscript.

WAR DIARY
or
INTELLIGENCE SUMMARY. Y/23 Trench Battery. R.A.

(*Erase heading not required.*)

Army Form C. 2118.

Place	Date	Hour	Summary of Events and Information	Remarks and references to Appendices
Hersent.	March 31st		Daltwaite J. Parry D. Pilkington N. Rice A. Rollins T. Smith G. Thomas T. Wilson H. —— These 2 Coy and men were withdrawn from the battery when it was decided that Light T.M. Btys. should consist of 50% infantry personnel. 23.11.15 ——. Cpl. Lavender (23 Div. Cyclist Coy) L/Cpl. Temple - Do. - Ptes Pickles J. & Thistle T. (8th Yorks) Ptes Barker T & Chalmers H. (11th West Yorks) & Pte Carter P. 10th West Ridings —— posted to complete personnel of Y/23 which was then the authorized Establishment for a T.M.B. 19.1.16. Gr Woodward W. wounded in action. 29.1.16. Gr. Ray A. " " " 30.1.16. Cpl Burns R.G.A., Grs. Ahern Alderson Allen Alday Ayto Batty Brown, Cocker, Dadford Durnford — posted from 1st Army School of Mortars when it was decided that a T.M.B. should consist of all R.A. personnel. 31.1.16. The aforementioned infantry were returned to their units.	Armd 2nd M.G. [illegible] D.P. Coles Capt 3/5 York R Cmdg Y/23 Trench Bty R.A.

2353 Wt. W2544/1454 700,000 5/15 D. D. & L. A.D.S.S./Forms/C. 2118.

Instructions regarding War Diaries and Intelligence Summaries are contained in F. S. Regs., Part II. and the Staff Manual respectively. Title pages will be prepared in manuscript.

WAR DIARY
or
INTELLIGENCE SUMMARY.
(Erase heading not required.)

Army Form C. 2118.

Y/23 Trench Battery R.A.
23rd Division

Place	Date	Hour	Summary of Events and Information	Remarks and references to Appendices
HERZEELE	March 31.		28.3.16. Gr. Sherman A. posted from B/103rd RFA	Amended [illegible] 2nd Lt. [illegible]
			30.3.16. Gr. Simpson A.P. " " C/103 R.F.A.	
			9.4.16. Grs Archer & Brown R.G.A. posted to X/23 T.M.B.	
			12.4.16. Gr. Ward J. Evacuated sick 12.4.16.	
			23.4.16 Gr. Boulton G. posted from C/104 Bde R.F.A.	
			29.4.16 G. Unswatt. G ——— C/105 29.4.16.	
			3.5.16. G. Dunford H. Evacuated sick	
			22.5.16. G. Sherman A. " "	
			24.5.16. G. Wood posted from C/106 R.F.A.	
			21.1.16 a/B.S.M. Bale wounded in action Albert	
			2.7.16. G. Sturdy H. " " "	
			25.7.16 Cpl Burns R. Posted to School of Mortars 4th Army	
			15.8.16. Grs Trayhan, McDonald & Sutton posted from 7/23 DAC	
			1.9.16 Grs Collis & Ellison attached as telephonists from C/102 RFA	
			14.9.16 G. Ellison returned to his unit.	
			3.10.16 Grs Steel G. & Davies G. posted from 2/23 D.A.C.	

D. P. Coles Lieut R. 3/2 York R.
Cmdg Y/23 Trench Bty R.A.

2353 Wt. W2544/1454 700,000 5/15 D. D. & L. A.D.S.S./Forms/C. 2118.

Instructions regarding War Diaries and Intelligence Summaries are contained in F. S. Regs., Part II. and the Staff Manual respectively. Title pages will be prepared in manuscript.

WAR DIARY
or
INTELLIGENCE SUMMARY.
(Erase heading not required.)

Army Form C. 2118.

Y/23 Trench Battery R.A.
23rd Division

Place	Date	Hour	Summary of Events and Information	Remarks and references to Appendices
HERZEELE	March 31	18.10.16	Gr Simpson A.S. Evacuated sick.	[illegible]
		19.12.16	Gr Price J. " "	
		20.12.16	Grs Harris Hopper Poole Smith, posted from 3/23 DAC	
		21.12.16	Cpl Davis wounded in action	
		24.12.16	Cpl Davis " "	
		26.12.16	Cpl Davis J.C. died of wounds.	
		25.12.16	Gr Smith G. Evacuated sick.	
		4.1.17	Gr Poole G. " "	
		16.1.17	Gr Harris T. " "	
		6.2.17	Gr Hopper T. " "	
		3.2.17	Gr Turner R. Posted from 3/23 D.A.C.	
		9.2.17	Gr Bell R " "	
		13.2.17	Gr Ander Posted from 3/23 D.A.C.	
		9.2.17	Gr Hawkins J. Posted from 3/23 D.A.C.	
		23.2.17	Gr Sutton R. Sent to Base (under age)	
		9.3.17	Gr Spear. H. posted from 3/23 D.A.C.	

D.H. Coles Lieut York R
3/12
Cmdg Y/23 Trench Battery RA

2353 Wt. W2544/1454 700,000 5/15 D. D. & L. A.D.S.S./Forms/C. 2118.

Instructions regarding War Diaries and Intelligence Summaries are contained in F. S. Regs., Part II. and the Staff Manual respectively. Title pages will be prepared in manuscript.

WAR DIARY
or
INTELLIGENCE SUMMARY. Y/23 Trench Battery R.A. 23rd Division.

(Erase heading not required.)

Army Form C. 2118.

Place	Date	Hour	Summary of Events and Information	Remarks and references to Appendices
HERZ[illegible]	[illegible] 151.		12.5.17 Gr. Owen a[illegible] posted from V/23. T.M.B.	Amended with 2" M.C. [illegible]
			27.5.17 Gr. Brown posted from X/23. T.M.B.	
			The above is a complete list of postings etc up to date.	
			D.A.P. Coles Lieut. 3/E. York. R. Comdg Y/23 Trench Bty. R.A.	

Re War Diary of

Y23 T M Bty

for

Novr. 1916

R.A. 23rd Division No: SL 37/2.

- 5 -

Headquarters,

23rd Division (A).

Herewith War Diary of T.M. Batteries, 23rd Div: for period June 7th to June 30th.

No further back records of the 2 D.T.M.Os who have been successively killed can be found.

X All documents were destroyed by shell fire during the recent operations.

B.G. McMurtrie Lieutenant,

11th July, 1917. Staff Lieutenant R.A. 23rd Division.

--------oOo--------

-6-

23rd Division No.A/802/18.

D.A.G.,
3rd Echelon, Base.

Forwarded.

H. C. Owen Capt
D.A.A.G.
for Major General,
July 11th 1917. Commanding 23rd Division.

23 DTM Bty
Vol 22
23
April

23rd Division

No. A/802/18.

R.A., 23rd Division.

For information.

E. F. Falkner

Lieut-Colonel,

10th July, 1917. A.A.& Q.M.G. 23rd Division.

R.A. 23rd Division No: S.L. 37/2

Headquarters,

23rd Division (A).

Reference your No: A/802/18 dated 28th ult:

Trench Mortar Batteries do not submit War Diaries. The D.T.M.O. submits a Diary similar to our F.A. Brigades.

Due to the changes and deaths of two of our D.T.M.Os, the Diaries for the months requested, are missing.

Based on the little material there is now available, Diary is now being written up for as long a period as possible, up to date.

B G McMurtrie Lieutenant,

4th July, 1917. Staff Lieutenant R.A. 23rd Division.

--------oOo--------

D.A.G., Base.

Forwarded.

Would you please say if this will be in order under the circumstances.

E F Faulkner [illegible]

Major General,
July 5th 1917. Commanding 23rd Division.

III

Head-quarters,

23rd.Division.

Yes, in the circumstances.

[signature]

Captain,
G.H.Qrs.,3rd.Echelon. D. A.A.G.,
7th.July, 1917. forD.A.G.

Head-quarters,

23rd. Division.

The Divisional T.M.Battery does not appear on any of the copies of receipts which have been sent you for April War Diaries.

Please forward the same, as it has not been received here.

G.H.Yates

Captain,
D. A. A. G.,
for D. A. G.

G. H. Qrs.,
3rd. Echelon.
23rd. June, 1917.

23rd Division.No.A/802/.18.

2

D.A.G.,
BASE.

The War Diaries in question were forwarded to you together with War Diaries of other Units of this Division on 6.5.17.

Acknowledgement thereto was received in this office on 19.5.17.

Lionel J Polgeon

2/Lieut.,for
D.A.A.G.,for
G.O.C.,23rd Division.

June 20th 1917.

Headquarters,

23 Division.

The War Diaries of the undermentioned Units have not been received for the months stated against them.

It is requested that they may be forwarded as soon as possible and the attention of the officers commanding be called to F.S.Regs.para.140.,subsection 2 and C.R.140/592 dated 12.12.15. +G.R01598

Unit.	Period.
Div Train	Apl 17
Div T M Bty	Apl 17

General Headquarters,
3rd Echelon,
15/6/1917.

for Major-General,
D. A. G.

Instructions regarding War Diaries and Intelligence Summaries are contained in F. S. Regs., Part II. and the Staff Manual respectively. Title pages will be prepared in manuscript.

WAR DIARY
or
INTELLIGENCE SUMMARY.
(Erase heading not required.)

Army Form C. 2118.

Place	Date	Hour	Summary of Events and Information	Remarks and references to Appendices
	1/4/17 to 5/4/17.		Training at Z Camp.	
	6/4/17.		Proceeded to Toronto Camp.	
	6/4/17 to 11/4/17		Training at Toronto Camp.	
	12/4/17		Proceeded to Winnipeg Camp.	
	12/4/17 to 13/4/17.		Training at Winnipeg Camp.	
	13/4/17.		Proceeded to Railway Dugouts & relieved 70th L.T.M.B. in the line (Right Sub-sector).	
	16/4/17.		Nothing to report.	
	17/4/17			
	18/4/17	10.30AM	3 rounds fired by us from our gun in Living Trench for registration purposes.	
	19/4/17.		Enemy sent over several rifle grenades and Light T.M. shells in the direction of Winnipeg St & Canada Trench. We retaliated effectively, firing 67 rounds in all.	
	20/4/17		21 rounds fired in registration & retaliation for enemy's rifle grenades.	
	21/4/17		During morning enemy fired 3 small aerial torpedoes near Canada Trench. We retaliated with 6 rounds, & enemy ceased firing.	

#353 Wt. W2544/1454 700,000 5/15 D. D. & L. A.D.S.S./Forms/C. 2118.

Instructions regarding War Diaries and Intelligence Summaries are contained in F. S. Regs., Part II. and the Staff Manual respectively. Title pages will be prepared in manuscript.

WAR DIARY
or
INTELLIGENCE SUMMARY.
(Erase heading not required.)

Army Form C. 2118.

Place	Date	Hour	Summary of Events and Information	Remarks and references to Appendices
	21/4/17	(Contd).	Late in the day 12 rounds were fired in retaliation for enemy's rifle grenades.	
	22/4/17		3 rounds fired for registration purposes on the camouflet blown near the Cutting at 4 A.m. 21/4/17.	
	23/4/17.		Canada Street & Winnipeg Street again bombarded with Light T.M. Shells. We retaliated & eventually silenced enemy's activity. Total rounds fired - 63. Relieved by 70th L.T.M.B. Proceeded to Erie Camp. ~~Left Erie Camp for Steenvoorde.~~	
	~~24/4/17~~ 24/4/17 to 28/4/17.		Training at Erie Camp, special attention being paid to tactical handling of Stokes mortars in open warfare & firing practice.	
	29/4/17		Proceeded to Steenvoorde.	
	30/4/17		Training in Steenvoorde area.	

4/5/17

A. Clarkson Capt.
O.C. 69th L.T.M.B.

Instructions regarding War Diaries and Intelligence Summaries are contained in F. S. Regs., Part II. and the Staff Manual respectively. Title pages will be prepared in manuscript.

WAR DIARY
or
INTELLIGENCE SUMMARY.
(Erase heading not required.)

Army Form C. 2118.

23 D T M Bty.

Vol 23

Place	Date	Hour	Summary of Events and Information	Remarks and references to Appendices
	1/5/17 to 10/5/17		STEENVOORDE Training Area. (8th, inspection by Brigadier)	
	11/5/17		moved to WINNIPEG CAMP.	
	11/5/17 to 18th		Training at WINNIPEG CAMP.	
	18/5/17		moved to Railway Dugouts & relieved 68th Bde in the line.	
	19/5/17		26 rounds fired (20 at 4.30 p.m., +6 at about 11 p.m.) in retaliation for 3 Heavy T.M.'s & 2 rifle grenades.	
	20/5/17		15 rounds fired in retaliation for a few heavy T.M.s, sent over near Grand Fleet St.	
	21/5/17		During the raid at 1 A.M. we fired 164 rounds on the pre-arranged targets. We also fired 78 rounds in retaliation for rifle grenades & heavy trench mortars.	
	22/5/17		We fired 71 rounds in retaliation for enemy rifle grenades and heavy T.M.'s.	
	23/5/17		We fired 17 (seventeen) rounds in retaliation for heavy T.M.s fired on St. Peters Street.	
	24/5/17		moved to Boeschepe Area, & carried out training.	
	25/5/17		" " Watou Area	
	26/5/17 to 31/5/17		Carried out training in Manoeuvre area.	

J.H. [illegible] Capt.
O.C. 69th L.T.M.B.

8353 Wt. W2544/1454 700,000 5/15 D. D. & L. A.D.S.S./Forms/C. 2118.

Instructions regarding War Diaries and Intelligence Summaries are contained in F. S. Regs., Part II. and the Staff Manual respectively. Title pages will be prepared in manuscript.

WAR DIARY
or
~~INTELLIGENCE SUMMARY.~~
(Erase heading not required.)

Army Form C. 2118.

23

T M Bty

Vol 21

Place	Date	Hour	Summary of Events and Information	Remarks and references to Appendices
	Mar 1st		Marched from MERCKEGHEM to training Area at EPERLECQUES.	
EPERLECQUES	Mar 2nd to 18th		Training and Recreation carried out in accordance with programmes	
	Mar 19th		Marched from EPERLECQUES to MERCKEGHEM.	
	Mar 20th		Marched from MERCKEGHEM to HOUTKERQUE Area.	
	Mar 21st		Marched from HOUTKERQUE Area to Z. Camp. ST JAN TER. BIEZEN	
	Mar 22nd to Mar 31st		Carried out training.	
	Mar 26th		Inspection by G.O.C. 2nd Army.	

A Clarkson. Capt
O.C. 69th Light Trench Mortar Battery

2353 Wt. W2544/1454 700,000 5/15 D. D. & L. A.D.S.S./Forms/C. 2118.

CONFIDENTIAL.

No. 1
Vol 24

WAR DIARY

23rd Divisional Trench Mortars.

June 7th — June 30th

1917

ORIGINAL.

R. [illegible] Capt
D.T.M.O. 23rd Divn

CPL POPE M.M.

54920

RFA

Army Form C. 2118.

Instructions regarding War Diaries and Intelligence Summaries are contained in F. S. Regs., Part II. and the Staff Manual respectively. Title pages will be prepared in manuscript.

WAR DIARY
or
INTELLIGENCE SUMMARY.
(*Erase heading not required.*)

Place	Date	Hour	Summary of Events and Information	Remarks and references to Appendices
HALIFAX CAMP 28.G.13.d.	1917 June 7th	3.10 am	In accordance with orders received from 23rd Div Arty at Zero hour for the attack on the MESSINES RIDGE the T.M. consisting of 8 2" mortars and 2 9.45" mortars opened fire on the enemy [illegible] [illegible] of the attack (the CLONMEL COPSE Area) [illegible] [illegible]. [illegible] the positions being [illegible] [illegible] fire. Altogether 800 rounds of 2" and 35 rounds of 9.45" were fired the only mortars left in action being 3 2" and 1 9.45". [illegible] slightly wounded [illegible] remained at duty.	
		12 noon	Capt. F.E.J. Hon, Instructor Second Army T.M. School, posted to the Division as D.T.M.O. and reported to H.Q. R.A. for duty.	[illegible]
	9th		D.T.M.O. took over from A/D.T.M.O. and made his H.Q.s in HEDGE St TUNNEL. X/23 T.M. Bty was sent to rest billets leaving Y/23 Z/23 and [illegible] Y/23 to get as many mortars as possible back into action and [illegible] ammunition [illegible] from 8 a.m. [illegible] on [illegible] or CLONMEL COPSE and all mortars [illegible] to break up any hostile [illegible] forming up for the counter attack in that neighbourhood. [illegible] [illegible] 1st Rounds 2" and 10 9.45" [illegible]	
			Lt B [illegible] 52 X/23 T.M. Bty (after 24 hours) rejoined from hospital. 1 N.C.O. [illegible] (gassed not [illegible])	F.F.C.
	9th–12th		Harassing fire continued. Military Medals awarded to Sergt Stevenson, Corp Pipe, Bdr Cope and Gnr White for gallantry [illegible] in a 9.45" mortar [illegible] fire.	F.F.C.
	13th		X/23 T.M.Bty relieved Y/23 and Z/23 in the line, the two latter returning to rest billets	F.F.C.
28.G.31.c.	14th		H.Q. Camp moved from Halifax Camp to field at 28.G.31.c. D.T.M.O. moved his H.Q. to new camp from the line. 6 medium mortars now in action.	F.F.C.
	16th		Lt Chapman who had been stationed at [illegible] during the previous fortnight [illegible] as connecting [illegible] between the batteries in the line and the camp and also [illegible] Capt [illegible] admission to hospital left after Cotton's arrival as A/D.T.M.O. withdrawn to the camp.	
	19th		X/23 T.M.Bty relieved by Z/23 T.M.Bty.	F.F.C.
	21st		Positions taken over by 24th Divisional Trench Mortars, mortars in the line being exchanged for mortars at camp. On this day there were 7 2" and 1 9.45 in action 2" with [illegible] 2 9.45 [illegible] into position.	F.F.C.
	22nd		Batteries complete with 2" mortars proceeded to rest billets near BOESCHEPE. 9.45" mortar handed over to X/24 T.M.Bty.	
	23rd		G.O.C. R.A. visited Billets and inspected the camp.	F.F.C.

D. D. & L., London, E.C.
(A7883) Wt W859/M1672 350,000 4/17 Sch. 52a Forms/C/2118/14

Sheet 2.

Army Form C. 2118.

Instructions regarding War Diaries and Intelligence Summaries are contained in F. S. Regs., Part II, and the Staff Manual respectively. Title pages will be prepared in manuscript.

WAR DIARY
or
INTELLIGENCE SUMMARY.
(Erase heading not required.)

Place	Date	Hour	Summary of Events and Information	Remarks and references to Appendices
REST BILLETS	1917			
Near BOESCHEPE	June 21st		Daily parades & inspections, also drill and rifle practice in accordance with instructions for training	
	– 26th		drawn up by D.T.M.O. 26th 2/Lt A.H. Campbell rejoined from hospital.	[illegible]
	27th	10.30am	Presentation of Military Medals to Sergt R[illegible] Corpl Allen Y/23 Sergt Fox[illegible] and Corpl [illegible] V/23 T.M. Bys	
			by G.O.C 23rd Divn at C/102 Bde R.F.A. wagon lines. All batteries marched to presentation. D.T.M.O. visited	
			Second Army T.M. School.	[illegible]
	28th		6" (Newton) T.M. borrowed from 2nd Army T.M. School for drill purposes	[illegible]
	29th		Lecture to Medium Batteries on 6" by D.T.M.O. 2/Lt Cochrane admitted to hospital	[illegible]
	30th		Nil	[illegible]

[signature illegible] D.T.M.O.
23rd Divn

D. D. & L., London, E.C.
(A7883) Wt. W859/M1672 750,000 4/17 Sch. 52a Forms/C/2118/14

C O P Y.
****

-5- R.A. 23rd., Division No:SL 37/2.

Hd. Qrs. 23rd. Division
No. A 802/18 d/-11/7/17.

Head-quarters,

23rd. Division. (A).

Herewith War Diary of T. M. Batteries, 23rd.Div. for period June 7th. to June 30th.

No further back records of the 2 D.T.M.Os who have been successively killed can be found.

All documents were destroyed by shell fire during the recent operations.

(Sgnd.) B.F.McMuntrie? Lieut.
Staff Lieut. R. A. 23rd.Divsn

11th. July, 1917.

-------------000--------------

-6- 23rd. Division No. A/802/18

D.A.G.,
3rd. Echelon, Base.

Forwarded.

(Sgnd.) H.C.Owen, Capt.,
D. A. A. G.,
for Major General,
Commanding 23rd. Division.

July, 11th. 1917.

--------------000-------------

Instructions regarding War Diaries and Intelligence Summaries are contained in F. S. Regs., Part II. and the Staff Manual respectively. Title pages will be prepared in manuscript.

WAR DIARY
or
~~INTELLIGENCE SUMMARY.~~
(*Erase heading not required.*)

Vol 25

SHEET. No.1

Army Form C. 2118.

23rd DIVISIONAL TRENCH MORTARS.

Place	Date	Hour	Summary of Events and Information	Remarks and references to Appendices
REST BILLETS NEAR BOESCHEPE	1917 July 1st		— NIL —	Y.S.C.
	July 2nd		D.T.M.O. went up to arrange with 24th Div T.M. taking over of their positions on 4th July	Y.S.C.
	July 4th	6 am	Left Rest billets and proceeded to HALLEBAST CORNER (Sheet 28 N.2.b.4.3) and took over from 24th Div	Y.S.C.
REF. MAP 1/40000 BELGIUM & FRANCE SHEET 28.			Y/23 T.M.Bty and 1/3 personnel of V/23 H.T.M.Bty to take over guns in action (6 2" and 3 9.45")	Y.S.C.
HALLEBAST CORNER 28 N.2.b.4.8		9.15 am	in neighbourhood of OBSERVATORY RIDGE. Batteries turned out to line the road for H.M. the King on his	Y.S.C. Appendix A
			way to VIERSTRAAT. One long 9.45" (Russian) mortar taken over from 24th Div making total of	Y.S.C.
			5 9.45" mortars and 12 2" mortars in charge. Canteen started for the men of the T.M. Batteries.	
		6.30 pm	D.T.M.O. visited the line and ordered 2 2" mortars in DAVIDSON ST (I.24.d) to be dismantled as	
			the emplacements were impossible to approach ~~[illegible]~~ owing to state of the trench, and had also been badly	
			damaged by shell fire. D.T.M.O. also examined small (7.6 cm) minenwerfer captured by 8th Battalion	
			York & Lancs Reg in position in IMAGE CRESCENT with a view to employing it against the enemy.	
			The M.W. was unsuitable. 23rd Div transferred from I Corps Second Army to II Corps Fifth Army.	Y.S.C.
	July 6th		One N.C.O. wounded, remained at duty.	Y.S.C.
	7th		12 rounds 2" fired at infantry request in retaliation.	Y.S.C.
	9th		X/23 T.M.Bty relieved Y/23 in the line and personnel of V/23 changed. All battery commanders [illegible]	
			went up in order to reconnoitre positions for mortars to engage enemy trenches on the right of the present [illegible]	Y.S.C.

D. D. & L., London, E.C.
(A7853) Wt W809/M1672 50,000 4/17 Sch 52a Forms/C/2118/14

SHEET. No. 2

Army Form C. 2118.

Instructions regarding War Diaries and Intelligence Summaries are contained in F. S. Regs., Part II. and the Staff Manual respectively. Title pages will be prepared in manuscript.

WAR DIARY
or
INTELLIGENCE SUMMARY.

(Erase heading not required.)

Place	Date	Hour	Summary of Events and Information	Remarks and references to Appendices
HALLEBAST CORNER	9th		D.T.M.O. accompanied G.O.C.R.A + BRIGADE MAJOR on reconnaissance of T.M. positions in the line, impossible to complete owing to heavy shelling. Report sent in to C.R.A on result of reconnaissance by battery commanders. 40 men provided from batteries at rest to work on [illegible] Ammunition Dump at [illegible]	Y.F.C.
	10th		G.O.C.R.A visited camp.	
	11th		D.T.M.O left to attend D.T.M.O's conference at Second Army Trench Mortar School.	Y.F.C.
	12th		N.C.O's and men attending course at 2nd Army T.M. School rejoined	Y.F.C.
	13th		D.T.M.O returned	
REF. MAP 1/10000 ZILLEBEKE	14th		G.O.C.R.A and B.M. with D.T.M.O. visited T.M. positions in the line. First two 6" Newton T.M.s arrived from base. Orders received to get them and 1 long 9.45 into action. Tunnel positions in rear of WINNIPEG ST handed over to 30th DIVISION. Arrangements made for getting ~~guns~~ mortars up the line cancelled owing to impending raid.	Y.F.C.
	15th		60 rounds 9.45 ammunition and Long (Russian) 9.45 mortar sent up to VALLEY COTTAGES also 2. 6" Mortars under 2/Lt Campbell. Heavy shelling of neighbourhood of TRANSPORT FARM made it necessary for wagons to go via YPRES & MENIN RD. Long 9.45 towed on its own carriages behind G.S. Wagons. One 6 inch mortar got up to HEDGE ST and the 9.45 to the REDAN. D.T.M.O. lectured 24th DIV T.M's on 6" and long 9.45 in the afternoon. 2/Lt Jackson joined from 23rd D.A.C.	APPENDIX. B. Y.F.C

D. D. & L., London, E.C.
(A7889) Wt. W809/M1672 50,000 4/17 Sch. 52a Forms/C/2118/14

SHEET. 3.
Army Form C. 2118.

Instructions regarding War Diaries and Intelligence Summaries are contained in F. S. Regs., Part II. and the Staff Manual respectively. Title pages will be prepared in manuscript.

WAR DIARY
or
INTELLIGENCE SUMMARY.
(Erase heading not required.)

Place	Date	Hour	Summary of Events and Information	Remarks and references to Appendices
HALLEBAST CORNER	1917. July 16		2/Lt Capey joined for duty + posted to 2/23 T.M. Bty. Carrying parties got up 25 9.45 bombs from VALLEY COTTAGES to THE REDAN. Hostile Shelling very heavy during the night and gas shells largely used. No casualties to 23rd Div T.M's but 24th Div T.M. party working with them had 1 killed and 3 wounded. B.C.	APPENDIX C.
	July 17th		10 9.45 Bombs, spare bed for 6" mortar and ammunition components for 100 rounds long 9.45" sent up to VALLEY COTTAGES. 6" ammunition did not arrive at dump in time to be sent up. 28 9.45 bombs got up from VALLEY COTTAGES to THE REDAN. 24th T.M's had 1 Officer killed and 8 O.R. wounded while engaged on this work. 23rd Div T.M.s Casualties Nil. B.C.	APPENDIX D.
	18th		2/Lt Moss and carrying party attempted to get remaining ammunition at VALLEY COTTAGES up to the line by daylight under cover of mist. Hostile shelling rendered this impossible however. 23rd Div T.M.s relieved in the line by 24th division during the evening. D.T.M.O's of both divisions visited line in connection with hand over, the long 9.45 and 1 6" T.M. were in action and ready to fire if required. The remaining 6 inch was at the position but had not been put in owing to there being no ammunition. B.C.	APPENDIX E
	19th	2.30 am	Vicinity of camp shelled for about an hour. 2/Lt Wise wounded but remained at duty. B.C.	
	20th		Carrying party of 39 N.C.Os + men left camp at 2.30 am and carried 64 6" Bombs via VINCE ST from ZILLEBEKE to HEDGE St. D.T.M.O. lectured 23rd + 24th division medium batteries on 6" ammunition. Lt McLachlan transferred to D/102 Bde R.F.A. 2/Lt Wise taking over command of X/23 T.M.Bty. B.C.	
	21st		Carrying party 50 N.C.O's + men got up 100 6" bombs by same route as on 20th left camp 2.30 am. Sixty men established. B.C.	

D. D. & L., London, E.C.
(A7883) Wt W8C9/M1672 30,000 4/17 Sch. 52a Forms/C/2118/14

SHEET .4.
Army Form C. 2118.

Instructions regarding War Diaries and Intelligence Summaries are contained in F. S. Regs., Part II. and the Staff Manual respectively. Title pages will be prepared in manuscript.

WAR DIARY
or
INTELLIGENCE SUMMARY.
(Erase heading not required.)

Place	Date	Hour	Summary of Events and Information	Remarks and references to Appendices
HALLEBAST CORNER	1917			
	July 22nd		Hostile Aeroplane dropped bombs round the camp about 10.25 pm. No damage done. All batteries inspected by D.T.M.O. in their new equipment. V.B.C.	
	23rd		G.O.C.R.A. inspected camp. Instruction in semaphore signalling begun for all batteries. V.B.C.	
	24th		2/Lt Thomson reported for duty on arrival from base. Posted to V/23 T.M.B. 2/Lt Campbell admitted to hospital sick. V.B.C.	
	25th		3 N.C.O's returned from Gas Course and began instruction of batteries in latest anti-gas measures. V.B.C.	
	26th		G.O.C.R.A. visited camp. V.B.C.	
	27th		Additional 6 inch ammunition being required by 24th T.M.s. Lt Cashan and 60 O.R. attempted to carry from new dump on KNOLL RD but only about 40 bombs got forward owing to hostile shelling and our own practice barrage which necessitated parties being withdrawn before hand in view of the retaliation. V.B.C.	
	28th		Lt Smith + 30 O.R's carried 6" bombs successfully in daylight leaving in G.S. wagons at 3.30 pm. R.A.M.C. Sergt lectured batteries on first aid. Neighbourhood of camp shelled about 9.0 pm. 1 O.R. wounded. V.B.C.	
	30th		R.A.M.C. Sergt instructed all batteries in stretcher drill both morning and afternoon. V.B.C.	
	31st	3.am	Stretcher bearing party 4 Officers + 100 O.R. left for line to work under 72 Field Ambulance at clearing wounded of 24th Division from the front line in SHREWSBURY FOREST via LARCHWOOD Dressing Station to LOCK 8 near VERMOZELE. Party organised in squads of 25 each under an officer and besides carrying stretchers worked the trolley system from LARCHWOOD to LOCK 8. Casualties 2 O.R. gassed (shell).	APPENDIX F.
		3.50am	Zero hour Third Battle of Ypres. V.B.C.	

V.B. [signature]
D.T.M.O. 23rd Div.

D. D. & L., London, E.C.
(A7853) Wt W809/M1672 350,000 4/17 Sch 52a Forms/C/2118/14

SECRET. APPENDIX A. COPY No 5

OPERATION ORDERS BY CAPT. V.E. COTTON. R.F.A

D.T.M.O 23rd DIVN.

1. 23rd Divnl. T.M's will relieve 24th Divnl. T.M's on July 4th.

2. 6 Lorries will be at the disposal of Batteries as under at 6 am. All Lorries to be loaded up & ready to move by 6.30 am.

X/23	- 1.	V/23	- 2.
Y/23	- 1	HQ	- 1.
Z/23	- 1.		

3. Horses under 2/Lt. W.K. Moses will proceed independently

4. Location of the new rest camp is Sheet 28 - H.2.B.4.8

5. On arrival at the Camp. 2" mortars will be handed over to 24th Divn. as follows:-

X/23 - 2. Y/23 - 4 & Z/23 - 3

Stores will be exchanged in accordance with arrangements made by Battery Commanders concerned. OC V/23 will take over 6" Heavy mortars from V/24.

Receipts will be obtained for all stores handed over & forwarded to this office

6. V/23 and 1 Officer & 1/3 personnel of V/23

will proceed to the line & take over all mortars in position, advising this office, as soon as the relief is complete. These Batteries will be relieved on 8th inst.

7. The ration wagon will report at Berthen at 6am 4th inst, and march with the Supply Column to the new refilling point.

8. The amount of amtn. taken over in the line will be reported immediately to this office by batteries concerned.

9. Acknowledge

3.7.17

[signature] Captain RA.
DTMO 23rd Divn

Copies to:-
OC. X. Y. Z. V/23
War Diary (2)
File.

SECRET

APPENDIX B

OPERATION ORDER No 2 BY CAPT M E COTTON
DTMO 23rd Divn

July 15th 1917

Copy No 9.

1. Z/23 TMB will be relieved by Y/23 on the night 15th/16th. The personnel of Z/23 TMB in the line will be relieved by personnel from HQ Camp.

2. 5 GS wagons from the DAC will draw 60 rds of 9.45" Ammn at the ARP [illegible] at 6 pm to-night.
X/23 will provide a loading party of 2 NCO's & 10 OR. On completion of loading the wagons will report to TM Camp.

3. 2 GS wagons will report at TM Camp at 6 pm and will be loaded with 10 rds of 9.45", 2 6" mortars complete with beds and 1 handcart. The long 9.45" with its carriages be attached to the 2 leading GS wagons.

4. The 7 GS wagons will proceed at 7 pm to UPPER HOUSE on OBSERVATORY RIDGE ROAD in charge of 2/Lt Campbell. There they will be at once off loaded and the Ammn and mortars taken up to the positions.
The GS wagons will return to the DAC under their own NCO.

5. OC 2/23 2/Lt [illegible] will arrange to have working parties to meet the wagons and improve the roadway. 2/Lt [illegible] will send a guide down to [illegible] to await the arrival of the wagons

6. The following personnel will be available for man-handling the mortars & carrying ammn:

2/23 – personnel at present in the line
V/23 – " " " " " "
Y/23 – all ranks
V/23 – relieving personnel
24th D.T.M. – 1 Officer & about 50 O.R.

The 3 last parties will march from camp at 7 pm in charge of 2/Lt [illegible]

7. OC 2/23 is responsible for getting 2 6" mortars to the position & will take charge of the personnel of Y/23 on arrival: 2/23 will return to camp as soon as the 6" mortars are got up to the position

8. 2/Lt Campbell will take charge of the 24th T.M. personnel & V/23 personnel & be responsible for getting the mortars & ammn up to the position

9. The personnel of 24th T.M. will return under their own Officer leaving the line at

SECRET

APPENDIX C.

OPERATION ORDERS No 3 By CAPT V.E. COTTON
D.T.M.O. 23rd DIVN

Copy No 9. 11th July 1917

1. The task allotted for the night 16/17th is:-
(a) To get the remaining 6" [illegible] from the neighbourhood of [illegible] to HEDGE ST
(b) To carry 18 rds of 9.45" from Valley Cottages to the Redan

2. Working parties will be as under:-
X/23 T.M. Battery
2 Offrs & about 50 ORs from 2nd Divnl T.M.s
Both parties will be under the command of OC X/23 and will parade at 6.30 pm. Batteries in the line will not be required for carrying.

3. If bombs are available a G.S. wagon with 10 9.45" bombs will report at the camp at 6.30 pm & will proceed to [illegible] HOUSE in charge of an NCO from X/23. 2 ORs from X/23 will accompany it. The above bombs are included in the total of 18 in para 1 (b)

4. Working parties will return to camp on completion of task.

5. 2/Lt Campbell will prepare 2 9.45" trucks for bomb-carrying & send them and the handcarts down to Valley Cottages as soon

2.45 am punctually. The retained portion of Y/23 will return as soon as the mortars have been got up to the position.

10. Every effort must be made to get mortars & emplacements up before daylight (3 am).

11. Acknowledge.

[illegible]
Captain RA
DTMO 23rd Divn

Copy No 1 to X/23 TMB
" " 2 " Y/23 "
3 " Z/23 "
4 " V/23 "
5 24th DTMO
6 2/Lt [illegible]
7 [illegible]
8-9 War Diary

and in hand to meet the amount of the outgoing finishes

b) OC Y/23 will send an orderly to inform OC X/23 if the 6" equipment has been got off from the Sidan during the day.

7. Acknowledge

[illegible]

Captain RA

DTMO 23rd Div

Copy No 1 to X/23 TMB
2 Y/23
3 Z/23
4 V/23
5 23rd DTMO
6 23rd Div Art
7 File
8+9 War Diary

SECRET OPERATION ... COTTON

APPENDIX D

D.T.M.O. 23rd Div

Copy No. 8 July 17th 1917

1. Task allotted :- 24th Divnl T.M's carrying 9.45 bombs (52) from the neighbourhood of Valley Cottages & [illegible] House to the Redan.
23rd Divnl T.M's loading conducting & unloading 320 rds 6", 10 9.45 bombs (included in above total) and components for 100 rds 9.45" also of [illegible] personnel carrying 9.45" components to the Redan

2. 24th Divl personnel will act independently under their own Officers

3. 23rd Divnl T.M's will provide parties as follows:-
Loading Party - X/23 - 2 NCOs & 15 ORs
Unloading Party } - Z/23 - 2 NCOs & 14 ORs
} Y/23 - 26 ORs

4. 2/Lt [illegible] will be in charge of the loading party which will parade punctually at 5.45 pm & will proceed to Dump at H1 central returning on completion of duty
2/Lt [illegible] will conduct the wagons loaded as follows:-
8 wagons each with 40 rds 6" Ammn complete
1 wagon containing 10 9.45" Bombs
1 " -do- component parts for 100 9.45" Bombs
The wagons will report at T.M. Camp [illegible] where they will be joined by the unloading party under
2/Lt [illegible] and then proceed via Valley Cottages

as far as practicable towards Redan House. As soon as they are unloaded 2/Lt Moses will conduct them back to No 3 Section DAC

5 When the party has completed unloading the wagons they will carry bomb ammunition to Hedge St Tunnels and guns components to the Redan

6 2/Lt Campbell will furnish a guide to meet 2nd Army T M party at Valley Cottages at 10 pm

7 Acknowledge

R. [illegible]
Captain RA
DTMO 23rd Div

Copy No 1 to X/23 TMB
2 Y/23
3 Z/23
4 V/23
5 DTMO [illegible]
6 2/Lt [illegible] [illegible]
7 File
8-9 War Diary

Secret

APPENDIX E

OPERATION ORDERS No 5 BY CAPT Y.E.C., T.M.O.
D.T.M.O. 23rd Div

Copy No 5 — 18th July 1917

1) 23rd Divnl T.M's will be relieved in the line by 24th Divnl T.M's this evening.

2) Relieving Batteries are leaving camp about 5.30 pm to-day.

3) The following will be handed over:-

a) by OC Y/23 to OC Y/24

1) In the line

2 6 inch Mortars complete with beds

1 Spare Bed

9 2" Mortars including extension frames & beds

Aeroplane Photographs & maps

2. In the Camp

1 6" Bed. Separate receipts will be taken for 6" equipment, 2" equipment & documents. All 2" gun stores will be brought down

b) by OC V/23 to OC V/24

1) In the line

1 Russian 9.45" Mortar complete with stores & carriages

2 Short 9.45" Mortars. Aeroplane photographs & maps

Separate receipts will be taken for long 9.45" equipment, short 9.45" equipment, & documents

2. In the Camp

Remainder of long 9.45" equipment

4. OC Y/23 will arrange to bring down the handcart at present in the line.

R Cotton
Captain RA
DTMO 23rd Div

Issued at 1.0 pm

Copy No 1 to OC Y/23
2 OC V/23
3 24th DTMO
4 File
5 & 6 War Diary

SECRET OPERATION. ORDERS No 6 APPENDIX F.

By. D.T.M.O. 23rd DIVN

Copy No 5. July 30th 1917

1. General Stretcher Bearing Party composed as under will report at HQ. 72nd. Field Ambulance, Dickebusch on the night 30th/31st at an hour to be notified later:-

2/Lt. Cheesman in command.

2/Lt. Moses, 2/Lt Capey, 2/Lt Thomson

Medium Batteries - 18 OR^s each

V/23 - 46 OR^s

2. Organization Parties will be formed as follows:-

Squad. No 1. 2/Lt Moses 18 OR^s of X/23 & 7 OR^s of V/23
- " - 2. 2/Lt Cheesman 18 OR^s of Y/23 & 7 OR^s of V/23
- " - 3. 2/Lt Capey 18 OR^s of Z/23 & 7 OR^s of V/23
- " - 4 2/Lt Thompson 25 OR^s of V/23

Officers will provide themselves with a Nominal Roll of their parties

3. Rations One days rations for consumption on 31st will be carried on the person. Cooked Rations for the 1st will be sent to ECLUSE TRENCH on the afternoon of the 31st. A hot meal will be provided before the party leaves camp.

4. Dress Arms & Blankets will not be carried. P.H. Helmets as well as Box Respirators will be taken.

5. Parade Squads will parade at 7 pm, fully equipped. Rations will be issued at this parade, also water bottles will be filled with cold tea.

6. Return Batteries will render a return to this office by 5 pm to-night showing:
(a) Total No of O.R.s remaining in camp
(b) Number of employed men giving details of employment.

7. Guard The Guard will be relieved at 6.45 pm to-day, under arrangements to be notified later.

8. Acknowledge

V. B. [signature]
Captain RA
DTMO 23rd Div

Copy No 1 to OC X/23
" 2 " " Y/23
" 3 " " Z/23
" 4 " " V/23
" 5 & 6 " War Diary
" 7 " File.

SECRET — OPERATION. ORDERS No 6

By. D.T.M.O. 23rd Divn

APPENDIX F.

Copy No 6 — July 30th 1917

1. General — Stretcher Bearing Party composed as under will report at HQ 72nd Field Ambulance Dickebusch on the night 30/31st at an hour to be notified later.–

2/Lt Cheesman in command
2/Lt Moses 2/Lt Lahey, 2/Lt Thomas
Medium Batteries – 18 O.R.s each
V/23 – 46 O.R.s

[Organisation]
2. Parties will be formed as follows:–

Squad No 1.	2/Lt Moses	18 O.Rs of X/23 & 7 O.Rs of V/23
– " – 2.	2/Lt Cheesman	18 O.Rs of Y/23 & 7 O.Rs of V/23
– " – 3.	2/Lt Lahey	18 O.Rs of Z/23 & 7 O.Rs of V/23
– " – 4.	2/Lt Thompson	25 O.Rs of V/23

Officers will provide themselves with a nominal Roll of their parties

3. Rations — One days rations for consumption on 31st will be carried on the person. Cooked Rations for the 1st will be sent to ECLUSE TRENCH on the afternoon of the 31st. A hot meal will be provided before the party leaves camp.

4. Dress — Arms & Blankets will not be carried. P.H. Helmets as well as Box Respirators will be taken.

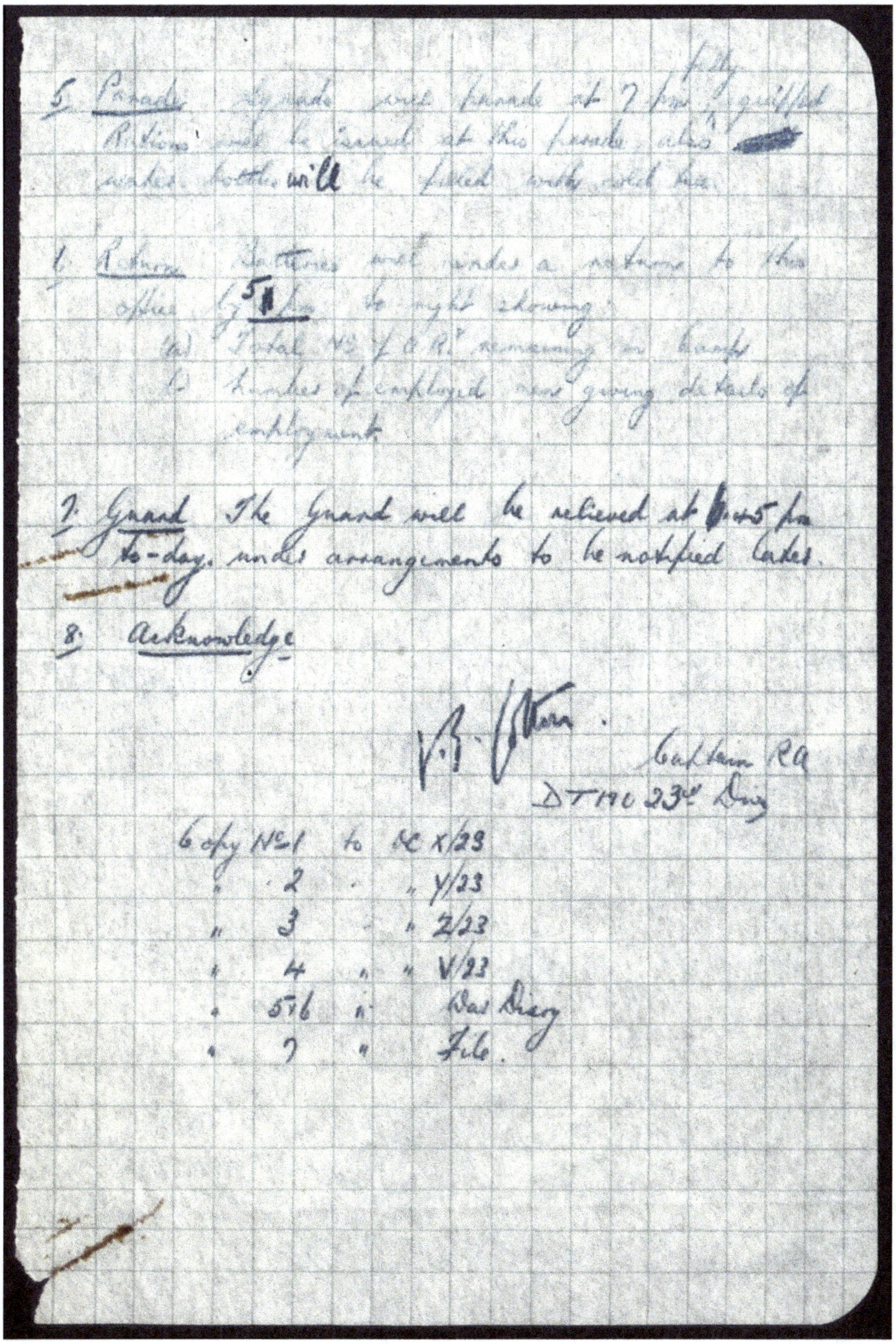

5. Parade. Squads will parade at 7 pm fully equipped. Rations will be issued at this parade, also water bottles will be filled with cold tea.

6. Return. Batteries will render a return to this office by 5 pm to-night showing:
   (a) Total No. of O.R. remaining in camp
   (b) Number of employed men giving details of employment.

7. Guard. The Guard will be relieved at [illegible]45 pm to-day, under arrangements to be notified later.

8. Acknowledge

[illegible signature]

Captain RA
DTMO 23rd Div

Copy No. 1 to OC X/23
" 2 " " Y/23
" 3 " " Z/23
" 4 " " V/23
" 5 & 6 " War Diary
" 7 " File.

Instructions regarding War Diaries and Intelligence Summaries are contained in F. S. Regs., Part II. and the Staff Manual respectively. Title pages will be prepared in manuscript.

WAR DIARY
or
~~INTELLIGENCE SUMMARY.~~
(Erase heading not required.)

Army Form C. 2118.

Place	Date	Hour	Summary of Events and Information	Remarks and references to Appendices
	1917 August			
	1 – 8		In training at LA WATINE.	
	9		Marched to EPERLECQUES AREA. Arrived at billets, MOULLE. 4.20pm.	
	10/23		Training	
	24		Moved to ABEELE AREA. Arrived in Billets 4.0p.m.	
	25		Moved by Bus to DICKEBUSH HUTS.	
	27		Moved to huts near DICKEBUSH	
	31		In huts.	

A Clarkson. Captain
O.C. 69th L.T.M. Battery.

Instructions regarding War Diaries and Intelligence Summaries are contained in F. S. Regs., Part II. and the Staff Manual respectively. Title pages will be prepared in manuscript.

23rd Divisional Trench Mortars.

WAR DIARY
or
~~INTELLIGENCE SUMMARY.~~
(Erase heading not required.)

Army Form C. 2118.

Vol 26

Place	Date 1917	Hour	Summary of Events and Information	Remarks and references to Appendices
Sheet 28. Belgium + France 1/40,000 N.2.b.4.8. HALLEBAST CORNER.	AUG 1.		Stretcher party from the line got back during the morning from 8 am to 1 pm. At 7.30 pm 3 Officers + 66 OR. went up by lorry to relieve stretcher bearers of 24th Div TMs. About 50 of this party where men who had only come down 6 hours before and were extremely exhausted. The remainder consisted of all employed men in camp including guard Officers servants cooks etc. Rained all day	Appendix A.
	2nd		Stretcher party relieved in the line at midday. Casualties 1 OR. gassed.	
	4th		1 Officer + 30 OR. stretcher bearing. Rained all day	
	5th		Stretcher bearers relieved by second party of same strength.	
	6th		All men down from the line.	
	9th		G.O.C.RA visited camp ~~[illegible]~~ and addressed the men on parade congratulating them on the work they had done during the past weeks.	
	13th		9 2inch T.M. taken over from 24th Div in camp in exchange for similar number stored in trench emplacements in HEDGE ST (E OF ZILLEBEKE). Disciplinary powers of Brigade commander + Company commander delegated by G.O.C.RA to DTMO. and battery commanders respectively. 1 Officer + 20 OR. assisted B/102 Bty in their wagon lines.	
	14th		4. 9.45 inch TM.s handed over to ~~[illegible]~~ V/18 T.M.Bty. 2/Lt Thomson admitted to hospital sick	

D. D. & L., London, E.C.
(A6839) Wt. W809/M1672 350,000 4/17 Sch 52a Forms/C/2118/14

23rd Divl Trench Mortars

SHEET. 2.

Army Form C. 2118.

Instructions regarding War Diaries and Intelligence Summaries are contained in F. S. Regs., Part II. and the Staff Manual respectively. Title pages will be prepared in manuscript.

WAR DIARY
or
~~INTELLIGENCE~~ ~~SUMMARY~~.
(Erase heading not required.)

Place	Date	Hour	Summary of Events and Information	Remarks and references to Appendices
	1917 Aug			
~~Ypres~~	15th		Moved to new camp at F24 a 5.5. Sheet 27 BELGIUM & FRANCE 1/40000. 8 lorries to transport personnel + equipment. In addition 20 men marched with No II Section 23rd D.A.C. to act as brakesmen. Move completed by 9 a.m. Batteries billeted in huts. Officers in bivouacks by D.A.C. lines	V.F.C.
Sheet 27 1/40000 F 24 a 5.5	16th		G.O.C. R.A. visited camp. Award of Military Medal to Grs Otty, Hill, McColl and Unsworth appeared in orders.	V.F.C.
	17th		Messing committee formed to supervise feeding of men in all four batteries	V.F.C.
	18th		D.T.M.O. accompanied 102 Brigade R.F.A. in reconnaissance of new Zone. G.O.C R.A. promised to consider the suggestion of attaching Officers to field batteries for instruction.	V.F.C.
	19th		Grs Fry and Curran tried by F.G.C.M.	V.F.C.
	21st		Lt Wise + 2/Lt Cheesman attached to 103 Bde R.F.A. temporarily for duty with field batteries	V.F.C.
	22nd		2/Lt Capey attached temporarily 103 Bde R.F.A. 2/Lt Thomson returned from hospital.	V.F.C.
	23rd		35 O.R. ranks posted to 102 Bde + 5 O.R. to 103 Bde for temporary duty in the line. Remaining men in camp formed into a composite battery for duties. Advanced signalling class formed.	V.F.C.
	24th		G.O.C.R.A. inspected camp.	V.F.C.
	26th		F.G.C.M. on Gr B. Curran promulgated. 2/Lt Moses went on leave. 2/Lt Wise admitted to hospital sick.	V.F.C.
	29th		G.O.C.R.A. visited camp. Duty men lent to neighbouring farmer for hop picking owing to damage to crop owing to recent gales.	V.F.C.

D. D. & L., London, E.C. (A7853) Wt W809/M1672 50,000 4/17 Sch. 52a Forms/C/2118/14

Instructions regarding War Diaries and Intelligence Summaries are contained in F. S. Regs., Part II. and the Staff Manual respectively. Title pages will be prepared in manuscript.

23rd Divl Trench Mortars

WAR DIARY
or
~~INTELLIGENCE~~ ~~SUMMARY~~.
(*Erase heading not required.*)

SHEET 3
Army Form C. 2118.

Place	Date	Hour	Summary of Events and Information	Remarks and references to Appendices
Sheet 27 1/40000 F24a.5.5.	30/8/17		Casualty - No 55970 Gr J. Redmond was killed by shell fire on 28/8/17 while attached to A/102 Bde RFA. Hop picking continued by duty men in Camp	AG
	31/8/17		Capt V.E. Cotton RFA D.T.M.O attached to H.Q.R.A. Capt A Goodfellow RFA V/23 HTMB takes over during his absence. Work continued at hop picking	AG

A Goodfellow Capt RFA
A/D.T.M.O 23rd RA

D. D. & L., London, E.C.
(A7883) Wt W809/M1672 50,000 4/17 Sch 52a Forms/C/2118/14

23rd Divl Trench Mortars

Vol 27

Army Form C. 2118.

Instructions regarding War Diaries and Intelligence Summaries are contained in F. S. Regs., Part II. and the Staff Manual respectively. Title pages will be prepared in manuscript.

WAR DIARY
or
~~INTELLIGENCE SUMMARY~~.

(*Erase heading not required.*)

Place	Date	Hour	Summary of Events and Information	Remarks and references to Appendices
Sheet 27 F24 a 5 5	1/9/17		Instruction in cable laying & repair by Sergt McGuire RA Signals and assistance given to neighbouring farmers – hop picking. All ORs bathed in the afternoon	A.G.
	2/9/17		General Cleaning up – Church parade at 10.30 am at Church Army Hut	A.G.
	3/9/17		40 ORs proceeded to the line to relieve T.M. personnel attached to Batteries. Lt A.D. Smith proceeded on leave to England.	
			2/Lt C.R. Cheesman & 2/Lt A.K. Carey returned from 103rd Brigade R.F.A.	A.G.
	4/9/17		D.T.M.O returned from attachment to R.A. H.Q.	J.G.
	5/9/17		Gnr McLean awarded 7 days F.P. No1 for overstaying leave.	J.G.
	6th		Lt Crehan & 6 OR. from 23rd D.A.C. left for course at 5th Army T.M. School. Subplatform for 6" Newton T.M. dug in for practice.	J.G.
Sheet 28. H34.a.	8th	9. am	~~9 am~~ Moved in 8 motor lorries to new camp near DICKEBUSCH, arriving about midday. ~~Ex~~ camping ground only no tents or shelters. Bivouac sheets & 4 tents drawn from Area Commandant also sandbags & timber from R.E. Park. T.M. Batteries & H.Q. RA only 23rd Divisional unit in forward area. Remainder of artillery round WESTOUTRE & infantry further back in rest billets	J.G.

A Goodfellow Capt R.F.A.
a/D.T.M.O 23rd R.A.

D. D. & L., London, E.C. (A7833) Wt W829/M1672 50,000 4/17 Sch. 52a Forms/C/2118/14

SHEET. 2.

23rd Divl Trench Mortars Army Form C. 2118.

WAR DIARY
or
~~INTELLIGENCE SUMMARY.~~

(Erase heading not required.)

Instructions regarding War Diaries and Intelligence Summaries are contained in F. S. Regs., Part II. and the Staff Manual respectively. Title pages will be prepared in manuscript.

Place	Date	Hour	Summary of Events and Information	Remarks and references to Appendices
Sheet 28 H34.a.	Sept 9th		D.T.M.O. arranged with RA 33rd Division to supply working party of 40 O.R. and 3 officers to work on new emplacements for 103 Bde RFA near MAPLE COPSE ZILLEBEKE. Daylight aeroplane raid round DICKEBUSH LAKE. Bombs just missed camp. One horse wounded severely.	R.C.
	10th		D.T.M.O. accompanied G.O.C RA at 5.30 to HOOGE and selected position for two 6" Newton Mortars at Stirling Castle. Camouflage secured also RE material and arrangements made for 3 ton lorry to be attached during period of getting up ammunition and working parties.	
		3.30am	Heavy Btty under Capt Goodfellow went up to dig 18 pdr emplacements as arranged.	R.C.
	11th		D.T.M.O. with Y & Z Batteries proceeded to Stirling Castle at 5.30 am to work on medium positions. Very good progress was made with the positions. X Battery under 2/Lt Capey was relieved from Capt Goodfellow's party at Maple Copse in order that they might assist at medium positions. Y & Z returned at 2.30 pm	A.G.
	12th		X Battery under 2/Lt Capey proceeded to medium positions at 5.30 am and remained until next morning. At 6.30 pm Y & Z.	

A Goodfellow Capt RFA
a/D.T.M.O. 23rd RA.

D. D. & L., London, E.C.
(A7551) Wt W809/M1672 350,000 4/17 Sch 52a Forms/C2118/14

Instructions regarding War Diaries and Intelligence Summaries are contained in F. S. Regs., Part II. and the Staff Manual respectively. Title pages will be prepared in manuscript.

WAR DIARY or ~~INTELLIGENCE SUMMARY.~~ 23rd Divl Trench Mortars

(Erase heading not required.)

Army Form C. 2118.

Sheet 3.

Place	Date	Hour	Summary of Events and Information	Remarks and references to Appendices
Sheet 28 H.34 a	12th contd		Batteries carried material to the positions. V Battery having completed field gun positions returned to Camp.	AG
	13th		X Battery returned to Camp at 9 pm. Z Battery & part of V Battery carried the 2-6" Mortars to the position. D.T.M.O visited the position at 10 am and found that good progress had been made, notwithstanding heavy shell fire. 2nd Lt E.R Chessman proceeded on leave.	AG
	14th		40. ORs V Battery proceeded to 103rd Bde to be attached 10 to each battery. Y Battery under 2/Lt Jackson (V Battery) proceeded to 6" position for work. One OR of Z battery wounded previous night. D.T.M.O. visited position in the afternoon. 2nd Lt W.K Moses returned from leave.	AG
	15th		X & Z Batteries carried ammunition to 6" positions, but only got 30 rounds up owing to heavy shell fire. One OR of X Battery wounded. 2nd Lt J.P Thomson returned from hospital and took charge of carrying party with 100 rds 6" ammunition	

A Goodfellow Capt RFA
A/D.T.M.O 23rd R.A

D. D. & L., London, E.C.
(A7883) Wt W809/M1672 50,000 4/17 Sch 52a Forms/C/2118/14

Instructions regarding War Diaries and Intelligence Summaries are contained in F. S. Regs., Part II, and the Staff Manual respectively. Title pages will be prepared in manuscript.

WAR DIARY 23rd Divl Trench Mortars
or
~~INTELLIGENCE SUMMARY.~~
(Erase heading not required.)

Army Form C. 2118.

Sheet 4

Place	Date	Hour	Summary of Events and Information	Remarks and references to Appendices
Sheet 28.	15th	Contd	& dumped there near Zillebeke	AG
H 34 a	16th		Y Battery relid with 2/Lt R Jackson at 6.30 am 1 Position completed & mortar mounted. Other positions well advanced but bed not up. X Battery with details from V & Z proceeded to the position to carry amm under 2/Lt W K Innes & 2/Lt A R Capey. Only 15 bombs were got up to position owing to very heavy shell fire. Lt A D Smith returned from leave.	AG
	17th		D.T.M.O visited position	AG
	18th		Y & Z Batteries & details of V Battery proceeded at 8 am to carry amm. & rations to position. 23 Rounds were got up. No 1 gun received direct hit destroying the gun and seriously damaging the position. Could get no other mortar in time to replace. 1 O.R. V Battery attached 103rd Bde wounded	AG.

A Goodfellow Capt R.F.A
A/D.T.M.O. 23rd R.A.

D. D. & L., London, E.C. (A7853) Wt W809/M1672 50,000 4/17 Sch. 52a Forms/C/2118/14

Instructions regarding War Diaries and Intelligence Summaries are contained in F. S. Regs., Part II. and the Staff Manual respectively. Title pages will be prepared in manuscript.

WAR DIARY or ~~INTELLIGENCE~~ SUMMARY. 23rd Divl Trench Mortars

(Erase heading not required.)

Army Form C. 2118.

Sheet 5

Place	Date	Hour	Summary of Events and Information	Remarks and references to Appendices
Sheet 28	19th		2/Lt W. K. Moses completed No 2 position & returned the ORs	
H 34 a			not required to fire the mortar. 10 ORs from DAC	
			reported at Camp to go to T.M. School. Orders with	
			Zero hour sent up to position to Lt Moses.	AG
	20th		At Zero the mortar only fired a few rounds when the	
			hook of elevating screw straightening out. Owing to time of	
			barrage being so short, it was impossible to repair in time	
			No casualties. Detachment returned to Camp. 20 ORs	
			from all batteries lent to ADMS to assist in stretcher work	AG
	21st		20 ORs all batteries relieved those lent to ADMS yesterday,	
			who had been working steadily for 24 hours.	AG
	22nd		20 ORs relieved ADMS party at 6 am. DTMO	
			proceeded to locate captured Bosche minnies. With the	
			G.O.C.R.A. got as far as Sanctuary Wood. Lively time.	AG
	23rd		Y & Z under Lt Smith salved the guns at Stirling Castle &	
			brought them to Jackdaw Dump.	AG

A Goodfellow Capt RFA
A/D.T.M.O. 23rd RA

D. D. & L., London, E.C. (A7853) Wt W829/M1672 50,000 4/17 Sch. 52a Forms/C/2118/14

Army Form C. 2118.

Instructions regarding War Diaries and Intelligence Summaries are contained in F. S. Regs., Part II. and the Staff Manual respectively. Title pages will be prepared in manuscript.

~~WAR DIARY~~ or INTELLIGENCE ~~SUMMARY~~. 23rd Divl Trench Mortars

(*Erase heading not required.*)

Sheet 6.

Place	Date	Hour	Summary of Events and Information	Remarks and references to Appendices
Sheet 28. H 34 a	24th		2nd Lt W K Moses with X Battery proceeded at 4 am to Jackdaw Dump with 4 GS wagons and brought the mortar ammn. back to Camp.	AG
	25th		Usual routine. Battery parades. ~~2nd~~ Lt W. H Graham returned from T M Course. 2nd Lt C R Chessman returned from leave.	AG
	26th		Usual parades. 10 OR ranks of X Battery attached to DAC.	AG
	27th		Usual routine Battery parades	AG
	28th		do. do	AG
	29th		do. do	AG
	30th		do do.	AG

A Goodfellow Capt RFA.
A D.T.M.O / 23rd R A.

D. D. & L., London, E.C. (A7883) Wt W809/M1672 350,000 4/17 Sch 52a Forms/C/2118/4

23rd Div Trench Mortars

Sheet 1

Vol 28

Army Form C. 2118.

Instructions regarding War Diaries and Intelligence Summaries are contained in F. S. Regs., Part II, and the Staff Manual respectively. Title pages will be prepared in manuscript.

WAR DIARY
or
~~INTELLIGENCE SUMMARY.~~
(*Erase heading not required.*)

Place	Date	Hour	Summary of Events and Information	Remarks and references to Appendices
Sheet 28	1/10/17		First of month finds us with D.T.M.O. on leave and 40 O.Rs attached	
H 34 a			to field batteries. Lt Curran Z Battery wounded. Lt Atkinson	
			V Battery accidentally injured in camp.	AG
	2/10/17		Lt [illegible] V/Battery wounded at [illegible] Farm. Capt	
			Waugh Z Battery [illegible] ([illegible]) [illegible] with D/103. Replaced	
			by Capt Pope V Battery	AG
	3/10/17		Nothing of incident. Usual parades in camp.	AG
	4/10/17		Usual parades & fatigues. Disposition of men is	
			as follows: In camp 44 (32 employed). Attached to F.A. Batteries	
			61, Leave 4. Hospital 3, On Course 1. Total 113 O.Rs	AG
	5/10/17		Nothing of incident. Usual parades & camp fatigues	AG
	6/10/17		10 O.Rs proceed for duty to D/103. This leaves a	
			total of 12 O.Rs in camp for all fatigues.	AG
	7/10/17		2 Lt Johnstone V Battery transferred to 9th [illegible]	
			as B.Q.M.S. Regret to lose the old man who was	
			in the Div. since formation in 1914.	AG

D. D. & L., London, E.C.
(A7853) Wt W809/M1672 50,000 4/17 Sch. 52a Forms/C/2118/14

23rd Mortars

Sheet 2

Army Form C. 2118.

Instructions regarding War Diaries and Intelligence Summaries are contained in F. S. Regs., Part II. and the Staff Manual respectively. Title pages will be prepared in manuscript.

WAR DIARY
or
~~INTELLIGENCE SUMMARY.~~

(Erase heading not required.)

Place	Date	Hour	Summary of Events and Information	Remarks and references to Appendices
Sheet 28	8th		Three officers detailed for duty in F.A. 2/Lt E.K. [illegible]	
H.24.a			to [illegible] – 2/Lt [illegible] to D/102. 2/Lt L. Jackson to	
			B/102. Fatigues in camp. 1 OR went on leave.	AG
	9th		Capt [illegible] V. Bacon gassed (slight) at D/103 and	
			sent to CCS. Fatigues in camp.	AG
	10th		Capt. [illegible] returned from leave [illegible] at once	
			to H.Q. L.A. to act as S.C. in the absence of Capt	
			Matthews. A.G. therefore continues in his [illegible]	
			position meantime. Camp fatigues.	AG
	11th		8 ORs attached to A/103 returned for 48 hours rest.	
			Usual camp fatigues.	AG
	12th		17 ORs returned from D/102 for rest. Nothing else	
			of importance occurred. Usual camp fatigues.	AG
	13th		Lt. [illegible] was attached to C/103. 2/Lt [illegible] to B/103	
			2/Lt L. Jackson returned for 24 hrs rest from B/102.	
			Usual parades & camp fatigues.	AG.

D. D. & L., London, E.C.
(A7883) Wt W809/M1672 350,000 4/17 Sch 52a Forms/C/2118/14

23rd Mortars

Army Form C. 2118.

WAR DIARY
or
~~INTELLIGENCE SUMMARY.~~
(Erase heading not required.)

Sheet 3

Instructions regarding War Diaries and Intelligence Summaries are contained in F. S. Regs., Part II, and the Staff Manual respectively. Title pages will be prepared in manuscript.

Place	Date	Hour	Summary of Events and Information	Remarks and references to Appendices
Sheet 28	14th		Cpl [illegible] wounded & [illegible] accidentally injured	
H 4 a			Lt A D Smith takes over [illegible] 2nd Lt Thompson [illegible] 10 [illegible]	
			attached [illegible] from TM School 10 OKs [illegible] X	
			returned from Camp [illegible] usual [illegible] fatigues	AG
	15th		Heavily [illegible] during the night. Nothing else of	
			importance. Usual parades & fatigues	AG
	16th		Parades as usual. Commencing [illegible] round	
			horses to prevent casualties from bomb splinters	AG
	17th		Parades as usual. Work on horse lines continued	
			10 OKs who were at TM school returned to DAC	AG
			Cpl Goodfellow returned	
	18th		2/Lt Thompson attached B/102. Some bombs fell	
			near Camp in the evening. Usual fatigues	AG
	19th		Nothing of importance	
	20th		Lt Cochran admitted to Hospital - gassed (slight). A band	
			which apparently was chosen from H Q reflects some [illegible]	
			[illegible] on us	AG

D. D. & L., London, E.C. (A7583) Wt W839/M1672 50,000 4/17 Sch 52a Forms/C/2118/14

23rd Mortars

Army Form C. 2118.

Sheet 4

Instructions regarding War Diaries and Intelligence Summaries are contained in F. S. Regs., Part II. and the Staff Manual respectively. Title pages will be prepared in manuscript.

WAR DIARY
or
~~INTELLIGENCE~~ SUMMARY.

(Erase heading not required.)

Place	Date	Hour	Summary of Events and Information	Remarks and references to Appendices
Sheet 28	21st		O.R.s returned from D/103. Also D/102. Usual	
H 33 a			parades & fatigues	AG
	22nd		Usual parades & fatigues. 15 O.R. loaned to D/102	
			to wash wagons. A/103 Wagon line was badly	
			bombed	AG
	23rd		Usual parades & fatigues in the morning.	AG
			Afternoon all available men went to A/103 who had	
			suffered heavy casualties	AG
	24th		Capt. [illegible] & Thompson returned to Camp. Fatigues	
			at A/103 & D/102	AG
	25th		Camp moved to Westoutre. Small [illegible] and	
			[illegible] as found. All O.R.s [illegible] returned	AG
Westoutre	26th		All ranks visited baths at [illegible] at 9 a.m.	
			clean change all round. Battery parades	AG
			[illegible] Jackson promoted [illegible]	

A6945 Wt. W11422/M1160 350,000 12/16 D. D. & L. Forms/C./2118/14.

23rd Division — Army Form C. 2118.

Sheet 5

Instructions regarding War Diaries and Intelligence Summaries are contained in F. S. Regs., Part II. and the Staff Manual respectively. Title pages will be prepared in manuscript.

WAR DIARY
or
~~INTELLIGENCE SUMMARY.~~
(Erase heading not required.)

Place	Date	Hour	Summary of Events and Information	Remarks and references to Appendices
Westoutre	27th	–	Battery parades – Inspection of personnel & Camp by A/D T M O	AG
	28th		[illegible] one week new [illegible], [illegible] & [illegible]. All ranks received from leave	AG
	29th		V/23 H T M B marched by order. Usual parades	AG
	30th		Capt Goodfellow appears to be transferred to another Bde. Heavy battery being made up to strength and remainder (82 ORs) will proceed to 102nd & 103rd Bdes on 2nd prox.	AG
	31st		Battery parades & fatigues	AG

A Goodfellow Capt RFA
A/D T M O 23rd D A

23RD DIVISION
DIVL ARTILLERY

23RD DIVL AMMN COLUMN

AUG 1915 - ~~FEB 1919~~ 1917 OCT

TO ITALY

23rd Division

121/7051

23rd Divl. A.C.

Vol I

Aug & Sept. 15

to

Feb '19

Army Form C. 2118.

WAR DIARY
or
INTELLIGENCE SUMMARY.
(*Erase heading not required.*)

Instructions regarding War Diaries and Intelligence Summaries are contained in F. S. Regs., Part II. and the Staff Manual respectively. Title pages will be prepared in manuscript.

Place	Date 1915 August	Hour	Summary of Events and Information	Remarks and references to Appendices
Bordon	20	4.30 pm	Received Orders to prepare for abroad. All Officers, N.C.O.s + Men recalled from leave.	EH
"	21		Drawing Stores + Mobilizing.	EH
"	22		Mobilization continued	EH
"	23		Mobilization completed. Awaiting final orders.	EH
"	24		Orders not yet received. Draft of 20 Gunners + 10 Drivers arrived from Preston. Lt R. S. Lippert joined to command No 1 Section.	EH
"	25		Final Orders received to proceed overseas. Draft of N.C.O.s arrived from Ballincollig.	EH
"	26	9 pm	Eight trains in detail for 23rd D.A.C. Commenced entraining about 9 p.m, remaining trains leaving at intervals of about 2 hours.	EH
"	27	8.30 am	Last train departed about 8.30 a.m.	
Southampton		10.30	Last train arrived about 10.30 a.m. Veterinary inspection of all animals as trains arrived. A few animals changed.	EH

2353 Wt. W2544/1454 700,000 5/15 D. D. & L. A.D.S.S./Forms/C. 2118.

Instructions regarding War Diaries and Intelligence Summaries are contained in F. S. Regs., Part II. and the Staff Manual respectively. Title pages will be prepared in manuscript.

WAR DIARY
or
INTELLIGENCE SUMMARY.
(Erase heading not required.)

Army Form C. 2118.

Place	Date	Hour	Summary of Events and Information	Remarks and references to Appendices
	August 1915		Embarkation commenced at about 12 noon. Three vessels the	
Southampton	27	12 noon	Maiden, Viper, & Westan Miller	EH
		3.55 pm	First Boat The Maiden sailed about 3.55 p.m	
Havre (Fine)	28	7 a.m	Commenced disembarkation	
		3 p.m	No 1 Section entrained for Audruicq 5 trains allotted for the whole column leaving at intervals of 4½ to 5 hours.	EH
In train (Fine)	29		En Route. Last train left Havre about Midday	EH
Audruicq (Showy)	30	7 a.m	Last train arrived; detrained at once and marched to the various Billets allotted – Headquarters at Chateau Behagle No 1 Section at La Recousse. No 2 + 3 Sections at Zouafques. Farmhouses being occupied as quarters, the Barns being used by the N.C.O's + Men, the animals being picquetted out + all Vehicles parked closed to the Hedges in the Field adjoining.	EH
Zouafques (Wet)	31	6 a.m	Party of 1 Officer + 18 men left to draw Ammunition from Railhead being conveyed to Sub Park by D A C Wagons + from there proceeded in Sub Park Motor Lorries.	
		1.30 pm	Party arrived with 4.5" Howitzer H.E.	EH

2353 Wt. W2544/1454 700,000 5/15 D. D. & L. A.D.S.S./Forms/C. 2118.

Army Form C. 2118.

Instructions regarding War Diaries and Intelligence Summaries are contained in F. S. Regs., Part II. and the Staff Manual respectively. Title pages will be prepared in manuscript.

WAR DIARY
or
INTELLIGENCE SUMMARY.
(Erase heading not required.)

Place	Date	Hour	Summary of Events and Information	Remarks and references to Appendices
Zouafques	1915 Sept 1st		The day spent in overhauling equipment, harness etc	
(Cloudy)		10 a.m.	Telephone connected with H.Q. R.A. 23rd Division.	EH.
"	2nd	9 a.m.	Route March of Section	
(Dull)		11 a.m.	" " "	
		2 p.m.	" " "	EH
"	3rd		Orders received to exchange H.E. 4.5 for Shrapnell 4.5	
(Rain)				EH.
"	4th	11 a.m.	Exchanged Ammunition as above with A + C Batteries 105th Brigade.	
(Still wet)		4 p.m.		EH.
		4.30 pm	Received instructions to be prepared to move shortly	
" (Dull)	5th		Completed the exchange of Ammunition with 105th Brigade	
		12 noon	Received Orders re March of following day	EH
" (Fine)	6th	8.30 a.m.	Commenced the March to Renescure via Houle Tilques (where we watered + fed) skirting St Omer; camped at Renescure for the night	EH
		5 p.m.	Arrived at Renescure	
Renescure	7th	10 a.m.	Route March to La Tir Anglais, via Sercus, Hazebrouck.	
(Fine)		5 p.m.	Reached La Tir Anglais + encamped for the night.	EH
La Tir Anglais	8th		Sections placed under Section Commanders for the day.	
(Fine)		12 noon	Telephone connected up	EH.
"	9th	6 a.m.	Lieut. Gaskell left with 3 G.S. Wagons of 4.5" Lyddite to join No 1 Section 20th D.A.C.	
(Fine)			to supply C/105th with Ammunition, at NEUF BERQUIN - ESTAIRES road.	EH.
"	10th	9 a.m.	Route March (practice) under O.C.	
(Fine)				EH.

Army Form C. 2118.

Instructions regarding War Diaries and Intelligence Summaries are contained in F. S. Regs., Part II. and the Staff Manual respectively. Title pages will be prepared in manuscript.

WAR DIARY
or
INTELLIGENCE SUMMARY.
(Erase heading not required.)

Place	Date 1915	Hour	Summary of Events and Information	Remarks and references to Appendices
Le Tir Anglais (Fine)	Sept 11th	8.30am	Another Practice Route March under O.C.	EH.
		10a.m.	Changed Ammunition (H.E for Shrapnell) for 104th Brigade	
" (Fine)	12th	9a.m.	Inspection by G.O.C. R.A. 23rd Division	EH.
			A quantity of 18 Pdr. Q.F. H.E tested and a report sent in that no fuzes could be set between 0 + 2 by hand.	
" (Fine)	13th	9a.m.	Retested the above fuzes with key fuze setting, borrowed from 103rd Bde Am Col. Two fuzes found defective, that is, could be set between 0 + 2, a report sent to H.Q. R.A. accordingly	EH
		2p.m.	Some 18 pdr. Ammunition which had got wet previously, was sent in to the Railhead at St Venant, which was replaced by new.	EH
" (Fine)	14th	5a.m.	D.A.C. parade to march to Froid Nid (Sheet Map 36 N.W.) A27.d.8.6	
Vieux Berquin	"	7.20a.m.	102nd 103rd + 104th Brigade Ammunition Columns joined the March	
Froid Nid (Fine)	"	10.30 a.m.	Arrived, found 27th D.A.C. still in occupation of our new Billets. Parked all the wagons under a long line of trees until	
		1.30 p.m.	Sections detailed to their Billets (Farms)	
		3.30pm	Orderlies sent to 102nd 103rd + 104th Bde Am. Cols for communication purposes	EH
Froid Nid (Fine)	15th		Order received that no 18 Pdr H.E. to be issued until further orders	
			Ammunition supplied to 19th Bde. Am. Col.	EH
" (Fine)	16th	10a.m.	Ammunition supplied to 103rd Brigade. Telephone connected to H.Q. 23rd Division	
		1p.m.	Two wagons under an Officer sent to Bethune to fetch bombs + deliver same to Bomb store. Out all night + returned at —	EH.

2353 Wt. W2544/1454 700,000 5/15 D. D. & L. A.D.S.S./Forms/C. 2118.

Army Form C. 2118.

Instructions regarding War Diaries and Intelligence Summaries are contained in F. S. Regs., Part II. and the Staff Manual respectively. Title pages will be prepared in manuscript.

WAR DIARY
or
INTELLIGENCE SUMMARY.
(Erase heading not required.)

Place	Date 1915	Hour	Summary of Events and Information	Remarks and references to Appendices
Froid Nid (Fine)	Sept. 17th	8.45 am		
		9 a.m	200 Grenades drawn from Railhead, St Venant and taken to Bomb Store.	
		2 p.m	500 Grenades taken to Bomb Store. Difficulty in getting Amtn from Sub Park	EH.
" (Fine)	18th		1500 Rds of Reserve 18 Pdr Q.F Amtn received from Sub Park	
		9 a.m	Amtn issued to 105th Bde Amtn Column	
		10 a.m	18 Pdr Q.F. H.E received from 102nd Brigade Am. Col.	
		1.45 p.m	Lt Cornwall with nine wagons sent to Railhead St Venant to draw 800 Grenades + to deliver same to Bomb Store	
		6 p.m	18 Pdr Q.F. H.E received from 103rd Bde Am. Col. 1200 rounds of reserve 18 Pdr Q F Amtn received from Sub Park	
		11 p.m.	Report rendered to G.O.C.R.A. that establishment of Amtn could not be got.	
" (Fine)	19th	8.30 a.m	O.C. + Adjt reported as ordered at H.Q. R.A. 23rd Div. re Expenditure of Amtn. Composite Section ordered to be formed for attachment to 8th D.A.C. for supply of Amtn to 103rd + 105th who also are attached to the 8th Div.	EH
		2 p.m	Final Orders re Composite Section received. Section formed, + made up to War Estab in Amtn. No 2 Section now reduced to S.A.A + Nos. 1 + 3 Sections left with only 18 Pdr. + S.A.A	
			During the day a fairly large amount of Amtn issued to Batteries	
		9.30 p.m	Arrival of large consignment of S.A.A. + 18 Pdr. Amtn to form a Park Dump Lt. Col. R. C Drury R.F.A appointed O.C. Refilling Point in addition to his other duties	EH.

2353 Wt. W2544/1454 700,000 5/15 D. D. & L. A.D.S.S./Forms/C. 2118.

Army Form C. 2118.

Instructions regarding War Diaries and Intelligence Summaries are contained in F. S. Regs., Part II. and the Staff Manual respectively. Title pages will be prepared in manuscript.

WAR DIARY
or
INTELLIGENCE SUMMARY.
(Erase heading not required.)

Place	Date	Hour	Summary of Events and Information	Remarks and references to Appendices
Froid Nid (Fine)	1915 Sept 20th		A very heavy day of Amtn receipts + issues	
		5 p.m	The Composite Section moved off to be attached in all respects under the Command of 8th D A C	EH
" (Fine)	21st		A very heavy day of Amtn supply both in and out.	
		11.16 p.m	Ordered not to draw any more Gun Ammunition until further orders received, nor to draw from Park Dump without first wiring H.Q. R.A 23rd Division	EH
" (Fine)	22nd	11a.m	A large consignment of 18 pdr Shrapnell issued to 104th Brigade	EH.

2353 Wt. W2544/1454 700,000 5/15 D. D. & L. A.D.S.S./Forms/C 2118.

Army Form C. 2118.

Instructions regarding War Diaries and Intelligence Summaries are contained in F. S. Regs., Part II. and the Staff Manual respectively. Title pages will be prepared in manuscript.

WAR DIARY
or
INTELLIGENCE SUMMARY.
(Erase heading not required.)

Place	Date	Hour	Summary of Events and Information	Remarks and references to Appendices
	1915 Sept			
Frezenberg (Fine during day – Thunderstorm)	23	4 30pm	Accident to a mule of No 3 Section on the road by its swerving on to an iron shod shaft of a civilian vehicle which entered the lung. Animal shot	
		5pm		EH
" (Damp Dull Dark night)	24		During the day a large amount of Ammunition received + sent to Bdes a first consignment of [illegible] Ammunition arrived. Three horses + 15 mules arrived Ammunition (Urgent) also arrived during the night.	
" (Wet dark night)	25	Early Morning	A mule of No 3 Section died from ruptured stomach. A good deal of Gun Ammunition in + out to 102nd Brigade + S.A.A in + out to 103 + 104 Bdes.	EH
" (Dull All day)	26	10am	A Subsection returned from Composite Section to No 2 Section. A very quiet day, until evening	EH
		9 45pm	Orders received to detach S.A.A. Section of No 1 Section for duty with 20th D.A.C. to supply 68th Bde	
		11.15pm	Detachment moved off	EH
" (Dull with slight showers during evening)	27		Another quiet day. About 1000 rounds of 18 Pdr withdrawn from 102nd Bde Am Colm.	
		8pm	Lt. Col. R. C. Drury R.F.A received notification of relief by Lt. Col. C.V.B. Kuper R.F.A Nine men inoculated by the M.O. during the day (First injection) Total [illegible] done in the Column 97%. EH	In future [illegible] will be [illegible] as follows:- 18 Pdr Shrap = A 18 Pdr H.E. = AX 4.5 Shrap = B 4.5 H.E. = BX
" (Dull + Heavy)	28		Quiet day. ~~[illegible]~~ Received instructions to rearrange Park Dump by increasing its strength by one quarter of 18 Pdr + 4.5 Amtn. Orders received + acted on that detachment of 20th D.A.C were to return	
		9 45pm	Have not yet arrived	EH

2353 Wt. W2544/1454 700,000 5/15 D. D. & L. A.D.S.S./Forms/C. 2118.

Army Form C. 2118.

Instructions regarding War Diaries and Intelligence Summaries are contained in F. S. Regs., Part II. and the Staff Manual respectively. Title pages will be prepared in manuscript.

WAR DIARY
or
INTELLIGENCE SUMMARY.

(Erase heading not required.)

Place	Date 1915	Hour	Summary of Events and Information	Remarks and references to Appendices
Froid Nid. (Wet)	Sept. 29.	12.30 a.m	Detachment from 20th D.A.C arrived.	3rd Corps No. A/6602/15
		9 a.m	Letter sent to 23rd Divl. Train asking them to test Motor Drivers + Mechanics with a view to transfer.	
		8 a.m	Composite Section arrived from 8th D.A.C. Sections reformed as originally Nos 1. 2 + 3. All surplus ammunition brought in to H.Q. by Sections this surplus was returned by Brigade Amn Columns. Orders received to send same to 23rd Sub Park.	EH
Froid Nid (Wet all Day)	30th		A quiet day	
		11 a.m	Lorries arrived to remove Ammunition as arranged 29.9.15.	
			Morning Order issued for all letters + Numerals which indicate formations to be at once obliterated and a red circle 10" in Diameter to be painted on both sides of each vehicle instead.	EH

23rd Division

121
7595.

23rd Divl: A.C.
Vol 2

Oct 15

Instructions regarding War Diaries and Intelligence Summaries are contained in F. S. Regs., Part II. and the Staff Manual respectively. Title pages will be prepared in manuscript.

WAR DIARY
or
INTELLIGENCE SUMMARY.
(Erase heading not required.)

Army Form C. 2118.

Place	Date 1915	Hour	Summary of Events and Information	Remarks and references to Appendices
Froid Nid (Dry but very cold)	Octr 1st		Nearly 5000 empty Cartridges cases sent to Railhead also a large consignment of ·303 Amtn which was picked up in the Trenches. Otherwise the day very quiet.	EH
Froid Nid (Fine)	2nd		A very heavy day of fatigues for the C R E 23rd Div. at ARMENTIERS. Lt. Col C V B Kuper R. F. A. was met by the Adjt at H.Q. R. A. CROIS DU BAC.	
		11a.m.	Lt Col. C. V. B. Kuper arrived & assumed Command of the D. A. C. No Orders received with regard to Lt Col. R. C. Drury. Three wagons sent to be attached to 23rd Salvage Corps for Fatigue work.	EH.
Froid Nid (Fine)	3rd	10a.m.	Church Parade taken by the Chaplain.	
		10.30a.m.	Orders received for Lt. Col. R. C. Drury to proceed to England and to report in writing to the War Office for instructions. (Hqrs 1st Army "A" A. Q's No D/609)	
		3.20p.m.	Departure of Lt Col. R. C. Drury from Steenwerck Station.	
		5p.m.	Visited by Lt Col commanding 3rd Corps Park who talked over positions of Park Dump etc with reference to convenience of motor lorry traffic. He promised to try & secure some covers for the Park Dump ammunition.	EH.
Froid Nid (Dull with showers)	4th		A very quiet day Adjutant sent for by A. P. M. with reference to two mules left behind at Renescure – Satisfactory reply given to A.P.M.	EH.
Froid Nid (Rain)	5th		Application made for S. Smith Greenleaf to be transferred to R. F. A. from A.S.C.	
		10a.m.	Lt. Col Kuper had all Officers N. C. O's & Men paraded (Taking over parade) & spoke to all ranks particularly on Discipline. Tarpaulins for Amtn Dump received.	EH.

2353 Wt. W2544/1454 700,000 5/15 D. D. & L. A.D.S.S./Forms/C. 2118.

Army Form C. 2118.

Instructions regarding War Diaries and Intelligence Summaries are contained in F. S. Regs., Part II. and the Staff Manual respectively. Title pages will be prepared in manuscript.

WAR DIARY
or
INTELLIGENCE SUMMARY.
(Erase heading not required.)

Place	Date	Hour	Summary of Events and Information	Remarks and references to Appendices
	1915 Octr.			
Froid Nid (Morning Dry but cloudy Afternoon Fine)	6th		Very quiet day. 200 men proceeded to the Divisional Baths.	
		10a.m	Interpreter arrived on posting to 23rd D.A.C.	
		5p.m.	30 men under an Officer sent to Steenwerck Railway Station for Horses + Mules.	EH.
Froid Nid (Fine)	7th.	1a.m	Arrival of 3 chargers 4 Riding Horses + 23 Mules	
		9a.m	Two wagons without teams lent to 103rd Brigade	
			Commenced Horse Standings for Hdqrs preparatory to removal to an Adjacent compound.	EH.
Froid Nid (Fine)	8th		Another very quiet day. O.C. visited G.O.C.R.A. to discuss various things in connection with the Column.	EH.
Froid Nid (Fine)	9th		Quiet day.	
		3p.m.	G.O.C.R.A. 23rd Division inspected the D.A.C. He appeared quite satisfied.	EH.
Froid Nid (Fine)	10th	10a.m	Divine Service. Received intimation we were getting shelters for the Troops. Official intimation of appointment of Lt. C. Hiscock as Adjutant to the 23rd D.A.C. with effect from 20.8.15. Published in R.A. Routine Orders. No 25 para 100 dated 10-10-15.	EH.

2353 Wt. W2544/1454 700,000 5/15 D. D. & L. A.D.S.S./Forms/C. 2118.

Instructions regarding War Diaries and Intelligence Summaries are contained in F. S. Regs., Part II. and the Staff Manual respectively. Title pages will be prepared in manuscript.

WAR DIARY
or
INTELLIGENCE SUMMARY.
(Erase heading not required.)

Army Form C. 2118.

Place	Date 1915	Hour	Summary of Events and Information	Remarks and references to Appendices
Froid Nid (Dull)	Octr 11th		A quiet morning	
		2 pm	Visited by G. O. C. 23rd Division fairly satisfactory with exception of No 1 Section. Sent for 18 Shelters for the men	EH.
Froid Nid (Fine)	12th		200 men to the Divisional Baths during the day	
		10 a m	Board of Officers assembled to examine six men for Cold Shoers	EH.
Froid Nid (Fine)	13th		The wearing of ~~flax~~ cotton shirts is now prohibited as the weather is setting in cold. Notification received of Divisional Boot shop for Repairs at Steenwerck being opened. Bricks for standings to be drawn from Armentières Station on receipt of Authority from C. R. E. A return rendered shewing Number of Bricks required.	EH.
Froid Nid (Fine)	14th	9 a.m	Four Gunners sent to each Brigade to be attached for training in the Firing Line & four Gunners sent back on loan to replace.	EH.
Froid Nid (Fine)	15th		Canteen for the D. A. C. opened for the sale of Beer only.	
		11.30	Draft of 12 men arrived from the Base & posted to the various Sections as required.	EH.
Froid Nid (Fine)	16th	~~[illegible]~~	~~[illegible]~~ Three Shoeing Smiths + 1 Driver arrived as a Draft. Two Shoeing Smiths to D. A. C. only S. S. Cpl + 1 Driver for Brigades. These to be sent off next day. 2/Lt A. Windsor assumed Command No 1 Section vice Lt. Lippett posted to No 3 Section as Subaltern.	EH.

2353 Wt. W2544/1454 700,000 5/15 D. D. & L. A.D.S.S./Forms/C. 2118.

Instructions regarding War Diaries and Intelligence Summaries are contained in F. S. Regs., Part II. and the Staff Manual respectively. Title pages will be prepared in manuscript.

WAR DIARY
or
INTELLIGENCE SUMMARY.
(Erase heading not required.)

Army Form C. 2118.

Place	Date 1915	Hour	Summary of Events and Information	Remarks and references to Appendices
Froid Nid (Fine)	Oct. 17th	9.30	Church Parade.	
		2 p.m	Three men recently arrived from Base left for Steenwerck Railhead en route for England on 7 day leave.	EH.
Froid Nid. (Fine)	18th		During the course of the day 200 men sent to the Divisional Baths. 24th Inf. Brigade arrived + attached to 23rd Division therefore notification sent to them shewing D.A.C position on Reference Map.	
		8 p.m.	Letter received stating the Park Dump should be returned to Railhead	EH.
Froid Nid. (Fine)	19th	11 a.m	Lorries arrived + commenced moving the Dump.	
		6 p.m	Second Consignment of Lorries arrived filled up with Ammunition + departed.	EH
Froid Nid (Fine)	20th	9.30.	Lorries to take remainder of dump arrived. All dump Ammunition + Empties clear of D.A.C. Small party inoculated against Enteric Fever.	EH.
Froid Nid (Fine but Cloudy)	21st		A very quiet day. Practically nothing doing all day.	
		10.30	Rain Commenced to fall.	EH.
Froid Nid (Dull)	22nd	9 a.m	Parade of 1 N.C.O + four men per Section with Utensils for Wood Cutting at LA MOTTE. All Brigades found a similar number – the whole rendezvoused at H.Q. 23rd D.A.C. + were handed over to Lt Powell of 103rd Brigade R.F.A. The [illegible] is for Horse Shelters &c.	EH.

Instructions regarding War Diaries and Intelligence Summaries are contained in F. S. Regs., Part II. and the Staff Manual respectively. Title pages will be prepared in manuscript.

WAR DIARY
or
INTELLIGENCE SUMMARY.
(Erase heading not required.)

Army Form C. 2118.

Place	Date 1915	Hour	Summary of Events and Information	Remarks and references to Appendices
Froid Nid (Dull Cold)	Oct 22nd	11.0 a.m.	Draft of four Drivers + 1 Bombr. arrived from the Base. These were posted to the various sections. 100 Bombs drawn from Bomb School and delivered to 21st Trench Mortar Battery. Cottage opposite No 2 Section Field placed out of Bounds on account of illness therein.	EH.
Froid Nid (Fine but misty)	23rd		1 Bombr + four drivers posted to Brigades. Order published forbidding the leakage of information. Transport Fatigues started for bringing in the wood from NIEPPE Forest; this to be continued daily. B.Q.M.S. Swan recommended for a Commission	EH.
Froid Nid (Cold turning to rain)	24th	noon	Divine Service. B.Q.M.S. Swan interviewed by G.O.C.R.A. Interview satisfactory. Very quiet day with the exception of Fatigues which were very heavy.	EH.
Froid Nid. (Very wet all day + windy)	25th		Woollen underclothing taken into wear. Exceptionally quiet day with Fatigues more or less normal.	EH.
Froid Nid. (Bright Day little rain night)	26th		Very quiet day except for heavy Fatigues.	EH.
Froid Nid (Wet)	27th		20 Smoke Helmets drawn for Drill purposes which is being carried out by Sections on alternate weeks. Arrangements made for promotion of N.C.O's. To Sergeant within Brigades. To Staff Sergts + W.O. class II by H.Q. R.A. To W.O. Class I by Records. Sgt Price A.V.C. posted to 35 Mobile Vety. Section + relieved by Sgt. Dunbar A.V.C.	EH.

2353 Wt. W2544/1454 700,000 5/15 D. D. & L. A.D.S.S./Forms/C. 2118.

Army Form C. 2118.

Instructions regarding War Diaries and Intelligence Summaries are contained in F. S. Regs., Part II. and the Staff Manual respectively. Title pages will be prepared in manuscript.

WAR DIARY
or
INTELLIGENCE SUMMARY.

(Erase heading not required.)

Place	Date 1915	Hour	Summary of Events and Information	Remarks and references to Appendices
Froid Nid (Rain all day)	Octr 28th		Intimation received Driver Cuffley under age. At own request was sent to England.	
		2.31pm	Left for Skinnock Railhead en route	
			Letter written to Y.M.C.A. asking if possible for the erection of a large tent or hut or Marquee for Recreation purposes for the winter	
		7pm	Lt Rhodes arrived on posting to the D.A.C.	EH.
Froid Nid (Dull)	29th		Expeditionary Force Canteen Bailleul approached re the supply of Dry Goods for 23rd D.A.C. Canteen. Quiet day except for Fatigues.	EH.
Froid Nid (Dull)	30th		Normal quantity of Ammunition received + issued. Lt. Rhodes posted to No 3 Section. Usual Fatigues.	
Froid Nid (Rain)	31st	noon	Divine Service.	EH.
		1pm	Dry Canteen opened in connection with wet Canteen Q/Mr placed in charge with two assistants. A day of extremely heavy Fatigues	EH.

2353 Wt. W2544/1454 700,000 5/15 D. D. & L. A.D.S.S./Forms/C. 2118.

HEADQUARTERS
23rd DIVISIONAL AMMUNITION COLUMN
No.
Date

23rd Division

23rd Divl: Ac.
Vol: 3

121
7656

Nov 15

HEADQUARTERS
23rd DIVISIONAL AMMUNITION COLUMN
No.
Date

Instructions regarding War Diaries and Intelligence Summaries are contained in F. S. Regs., Part II. and the Staff Manual respectively. Title pages will be prepared in manuscript.

WAR DIARY
or
INTELLIGENCE SUMMARY.

(Erase heading not required.)

Army Form C. 2118.

Place	Date 1915	Hour	Summary of Events and Information	Remarks and references to Appendices
Froid Nid (Rain all day)	NOV. 1st	12 p.m	The Adjutant Lt E. Hiscock R.F.A. admitted to Convalescent Depôt Steenwerck, Fever and Bad arm, result of Anti-Titanic Serum Injection. Lt F. G. Squire R.F.A. deputed to carry out duties of Adjutant during his absence.	
			Quiet day. Normal receipt + issue of Ammunition.	EH
Froid Nid (Dull)	2nd	9 a.m	Draft of 32 men arrived from the Base + posted to Sections.	
			200 men proceeded to the Divisional Baths during the day.	
		noon	7 wagons detailed to proceed to Bomb School and convey Bombs to the 69th Brigade. Arrangements made for Hot Coffee late at night + early morning for men on Fatigues. Two men struck off the strength on evacuation. usual Fatigues.	EH
Froid Nid (Wet)	3rd	8 a.m	Additional wagons sent for conveyance of Bombs as above.	
			7 Gunners + 21 Drivers posted to Brigades.	
			Very heavy Fatigues including delivery of Shells to Durham Howitzer Brigade.	
		8 p.m	Two Officers (Lts. Campbell + Brock) arrived from the Base.	
		8.35 p.m	Warrant + Special leave arrived for Lt. Lippert - urgent private affairs.	EH
Froid Nid (Fine)	4th	4.30 a.m	Lt. Lippert departed on 7 days leave to England	
		11.30 a.m	Remounts fetched from Railhead.	
		1.45 p.m	Lts. Brock + Campbell reported to G.O.C.R.A. on arrival. Animals for racking paraded at Croix du Bac.	
			Case diagnosed as measles sent to Hospital. Certain men (contacts) therefore isolated for all purposes. Normal receipts + issue of ammunition also Fatigues.	EH.

2353 Wt. W2544/1454 700,000 5/15 D. D. & L. A.D.S.S./Forms/C. 2118.

Instructions regarding War Diaries and Intelligence Summaries are contained in F. S. Regs., Part II. and the Staff Manual respectively. Title pages will be prepared in manuscript.

WAR DIARY
or
INTELLIGENCE SUMMARY.

(Erase heading not required.)

Army Form C. 2118.

Place	Date 1915	Hour	Summary of Events and Information	Remarks and references to Appendices
Froid Nid (Fine)	Nov 5th		Lt R. S. de S Brock posted to No 1 Section Lt L S Campbell posted to No 2 Section 1 Horse + 17 mules taken on the strength + distributed to Sections.	EH.
Froid Nid (Fine)	6th	10 a m	Lieut A Goodfellow (No 2 Section) 2nd Lieut E L Bowley (No 1 Section) departed on posting to 103rd + 104th Brigades respectively.	
		Noon	Two field forges received + issued one to No 1 Section for their own + Hdqrs use the other to No 2 Section for theirs + No 3 Sections use. Rather heavy Fatigues Normal ammunition receipts + issues.	EH
Froid Nid (Fine)	7th		1 Bdr + 6 Drivers struck off the strength on evacuation out of the Divisional Area	
		Noon	Divine Service – Capt Birch O.C No 3 Section admitted to Hospital Light Fatigues + no Ammunition in or out.	EH
Froid Nid (Dull)	8th		Lt Gaskell (No 3 Section) admitted to Hospital Sheenwick sick. Lt R H Rhodes assumed Command of No 3 Section.	
		9 a m	203 Mules under 2nd Lt Warden moved off to Merville there to be exchanged for 201 light + heavy draught horses from the Meerut Division. Letter received from Records that H R H Princess Marys Gifts for men of this Division would be kept for delivery by Secretary Royal Artillery Institution No fatigues on account of exchange of animals	EH

2353 Wt. W2544/1454 700,000 5/15 D. D. & L. A.D.S.S./Forms/C. 2118.

Army Form C. 2118.

Instructions regarding War Diaries and Intelligence Summaries are contained in F. S. Regs., Part II. and the Staff Manual respectively. Title pages will be prepared in manuscript.

WAR DIARY
or
INTELLIGENCE SUMMARY.
(Erase heading not required.)

Place	Date 1915	Hour	Summary of Events and Information	Remarks and references to Appendices
Froid Nez (Damp)	Nov. 9th	6am – 1pm	Two hundred men attended the Divisional Baths. B.Q. Sergt Major, No 3 Section struck off the Strength on evacuation out of the Divisional Area, H.Q. R.A. asked to post a Successor Sergeant Farrier taken on the Strength + posted to No 2 Section. Fatigues + Ammunition light.	EH.
Froid Nez (Wet)	10th		Orders issued that Sections must keep a correct record of registered Nos of G. S. Wagons with dates of loaning + returning. Sergeant Farrier taken on the Strength + posted to No 1 Section. All contacts of Measles case Medically examined Two Gunners + four Drivers posted to the various Brigades. Normal Fatigues + Ammunition.	EH
Froid Nez (Showery)	11th		Brigades drew a considerable number of various Gun ~~[illegible]~~ Stores to complete them. A day of very heavy issues + receipts of Ammunition. Very heavy Fatigues.	EH.
Froid Nez (Wet)	12th	Noon	The Adjutant (Lt E. Hiscock) returned from Hospital, Shenwick. Two Drivers taken on the Strength on return from Hospital. 10 men per Section attended the presentation of the Military Cross to Lt. Van Gulken R.F.A. Promotions made of N.C.O.s to fill existing vacancies. Very heavy Fatigues Heavy issues + receipts of Ammunition	EH.

Instructions regarding War Diaries and Intelligence Summaries are contained in F. S. Regs., Part II. and the Staff Manual respectively. Title pages will be prepared in manuscript.

WAR DIARY
or
INTELLIGENCE SUMMARY.

(Erase heading not required.)

Army Form C. 2118.

Place	Date	Hour	Summary of Events and Information	Remarks and references to Appendices
	1915			
Froid Nez (Damp)	Nov. 13th		Information of Promotion of B.Q.M.S. Swan W. J. to 2nd Lieut received + instructions for him to proceed to Havre for instructions. — Left Steenwerck Railhead 7 p.m. en route to the Base.	
		2.15pm	All horses paraded on Road for Inspection by D.D.R. 1st Army 17 horses + 4 mules earmarked to go to Veterinary Section for Rest at a future date. Heavy Fatigues. Normal Ammunition.	EH.
Froid Nez (Cold)	14th		Orders issued for Gun Ammunition in future to be issued according to the number of Fuze lot.	
		Noon	Divine Service.	
			B.Q.M.S. struck off the Strength on promotion to 2nd Lieut + departure to the Base.	
			Regt Sergt Major struck off the Strength on evacuation out of the Divisional Area. Application to H.Q.R.A. for both vacancies to be filled. Normal Fatigues.	EH.
Froid Nez (Wet)	15th		1 Bdr 1 Shoe Smith + 5 Drivers struck off the Strength on evacuation out of the Divisional Area.	
			B.Q.M.S. posted to D.A.C.	
			B.S. Mjr. reported his arrival + posted to No 3 Section.	
			Very quiet day.	EH.

Army Form C. 2118.

WAR DIARY
or
INTELLIGENCE SUMMARY.
(Erase heading not required.)

Instructions regarding War Diaries and Intelligence Summaries are contained in F. S. Regs., Part II. and the Staff Manual respectively. Title pages will be prepared in manuscript.

Place	Date 1915	Hour	Summary of Events and Information	Remarks and references to Appendices
Froid Nard (Dull)	Nov 16th		1 Driver taken on the Strength on return from Convalescent Station. Very heavy call for Ammunition from Brigades especially 4.5 Howitzer. Very heavy Fatigues.	EH
Froid Nard (Fine)	17th		One Shoe Smith & 1 Driver taken on the Strength on return from Hospital. Certain promotions & postings made amongst the Sections to complete to Establishment. Heavy Receipts of Ammunition & Fatigues.	EH
Froid Nard (Wet)	18th	10.30	Six G. S. Wagons (unhorsed) loaned to Divisional Supply train for an indefinite period. A very quiet day with normal fatigues.	EH
Froid Nard (fine)	19th		A Draft of horses & mules received. One Driver from the Base met at Railhead & taken on the Strength. Information that Leave for the Division had been opened (7 days) commencing 23-11-15. 7 tickets every five days allotted to D.A.C subdivided into 2 per Section + 1 H.Q. including Officers. Heavy Fatigues Normal Ammunition transactions.	EH
Froid Nard (Dull)	20th		14 Mouth Organs purchased from England for the Recreation of the Troops and issued to Sections. 1 Bomb. 1 Gunner & 3 Drivers struck off the Strength on Evacuation. Quiet day.	EH.

2353 Wt. W2544/1454 700,000 5/15 D. D. & L. A.D.S.S./Forms/C. 2118.

Instructions regarding War Diaries and Intelligence Summaries are contained in F. S. Regs., Part II. and the Staff Manual respectively. Title pages will be prepared in manuscript.

WAR DIARY
or
INTELLIGENCE SUMMARY.
(Erase heading not required.)

Army Form C. 2118.

Place	Date	Hour	Summary of Events and Information	Remarks and references to Appendices
	1915			
Froid Nid (Cold)	Nov. 21st	Noon	Divine Service.	
			Certain promotions + postings made to equalize + complete Sections	
			Normal Fatigues + Ammunition transactions	EH
Froid Nid (Frost)	22nd		An exceedingly quiet day. 54 Rounds of Defective 18 pdr drawn from 103rd R.A.C.	
			Temp. acting Sgt. Sgt. Major arrived on posting to D.A.C.	EH
Froid Nid (Wet)	23rd	5.20 a.m.	1st leave party including 2nd Lt E Hiscock the Adjutant departed	
			from Steenwerck Railhead en route for England.	
			2nd Lieut F G Squire deputed to carry on the duties of Adjutant	
			during 2nd Lt E Hiscocks absence on leave. Above 54 Rounds	
			conveyed to Hazebrouck and handed over to Inspector of Ordnance	
			Offr taken on the Strength on return from Hospital	
			1 Sh Cpl 1 Wheeler Cpl. 2 Saddler Stitchers + 2 Gunners having reported	
			their arrival from the Base taken on the Strength + posted	
			Normal day as regards Ammunition + Fatigues	EH
			14 horses + 4 mules taken to Steenwerck Railhead for evacuation under	
Froid Nid (Cold + Dull)	24th	7 a.m.	Orders of D.D.R. 1st Army.	
			One Gunner + one Shoeing Smith posted on arrival from the Base	
			Bdr. taken on the Strength on return from Hospital	
			Heavy Fatigues Light receipts + issues of Ammunition.	EH

2353 Wt. W2544/1454 700,000 5/15 D. D. & L. A.D.S.S./Forms/C. 2118.

Instructions regarding War Diaries and Intelligence Summaries are contained in F. S. Regs., Part II. and the Staff Manual respectively. Title pages will be prepared in manuscript.

WAR DIARY
or
INTELLIGENCE SUMMARY.
(Erase heading not required.)

Army Form C. 2118.

Place	Date 1915	Hour	Summary of Events and Information	Remarks and references to Appendices
Froid Nez (Wet)	Nov. 25th		1 Gunner on return from Hospital taken on the Strength and posted to No 3 Section.	
			One Shoe Smith & 3 Drivers taken on the Strength from the Base.	
			Heavy Fatigues Normal Ammunition.	EH.
Froid Nez (Dull)	26th		6 a.m. to 1 p.m. 200 men attended the Divisional Baths	
			Heavy day for Fatigues otherwise very quiet.	EH.
Froid Nez (Frost)	27th		2nd Lieut Halliwell on arrival posted to No 1 Section.	
			Mules transferred amongst Sections to equalise.	
			New arrangement whereby La Motte Forest Party proceeds to midday	
			Billets overnight & returns the following day.	EH.
			Quiet day	
Froid Nez (Frost)	28th		Two A/Bdrs. 1 Gunner & 4 Drivers taken on the Strength on arrival from the Base.	
			1 Sergt 7 Drivers struck off the Strength on evacuation out of the Divisional Area	
		4 a.m.	Second Leave party departed for England.	
			Normal Fatigues. Very heavy issues of H.E. Ammunition	EH.

2353 Wt. W2544/1454 700,000 5/15 D. D. & L. A.D.S.S./Forms/C. 2118.

Army Form C. 2118.

Instructions regarding War Diaries and Intelligence Summaries are contained in F. S. Regs., Part II. and the Staff Manual respectively. Title pages will be prepared in manuscript.

WAR DIARY
or
INTELLIGENCE SUMMARY.
(Erase heading not required.)

Place	Date 1915	Hour	Summary of Events and Information	Remarks and references to Appendices
Froid Nid (Wet)	Novr. 29th	3pm	Lecture under the auspices of the A. D. V. S. in No 3 Section Compound for officers + N. C. O's of that Section.	
			Light Fatigues. Very heavy issues + receipts of H.E. Ammtn.	EH
Froid Nid (Mild turning to Rain)	30th		Exchange of a Gunner with the 8th Division	
		3pm	Lecture under the Auspices of the A.D.V.S. for Officers + N. C. O's of Nos. 1 + 2 Sections. Le Motte stopped temporarily on account of Thaw affecting the road &c.	
			Normal Fatigues. Heavy Ammunition in + out.	EH

2353 Wt. W2544/1454 700,000 5/15 D. D. & L. A.D.S.S./Forms/C. 2118.

23rd 8 Mc.

Vol: 4

121
7911

HEADQUARTERS
No.
Date
23rd DIVISIONAL AMMUNITION COLUMN

Army Form C. 2118.

Instructions regarding War Diaries and Intelligence Summaries are contained in F. S. Regs., Part II. and the Staff Manual respectively. Title pages will be prepared in manuscript.

WAR DIARY
or
INTELLIGENCE SUMMARY.
(Erase heading not required.)

Place	Date 1915	Hour	Summary of Events and Information	Remarks and references to Appendices
Froid Nid (Fine)	Decr 1st		Promotion of N.C.Os to fill existing vacancies. Second Lieuts. E Middleton and C. Musquith posted to Nos 1 and 2 Sections respectively. 2nd Lieut. L. S. Campbell struck off strength on departure to 102nd Brigade. Normal Ammunition + Fatigues.	EH.
Froid Nid (Wet)	2nd		Rather heavy Fatigues otherwise an unusually quiet day. Ammunition light.	EH.
Froid Nid (Wet)	3rd		Eight Gunners and 7 Drivers posted to various Sections on arrival from the Base, Havre. Appointments made to complete to establishment. Normal receipts of Ammunition. Fatigues as usual.	EH.
Froid Nid (Wet)	4th		15 Gunners and 15 Drivers posted to the various Brigades of the Division. Fatigues and ammunition somewhat light.	EH.
Froid Nid (Fine day wet in eve.)	5th		Fatigue work on Remounts at Railhead. Normal issues and receipts of Ammunition also Fatigues.	EH.
Froid Nid (Dull - Wet)	6th		Brig. General Stokes, 3rd Corps visited and inspected the D.A.C. Orders received to be in readiness to hand over Mules, L.D. Horses and harness in exchange for H.D. Fatigues and Ammunition as usual.	EH.

2353 Wt. W2544/1454 700,000 5/15 D. D. & L. A.D.S.S./Forms/C. 2118.

Instructions regarding War Diaries and Intelligence Summaries are contained in F. S. Regs., Part II. and the Staff Manual respectively. Title pages will be prepared in manuscript.

WAR DIARY
or
INTELLIGENCE SUMMARY.
(Erase heading not required.)

Army Form C. 2118.

Place	Date	Hour	Summary of Events and Information	Remarks and references to Appendices
	1915 Decr			
Frond Mid (Bright changing to Wet)	7th		Very large issue of Ammunition Fairly heavy Fatigues otherwise everything normal	EH.
Frond Mid (Bright and Windy)	8th		Authority obtained from Le Maire Steenwerck for part of No 2 Section to occupy another Field adjoining their Compound Divisional Rent Officer advised accordingly Normal day as regards Ammunition + Fatigues.	EH.
Frond Mid (Wet + very cold)	9th		Establishment of Ammunition to be carried by Sections revised under authority of H.Q. R.A. Ammunition Normal Fatigues heavy	EH.
Frond Mid (Wet)	10th		An exceedingly quiet day.	EH.
Frond Mid (Very Wet)	11th		All Vehicles parked on right side of road outside Section Compounds in accordance with G.O.C. Orders. Another quiet day as regards Ammunition and Fatigues.	EH.
Frond Mid (Dull, Wet + cold)	12th	11.30am	Divine Service 1 W.O. (class II) 1 Bdr, 2 Gnrs + 5 Drivers struck off the Strength on Evacuation out of the Divisional Area Normal receipts + issues of Ammunition also Fatigues.	EH.

Army Form C. 2118.

WAR DIARY
or
INTELLIGENCE SUMMARY.
(Erase heading not required.)

Instructions regarding War Diaries and Intelligence Summaries are contained in F. S. Regs., Part II. and the Staff Manual respectively. Title pages will be prepared in manuscript.

Place	Date	Hour	Summary of Events and Information	Remarks and references to Appendices
	1915			
Froid Nid (Bright, Cold)	Decr. 13th		A very quiet day. Nothing whatever to report.	EH.
Froid Nid (Fair)	14th		Percentage of men to Divisional Baths for Bathing. Establishment of A + AX. per Section further revised. Fatigues - Heavy, Ammunition - light.	EH.
Froid Nid (Dull Raw Day)	15th		Arrangements made for Ammn to be conveyed direct from Ammn. Sub. Park to the Sections direct. One mule died + one destroyed.	EH.
Froid Nid (Dull & Cold)	16th		10 Drivers having reported their arrival, taken on the Strength + posted to Sections. One mule struck off the Strength having died. Promotions, appointments + postings made to fill existing vacancies. 1 N.C.O. + 10 men per Section attached from Infantry for purpose of making Horse Standings and Shelters. Ammunition - Normal Fatigues - Heavy.	EH.
Froid Nid (Fine Cold)	17th		Very quiet day except for Fatigues which were very heavy. Ammunition - light.	EH.
Froid Nid (Dull)	18th		One Fitter S/Sgt 1 Saddler, 3 Wheelers + 6 Gunners taken on the Strength on arrival from Base + posted to Sections. Three Drivers ~~....~~ struck off the Strength on Evacuation. Ammunition + Fatigues - Normal	EH.

Army Form C. 2118.

Instructions regarding War Diaries and Intelligence Summaries are contained in F. S. Regs., Part II. and the Staff Manual respectively. Title pages will be prepared in manuscript.

WAR DIARY
or
INTELLIGENCE SUMMARY.
(Erase heading not required.)

Place	Date 1915	Hour	Summary of Events and Information	Remarks and references to Appendices
Froid Nid (V. Wet)	Decr. 19th		1 Corporal and 1 Driver struck off the Strength on evacuation. 1 Fitter Sff Sergt, 1 Fitter Corporal, 1 Wheeler, 1 Saddler, 6 Gunners + 5 Drivers posted to various Brigades. Ammunition and Fatigues light.	EH.
Froid Nid (Dull Heavy)	20th		Old bricks from dismantled buildings fetched from Firing lines for making Horse Standings. Saddler appointed to fill an existing vacancy. Certain inter postings made to equalise personnel in Sections. Ammunition – Normal.	EH.
Froid Nid (Rain)	21st		21 Horses, 54 Mules (1 dead) struck off the Strength evacuated to Mobile Vety Section. S/Smith promoted Corporal to complete to Establishment. Wood cutting party returned from La Motte (Forest Nieppe) with all Camp Equipment consequently La Motte Fatigues cease from this date. Ammunition issues + receipts normal.	EH.
Froid Nid (Brighter)	22nd	2 pm	Medical Examination of all men commenced. Inspection of all animals. H. D. Horse struck off the Strength on evacuation.	EH.
Froid Nid (V. Wet)	23rd		Lieut. R. Lippert R. F. A. struck off the Strength on arrival in England. Men employed on Fatigues with Remounts at Railhead. 21 Horses received from Railhead for D. A. C. + brought on Strength. Fatigues heavy. Ammunition a little more than usual.	EH.

2353 Wt. W2544/1454 700,000 5/15 D. D. & L. A.D.S.S./Forms/C. 2118.

Army Form C. 2118.

Instructions regarding War Diaries and Intelligence Summaries are contained in F. S. Regs., Part II. and the Staff Manual respectively. Title pages will be prepared in manuscript.

WAR DIARY
or
INTELLIGENCE SUMMARY.
(Erase heading not required.)

Place	Date 1915	Hour	Summary of Events and Information	Remarks and references to Appendices
Froid Nid (Wet-Dull)	Decr. 24th		Supply of Bricks obtained from demolished houses in the Firing Line for making Horse Standings. Ammunition - Normal Fatigues - heavy.	EH.
Froid Nid. (Showery)	25th		A small number of L.D Horses exchanged with another Division for H.D. 25 H.D. Horses taken over from the 20th Division. 6 G.S. Wagons loaned to 105th How Brigade. One Mule died, struck off Strength accordingly. Receipts + issues of Ammunition very heavy. Fatigues light	EH.
Froid Nid (Bright Day)	26th	11.15a	Divine Service and Holy Communion. S/Smith + Gunner struck off the Strength on evacuation. Ammunition above normal - Fatigues exceedingly light.	EH.
Froid Nid (& Windy with showers)	27th	11a.m.	O.C. met all Officers. Fd Genl Court Martial Sgt A McColl No 1 Section. Receipts + issues of Ammunition heavy Fatigues very heavy.	EH.
Froid Nid (Fair)	28th		Order republished for all men to be in Billets by 8-30 p.m. Divisional Baths utilised by D.A.C. Five L.D. horses taken on Strength from D.L.O.Y. Ammunition normal. Fatigues very heavy.	EH.

Instructions regarding War Diaries and Intelligence Summaries are contained in F. S. Regs., Part II. and the Staff Manual respectively. Title pages will be prepared in manuscript.

WAR DIARY
or
INTELLIGENCE SUMMARY.
(Erase heading not required.)

Army Form C. 2118.

Place	Date	Hour	Summary of Events and Information	Remarks and references to Appendices
	Decr 1915			
Froid Nid (Fine)	29th		Lieut. J U Gaskell R.F.A struck off the Strength Authority A/778 A.G.'s Office. Fatigues Normal. Ammunition Heavy.	EH.
Froid Nid (Dull)	30th		9 Gunners 8 Drivers taken on the Strength on arrival from the Base, Havre. 11 Gunners 6 Drivers struck off the Strength on posting to Brigades. Fatigues heavy – Ammunition Normal.	EH.
Froid Nid (Wet)	31st		Postings amongst Sections to equalize personnel. 4 Gunners & 1 Saddler taken on the Strength on arrival from the Base, Havre. G.O.C. R.A. inspected the animals of the D.A.C. at Watering Order. Issues & Receipts of Ammunition also Fatigues somewhat heavy.	EH.

2353 Wt. W2544/1454 700,000 5/15 D. D. & L. A.D.S.S./Forms/C. 2118.

23rd Divl Al Column

Vol: V

Instructions regarding War Diaries and Intelligence Summaries are contained in F. S. Regs., Part II and the Staff Manual respectively. Title pages will be prepared in manuscript.

WAR DIARY
or
INTELLIGENCE SUMMARY.
(Erase heading not required.)

36th 23rd DAC

Army Form C. 2118.

Place	Date 1916	Hour	Summary of Events and Information	Remarks and references to Appendices
Froid Nid (Fair)	Jan 1st		2Lt M A Hogarth taken on the Strength on reporting his arrival and posted to No 3 Section. Arrangements made whereby the Section on Duty does all D.A.C. Fatigues for the day except Ammunition which is done by the respective Sections concerned.	
		11 a.m.	Conference of Section Commanders with OC.	EH.
Froid Nid (Damp)	2nd	11.45 a.m.	Divine Service. Saddler posted to Brigade. 1 Corpl 2 Drivers struck off the Strength on Evacuation. Fatigues and ammunition normal.	EH.
Froid Nid (Dry Cold)	3rd		All Farm houses except Billets placed out of Bounds.	
		6.15 p.m.	D.A.C. Concert held at Steenwerck. Ammunition receipts and issues rather heavy.	EH.
Froid Nid (Fine)	4th		Three Officers 3 Sergts + 3 Corpls temporarily attached from the Bdes to the D.A.C. by G.O.C. R.A. to assist generally in the Sections. Three N.C.Os + 30 men (Infantry) temporarily attached to the DAC by Orders of G.O.C. for working on erection of Horse Standings etc. S/S Corpl taken on the Strength + posted to No 2 Section. Ammunition normal.	EH.
Froid Nid (Cold)	5th		Lecture given on Ammunition + its marks to Officers + N.C.Os. Horses of No 2 Section Malleined. Ammunition Normal.	
		2 p.m.	Court of Inquiry held on damage etc. of two hut shelters.	EH.

2353 Wt. W2544/1454 700,000 5/15 D. D. & L. A.D.S.S./Forms/C. 2118.

Army Form C. 2118.

WAR DIARY
or
INTELLIGENCE SUMMARY.
(Erase heading not required.)

Instructions regarding War Diaries and Intelligence Summaries are contained in F. S. Regs., Part II. and the Staff Manual respectively. Title pages will be prepared in manuscript.

Place	Date 1916	Hour	Summary of Events and Information	Remarks and references to Appendices
Froid Nid (Sunny)	Jan 6th		Lecture to Officers & N.C.O's on Ammunition, Mortars &c. One Mule died. Very quiet day.	EH.
Froid Nid (Fine)	7th		One mule struck off the Strength – died. Lecture to Officers & N.C.O's on Ammunition &c. Censorship regulations republished in D.A.C. Orders. Another Quiet day.	EH.
Froid Nid (Showery)	8th		Orders published for the return of all Empty Cartridge Cases to Sub Park. 8 Gunners for Water duties posted to Brigades. 3 Gunners & 22 Drivers posted to Brigades. 2 Gunners for Water duties and one driver posted to Sections. Lecture to Officers & N.C.O's on Ammunition. S/Bdr (V) struck off the Strength detained in Hospital in Ireland whilst on leave. Heavy Ammn. Receipts and issues.	EH.
Froid Nid (Wet)	9th		2/Lt C. Musgrith ~~posted~~ transferred EH. from No 2 to No 3 Section vice Lt. M. A. Hogarth transferred No 3 to No 2 Section. 1 S Smith & 3 Drivers struck off the Strength on evacuation out of the Divisional Area. 1 Horse & 1 Mule to the Mob. Vet. Section & 1 Mule died struck off the Strength. 103 Mules L.D. on arrival taken on the Strength and distributed to Sections. Usual Ammunition Lecture given. Divine Service. Orders issued to Section Commanders to make arrangements for washing & Hair cutting. Expense to be borne by the Public. Heavy Ammn. & Fatigues.	EH.

2353 Wt. W2544/1454 700,000 5/15 D. D. & L. A.D.S.S./Forms/C. 2118.

Instructions regarding War Diaries and Intelligence Summaries are contained in F. S. Regs., Part II. and the Staff Manual respectively. Title pages will be prepared in manuscript.

WAR DIARY
or
INTELLIGENCE SUMMARY.
(Erase heading not required.)

Army Form C. 2118.

Place	Date 1916	Hour	Summary of Events and Information	Remarks and references to Appendices
Frois Mid (Wet)	Jan 10th		One horse struck off Strength on evacuation to Mobile Vety. Section. Y M C A Hut opened at Bac St. Maur. Bathing at Divl. Baths.	
		5pm.	Veterinary Lecture given to Officers + N. C. O's and Artificers concerned. Normal receipts + issues of Ammunition.	EH.
Frois Mid (Damp)	11th		Two Gunners struck off the Strength on departure to Base as P.B men - Medical Authority. 1 Horse + 1 Mule struck off on evacuation to Mob. Vet. Sec. Farrier at own request reverts to Corporal. Usual receipts and issues of Ammunition.	EH.
Frois Mid (Dry Cold)	12th	6.30pm	Camp Fire Alfresco Concert held. Very quiet day.	EH.
Frois Mid (Cold, Bright)	13th		2 horses + 1 mule struck off Strength on evacuation also 1 mule on destruction. Issues and receipts of Ammunition - Normal.	EH.
Frois Mid (Cold)	14th		Court of Enquiry re Huts re-assembled to examine further witnesses now available. 1 Bomb. 2 Saddlers and 6 Gunners taken on the Strength on arrival from the Base. Usual Ammunition Lecture. Inspection of No 1 Section by the O.C. Issues + Receipts of Ammunition - Light.	EH.

2353 Wt. W2544/1454 700,000 5/15 D. D. & L. A.D.S.S./Forms/C. 2118.

Instructions regarding War Diaries and Intelligence Summaries are contained in F. S. Regs., Part II. and the Staff Manual respectively. Title pages will be prepared in manuscript.

WAR DIARY
or
INTELLIGENCE SUMMARY.
(Erase heading not required.)

Army Form C. 2118.

Place	Date 1916	Hour	Summary of Events and Information	Remarks and references to Appendices
Froid Nid (Dull + Damp)	Jan 15		Lecture on Ammunition Marks &c to Officers & N.C.Os. One Mule (Mob Vety Section) One horse (destroyed) struck off Strength. Ammunition receipts + issues Normal Inspection No 2 Section by O.C.	EH.
Froid Nid (Fine)	16	noon	Divine Service. 1 Driver struck off the Strength on transfer to Royal Flying Corps. 1 Bdr 2 Saddlers + 4 Gunners struck off the Strength on posting to Brigades. Inspection No 3 Section by O.C. Ammunition rather heavy. 2nd Lieut C. C. Bartlett on Strength on arrival.	EH.
Froid Nid (Dull + Damp)	17		One mule (evacuated) One mule (destroyed) struck off Strength. S/Smith Corpl. struck off strength on posting to 10th Bde R.F.A. Receipts + issues of Ammunition - light.	EH.
Froid Nid (Dull Wet)	18		Major G M A Gregory R.F.A. + Capt J A French R.F.A brought on Strength on reporting their arrival + posted to Command Nos 3 + 1 Sections respectively. 2nd Lieut C C Bartlett posted to No 3 Section vice 2nd Lieut C Musgrave transferred to 102nd Brigade R.F.A.	EH.
			G.O.C. R.A. inspected No 1 Section in full F.S. Marching Order. 1 Sergeant 1 Far. Sgt + 16 Drivers taken on the Strength	

2353 Wt. W2544/1454 700,000 5/15 D. D. & L. A.D.S.S./Forms/C. 2118.

Army Form C. 2118.

WAR DIARY
or
INTELLIGENCE SUMMARY.
(Erase heading not required.)

Instructions regarding War Diaries and Intelligence Summaries are contained in F. S. Regs., Part II. and the Staff Manual respectively. Title pages will be prepared in manuscript.

Place	Date 1916	Hour	Summary of Events and Information	Remarks and references to Appendices
Froid Nez (Dull. Wet)	Jan 18th	(contd)	2 Gnrs + 3 Drvs struck off Strength on evacuation out of the Divl Area. Two horses evacuated to Mob. Vet Sec and struck off Strength. Postings of N.C.Os + men to Sections to complete to Establishment. Fortnightly Inspection of Gas Helmets ordered. Ammunition - Normal	EH.
Froid Nez (Fine windy at night)	19th		One charger struck off Strength on transfer to Brigade. 1 Horse struck off on evacuation. Inspection of No 3 Section in F.S. Marching Order by G.O.C. R.A. Ammunition rather heavy.	EH.
Froid Nez (Fair showery)	20th		Two Drivers mustered Gunners. Sundry Postings made to equalize Sections. 7 Drivers each to 102nd + 104th Brigades R.F.A. Two horses + 1 Mule struck off on evacuation. Ammunition - Normal.	EH.
Froid Nez (Dull windy)	21st		Inspection of No 2 Section in F.S. Marching Order by G.O.C. R.A. Fatigues rather heavy. Issues + receipts of Ammunition light.	EH.
Froid Nez Dull. Wet + windy)	22nd		10 Gunners taken on the Strength on arrival from the Base. 1 Mule died + struck off Strength accordingly. Sergeant appointed Acting B.Q. Sgt. Mjr. to No 2 Section. Ammunition - Normal	EH.

Army Form C. 2118.

Instructions regarding War Diaries and Intelligence Summaries are contained in F. S. Regs., Part II. and the Staff Manual respectively. Title pages will be prepared in manuscript.

WAR DIARY
or
INTELLIGENCE SUMMARY.
(*Erase heading not required.*)

Place	Date	Hour	Summary of Events and Information	Remarks and references to Appendices
	1916 Jan			
Froid Nez (Fine)	23rd		7 Drivers and 3 Gunners taken on the Strength on arrival from the Base. 4 Drivers struck off the Strength on Evacuation.	
		noon	Divine Service. Eight Gunners struck off the Strength on departure to Brigades. Ammunition – normal.	EH.
Froid Nez (Bright)	24th		One Gunner and one Driver brought on the Strength on arrival from the Base. 29 Horses + Mules brought on the Strength on arrival from Remount Depot and distributed as required to Sections. One horse and one driver struck off the Strength on transfer to Brigade. Special Orders against Fire issued. Ammunition – light.	EH.
Froid Nez (Bright Cold)	25th		One horse evacuated and struck off accordingly. Troops to Divl. Baths. Very quiet day.	EH.
Froid Nez (Fine)	26th		1 Driver struck off the Strength on evacuation. Farr. Sgt. taken on the Strength on arrival & posted to No 3 Section to complete to Establishment. Another very quiet day.	EH.
Froid Nez (Dull with rain)	27th		3 Gunners + 6 Drivers struck off the Strength on posting to Brigades. 3 Mules evacuated to Mobile Vety Section. Receipts + Issues of Ammunition Heavy.	EH.

Army Form C. 2118.

WAR DIARY
or
INTELLIGENCE SUMMARY.

(Erase heading not required.)

Instructions regarding War Diaries and Intelligence Summaries are contained in F. S. Regs., Part II. and the Staff Manual respectively. Title pages will be prepared in manuscript.

Place	Date 1916	Hour	Summary of Events and Information	Remarks and references to Appendices
Froid Nid (Fair)	Jan 28th		One man per Section sent on a course of instruction in the repair of Gun Books. Orders issued that Sections must not supply Primers except in exchange for Miss fires or otherwise defective ones. Very heavy demands for Ammunition throughout the day.	EH.
Froid Nid (Fine)	29th		Troops sent to Divisional Baths throughout the day. Two Drivers brought on the Strength on arrival from the Base. Very heavy receipts and issues of Ammunition.	EH.
Froid Nid (Dull, Heavy Mist)	30th		Establishment of A + A X carried in the Sections amended. Capt L. H. P. Birch R.F.A. struck off the Strength on evacuation to England. 1 S/Smith 4 Drivers struck off the Strength on evacuation out of the Divisional Area. Re-issue of certain maps + old ones called in.	EH.
		Noon	Divine Service. One horse and one Mule evacuated. Ammunition light.	
Froid Nid (Cold)	31st		One horse and four mules struck off on Evacuation. 6 Wagons per Section to be kept continually loaded with Amtn. ready to move off at a minutes notice. Ammunition light.	
		9 a.m.	S/Smith arrived from General Base No 2. Officers + N.C.O's attached from Bdes returned to their Units.	EH.

2353 Wt. W2544/1454 700,000 5/15 D. D. & L. A.D.S.S./Forms/C. 2118.

ON HIS MAJESTY'S SERVICE.

Confidential

DG

War Diary
of
23rd Divl. Ammn Col; R.F.A.

Not Signed

From 1. 2. 16. To 29. 2. 16.

(Volume 1.)

23rd DAC.
Vol: 6

Army Form C. 2118.

WAR DIARY
or
~~INTELLIGENCE SUMMARY.~~
(Erase heading not required.)

Instructions regarding War Diaries and Intelligence Summaries are contained in F. S. Regs., Part II. and the Staff Manual respectively. Title pages will be prepared in manuscript.

Place	Date 1916	Hour	Summary of Events and Information	Remarks and references to Appendices
Froid Nid. (Bright - Cold)	Feb 1st		One man struck off the Strength on transfer as Munition worker to England. Ammunition very light.	EH.
Froid Nid (Bright morng Cloudy to slight rain)	2nd		One S/Smith taken on the Strength on arrival from the Base. Two horses + Two mules struck off the Strength on evacuation to Mobile Vety. Section. Promotions + postings made amongst Sections to complete to Establishment. Ammunition very light.	EH.
Froid Nid (Fairly Bright but Cold + Windy)	3rd		One A/Bdr. + four Gunners taken on the Strength on arrival from the Base. Reversion at own request of Cpl. to Gunner. Promotion + posting made to fill vacancy. Ammunition light.	EH.
Froid Nid (V. Windy. Dull to Rain)	4th		A/Bdr. + 4 Gunners struck off the Strength on posting to Brigades. Bombardier promoted to complete to Establishment.	
		10.20 a.m.	Inspection of all animals by G.O.C.R.A., D.R.S. + D.V.S. Ammunition normal.	EH.
Froid Nid. (Bright)	5th		Wheeler struck off the Strength on transfer to another Division. One mule struck off on evacuation to Mobile Vety. Section. Ammunition light.	EH.
Froid Nid (Fair Rain.)	6th		Two Officers and 8 men brought on the Strength on arrival from the Base. 1 Cpl., 1 S/Smith, 1 Gnr. + 2 Dvrs struck off the Strength on evacuation out of the Divisional Area. Mule struck off dead.	EH

Army Form C. 2118.

Instructions regarding War Diaries and Intelligence Summaries are contained in F. S. Regs., Part II. and the Staff Manual respectively. Title pages will be prepared in manuscript.

WAR DIARY
or
~~INTELLIGENCE SUMMARY.~~
(Erase heading not required.)

Place	Date	Hour	Summary of Events and Information	Remarks and references to Appendices
	1916 Feb			
Froid Nid	6th	11.15	Received by telephone practice Gas Alarm. Informed all Sections.	
	(contd.)	11.54	All D.A.C. harnessed up on the road ready to move off in F.S.M. Order.	
		11.57	H.Q. R.A. so informed.	
			Infantry detachments returned to their own Units.	
			Bdr. promoted Cpl. to fill an existing vacancy.	
			Ammunition light.	EH.
Froid Nid (Fair to Bright Cold Wind)	7th		Received official intimation of move of 23rd Division into the Reserve area. Programme for D.A.C. to move No1 Section + H.Q. 19-2-16 No2 Section 20.2.16 No3 Section 21-2-16 the corresponding Units of the 34th Divisions to take over on same day.	EH.
			Sergeant reduced to Gunner by G.O.C. 3rd Corps for Inefficiency.	
			Two Officers struck off the Strength on posting to Brigades.	
			S.Smith posted to Section.	
			8 horses + 3 mules are struck off on evacuation to Mobile Vety Section.	
			Ammunition very light.	
Froid Nid (Dull turning to rain)	8th		Three Gunners and four drivers struck off the Strength on posting to Brigades. One S.Smith taken on the Strength on arrival from the Base. Ammunition very light.	EH

2353 Wt. W2544/1454 700,000 5/15 D. D. & L. A.D.S.S./Forms/C. 2118.

Army Form C. 2118.

WAR DIARY
or
~~INTELLIGENCE SUMMARY.~~
(Erase heading not required.)

Instructions regarding War Diaries and Intelligence Summaries are contained in F. S. Regs., Part II. and the Staff Manual respectively. Title pages will be prepared in manuscript.

Place	Date 1916	Hour	Summary of Events and Information	Remarks and references to Appendices
Froid Nid (Clear Bright)	Feby 9th		Four Officers taken on the Strength on arrival from the Base An exceedingly quiet day.	EH.
Froid Nid (Fine)	10th		Promotions + postings made to complete to Establishment in Sections.	
		noon	G. O. C. R. A. 3rd Corps visited D. A. C	
		6pm	Examination of Officers and Nos. 1 in Ammunition by Brigade Major R. A Sundry preparations made for moving. Ammunition light.	EH.
Froid Nid (Wet all day)	11th		Four Officers struck off the Strength on posting to Brigades. Orders to fill up with Ammunition to Establishment. Quiet day.	EH.
Froid Nid. (Dull and Cold)	12th		11 Gunners and 3 Drivers brought on the Strength on arrival from the Base Ammunition to complete to Establishment received. O.C. + Adjutant ~~[illegible]~~ EH viewed new area to be occupied by the D. A. C.	EH.
Froid Nid (~~Fair~~)	13th		11 Gunners + 3 Drivers struck off the Strength on posting to Brigades 1 S/Smith Cpl. + 3 Drivers struck off the Strength on Evacuation. Posting of N. C. O.s in Sections Very heavy demands for Ammunition. Column emptied + refilled from Sub. Park.	EH.

Instructions regarding War Diaries and Intelligence Summaries are contained in F. S. Regs., Part II. and the Staff Manual respectively. Title pages will be prepared in manuscript.

WAR DIARY
or
~~INTELLIGENCE SUMMARY.~~
(Erase heading not required.)

Army Form C. 2118.

Place	Date 1916	Hour	Summary of Events and Information	Remarks and references to Appendices
Froid Nid (Fair & Bright V. Windy)	Feb. 14th		Two Gunners brought on Strength. One H.D. horse struck off the Strength on Evacuation. Visit from G.O.C. R.A. Quiet day.	EH.
Froid Nid (Dull Rain & Windy all day)	15th	6 p.m. 8.20 p.m.	S. Smith brought on the Strength on return from Hospital. Lectures to all Officers and N.C.O's on Ammunition. 1 Cpl. + 11 Drivers arrived from the Base. 1 Riding Horse + 9 Mules arrived from Remounts. Ammunition – Normal.	EH.
Froid Nid Dull (Slight rain V. Windy)	16th		One L.D. horse struck off on evacuation. ~~One Corpl~~ 11 Drivers brought on the Strength. 1 Riding Horse + 9 Mules brought on the Strength + distributed to Sections as required. Fascines drawn for Section Compounds. Ammunition light.	EH.
Froid Nid (V. Windy)	17th		One horse struck off the Strength on evacuation. Orders issued for all S.A.A. to be packed in wagons and taken to new area on moving. Ammunition – Normal.	EH.
Froid Nid (V. Wet H. Wind).	18th	6.30 a.m.	50 Men under an Officer proceeded on a days fatigue for 1st Army. The following orders issued as regards Ammunition when moving:–	EH.

2353 Wt. W2544/1454 700,000 5/15 D. D. & L. A.D.S.S./Forms/C. 2118.

Army Form C. 2118.

WAR DIARY
or
~~INTELLIGENCE SUMMARY.~~
(Erase heading not required.)

Instructions regarding War Diaries and Intelligence Summaries are contained in F. S. Regs., Part II. and the Staff Manual respectively. Title pages will be prepared in manuscript.

Place	Date 1916	Hour	Summary of Events and Information	Remarks and references to Appendices
Froid Nid	Feb. 18th		All Gun ammunition will be handed over to 34th Division Am. Col. by Sections less one wagon load of 4.5 Howitzer which will consist of 46 Rnds B X and 20 Rnds B which will accompany Sections into New area – An Officer, Ammn N.C.O. + one Gunner to go + take over Amn from their corresponding Section 34th D A C the day prior to move. All Gun Book to be handed over to the incoming Unit	
			Ammunition – light.	
Froid Nid (C Wind. Fair)	19th	9.15am	Headquarters and No 1 Section moved off in F.S. Marching Order to New Area.	E.H.
		11.30am	Arrived and occupied Billets vacated by 34th D A C.	E.H.
Thary Berquin (Bright Frost)	20th	9.15a	No 2 Section moved off as above and at about	
		11.30a	Arrived and occupied Billets vacated by 34th D.A.C.	E.H.
Neuf Berquin (Dull Cold) Neuf Berquin	21st	9.15a	No 3 Section moved off as above and at about	
		11.30a	Arrived and occupied Billets vacated by 34th D.A.C. Redistribution of Billets and standings consisting of standings (fair rather small) for H.Q. Nos 1 + 2 Sections none however for No 3 Section. All Ranks billeted in Farm houses Barns + Cottages. All vehicles parked on the road. The new area commences 1 mile N west of Estaires along the main road to ½ mile short of NEUF BERQUIN the Units being in the following order No 3 Section, No 2 Section + Headquarters. ~~&~~ No 1 Section. One Mule struck off the Strength – deceased.	E.H.

2353 Wt. W2544/1454 700,000 5/15 D. D. & L. A.D.S.S./Forms/C. 2118.

Instructions regarding War Diaries and Intelligence Summaries are contained in F. S. Regs., Part II. and the Staff Manual respectively. Title pages will be prepared in manuscript.

WAR DIARY

or

~~INTELLIGENCE SUMMARY.~~

(Erase heading not required.)

Army Form C. 2118.

Place	Date	Hour	Summary of Events and Information	Remarks and references to Appendices
~~[illegible]~~ Neuf Berquin (V. Cold. Snow nearly all day)	1916 Feb. 22nd		Attached to the 8th Division for Rations & Forage Inaugurated a Regtl Mil Police – 1 Gunner per Section under a N.C.O. 1 Driver struck off the Strength on admission to Hospital whilst on leave to England 1 Gnr + 3 Drs struck off the Strength on Evacuation Chaff Cutters hired + allotted one each to Hdqrs + Sections. Arrangements made for washing of Mens Clothing. Ammunition light	EH
Neuf Berquin (Snow all day)	23rd		1 Gunner struck off the Strength on evacuation. Ammunition Nil. Intimation received that a move may be imminent.	EH.
Neuf Berquin (Bright)	24th		Strict Orders issued for the application of Whale Oil and Anti Frostbite Grease during the inclement weather. Exceedingly quiet day.	EH
Neuf Berquin (Snow Dull)	25th		Two Drivers brought on the Strength Another very quiet day.	EH.
Neuf Berquin (Dull morn – Bright) Thaw set in	26th		A driver mustered Gunner. One Corporal Two wheelers 5 Gunners for Water duties, 4 Howitzer Gunners, 10 R.F.A. Gunners + 5 Drivers brought on the Strength. Another quiet day. Thaw precautions taken	EH.

Army Form C. 2118.

WAR DIARY

or

~~INTELLIGENCE SUMMARY.~~

(Erase heading not required.)

Instructions regarding War Diaries and Intelligence Summaries are contained in F. S. Regs., Part II. and the Staff Manual respectively. Title pages will be prepared in manuscript.

Place	Date 1916	Hour	Summary of Events and Information	Remarks and references to Appendices
Neuf Berquin (Damp Raw Misty day)	Feb. 27th		Orders issued for frequent lectures on Ammunition to be held 1/4 hours Physical Drill instruction daily instituted Ammunition [illegible]	EH
Neuf Berquin (Very damp & Misty)	28th		Two Corporals, Two Bombardiers, One Wheeler, Twenty Gunners and Thirteen Drivers are hereby struck off the strength on posting to Brigades. Postings made to Sections. Harness & Animals of No 1 Section inspected by C.O.	EH.
Neuf Berquin Bright-dull with rain in afternoon Dull Raw Night Sanchy	29th	4.30am	Received Orders from H.Q. R.A. to move off as a whole in F.S.M.O. at 10 a.m. Destination Pernes via Merville, St Venant, Lillers and Auchy.	
		10.15am	Moved off with all personnel Animals Wagons & Amtn.	
		10.30pm	Arrived after a 30 miles march. Wagons parked on Roadside, Horses picketted in Fields. Men billetted in Barns Farms & Houses. Driver appointed Wheeler with effect from 1-1-16. 27 L.D. Mules brought on Strength & distributed to Sections	EH.

ON HIS MAJESTY'S SERVICE.

Confidential.

D

War Diary
of
23rd Divisional Ammn Column
from 1-3-16. to 31-3-16
Volume 1.

23 Dw
A Col
Vol 7

23 D A C

Army Form C. 2118.

WAR DIARY
or
~~INTELLIGENCE SUMMARY.~~
(Erase heading not required.)

Instructions regarding War Diaries and Intelligence Summaries are contained in F. S. Regs., Part II. and the Staff Manual respectively. Title pages will be prepared in manuscript.

Place	Date 1916	Hour	Summary of Events and Information	Remarks and references to Appendices
SACHIN (Fine)	Mch 1st		Spent in Parking Vehicles conveniently on the roadside and making best possible arrangements as regards men and animals.	EH.
SACHIN (Fine)	2nd		Spent in cleaning Harness and Wagons after the March	
SACHIN (Dull-Snow)	3rd		Another quiet day spent in overhauling + preparing for a further March	EH.
SACHIN. (Snow All day)	4th		Orders published that no Soldier may part with any of his kit, Rations or other Government property to Civilians.	
			Orders issued with regard to Road discipline.	
			One Driver struck off the Strength on departure to Railway Depot, AUDRUICQ for transfer to Railway Troops.	
		10am	Field General Court Martial held at Headquarter Billet to try No 84667 Gunner W. Haynes No 1 Section for refusing to obey a lawful command given by his superior Officer.	
SACHIN (Snow)	4th		Received Orders to unload three G. S. Wagons per Section and dump the Ammunition, Rationing the men and animals for two days all to be held in readiness for temporary attachment to 102nd 3rd + 4th Brigades respectively at a moments notice.	EH.

2353 Wt. W2544/1454 700,000 5/15 D. D. & L. A.D.S.S./Forms/C. 2118.

Army Form C. 2118.

WAR DIARY
or
~~INTELLIGENCE SUMMARY.~~
(Erase heading not required.)

Instructions regarding War Diaries and Intelligence Summaries are contained in F. S. Regs., Part II. and the Staff Manual respectively. Title pages will be prepared in manuscript.

Place	Date 1916	Hour	Summary of Events and Information	Remarks and references to Appendices
SACHIN (Snow)	Mch 5th (contd)	10 pm	Orders received for the aforementioned wagons to proceed at once to the Brigades to which allotted. Also for the D.A.C. to be in readiness to move on the 7.3.16.	
SACHIN. (Fair)	5th		Bombardier reverted to Gunner at own request. A very quiet day.	EH.
SACHIN (Snow – All day)	6th		1 Cpl 1 Bdr. 1 Gunner + 2 Drivers struck off the Strength on evacuation. Order issued forbidding Clipping of Animals.	EH.
		11.15 am	Court Martial Parade. No 84667 Gnr W. Haynes sentenced to 42 days detention. Commuted by G.O.C. R.A. to 42 days F.P. No. 1. Received Orders to March out 8.3.16.	EH
SACHIN (Snow – All day)	7th		Bdr. reverts to Gunner at own request. Gunner brought on the Strength on return from Hospital. Preparations made for Marching Out. A/Bdr reverted to Gunner for Neglect of Duty.	EH
SACHIN (Fair)	8th	6 am	Billetting party consisting of 1 Officer, Interpreter + 4 N.C.Os, moved off.	
		8.45 am	The D.A.C. moved off as a whole	
GAUCOURT			Arrived parked Vehicles on Roadside, Animals watered fed + stabled in Horse Shelters. Men billetted in Farms Barns &c.	EH

Instructions regarding War Diaries and Intelligence Summaries are contained in F. S. Regs., Part II. and the Staff Manual respectively. Title pages will be prepared in manuscript.

WAR DIARY
or
~~INTELLIGENCE SUMMARY.~~
(*Erase heading not required.*)

Army Form C. 2118.

Place	Date 1916	Hour	Summary of Events and Information	Remarks and references to Appendices
GAUCOURT (Fair-cloudy-Snow)	Mch 9th		Communications opened with Brigades + H.Q.R.A. Section Offices obtained + opened. Ammunition of various kinds received + issued. Otherwise the day spent in settling down.	EH
CAUCOURT (Dull-Cold)	10th		Saddler struck off the Strength on posting to the Base. Orders issued against troops entering Estaminets or Houses of Refreshment during prohibited hours Enr brought on the Strength. Driver struck off on evacuation. Ammunition in and out fairly heavy.	EH.
CAUCOURT (Dull-Rain)	11th		Orders issued that No1 Section will supply "Very Lights" No2 Section "Rockets" and No3 Section "Grenades" as required by troops in the firing line. 1 G.S. wagon to be used for Grenades and to carry 1380. All S.A.A. Wagons to carry 41 Boxes S.A.A. The Establishment of Very Lights + Rockets to be 200 and 50 respectively. 1 Bdr and 33 O.R. taken on the Strength on arrival from the Base and attached to Sections. 100 L.D. Horses + Mules brought on the Strength on arrival from Base Remount Depot.	EH
CAUCOURT (Fine Fairly clear)	12th		Establishment of Very Lights + Rockets amended to 500 + 50 respectively.	
		11 a.m.	Divine Service for C of E + R.C's. Bomb. promoted to fill existing vacancy. Ammunition fairly heavy.	EH

2353 Wt. W2544/1454 700,000 5/15 D. D. & L. A.D.S.S./Forms/C. 2118.

Instructions regarding War Diaries and Intelligence Summaries are contained in F. S. Regs., Part II. and the Staff Manual respectively. Title pages will be prepared in manuscript.

WAR DIARY
or
~~INTELLIGENCE SUMMARY.~~
(Erase heading not required.)

Army Form C. 2118.

Place	Date 1916	Hour	Summary of Events and Information	Remarks and references to Appendices
CAUCOURT (Bright-Clear)	Mch 13th		Lieut T Davies (D.O) R.A. brought on the Strength on arrival from 14th Div. and posted to No 1 Section. 2nd Lieut C Middleton & 2nd Lieut A Windsor transferred from No 1 Section to No 3 Section. A quiet day.	EH
CAUCOURT (Bright-Clear)	14th		Lt Col C.V.B. Kuper R.F.A. struck off the Strength on departure to England. Col. C.A.P. Holday R.F.A. brought on the Strength on arrival to command. Gnr & Dvr. brought on the Strength. 1 Bdr 10 Gnrs & 12 Dvrs struck off the Strength on posting to Brigades. Orders issued for all Wagons to be washed down daily. Postings made amongst Sections. One horse brought on the Strength. 52 Horses struck off the Strength on being taken over by other Units of the Division.	EH
CAUCOURT (Dull-Fine)	15th		Lieut T. Davies (D.O.) R.A. posted to No 3 Section to command. 2Lt A. Windsor and one horse transferred from No 3 Section to No 1 Section	
		8.30am	No 2 Section moved off in F.S.M.O. to Barlin to join the 2nd D.A.C. Gnr. struck off the Strength on posting to 105th Bde.	EH
CAUCOURT (Dull)	16th		Ammunition both in and out rather heavy otherwise a quiet day.	EH

2353 Wt. W2544/1454 700,000 5/15 D. D. & L. A.D.S.S./Forms/C. 2118.

Army Form C. 2118.

WAR DIARY
or
~~INTELLIGENCE SUMMARY.~~
(Erase heading not required.)

Instructions regarding War Diaries and Intelligence Summaries are contained in F. S. Regs., Part II. and the Staff Manual respectively. Title pages will be prepared in manuscript.

Place	Date 1916	Hour	Summary of Events and Information	Remarks and references to Appendices
CAUCOURT (Fair)	Mch 17th	9 a.m	No 1 Section inspected in F. S. M. O. by the OC	
		9.45 a.m	No 2 Section inspected in F. S. M. O. by the OC.	
			1 H.D Horse + 1 Mule struck off the Strength on evacuation	
			Ammunition - Normal	EA
CAUCOURT (Dull - Bright)	18th		Major G. M. A. Gregory R. F. A. struck off the Strength with effect from 12.3.16 - Authority 1st Army No 3527/20 A - dated 12.3.16.	
			Lieut G. H. Rhodes struck off the Strength on transfer to 14th Division with effect from 14.3.16	
			1 Bdr & 3 Gnrs brought on the Strength on arrival from the Base and attached to Sections. Corporal reverted to Gunner at own request	
			Dvr brought on the Strength and posted to No 3 Section from 14th Division.	
			Wagons loaned to Batteries to assist in Move.	EA
CAUCOURT (Fine)	19th	8 a.m	Billetting party left for BRUAY	
		10.40 a.m	Divine Service for R. Cs.	
		11.15 a.m	Divine Service for C of E.	
			Gnr struck off the Strength on evacuation.	
			Mule struck off the Strength on evacuation	EA.
CAUCOURT (Fine - Cloudy)	20th	9 a.m	No 3 Section, No 1 Section + Hdqrs moved off in F S M O for BRUAY via HERMIN, REBREUVE & MAISNIL Officer remained behind to collect and ascertain correctness of all Claims which were nil.	EA.

2353 Wt. W2544/1454 700,000 5/15 D. D. & L. A.D.S.S./Forms/C. 2118.

Army Form C. 2118.

Instructions regarding War Diaries and Intelligence Summaries are contained in F. S. Regs., Part II. and the Staff Manual respectively. Title pages will be prepared in manuscript.

WAR DIARY
or
~~INTELLIGENCE SUMMARY.~~
(Erase heading not required.)

Place	Date 1916	Hour	Summary of Events and Information	Remarks and references to Appendices
BRUAY (Fine - Cloudy)	Mch 20th	11.30am	Arrived. Nine mules brought on the Strength and issued to Sections	EH
BRUAY (Dull Damp)	21st		O. C. Nos. 1 & 3 Sections proceeded to 2nd D. A. C. to inspect Billets and Standings they will eventually take over at BARLIN 13 H.D exchanged with 34th Div for 20 L.D. at LOCON	EH
BRUAY (Wet)	22nd		Quiet day spent in Wagon washing, greasing, & cleaning of harness preparatory to another move.	EH
BRUAY (Dull rain)	23rd		Lt Col. H. Biddulph brought on the Strength on arrival to Command VICE Col. Hobday Orders issued to Hay & Shaw band the spokes of all wheels. Officers arrived from 2nd D. A. C. to inspect this Units Billets and Standings prior to taking over.	EH
BRUAY. (Snow all day)	24th		Two S. Smiths, 1 Gnr. and 5 Drivers struck off the Strength on evacuation. 25 O.R. brought on the Strength on arrival from Base & attached to Sections. One Riding horse struck off the Strength on evacuation. Col. Hobday departed for England to report to War Office.	
		9am	No 1 Section & H.Q. moved off in F. S. M. O. for Barlin.	
		10am	No 3 " moved off in F. S. M. O. for Barlin.	EH

2353 Wt. W2544/1454 700,000 5/15 D. D. & L. A.D.S.S./Forms/C. 2118.

Army Form C. 2118.

Instructions regarding War Diaries and Intelligence Summaries are contained in F. S. Regs., Part II. and the Staff Manual respectively. Title pages will be prepared in manuscript.

WAR DIARY

or

~~INTELLIGENCE SUMMARY.~~

(Erase heading not required.)

Place	Date 1916	Hour	Summary of Events and Information	Remarks and references to Appendices
BARLIN (Fairly Bright Afternoon)	Mch 24th	noon	The D.A.C including No 2 Section arrived. Vehicles parked in Fields and Side Roads. Men in huts left by the French and Animals on Standings.	EA.
BARLIN (Dull Wet)	25th		4 Drivers brought on the Strength + posted to Sections 1 Mule struck off the Strength on evacuation. A. S. C. Forage Wagons with horses Drivers + loaders returned to Divl Train charger struck off the Strength on transfer to Brigade. Gnr + Dvr struck off the Strength on posting to a Brigade.	EA.
BARLIN (Wet morning Brighter Afternoon)	26th	11am	Divine Service for non conformists	
		3pm	Divine Service for Church of England Dvr. brought on the Strength on return from Hospital One mule struck off on evacuation 12 H.D. Horses struck off on being taken over by 12th Div. 45 L.D. Horses brought on the Strength on arrival from Base Ammunition of various sorts fairly heavy. 2 Officers 21 O.R. attached St. Venant for Trench Mortar Battery	EA.
BARLIN (Dull Wet)	27th		4 Drivers struck off the Strength on evacuation. 74 men attended Bathing Parade 3 Bdrs + 12 men attached to Brigade for Signalling Course. Baggage wagons returned to A. S. C. 13 Gunners + 10 Drivers struck off the Strength on posting to Brigades.	EA.

2353 Wt. W2544/1454 700,000 5/15 D. D. & L. A.D.S.S./Forms/C. 2118.

Instructions regarding War Diaries and Intelligence Summaries are contained in F. S. Regs., Part II. and the Staff Manual respectively. Title pages will be prepared in manuscript.

WAR DIARY
or
INTELLIGENCE SUMMARY.
(Erase heading not required.)

Army Form C. 2118.

Place	Date	Hour	Summary of Events and Information	Remarks and references to Appendices
	1916 Mch			
BARLIN	27th		G.O.C. R.A. ~~arrived~~ visited D.A.C.	
			A.D.V.S. & O.C. inspected Horses of 23rd D.A.C. and reclassified same as regards H.D. & L.D.	E.H.
BARLIN (Fine)	28th		13 Gunners & 10 Drivers struck off the Strength on posting to Bdes.	
			Court of Enquiry held as to G.S. Wagon damaged.	
			1 S/Smith brought on the Strength on return from hospital	
			1 L.D. Horse & 1 Mule struck off on evacuation to Mobile Vety. Sec.	
			74 O.R. Bathed at Shower Baths at Pitheads 28 Centimes per man.	
			Promotions made to complete to Establishment.	
			Orders issued for N.C.O.s to be dealt with by O.C. not Section Commdrs. also for all Defaulters to parade at H.Q. D.A.C. and be inspected by the D.A.C. Orderly Officer.	[signature]
BARLIN (Fine)	29th		1 A/Bdr. brought on the Strength on arrival from Base.	
			Medical Inspection of No 1 Section.	
			144 attended the Baths	
			Four Gunners sent to each Brigade for a weeks course of Gunnery.	
			1 Horse and 1 Mule struck off on evacuation.	
			Ammunition Normal	
			Lieut & Adjt. G. Hancock R.F.A. proceeded on 8 days leave to England	
			2Lt. F.G. Squire R.F.A. detailed to officiate in his absence	[signature]

Instructions regarding War Diaries and Intelligence Summaries are contained in F. S. Regs., Part II. and the Staff Manual respectively. Title pages will be prepared in manuscript.

WAR DIARY
or
INTELLIGENCE SUMMARY.
(Erase heading not required.)

Army Form C. 2118.

Place	Date	Hour	Summary of Events and Information	Remarks and references to Appendices
	1916			
BARLIN (Bright)	Mch 30th		Three G. S. Wagons with 6 S. Sets of Wheel and 12 S. Sets of Lead Harness handed over to Ordnance Officer, Railhead, BRUAY for transmission to Base. this with the one handed to 47th Div reduces establishment to 94 G. S. Wagons with complement of Drivers Animals and Harness.	
			18 L.D. Horses handed over to 34th Div. in connection with above.	
			Farrier Sergeant brought on the Strength and posted to No 1 Section to fill an existing vacancy.	
			1 Riding horse struck off Strength.	
			72 O.R. attended Baths	
			H.Q. medically inspected	
			Transfer of No 3 Section to new site commenced.	[illegible]
BARLIN (Fair)	31st		1 Horse struck off on evacuation 1 Mule struck off dead.	
			144 attended Bathing Parades	
			Ammunition normal. Quiet day generally.	[illegible]

2353 Wt. W2544/1454 700,000 5/15 D. D. & L. A.D.S.S./Forms/C. 2118.

Instructions regarding War Diaries and Intelligence Summaries are contained in F. S. Regs., Part II. and the Staff Manual respectively. Title pages will be prepared in manuscript.

WAR DIARY
or
INTELLIGENCE SUMMARY.
(Erase heading not required.)

Army Form C. 2118.

23 DAC
Vol 7

Place	Date 1916	Hour	Summary of Events and Information	Remarks and references to Appendices
BARLIN (Bright)	April 1st		One driver brought on the Strength on return from Hospital An exceedingly quiet day	EH.
BARLIN (Fine)	2nd		Divine Service - R.Cs 7 a.m. C. of E. 2.45 p.m. Non-conformist 6 p.m. One G.S. Wagon 6 Mules and 3 Drivers attached to 23rd Salvage Corps. Postings of N.C.O's amongst Sections to equalize. Ammunition Normal.	EH.
BARLIN (Sunny)	3rd		Two drivers struck off the Strength on departure to the Base as medically unfit for the Front Receipts + Issues of Ammunition - Normal.	EH.
BARLIN (Fine)	4th		Visit by G.O.C. 23rd Division. 1 Corpl. 1 Bdr + 1 Dvr struck off the Strength on evacuation out of the Divl. Area. 54 O.R. brought on the Strength on arrival from the Base. 1 Mule struck off the Strength on evacuation to Mob Vet Sec Ammunition - Normal.	EH.
BARLIN (Cold)	5th		One horse struck off the Strength on Evac. to Mob. Vet. Sec. Ammtn - Normal. Generally a quiet day.	EH.

2353 Wt. W2544/1454 700,000 5/15 D. D. & L. A.D.S.S./Forms/C. 2118.

Instructions regarding War Diaries and Intelligence Summaries are contained in F. S. Regs., Part II. and the Staff Manual respectively. Title pages will be prepared in manuscript.

WAR DIARY
or
~~INTELLIGENCE SUMMARY.~~
(Erase heading not required.)

Army Form C. 2118.

Place	Date	Hour	Summary of Events and Information	Remarks and references to Appendices
	1916			
BARLIN (Dull - Rain night)	April 6th		43 O.R. posted to Brigades and struck off the Strength A/B.S.M. confirmed in his rank as B.S.M. Medical Inspection of newly joined draft. Ammunition Receipts + Issues - Normal.	EH.
BARLIN (Dull Cold)	7th		2nd Lt C G Bartlett R.F.A. detailed for duty with Z/23 Trench Mortar Battery. Medical Inspection of all newly joined men. Watering Orders published Ammunition - Normal	EH.
BARLIN (Bright)	8th		Orders issued that no Empty Cartridge Cases may be accepted unless packed in Boxes. Quiet day with the usual receipts and issues of Ammunition.	EH.
BARLIN (Fine)	9th		Divine Services for C. of E. Nonconformists and R. C's. Twenty O.R. taken on the Strength on arrival from the Base Ammunition receipts and issues normal.	EH
BARLIN (Dull Cold)	10th		1 Driver struck off the Strength on evacuation out of the Divl Area Quiet day spent in overhauling vehicles &c Ammunition Receipts and issues as usual.	EH.

2353 Wt. W2544/1454 700,000 5/15 D. D. & L. A.D.S.S./Forms/C. 2118.

Instructions regarding War Diaries and Intelligence Summaries are contained in F. S. Regs., Part II. and the Staff Manual respectively. Title pages will be prepared in manuscript.

WAR DIARY
or
~~INTELLIGENCE SUMMARY~~.

(Erase heading not required.)

Army Form C. 2118.

Place	Date 1916	Hour	Summary of Events and Information	Remarks and references to Appendices
BARLIN (Wet)	April 11th	9 a.m	G.O.C. R.A visited the D.A.C	
		11 a.m	All animals inspected by the D.D.V.S and the Clipping of all Animals ordered.	
			1 Fitt. Bdr 4 Gnrs and 8 Drivers struck off the Strength on ~~[illegible]~~ Posting to Brigades.	
			140 men paraded and Marched to the Baths.	
			Ammunition - Normal.	EH.
BARLIN (Dull, Cold Wet, Windy)	12th		Orders issued as to the number of Employed men allowed per Section	
			Exchange of four Gunners with each Brigade for training	
			All Blankets disinfected.	
			All undercoats fur called in and returned to Ordnance	
			Ammunition - Normal	EH.
BARLIN (Bright Showery)	13th		One Gunner brought on the Strength on return from Hospital.	
			All leave to the United Kingdom stopped until further Orders.	
			Cases of Drunkenness not to be disposed of without reference to H.Q. R.A.	
			2nd Lieut. R. S. de S. Brock R.F.A. 1 N.C.O. and 5 O.R. attached to A/23rd Trench Mortar Battery for duty.	
			Promotions made to fill existing vacancies.	
			The usual receipts and issues of Ammunition.	EH.

2353 Wt. W2544/1454 700,000 5/15 D. D. & L. A.D.S.S./Forms/C. 2118.

Instructions regarding War Diaries and Intelligence Summaries are contained in F. S. Regs., Part II. and the Staff Manual respectively. Title pages will be prepared in manuscript.

WAR DIARY
or
~~INTELLIGENCE SUMMARY.~~
(Erase heading not required.)

Army Form C. 2118.

Place	Date	Hour	Summary of Events and Information	Remarks and references to Appendices
	1916 April			
BARLIN (Windy Showery)	14th		2nd Lieut. G C Doddemeade having reported his arrival from No 2 General Base, Havre brought on the Strength and temporarily attached to No 1 Sec. 24 Other Ranks brought on the Strength on arrival from the Base 140 Men attended the Baths Ammunition Normal.	EH.
BARLIN (Bright Windy Showery)	15th		24 O.R. struck off the Strength on posting to Brigades 1 Horse struck off the Strength - dead. 140 men paraded for the Baths. Usual receipts and issues of Ammunition	EH.
BARLIN (Fair)	16th		One ?Bdr and 1 Dvr struck off the Strength on evacuation out of the Divisional Area Divine Service - C of E 2.45 pm - R.C. 2.45 pm - Non conformists 7 pm 1 L D Horse destroyed and struck off the Strength Ammunition Normal.	EH.
BARLIN (Wet-Windy)	17th		1 Horse struck off the Strength on evacuation to Mob. Vety Section. 140 men paraded for Baths Quiet day Ammunition - Normal	EH.

Army Form C. 2118.

Instructions regarding War Diaries and Intelligence Summaries are contained in F. S. Regs., Part II. and the Staff Manual respectively. Title pages will be prepared in manuscript.

WAR DIARY
or
INTELLIGENCE SUMMARY.
(Erase heading not required.)

Place	Date	Hour	Summary of Events and Information	Remarks and references to Appendices
	1916			
BARLIN (Wet. Cold. Windy)	Apl. 18th		Orders issued forbidding all correspondence etc with Strangers	
			1 Driver struck off the strength on posting to a Brigade	
			1 Mule (dead) struck off the strength	
			A/Bdr reverted to permanent rank of Gunner	
			Ammunition somewhat scarce Brigades completing to Establishment	EH.
BARLIN (Wet. Cold Windy)	19th		Two mules struck off the strength on evacuation to Mob Vety Sec	
			S/Smith promoted Corporal to fill an existing vacancy	
			Ammunition Normal	EH.
BARLIN (Wet Morn Fine day)	20th		1 Officer, 30 O.R. and 50 Animals attached to 2nd D.A.C.	
		8.45am	No 1 Section moved off in F.S.M.O.	
		9.45am	No 2 Section (less detachment) moved off in F.S.M.O.	
		10.45am	No 3 Section moved off in F.S.M.O.	
		11am	H.Q. moved off each Unit arriving an hour later at	
BRUAY			Took over Billets and horse standings vacated by the Relieving Unit viz: 2nd D.A.C.	
			Men billetted in Barns Sheds and Houses, Horses under Shelters all on the BRUAY - BETHUNE main road situated on the extreme edge of Bruay.	EH.

2353 Wt. W2544/1454 700,000 5/15 D. D. & L. A.D.S.S./Forms/C. 2118.

Instructions regarding War Diaries and Intelligence Summaries are contained in F. S. Regs., Part II. and the Staff Manual respectively. Title pages will be prepared in manuscript.

WAR DIARY
or
~~INTELLIGENCE SUMMARY.~~
(Erase heading not required.)

Army Form C. 2118.

Place	Date 1916	Hour	Summary of Events and Information	Remarks and references to Appendices
BRUAY. (Fine-Dull)	April 21st		1 Horse struck off the Strength on evacuation to Vety Mob Section. 2 N C O's and 20 Drivers brought on the Strength on arrival from the Base. Quiet day cleaning harness &c after the Move	EH.
BRUAY (Wet)	22nd		2nd Lieut E Middleton R.F.A struck off the Strength on evacuation out of the Country Authority War Office A.G. 4 a dated 13-4-16. S Smith taken on the Strength on arrival from the Base. 1 Sgt 1 Bomdr and 12 Gunners attached to the T M Batteries for instruction. Amended detail published.	EH.
BRUAY (Bright)	23rd		Five Officers temporarily brought on the Strength on arrival from the Base. 9 Drivers struck off the Strength on ~~evacuation~~ posting. to Brigades. 1 Sgt 1 Gnr + 4 Drivers struck off the Strength on evacuation. Postings made amongst Sections to equalize. 3 men attached to each Brigade for a course of Signalling whilst in rest. G S Wagon with Drivers Animals + Harness complete transferred from No 1 Section to No 3 Section for the carriage of Bombs. Divine Services — R. C's 8 30 a.m. C. of E. 9 30 a.m.	EH.

2353 Wt. W2544/1454 700,000 5/15 D. D. & L. A.D.S.S./Forms/C. 2118.

Instructions regarding War Diaries and Intelligence Summaries are contained in F. S. Regs., Part II. and the Staff Manual respectively. Title pages will be prepared in manuscript.

WAR DIARY
or
~~INTELLIGENCE SUMMARY.~~
(*Erase heading not required.*)

Army Form C. 2118.

Place	Date 1916	Hour	Summary of Events and Information	Remarks and references to Appendices
BRUAY (Bright - Mild)	April 24th		A General holiday by order of G.O.C. R.A as far as the care of the Animals would admit.	
BRUAY (Clear)	25th		Two Officers left for Brigades and 2Lt A M Campbell & 2Lt M.D McKenzie posted to No 1 Section, 2Lt G C Doddemeade & 2Lt H E Thompson posted to No 3 Section. 1 Gunner on arrival from the Base brought on the Strength 1 Sgt + 1 Gnr struck off the Strength on evacuation. 100 men paraded for the Baths. Orders issued to cease clipping animals unless lousy.	EH
BRUAY (Bright)	26th		1 Sgt brought on the Strength on return from Hospital. 1 Cpl + 1 Bdr struck off the Strength on posting to a Brigade. 1 Horse struck off the Strength on evacuation to Mob Vety Section. Leave to United Kingdom re-opened. 300 All Ranks detailed for Gas Demonstration at H.Q. R.A. 100 men paraded for Baths. Promotions Appointments and Postings made in Sections to fill existing vacancies.	EH.
BRUAY (Bright)	27th		2 Drivers struck off the Strength on evacuation. 100 men paraded for Baths A quiet day	EH.

2353 Wt. W2544/1454 700,000 5/15 D. D. & L. A.D.S.S./Forms/C. 2118.

Army Form C. 2118.

Instructions regarding War Diaries and Intelligence Summaries are contained in F. S. Regs., Part II. and the Staff Manual respectively. Title pages will be prepared in manuscript.

WAR DIARY
or
INTELLIGENCE SUMMARY.
(Erase heading not required.)

Place	Date 1916	Hour	Summary of Events and Information	Remarks and references to Appendices
BRUAY (Bright)	April 28th		12 Gunners + 3 Drivers brought on the Strength on arrival from the Base. 2 Horses struck off the Strength on evacuation to Mob. Vety Section. 1 Mule (died) struck off the Strength 100 men paraded for the Baths. Field General Court Martial on Saddler Willis Teale No 3 Section for Drunkenness.	EH.
BRUAY (Fine)	29th		Dvr. brought on the Strength on arrival from Hospital. Orders issued for all ranks to be in their Billets by 9 p.m 100 men paraded for Baths. H. A. Windsor posted to command No 3 Section.	EH.
BRUAY (Fine)	30th		9 ~~Drivers~~ Gunners + 3 Drivers struck off the Strength on posting to Brigades. 1 Gnr. - 3 Drvs. Struck off the Strength on evacuation. Inspection by G. O. C. R. A. of Hdqts Nos 2 + 3 Sections. 150 All ranks detailed for Gas Demonstration at H. Q. R. A.	EH.

23 Div Am Col
Vol 9

Army Form C. 2118.

Instructions regarding War Diaries and Intelligence Summaries are contained in F. S. Regs., Part II. and the Staff Manual respectively. Title pages will be prepared in manuscript.

WAR DIARY
or
INTELLIGENCE SUMMARY.
(Erase heading not required.)

Place	Date 1916	Hour	Summary of Events and Information	Remarks and references to Appendices
BRUAY (Fine)	May 1st		Bdr brought on the Strength on arrival from the Base. 1 Gnr 5 Drs struck off the Strength on evacuation out of the Divl Area. Quiet day.	EH
BRUAY (Fine Cloudy Showers)	2nd		80 men paraded for Baths. Inspection of No 1 Section in F.S.M.O. by G.O.C. R.A. Another quiet day.	
BRUAY (Fine but Showery)	3rd		Driver brought on the Strength on return from Hospital. 1 H.D. Horse struck off the Strength (dead)	EH
BRUAY (Fine)	4th		1 Dvr from Base & 1 Dvr returning from Hospital brought on the Strength. 1 Mule struck off the Strength on evacuation to Mob. Vet. Sec. Rifle drill ordered daily in the early mornings. Bran mash ordered once a week for all Animals. 80 men paraded for Baths.	EH EH
BRUAY (Dull Sultry)	5th		80 men paraded for Baths. 3 Gnrs permanently posted to Trench Mortar Batteries. 2/Lt C. G. Bartlett re posted from Trench Mortar Batteries to D.A.C.	EH

Instructions regarding War Diaries and Intelligence Summaries are contained in F. S. Regs., Part II. and the Staff Manual respectively. Title pages will be prepared in manuscript.

WAR DIARY
or
INTELLIGENCE SUMMARY.
(Erase heading not required.)

Army Form C. 2118.

Place	Date 1916	Hour	Summary of Events and Information	Remarks and references to Appendices
BRUAY (Fine-Windy)	MAY 6th		1 Dvr. struck off the Strength on evacuation out of the Divl. Area. 1 Mule struck off the Strength on evac. to the Mob. Vet. Sec. 80 men paraded for Baths. Orders issued for 3 men to be always in the Farriers Shop under training and 1 man in the Saddlers Shop under instruction.	EH
BRUAY (Fair)	7th		C. of E. parades at 11 + 6. A very quiet day.	EH
BRUAY (Dull with Rain)	8th		80 men paraded for Baths. 1 Bdr. brought on the Strength on arrival from the Base. 3 Mules struck off the Strength on evacuation to the Vet. Mob. Sec. Orders issued for the weekly inspection of all Hands by M.O. i/c.	EH
BRUAY (Rain with cold wind)	9th		80 men paraded for Baths. Two mules struck off the Strength, 1 lost, 1 to Mobile Veterinary Section Two Drivers brought on the Strength from the Base.	EH.
BRUAY (Cloudy cold Bright)	10th		Visit from the G.O.C. R.A. Orders received for the move of the D.A.C. to BRUAY. 80 men paraded for Baths. 5 Horses + 3 Mules struck off the Strength on evacuation to the Mob. Vet. Sec.	EH.

2353 Wt. W2544/1454 700,000 5/15 D. D. & L. A.D.S.S./Forms/C. 2118.

Army Form C. 2118.

WAR DIARY
or
~~INTELLIGENCE SUMMARY.~~
(*Erase heading not required.*)

Instructions regarding War Diaries and Intelligence Summaries are contained in F. S. Regs., Part II. and the Staff Manual respectively. Title pages will be prepared in manuscript.

Place	Date 1916	Hour	Summary of Events and Information	Remarks and references to Appendices
BRUAY. (Dull-Chilly)	MAY 11th		80 men paraded for Baths Orders issued urging the necessity of re-inoculation 7 Mules struck off the Strength on evacuation to Mob. Vety. Section 15 H.D. Horses struck off the Strength on transfer to No 1 Field Remount Depot Orders issued for All Water troughs to be taken when the Unit marches away. Orders issued for an Officer N.C.O. + 3 men per Section to go in advance and take over Amtn &c.	EA
BRUAY (Dull)	12th		80 men paraded for Baths. 1 Gnr struck off the Strength on evacuation out of the Divl. Area 6 Drs brought on the Strength on return to their Unit 24 men brought on the Strength on arrival from the Base	EA.
BRUAY (Dull-Cold)	13th		Rifle Inspection by the C.O. 80 men paraded for Baths. Preparations made for the impending move	EA.
BRUAY. (Dull-Damp)	14th		Quiet day spent in getting ready to move the following day. The Adjutant attended conference at H.Q. R.A. when abolition of Artillery Brigade Amtn. Cols and the reorganisation of the D.A.C. was decided to commence at once. All preparations made accordingly.	EA.

2353 Wt. W2544/1454 700,000 5/15 D. D. & L. A.D.S.S./Forms/C. 2118.

Instructions regarding War Diaries and Intelligence Summaries are contained in F. S. Regs., Part II. and the Staff Manual respectively. Title pages will be prepared in manuscript.

WAR DIARY
or
~~INTELLIGENCE SUMMARY.~~
(Erase heading not required.)

Army Form C. 2118.

Place	Date 1916	Hour	Summary of Events and Information	Remarks and references to Appendices
BRUAY (Wet - Clear)	MAY 15th	8 a.m.	No 1 Section moved off	
		9 a.m.	No 3 Section and Hdqrs moved off	
		10 a.m.	No 2 Section moved off. The Unit about an hour after arriving at	
BARLIN			and relieving the 2nd D.A.C.	
			Later, part of No 1 Section marched to Fosse 7 near Barlin and joined the old 105th Brigade Ammn. Col. the whole becoming No 3 Section of the new 23rd D.A.C.	
			Part of No 2 Section marched to HERSIN and joined the old 103rd Bde Ammn. Col. the whole becoming No 2 Section of the new 23rd D.A.C	
			Part of No 3 Section marched to LA THIEULOYE and joined the old 104th Bde Am. Col. the whole becoming No 1 Section. These 3 Sections with Hdqrs forming "A" Echelon of a reorganised Div. Am. Col.	EH
BARLIN (Bright)	16th		A number of Personnel + Vehicles formed to join the old 102nd B.A.C which marched into BARLIN the whole forming No 4 Section 23rd Div Am Col	
		noon	All 23 Div. R.A. Brigade Columns + old 23rd D.A.C ceased to exist. The new 23rd D.A.C. with 4 Sections came into being.	EH
			Departure of D.A.C. Details by Road to Calais.	
BARLIN. (Fine)	17th	[illegible]	Arrangements made as regards surplus personnel and animals on reorganization. Postings made to Brigades	EH

2353 Wt. W2544/1454 700,000 5/15 D. D. & L. A.D.S.S./Forms/C. 2118.

Instructions regarding War Diaries and Intelligence Summaries are contained in F. S. Regs., Part II. and the Staff Manual respectively. Title pages will be prepared in manuscript.

WAR DIARY
or
INTELLIGENCE SUMMARY.

(*Erase heading not required.*)

Army Form C. 2118.

Place	Date	Hour	Summary of Events and Information	Remarks and references to Appendices
	1916	9.45	Parade of D. A. C. Details to proceed to Calais by Rail	
BARLIN (Fine)	MAY 18th		Officer and N.C.O. detailed for 3 day course of Instruction on Gas. Saddler struck off the Strength on Evacuation out of the Divl Area Postings made amongst Sections Usual receipts and issues of Ammunition.	EH.
BARLIN (Fine)	19th	~~9.45~~	~~Parade of D. A. C. Details to proceed to Calais by Rail~~ EH Orders issued for Nos 1. 2. + 3 Sections to each have 4 sub sections and No 4 6 sub sections. All ~~[illegible]~~ Vehicles to be equally distributed amongst these sub sections. All surplus vehicles on reorganization despatched to CALAIS by Rail @ 3pm Postings among Sections.	EH
BARLIN (Fine)	20th		2 Gunners + 1 Driver struck off the Strength on posting to Brigades 1 Horse struck off the Strength on posting to Brigade. Ammunition - Normal.	EH
BARLIN (Fine)	21st		Orders issued for all Stables to be lime washed and all brushes disinfected. Driver brought on the Strength on arrival from the Base.	EH
BARLIN (Dull. Rain Cool)	22nd		Postings made to equalize Sections 1 Driver struck off the Strength on evacuation out of the Divisional Area 2/Lt J. H. Hutchinson attached to No 4 Section " G. H. Hamer attached to No 1 Section + " N. C. Brown attached to No 3 Section	EH

2353 Wt. W2544/1454 700,000 5/15 D. D. & L. A.D.S.S./Forms/C. 2118.

Instructions regarding War Diaries and Intelligence Summaries are contained in F. S. Regs., Part II. and the Staff Manual respectively. Title pages will be prepared in manuscript.

WAR DIARY
or
~~INTELLIGENCE SUMMARY.~~
(Erase heading not required.)

Army Form C. 2118.

Place	Date 1916	Hour	Summary of Events and Information	Remarks and references to Appendices
BARLIN (Fine-Cloudy)	MAY 23rd		1 Gnr brought on the Strength on return to the D.A.C. 5 men struck off the Strength on evacuation out of the Divl. Area. 2 Mules struck off the Strength on evacuation to the Mob. Vet. Sec.	EH
BARLIN (Dull)	24th		1 Driver brought on the Strength on discharge from Hospital + posted to No 4 Section. 12 Gunners brought on the Strength on arrival from the Base. 2 Officers + 20 OR having arrived from A/23 Trench Mortar Battery brought on the Strength and temporarily attached to No 4 Section.	EH
BARLIN (Dull Showery)	25th		2 L. D. Horses struck off the Strength on evacuation out of the Divl. Area. Postings made to Brigades &c. A quiet day	EH
BARLIN (Fair)	26th		1 Driver struck off the Strength on evacuation out of the Divl. Area 1 Driver struck off the Strength on posting to 102nd Bde	EH
BARLIN (Fine)	27th		Daily Routine issued for all Sections. 2Lt. G. H. Hawkins Lt. N. C Brown + 2Lt. J. H. Hamer posted to 105th Bde R.F.A. Wheeler brought on the Strength on arrival from the Base. Capt J. A. French posted to Tempy Command of No 3 Section on arrival from the Base. 2Lt. Elssop posted to No 3 Section on arrival after receipt of a Commission from the Ranks. No 69711 Dvr. Pilbury returned after being absent 6 months in England having been taken ill whilst on leave.	EH

Instructions regarding War Diaries and Intelligence Summaries are contained in F. S. Regs., Part II. and the Staff Manual respectively. Title pages will be prepared in manuscript.

WAR DIARY
or
~~INTELLIGENCE SUMMARY.~~
(Erase heading not required.)

Army Form C. 2118.

Place	Date 1916	Hour	Summary of Events and Information	Remarks and references to Appendices
BARLIN (Fine)	MAY 28th	2.30pm	Divine Service	
			Driver + S/Smith posted on return from Hospital to Sections	
			1 Driver struck off the Strength on posting to a Brigade.	
			1 Mule + 1 Horse struck off the Strength on evacuation to Mobile Vety Section.	EH
BARLIN (Fine)	29th		1 Sergeant brought on the Strength on arrival from the Base	
			1 Horse + 3 Mules struck off on evacuation to the Mobile Veterinary Section.	
			Section Commanders impressed with the necessity of weekly Medical Examination of all ranks for Scabies	EH
BARLIN (Fine)	30th		1 Driver 1 Gunner + 1 S/Smith struck off the Strength on posting to Brigades	
			Orders issued re the markings of all Vehicles.	
BARLIN (Bright)	31st		Examination of and report on all 4.5 Amm. Baskets ordered.	EH
			Three Drivers mustered Gunners.	
			Orders issued re trial of certain cases by C.O. and not Section Commanders.	
			Dr. Pilsbury again admitted into Hospital.	EH

2353 Wt. W2544/1454 700,000 5/15 D. D. & L. A.D.S.S./Forms/C. 2118.

WAR DIARY
or
INTELLIGENCE SUMMARY.
(Erase heading not required.)

Army Form C. 2118.

Instructions regarding War Diaries and Intelligence Summaries are contained in F. S. Regs., Part II. and the Staff Manual respectively. Title pages will be prepared in manuscript.

23 D. Am Col
Vol 10

Place	Date 1916	Hour	Summary of Events and Information	Remarks and references to Appendices
BARLIN. (Fine)	JUNE 1st		1 Horse struck off the Strength on evacuation to the Mob. Vety Sec. Postings amongst Sections. Lt Col W. A. Nicholson (105th Bde Commander) assumed Command of the 23rd D.A.C. in addition to his other duties.	EH.
BARLIN (Fine)	2nd		Order issued for all Mules not clipped to be clipped at once. Driver mustered Gunner. 3 Drivers brought on the Strength on arrival from the Base also 1 Fitter, 2 W/Bdrs and 4 Gnrs.	EH.
BARLIN (Fine)	3rd		Strict Orders issued for all Water Troughs to be kept thoroughly clean. 1 Dvr struck off the Strength. A very quiet day.	EH.
BARLIN (Dull Cold Windy)	4th	11 a.m.	Divine Service. 1 Horse struck off the Strength on evacuation to the Mobile Veterinary Section. All 4.5" Howitzer Shrapnel Baskets to be converted to carry 4.5" H.E. Shell. All 4.5" Howitzer Ammunition Baskets to be fitted with shoulder wedges for Shell. All wedges to be used at all times when packing 4.5" H.E. Shell.	EH.
BARLIN (Dull)	5th		1 Mule struck off the Strength having died. Tally taken of number of Horses from all Units using the Water Troughs. Visited by G.O.C. R.A.	EH.

2353 Wt. W2544/1454 700,000 5/15 D. D. & L. A.D.S.S./Forms/C. 2118.

Army Form C. 2118.

Instructions regarding War Diaries and Intelligence Summaries are contained in F. S. Regs., Part II. and the Staff Manual respectively. Title pages will be prepared in manuscript.

WAR DIARY
or
INTELLIGENCE SUMMARY.
(Erase heading not required.)

Place	Date 1916	Hour	Summary of Events and Information	Remarks and references to Appendices
BARLIN (Heavy with showers - Bright)	June 6th		1 Horse struck off the Strength on evacuation to Mobile Veterinary Section. 2 a/Bdrs 1 Fitter and 4 Gunners struck off the Strength on posting to 165th Brigade R.F.A. 30 men brought on the Strength on arrival from the Base Postings amongst Sections 3 Drivers struck off the Strength on evacuation out of the Divisional Area	EH.
BARLIN (Dull)	7th		2 Horses struck off the Strength on evacuation to the Mob. Vet. Sec. A very quiet day.	EH.
BARLIN (Bright - Dull - Rain)	8th		1 Far Sgt 1 Cpl S.S. 1 a/Bdr 16 Gnrs 8 Drvs + 2 Shsmiths struck off the Strength on posting to Brigades. Ldr reverts at own request to permanent rank of Driver. Postings amongst Brigades Sections.	EH.
BARLIN (Dull - Showery)	9th		Lieut H. Cornwell R.F.A. brought on the Strength on arrival and attached to No 1 Section. Another quiet day	EH.
BARLIN (Dull - Thunder - Rain)	10th		Capt. H C Courage brought on the Strength on arrival and posted to Command of No 3 Section. 1 Gunner struck off the Strength on evacuation out of the Divl. Area.	EH.

Army Form C. 2118.

Instructions regarding War Diaries and Intelligence Summaries are contained in F. S. Regs., Part II. and the Staff Manual respectively. Title pages will be prepared in manuscript.

WAR DIARY
or
INTELLIGENCE SUMMARY.
(Erase heading not required.)

Place	Date 1916	Hour	Summary of Events and Information	Remarks and references to Appendices
BARLIN (Thunder Storm with rain - Dull)	JUNE 11th		1 Bdr and 1 Dr. struck off the Strength on evacuation out of the Divl Area. 1 Horse struck off the Strength on evacuation 1 Gnr + 1 Dvr brought on the Strength on posting from Brigade	EH.
		11 a.m.	Divine Service Orders issued that Ammunition must not be dumped on the ground but raised at least 4 to 6 inches therefrom.	
BARLIN (Dull - Cold - Wet)	12th		1 Dvr. struck off the Strength on evacuation out of the Divl. Area. Visits from + to 47th Division re taking over of Billets Offices &c. Otherwise a quiet day.	
BARLIN (Dull Cold - Wet)	13th		Two mules struck off the Strength Laid down that the Strength of Rifles per Section is 147. Order re published that all men on leave losing their warrants shall forfeit all leave for 1 year and pay their own fare back to France.	EH.
BARLIN (Dull + Cold)	14th	10 a.m.	Headquarters removed from Chateau to a small Farm handing over the former to the 47th Division 3 Horses struck off the Strength on evacuation to the Mob. Vety Sec Baggage + Supply wagons attached to the Sections from Divl Train.	EH.
BARLIN (Dull - Cold)	15th		Orders issued that men re engaging for duration of War are not now entitled to the months furlough.	
		11 p.m.	Standard Time changed by advancing all clocks one hour.	EH.

2353 Wt. W2544/1454 700,000 5/15 D. D. & L. A.D.S.S./Forms/C. 2118.

Army Form C. 2118.

Instructions regarding War Diaries and Intelligence Summaries are contained in F. S. Regs., Part II. and the Staff Manual respectively. Title pages will be prepared in manuscript.

WAR DIARY
or
~~INTELLIGENCE SUMMARY.~~
(Erase heading not required.)

Place	Date 1916	Hour	Summary of Events and Information	Remarks and references to Appendices
BARLIN (Fine - Cold)	JUNE 16th		Capt. C D W Archer assumed Command of the 25th D.A.C.	
			8 Gunners detailed Six Section for Hy Trench Mortar Batteries.	
			Lieut H. Cornwell detailed to remain behind 3 hours after last party vacates for purpose of Claims etc.	
			Section Commanders to send forward N.C.O.s to ascertain exact locations of Billets, return & conduct Sections there.	
			N.C.O.s & men attached to A/25 T.M. Battery returned to Sections on disbanding of this Battery.	
		11 a.m	No 4 Section moved off	
		noon	H.Q. Nos 1, 2 & 3 Sections moved off.	
TANGRY		4.30	Hdqrs & No 4 Section arrived. Horses in Fields, Vehicles on Roadside & Fields	
		4.45	Nos 1 & 2 Sections arrived at SAINS-les-PERNES Horses in Field Vehicles on Roadside	
		6.30	No 3 Section arrived at TANGRY Horses in Fields Vehicles on Roadside & Fields. All men of the D A C billetted in Barns.	EA.
TANGRY (Fair)	17th	7 a.m	Nos 1 & 2 Sections moved off	
		7.30 a	No 3 Section moved off	
		8 a.m	H.Q. & No 4 Section moved off	
ROQUITOIRE		3.15 pm	No 1 Section arrived & billetted at QUEUSTEDE	Horses & Vehicles in Fields used for the purpose previously
		"	No 2 Section arrived & billetted at ROQUEUTOIRE	
		4 pm	No 3 Section arrived and billetted at QUEUSTEDE	Men in Barns and outbuildings.
		4.15 pm	No 4 Section arrived and billetted at ECQUES	EA.

Instructions regarding War Diaries and Intelligence Summaries are contained in F. S. Regs., Part II. and the Staff Manual respectively. Title pages will be prepared in manuscript.

WAR DIARY
or
INTELLIGENCE SUMMARY.
(Erase heading not required.)

Army Form C. 2118.

Place	Date 1916	Hour	Summary of Events and Information	Remarks and references to Appendices
ROQUITOIRE (Fine - Cloudy)	JUNE 18th		Overhauling grooming and generally cleaning up.	
			Orders published with regard to men injured through tampering with detonators fuzes &c.	
			Orders issued re Discipline on line of March.	
ROQUITOIRE (Dull Misty)	19th		1 Bdr 1 Whr. 16 Gunners and 9 Drivers struck off the Strength on posting to Bdes	E.H.
			1 Bdr 1 Sfsmith 1 Gunner and 3 Drivers struck off the Strength on evac. out of Divl Area	
		5 a.m	No 1 Section moved off for Manoeuvres.	
		5.30 a.m	Nos. 2 + 3 Sections moved off for Manoeuvres.	
			No 4 Section did not move off	
		7.30 a.m	Hdqrs moved off for Manoeuvres.	
			No 2 Section on return moved into Marne (Roquitoire)	
			Nos 1 + 3 Sections + H.Q. returned to the respective billets they previously occupied.	
ROQUITOIRE (Rain - Fair)	20th		A quiet day spent in overhauling grooming and cleaning up generally	E.H.
ROQUITOIRE (Dull)	21st		1 Bdr 1 Gnr + 4 Drvs struck off the Strength on evacuation out of the Divl Area	E.H.
			1 Dvr taken on the Strength on return from Hospital.	
			Orders issued for Section Commanders to indent direct for their Iron Rations.	E.H.
ROQUITOIRE (Sulky)	22nd		1 Bdr + 7 Gnrs struck off the Strength on posting to 10th Bde R.F.A.	
			Orders issued all Ammunition to be kept on Vehicles as far as possible Dumping not being permissible.	E.H.

2353 Wt. W2544/1454 700,000 5/15 D. D. & L. A.D.S.S./Forms/C. 2118.

Instructions regarding War Diaries and Intelligence Summaries are contained in F. S. Regs., Part II. and the Staff Manual respectively. Title pages will be prepared in manuscript.

WAR DIARY
or
INTELLIGENCE SUMMARY.
(Erase heading not required.)

Army Form C. 2118.

Place	Date	Hour	Summary of Events and Information	Remarks and references to Appendices
	1916 JUNE			
ROQUITOIRE (Sultry – Thunder – Rain – Fair)	23rd		All Orderlies with Brigades to be recalled to their respective Sections. Medical Inspection of All Ranks in each Section – Weights.	
ROQUITOIRE (Sunny with Clouds)	24th		Major H. G. Buchanan R. F. A. brought on the Strength on rejoining [illegible] arrival from 1st Division to command the 23rd D. A. C.	EH.
			1 Gunner 1 Dvr brought on the Strength on arrival from the Base 1st Div. 1 Mule struck off the Strength on evacuation to Mob. Vety Section.	
ROQUITOIRE (Hot, Sunny)	25th		During the day the D. A. C marched out H.Q. & No 1 Section to entrain at Lillers No 2 Section at Berguette & Nos 3 & 4 Sections at Aire the trains running at 3 hour intervals for LONGEAU (AMIENS) detrained there for	EH.
ARGŒUVES (Showery)	26th		Picketted Horses and parked Vehicles. Spent remainder of day in Grooming and cleaning up generally.	EH.
ARGŒUVES (Showery)	27th		1 Horse struck off the Strength on evacuation to Mob. Vety Section. Postings amongst Sections. ~~[illegible] Parade~~	EH.
ARGŒUVES (Dull)	28th		1 Bdr. 2 Gnrs. + 4 Drivers struck off the Strength on evacuation out of the Divl. Area. 1 Gnr brought on the Strength + posted to No 4 Section.	EH. EH.

2353 Wt. W2544/1454 700,000 5/15 D. D. & L. A.D.S.S./Forms/C. 2118.

Instructions regarding War Diaries and Intelligence Summaries are contained in F. S. Regs., Part II. and the Staff Manual respectively. Title pages will be prepared in manuscript.

WAR DIARY
or
INTELLIGENCE SUMMARY.
(Erase heading not required.)

Army Form C. 2118.

Place	Date	Hour	Summary of Events and Information	Remarks and references to Appendices
	1916			
ARGOEUVES (Fair)	JUNE 29th		3 Mules struck off the Strength on evacuation to Mobile Vety Section	
			1 Gnr 1 Dvr struck off the Strength on posting to Bdes.	
			1 Bdr + 1 Gnr brought on the Strength on return from Hospital.	
			F.G.C.M. at 104th Bde R.F.A. Wagon lines on a Driver + Gunner of D.A.C for "Drunkenness"	EH
ARGOEUVES (Sunshine)	30th		6 Horses struck off the Strength on evacuation to Mob. Vety. Section.	
		1 p.m.	Received Orders to be on the road at Dreuil Church by 2 p.m.	
		2 30	D.A.C on the road + proceeded to DREUIL	
		4 p.m.	D.A.C left Dreuil + marched in the following order - H.Q. Nos 1 2 3 + 4 Sections - via South side of the River SOMME to AMIENS thence via South Side of the Citadelle to	EH
ALLONVILLE		6.30 p.m.	Arrived. Parked Vehicles + Picketed Animals.	EH

Instructions regarding War Diaries and Intelligence Summaries are contained in F. S. Regs., Part II. and the Staff Manual respectively. Title pages will be prepared in manuscript.

WAR DIARY
or
INTELLIGENCE SUMMARY.
(Erase heading not required.)

Army Form C. 2118. July

23

DAC 23 DW

VOL 11

Place	Date	Hour	Summary of Events and Information	Remarks and references to Appendices
	1916 JULY			
ALLONVILLE Fine	1st	6.15 pm	Received orders to be ready to move off at 7 pm	
		7 pm	Ready	
		10 pm	Moved off in following order HQ Nos 1. 2. 3 & 4 Sections	
BEAUCOURT		11.45 pm	Arrived and Bivouaced in Fields &c.	SH.
BEAUCOURT Fine	2nd		1 Dvr brought on the strength on return from Hospital. 1 Horse struck off the strength on evacuation to Mob Vet Section. 1 Gnr struck off the strength on posting to 103rd Bde. R.F.A. 2nd Lieuts C. Gibson and A.E.G. KNIGHT struck off the strength on posting to 103rd Brigade R.F.A.	SH.
BEAUCOURT Fine	3rd		1 Sergt posted to 102nd Brigade R.F.A. and 1 Cpl posted therefrom to D.A.C. 1 B.S.M. struck off the strength on posting to a Brigade.	SH.
BEAUCOURT Fine	4th		Quiet day spent in Grooming Harness cleaning and cleaning Camp up generally	SH.
BEAUCOURT Fine	5th		1 Horse struck off the strength on evacuation to Mob Vet Sec. Quiet day spent in improving the Camp &c.	
		10 pm	The whole D.A.C moved off	
~~BEAUCOURT~~	~~6th~~		~~[illegible]~~	SH.
ALBERT Dull & cold.	6th	2 am	Arrived Bivouaced out. All Sections alongside each other	
		9.30 pm	Moved out and marched to DERNANCOURT.	SH.

2353 Wt. W2544/1454 700,000 5/15 D. D. & L. A.D.S.S./Forms/C. 2118.

Instructions regarding War Diaries and Intelligence Summaries are contained in F. S. Regs., Part II. and the Staff Manual respectively. Title pages will be prepared in manuscript.

WAR DIARY
or
INTELLIGENCE SUMMARY.
(Erase heading not required.)

Army Form C. 2118.

Place	Date 1916 July	Hour	Summary of Events and Information	Remarks and references to Appendices
DERNANCOURT Dull + cold.	6th	11.30pm	Arrived and Bivouaced just outside the Village. H.Q. + No 3 Section with Nos 1. 2. 4 Sections together near at hand. A Dump formed and worked by the D.A.C. near ALBERT.	
DERNANCOURT Raining + Dull	7th		1 Gnr + 1 Dvr struck off the strength. 1 Horse + 1 Mule struck off the strength on evacuation to Mob. Vet. Sec. Driver posted to 103rd Bde. Orders issued for All Gun parts in whatever condition to be returned to I. O. Ms Workshop. Lieut D HERRSCHORN struck off the strength - sick in England. 2nd Lieut P. HENDRY brought on the strength on arrival and posted to No 3 Section.	EH EH
DERNANCOURT Dry + Cloudy	8th		1 Cpl. + 1 Dvr. struck off the strength on evacuation out of the Divl. Area. Camp here improved. Very busy day at the Dump with relays of Fatigue parties.	EH
DERNANCOURT Dry + Cloudy	9th		Very busy night + day at the Ammunition Dump. Also Fatigues for Brigades Batteries &c.	EH

Instructions regarding War Diaries and Intelligence Summaries are contained in F. S. Regs., Part II. and the Staff Manual respectively. Title pages will be prepared in manuscript.

WAR DIARY
or
INTELLIGENCE SUMMARY.
(Erase heading not required.)

Army Form C. 2118.

Place	Date	Hour	Summary of Events and Information	Remarks and references to Appendices
	1916 July			
DERNANCOURT Fine. One shower of rain	10th		2nd Lieuts M.D. MACKENZIE & J.H. HUTCHINSON struck off the strength on posting to 102nd Brigade R.F.A. Very busy night and day at the Dump; a roadway made there to assist traffic.	E.H.
DERNANCOURT Fair	11th		Orders issued re Estaminets being open to Troops between 12 & 2 instead of 11 & 1. Very busy at the Dump also on Fatigues for Salvage Corps.	E.H.
DERNANCOURT Cloudy but dry.	12th		1 Sgt 1 Gnr & 2 S/Smiths brought on the strength on arrival from the Base. Very busy at the Dump and on Fatigues.	E.H.
DERNANCOURT. Cloudy but dry	13th		Estaminets placed out of bounds between the hours of 12 noon to 2 pm & from 6 pm to 8 pm. Dump work carried on & usual Salvage Corps fatigues. One horse died from wounds. Orders published re looting, & throwing BOMBS in river ANCRE. 2nd Lieut L.A. Dent taken on the strength & posted to No 4 Section.	E.H.
DERNANCOURT. Fair One shower in the morning	14th		Sergt Bowers (A.C.) posted to 35th Div H.Q.R.A. on promotion. 1 Sgt 1 Gnr & 2 S/Smiths posted to Brigades. 2nd Lieuts Mills & Granshaw taken on D.A.C. strength with effect from 6.7.16. Dump & Salvage Corps work as usual.	E.H.

2353 Wt. W2544/1454 700,000 5/15 D. D. & L. A.D.S.S./Forms/C. 2118.

Army Form C. 2118.

WAR DIARY
or
INTELLIGENCE SUMMARY.
(Erase heading not required.)

Instructions regarding War Diaries and Intelligence Summaries are contained in F. S. Regs., Part II. and the Staff Manual respectively. Title pages will be prepared in manuscript.

Place	Date	Hour	Summary of Events and Information	Remarks and references to Appendices
DERNANCOURT. Fine with clouds.	15th	2.0 am	Arrival of No 2 Section 1st Div Am Col on being attached to 23rd D.A. Usual Dump & Salvage Corps work. A good supply of S A A delivered forward.	E.H.
DERNANCOURT. Fine morn Dull afternoon Wet evening	16th		One horse evacuated to mobile Vety Section. Usual Dump & Salvage Corps fatigue. Orders received for Nos 1 & 2 Sections, & also the Section of 1st D.A.C to move nearer ALBERT. viz to E.10.c Sheet map FRANCE 62D. Move completed by 7.0 pm. This to supply wagon lines which have moved forward.	E.H.
DERNANCOURT Dull cloudy day. One slight shower.	17th	10.30 am	H.Q. D.A.C moved to join Nos 1 & 2 Sections, where they arrived at 11.0 am. Section of 1st D A C moved off to rejoin their own unit. Ammn supply heavy. Orders published re increase of mange amongst horses & copy of memorandum on the subject sent out to Sections. Usual Dump, & Salvage Corps fatigue.	
ALBERT.		4.30 pm	No 3 Section received orders to join up with H Q & Nos 1 & 2 Sections.	
		7.0 pm	No 3 Section joined up. This to supply 104th Bde, whose wagon lines have gone forward. Ammn supply heavy.	E.H.
ALBERT. Dull cold day. Clear night	18th		One Driver struck off on evacuation. Usual Dump & Salvage Corp fatigue. Ammn supply above normal. Orders received re No 4 Section to move to E 3 d Sheet map FRANCE 62D.	
		4.0 pm	Move of No 4 Section completed.	E.H.

2353 Wt. W2544/1454 700,000 5/15 D. D. & L. A.D.S.S./Forms/C 2118.

Instructions regarding War Diaries and Intelligence Summaries are contained in F. S. Regs., Part II. and the Staff Manual respectively. Title pages will be prepared in manuscript.

WAR DIARY
or
INTELLIGENCE SUMMARY.
(*Erase heading not required.*)

Army Form C. 2118.

Place	Date	Hour	Summary of Events and Information	Remarks and references to Appendices
ALBERT Bright a few clouds.	July 19th		Usual Dump & Salvage Corps fatigues, also R.E. fatigues. Ammn now coming in fairly fast. One ~~mule~~ Eng mule struck off the strength on evacuation, & also one horse.	EA.
	20th		2nd Lieut Patterson. G.L. joined from the Base & posted to No 1 Section.	
ALBERT Bright day			A draft of ~~1~~ 8th 1 NCO 8th, 2 Saddlers, 22 Telephonists, 3 Gunners & 6 Drivers joined from No 2 General Base & temporarily attached to Sections. Three mules struck off the strength on evacuation. One gunner, attached to/102nd Bde reported killed in action, on 14.7.16. 2nd Lieut W. Cranshaw posted to 104th Bde, by HQRA, 23rd Div with effect from 21.7.16. One Gunner returned from TM Batteries, & posted, supernumerary, to No 4 Section. Orders published re animals not to be exercised on roads. Usual Dump & Salvage Corps fatigues, also RE fatigue.	EA.
ALBERT Clear & bright	21st	5.0am	Party of 20 men paraded under the Adjutant to go to Mericourt to detrain & distribute Remounts. 14 horses were brought back for D.A.C, & brought on the strength. The above draft which arrived 20.7.16 were sent to Brigades on posting by H.Q.R.A. 23rd Div. Notification received that Sergt Revill (A.C.) had, this day, been despatched to join 23rd D.A.C, as Artillery Clerk for this unit.	EA.

2353 Wt. W2544/1454 700,000 5/15 D. D. & L. A.D.S.S./Forms/C. 2118.

Instructions regarding War Diaries and Intelligence Summaries are contained in F. S. Regs., Part II. and the Staff Manual respectively. Title pages will be prepared in manuscript.

WAR DIARY
or
INTELLIGENCE SUMMARY.
(*Erase heading not required.*)

Army Form C. 2118.

Place	Date	Hour	Summary of Events and Information	Remarks and references to Appendices
ALBERT. Dull morning Bright afternoon	July 22nd		40 Gunners sent to Brigades to assist in the gun line. 60 O.R. of T.M. Batteries to be loaned each day to assist in Dump work. Usual Salvage Corps + RE fatigue. 1 Gunner struck off the strength, Killed in action whilst attached to A/103 Bde R.F.A., on 20-7-16.	EH.
ALBERT. Dull day.	23rd		Usual Salvage Corps + RE Fatigue. Received orders to move to new area viz E 3. Sheet Map 62.D FRANCE. Orders issued to "A" Echelon accordingly. Sergt (A.C.) Revill arrived from Artillery 3rd Echelon, to fill existing vacancy.	EH.
ALBERT Bright Day	24th		Moved to new area IZ E.3. Sheet, Map 62.D of FRANCE. 2 Horses lost in action struck off. Instructions received to be prepared for large calls of Ammunition. 19 D.A.C. left 5030 AX + 600 BX at Dump, being replaced by a similar quantity	
ALBERT Bright Day	25th		Cpl. Beacham struck off strength 23/7/16. Cpl. Cash posted 103 Bde 25/7/16. Complaint* from 3rd Corps re Billets when vacated, left in a dirty condition. 2 G.S. Wagons to proceed to Divisional Store, Rue-de-la-PAPETERIE, ALBERT, E.4.b-2-3 at 10. am 26/7/16.	*: Does not refer to this unit.
ALBERT Bright Day	26th		12 Drivers + 24 horses posted to 103 Bde 24/7/16. 10 G.S. Wagons to report to 'C' Lab Bn. at Becourt Wood Store Dump, X 25. D. 82. at 8.30 a.m. 27/7/16. Sgt. Stephenson posted to Heavy T.M. Bty. 26/7/16.	

2353 Wt. W2544/1454 700,000 5/15 D. D. & L. A.D.S.S./Forms/C. 2118.

Instructions regarding War Diaries and Intelligence Summaries are contained in F. S. Regs., Part II. and the Staff Manual respectively. Title pages will be prepared in manuscript.

WAR DIARY
or
INTELLIGENCE SUMMARY.
(Erase heading not required.)

Army Form C. 2118.

Place	Date	Hour	Summary of Events and Information	Remarks and references to Appendices
ALBERT Bright day	27th		Dump & Salvage work as usual. 2/Lt. Heddy posted to 102 Bde 28/7/16 one horse struck off.	EH
ALBERT Bright Day	28th		2/Lts. Lock, Golding, Kellie, Dean, Fairchild & Clark taken on strength 1 N.C.O. & 3 men struck off 1 W.O. (Class II) 1 N.C.O. & 11 other ranks taken on strength.	
ALBERT Bright Day	29th		1 N.C.O. & 1 man wounded. Lieut H. Cornwell, 2/Lieut W. D. G. Mills, 2/Lieut L. G. Lock, & 2/Lieut H. K. L. Fairchild struck off the strength 1 W.O. (Class II) & 10 other ranks posted to Brigades, 2 Dvrs. brought on strength	EH
ALBERT Bright Day Hot	30th		Usual fatigues, 1 N.C.O. & 6 men struck off the strength. 22 [illegible] brought on the strength. 1 man to [illegible]. 5 N.C.Os. brought on the strength	EH
ALBERT Bright Day very Hot	31st		7 N.C.Os. & 4 other ranks struck off the strength. 5 Cpls. & 2 other ranks posted to Bdes &c. Several promotions & appointments made. 1 mule struck off the strength. Usual fatigues.	EH EH

23rd Divisional Artillery.

23rd DIVISIONAL AMMUNITION COLUMN

AUGUST 1 9 1 6

"A"

23 DIVISION

Herewith War
Diary 23 DAC
for month of August
1916 –

H Lanell [illegible]
a/Staff Capt
HQRA
23 Div

ACS

3/9/16

Instructions regarding War Diaries and Intelligence Summaries are contained in F. S. Regs., Part II. and the Staff Manual respectively. Title pages will be prepared in manuscript.

WAR DIARY
or
INTELLIGENCE SUMMARY.
(Erase heading not required.)

Army Form C. 2118.

Amm Col

Vol 12

Place	Date	Hour	Summary of Events and Information	Remarks and references to Appendices
ALBERT Bright Day	1 8/16		1 Cpl. posted to 103 Bde. Grs. Constable & Barton "killed in action" 30 7/16. 2 Cpls. & 4 Gunners struck off the strength. 1 Horse & 2 Mules struck off.	EH.
ALBERT Bright Day	2 8/16		2 Cpls. reverted at own request. 1 man died from wounds, & struck off the strength. 1 Mule struck off the strength. Usual fatigues.	EH.
ALBERT Clear Day Hot.	3 8/16		Usual promotions in D.A.C. 3 L.D. Horses struck off. – Establishment of each Section of "A" Echelon increased by 5 "Gunners", 1 Fitter, 2 Shoeing Smiths, 2 Telephonists, 25 Grs. & 13 Drs. joined from Base.	EH.
ALBERT Bright Day	4 8/16		Usual fatigues. 2/Lt. L. A. Dent & 2/Lt. G. L. Paterson, posted to 103 Bde. 4/8/16. 1 fitter, 2 telephonists, & 48 other ranks posted to Bdes. 2 S/S. posted to No. 1 Section. – Capt. Archer ordered to D. R. S.	EH.
ALBERT Bright Day	5th.		2/Lt. W. J. S. Dowson & Tempy. 2/Lt. C. H. Campbell joined 5/8/16. 2 N.C.Os. & 1 man struck off the strength. G. R. O. 1714 of 4/8/16, re enemy documents republished in orders. Usual fatigues. G.O.C. R.A. visited Camp.	EH.
ALBERT Bright Day	6 8/16		5 men posted to 105 Bde. 1 Cpl. taken on the strength. 1 L.D. horse struck off. 2/Lt. L. L. Kellie posted to 102 Bde. – Various fatigues.	EH.

2353 Wt. W2544/1454 700,000 5/15 D. D. & L. A.D.S.S./Forms/C. 2118.

Instructions regarding War Diaries and Intelligence Summaries are contained in F. S. Regs., Part II. and the Staff Manual respectively. Title pages will be prepared in manuscript.

WAR DIARY
or
INTELLIGENCE SUMMARY.
(Erase heading not required.)

Army Form C. 2118.

Place	Date	Hour	Summary of Events and Information	Remarks and references to Appendices
ALBERT Bright Day	7 8/16		2/Lt Campbell posted to 105 Bde. 2 Officers, 1 N.C.O. & 7 other ranks struck off the strength. 8 L.D. Horses struck off. Usual fatigues.	EH
ALBERT Bright Day	8 8/16		III Corps Routine Order 131 of 1916 re occupation of land published. Usual fatigues & ammunition supply.	EH
ALBERT Bright Day	9th		1 man posted to 103 Bde. 34 Mules taken on strength. 23 D.A. attached to O.O. III Corps Troops for Ordnance Services on departure of Division.	
			G.R.O. 589, republished re visiting area of French or Belgian Armies.	EH
ALBERT Dull Day	10th		1 N.C.O. struck off the strength. 1 Fitter S. Sergt & 85 Men taken on the strength. Usual fatigues & ammunition supply.	EH
ALBERT Bright Day	11th		71 men posted to Brigades & struck off the strength. 1 L.D. Horse & 1 Mule struck off the strength. Order published re N.C.T. charges being Reps dry. Instructions received to join 2nd Army, probable date of move 17/8/16. Usual fatigues	EH
ALBERT Bright Day	12th		Section Commanders reminded that on leaving the area, they march with ammunition complete. X.Y.Z. T.M. Btys attached for rations from 13th. All 3 Batteries to be at FRECHINCOURT on 14 8/16 Capt FRENCH + 5 N.COs detailed as Billeting party in new area.	EH

3353 Wt. W2544/1454 700,000 5/15 D. D. & L. A.D.S.S./Forms/C. 2118.

Instructions regarding War Diaries and Intelligence Summaries are contained in F. S. Regs., Part II. and the Staff Manual respectively. Title pages will be prepared in manuscript.

WAR DIARY
or
INTELLIGENCE SUMMARY.

(Erase heading not required.)

Army Form C. 2118.

Place	Date	Hour	Summary of Events and Information	Remarks and references to Appendices
ALBERT. Bright Day	13/8/16		2 men struck off the strength. Dr. Green died from injuries 31/7/16. 6 Horses struck off the strength. D.A.C. to march to BEAUCORT. All maps to be handed over to 47 D.A.C. on leaving area. Ammunition return to be handed in before moving off.	E.H.
ALBERT Dull Day	14/8/16		3 men struck off the strength. D.A.C. moved to BEAUCOURT.	E.H.
BEAUCOURT Dull Day	15/8/16		Instr. received for D.A.C. to proceed to QUEERIEUX on 16/8/16. 1 Horse & Mule struck off strength 14/8/16. Sections to detail 2 men each for Sanitary Duties.	E.H.
QUEERIEUX	16/8/16		D.A.C. marched to QUEERIEUX. Camped in wood.	E.H.
	16/8/16		Part of D.A.C. marched to LONGUEAU & entrained for new area	E.H.
QUEERIEUX	17/8/16		1st part of D.A.C. arrived at CASSELL & detrained. Remainder of D.A.C. left QUEERIEUX & marched to LONGEAU & entrained for new area.	E.H.
GODEWAERVEDE	18/8/16		D.A.C. took up positions: H.Q. at 18.a.55 No. 1 Section:- Q 10.d.9.7. No. 2 Section Q.23.a.4.4. No. 3 Sect. Q.17.b.69 No. 4 Section. P.24.A.8.3. — Map reference, sheet 27. S.E.	E.H.

2353 Wt. W2544/1454 700,000 5/15 D. D. & L. A.D.S.S./Forms/C. 2118.

Army Form C. 2118.

Instructions regarding War Diaries and Intelligence Summaries are contained in F. S. Regs., Part II. and the Staff Manual respectively. Title pages will be prepared in manuscript.

WAR DIARY
or
INTELLIGENCE SUMMARY.
(Erase heading not required.)

Place	Date	Hour	Summary of Events and Information	Remarks and references to Appendices
GODEWAERSVELDE	18/8/16		Received instructions to proceed into forward area. 8 men joined from Base & posted to D.A.C. Orders re troops being properly dressed when leaving billets.	E.H.
—"—	19/8/16		Capt. C.D.W. ARCHER, struck off the strength 18/8/16, 6 N.C.O. & men, 1 Saddler, 1 Wheeler, 1 fitter, joined from Base & posted to Bdes 18/8/16. 2/Lt. W.G. DAWSON, detailed for course at 2nd Army School. Orders issued for move of D.A.C. on 20/8/16.	E.H.
LEMENAGATTE	20/8/16		D.A.C. marched & took up positions. – H.Q. B.19.b.7.7. No 1 Section, B19.a.2.2. No 2 Section, B19.b.2.5. No 3 Section, B14.c.1.1 – No 4 Section, B14.d.3.7 } Sheet 36 1/40,000	E.H.
—"—	21/8/16		5 men taken on strength. Notification recd that D.D.V.S. will see animals of D.A.C. not suitable for duty on 22/8/16.	E.H.
—"—	22/8/16		2 men struck off the strength. 1 man posted to No 1 Section. R.E. & Dump fatigues.	E.H.
"	23/8/16		Routine Order republished re cleaning rifles. R.E. & Dump fatigues	E.H.

Instructions regarding War Diaries and Intelligence Summaries are contained in F. S. Regs., Part II. and the Staff Manual respectively. Title pages will be prepared in manuscript.

WAR DIARY
or
INTELLIGENCE SUMMARY.
(Erase heading not required.)

Army Form C. 2118.

Place	Date	Hour	Summary of Events and Information	Remarks and references to Appendices
LEMENA GATTE	24/8/16		3 men struck off the strength. Usual fatigues	EH.
— "	25/8/16		35 N.C.O's & men taken on the strength. Order re men of Trench Mortar Batteries being borne supernumerary to Est. 3 men struck off the strength. R.E. & Dump fatigues.	EH.
— " —	26/8/16		25 N.C.O's & men posted to Bdes & struck off the strength 26/8/16. 12 Second Lieutenants joined from Base. 12 Mules & 3 L.D. Horses struck off the strength. Usual fatigues.	EH.
— " —	27/8/16		X/23 T.M. Bty posted to No. 1 Section. Lt Ewart 2/D.A.C. exchanged with 2/Lt W.H. DEAN, 23rd D.A.C. 10 Officers struck off the strength.	EH.
— " —	28/8/16		2/Lt R. GILDER posted to No 4 Section, 2/Lieut S.C. NIRDINGTON posted to 3 Section, 1 Sgt. posted to 104 Bde. "A" Echelon to vacate position on 29/8/16.	
PAPOT	29/8/16		Y/23. T.M. Bty posted to No. 2 Section. "A" Echelon marched & took up positions: — 1 Sect. B.3.d.6.9, 2 Sect. – B.3.d.½.9, No 3 Sect. – B.8.a.8.8, HQ – B.8.a.8.8. Usual fatigues.	EH.

2353 Wt. W2544/1454 700,000 5/15 D. D. & L. A.D.S.S./Forms/C. 2118.

Army Form C. 2118.

Instructions regarding War Diaries and Intelligence Summaries are contained in F. S. Regs., Part II. and the Staff Manual respectively. Title pages will be prepared in manuscript.

WAR DIARY
or
INTELLIGENCE SUMMARY.
(Erase heading not required.)

Place	Date	Hour	Summary of Events and Information	Remarks and references to Appendices
PAPOT	30/8/16		Z/23. T.M. By posted to the 3 Sections. 1 Mule struck off strength 12 L.D. horses taken on strength, 6 N.C.O. & men selected for Trench Mortar Course commencing 2/9/16	EH
PAPOT	31/8/16		12 L.D. Horses posted to the 3 Sections – 3 men struck off the strength – Usual fatigues.	EH.

[illegible signature]
LT. COL. R.F.A.
COMMDG. 23RD DIV. ... COL.

2353 Wt. W2544/1454 700,000 5/15 D. D. & L. A.D.S.S./Forms/C. 2118.

Instructions regarding War Diaries and Intelligence Summaries are contained in F. S. Regs., Part II. and the Staff Manual respectively. Title pages will be prepared in manuscript.

WAR DIARY
or
INTELLIGENCE SUMMARY.
(*Erase heading not required.*)

Army Form C. 2118.

Vol 13

Place	Date	Hour	Summary of Events and Information	Remarks and references to Appendices
PAPOT	1/9/16		1 N.C.O. & 11 Gunners posted to Bdes & struck off the strength. 26 Drivers taken on the strength. 10 G.S. wagons sent from 32 [illegible]	E.A.E.
— " —	2/9/16		16 Drivers posted to Bdes, & struck off the strength. 2/Lt D.F. CRUX posted to 52 A.A. Bty. 6 N.C.Os & men posted to V/23. T.M. Bty	E.A.E.
"	3/9/16		6 men struck off the strength, 1 man killed in action. Class at Gas school for instruction on 4/9/16. Usual fatigues.	E.A.E.
— " —	4/9/16		1 W.O. & 54 other ranks taken on strength from 103-4-5 Brigades. 13 horses taken on strength 4/9/16. 3 men struck off strength. 5 horses struck off strength. B.Q.M.S. Bell posted to H.Q. D.A.C. 4 men posted to C/102 Bde.	E.A.E.
Heavy Rain	5/9/16		4 fitters posted to Sections. 3 N.C.Os & 1 S.S. 3 horses posted to No 2 Section. 4 N.C.Os & men struck off strength. Usual fatigues	E.A.E.
PAPOT	6/9/16		6 Gunners posted to C/102 Bde. 2 men admitted hospital. G.R.O. 1779 republished re opening Ammunition boxes. Usual fatigues	E.A.E.

2353 Wt. W2544/1454 700,000 5/15 D. D. & L. A.D.S.S./Forms/C. 2118.

WAR DIARY

or

INTELLIGENCE SUMMARY.

(Erase heading not required.)

Army Form C. 2118.

Instructions regarding War Diaries and Intelligence Summaries are contained in F. S. Regs., Part II. and the Staff Manual respectively. Title pages will be prepared in manuscript.

Place	Date	Hour	Summary of Events and Information	Remarks and references to Appendices
PAPOT Bulger Day	7/9/16		R.O. 452 of 1916, re despatch of letters, re published. 1 N.C.O. & 1 Man struck off the strength. Orders received for D.A.C. to march on 9/9/16.	E.A.E.
— " —	8/9/16		Waterproof sheets not to be carried on off horses. Bathing in Canals permitted. 1 Sft. struck off strength. Usual fatigues.	E.A.E.
	9/9/16		D.A.C. marched to SCHAEXKEN, and bivouaced. Nos 1 & 2 Sections at R.29.c.1.7, No 3 Section X.4.0.7.2. No 4 Section R.33.b.9.0..	E.A.E.
SCHAE-XKEN	10/9/16		46 W.O.s N.C.O.s & Artificers posted to Base & struck off strength. Dr. Bonas for trial by F.G.C.M. 16 horses taken on strength & posted to No 1 Section. Orders received to entrain on 12/9/16	E.A.E.
— " —	11/9/16		2 men posted to X, Y & Z Bys. 2 men admitted hospital. 13 horses taken on strength & posted to 3 Section. 2 horses struck off	E.A.E.
	12/9/16		D.A.C. marched to BAILLEUL & entrained for new area.	E.A.E.
St. GRATIEN	13/9/16		D.A.C. arrived & bivouaced at St. GRATIEN. 1 man struck off strength	E.A.E.
— " —	14/9/16		Nos 1 & 2 Sections moved to forward area. Instructions received for D.A.C. to be ready to move at 2 hours notice. 2 men struck off strength.	E.A.E.

Instructions regarding War Diaries and Intelligence Summaries are contained in F. S. Regs., Part II. and the Staff Manual respectively. Title pages will be prepared in manuscript.

WAR DIARY
or
INTELLIGENCE SUMMARY.
(Erase heading not required.)

Army Form C. 2118.

Place	Date	Hour	Summary of Events and Information	Remarks and references to Appendices
St GRATIEN	15/9/16		50 N.C.Os & men joined from Base & taken on strength. 17 horses taken on strength. 17 N.C.Os & men posted to 104 Bde	E.A.E.
"	16/9/16		33 N.C.Os & men posted to Brigades. 2 men to Hospital.	E.A.E.
"	17/9/16		4 men posted from 1/23 Bty to Z/23 Bty & 4 men from Z/23 Bty to 1/23 Bty	E.A.E.
"	18/9/16		4 horses struck off strength. 2 men admitted to hospital. Instructions received to proceed to LAVEVILLE on 19/9/16	E.A.E.
"	19/9/16		H.Q. & Nos 3 & 4 Sections marched to and billeted at LAVEVILLE. 1 N.C.O. & 4 men struck off strength. 6 horses struck off strength.	E.A.E.
LAVEVILLE	20/9/16		43 N.C.Os & men joined from Base. 2/Lt. T. G. KENNEDY joined 18/9/16. R.E. & other fatigues. S.S. Cpl. Smith killed	E.A.E.
"	21/9/16		Sick of D.A.C. to report to 45th F.A. D.A.D.O.S. at ALBERT. Usual fatigues	E.A.E.
"	22/9/16		43 N.C.Os & men posted to Brigades & struck off strength. Fatigues.	E.A.E.
"	23/9/16		H.Q. D.A.C. marched & bivouaced in BEAUCOURT Wood. 5 Sergts joined from Base taken on strength.	E.A.E.

2353 Wt. W2544/1454 700,000 5/15 D. D. & L. A.D.S.S./Forms/C. 2118.

Instructions regarding War Diaries and Intelligence Summaries are contained in F. S. Regs., Part II. and the Staff Manual respectively. Title pages will be prepared in manuscript.

WAR DIARY
or
INTELLIGENCE SUMMARY.
(Erase heading not required.)

Army Form C. 2118.

Place	Date	Hour	Summary of Events and Information	Remarks and references to Appendices
BEECOURT WOOD	24 9/16		5 Sgts posted to Bdes. Lieut E. HISCOCK attached to A/104 Bde. Lieut E. A. EWART assumes duties of Acting Adjutant.	E.A.E.
—"—	25 9/16		24 Mules joined & posted to Sections. 1 NCO posted to 103 Bde.	E.A.E.
—"—	26 9/16		Lieut A. GOODFELLOW taken on strength 24/9/16. 2 Sgts from Base taken on strength. 6 men struck off. G.O.C. R.A. visited dump.	E.A.E.
—"—	27 9/16		2Lt R. L. CRUX rejoined 27/9/16. 33 N.C.Os & men taken on the strength. 2 Sgts posted to Bdes & struck off strength. Usual fatigues.	E.A.E.
—"—	28 9/16		25 Drivers taken on strength, 3 men to hospl. Usual fatigues	E.A.E.
—"—	29 9/16		33 NCOs & men posted to Bdes & Sections. 4 men admitted to hospital. 1 horse struck off. Usual fatigues	E.A.E.
—"—	30 9/16		8 Drivers posted to Bdes & struck off strength. 1 man wounded in action. 4 men to hospital. Instructions received to put clocks back 1 hour at 1 am 1/10/16	E.A.E.

2353 Wt. W2544/1454 700,000 5/15 D. D. & L. A.D.S.S./Forms/C. 2118.

23

Army Form C. 2118.

Vol 14

Instructions regarding War Diaries and Intelligence Summaries are contained in F. S. Regs., Part II. and the Staff Manual respectively. Title pages will be prepared in manuscript.

WAR DIARY
or
INTELLIGENCE SUMMARY.

(Erase heading not required.)

Place	Date	Hour	Summary of Events and Information	Remarks and references to Appendices
BEECOURT WOOD	1/10/16		2 men to hospital. R.E. & Dump fatigues	E.A.E.
	2/10/16		3 men to hospital. 1 man struck off strength. Usual fatigues	E.A.E.
"	3/10/16		7 men to hospital. 2 men struck off strength. Usual fatigues	E.A.E.
"	4/10/16		Various promotions made in D.A.C. 2 N.C.O. & 5 men to T.M. Course	E.A.E.
"	5/10/16		5 men to hospital. 2/Lt. H.E. THOMPSON & 2 O.R. wounded	E.A.E.
			2 Sergts. posted to Bde. Usual fatigues	
"	6/10/16		3 men to Hospital. R.E. & Dump fatigues	E.A.E.
"	7/10/16		4 men from hospital. 1 horse struck off strength. Orders received for D.A.C. to move to St Gratien on 9/10/16	E.A.E.
"	8/10/16		11 Mules joined D.A.C. 1 man struck off. 1 man killed in action. 4 men discharged hospital. Usual fatigues	E.A.E.
"	9/10/16		D.A.C. marched to & billeted at MIRVAUX	E.A.E.
MIRVAUX	10/10/16		1 horse struck off, 1 man to Base under age. – Various fatigues	E.A.E.
"	11/10/16		4 Mules struck off the strength. 1 man posted to D/83 Bde. fatigues	E.A.E.
"	12/10/16		23 N.C.Os & men taken off strength. 2 men to hospital – fatigues	E.A.E.
"	13/10/16		1 man from hospital. Instructions to send 1 Sect to G.1.b. 14/10/16	E.A.E.

2353 Wt. W2544/1454 700,000 5/15 D. D. & L. A.D.S.S./Forms/C. 2118

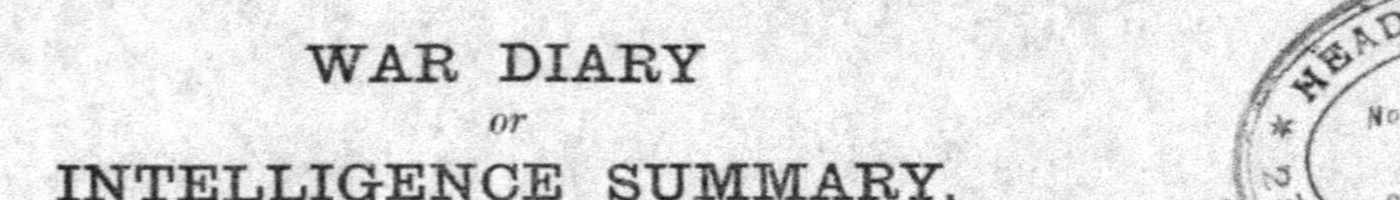

Instructions regarding War Diaries and Intelligence Summaries are contained in F. S. Regs., Part II. and the Staff Manual respectively. Title pages will be prepared in manuscript.

WAR DIARY
or
INTELLIGENCE SUMMARY.
(Erase heading not required.)

Army Form C. 2118.

Place	Date	Hour	Summary of Events and Information	Remarks and references to Appendices
MIRVAUX	14/10/16		38 men joined from Base. 34 horses struck off. 10 men from T.M. Course	E.A.E.
"	15/10/16		38 N.C.Os. & men posted to Bdes. & struck off the strength	E.A.E.
"	16/10/16		Sergt. Ball posted to Y/23 T.M. Bty. Various fatigues	E.A.E.
"	17/10/16		3 men struck off the strength.	E.A.E.
"	18/10/16		1 Man to hospital. Usual fatigues	E.A.E.
"	19/10/16		5 men struck off the strength. 1 Man to 24 D.A.	E.A.E.
"	20/10/16		3 Section joined from BEECOURT. No 1 Section left for BEECOURT. 4 men struck off strength. Fatigues	E.A.E.
"	21/10/16		2/Lt. PALMER to hospital. 4 men to hospital. Usual fatigues	E.A.E.
"	22/10/16		62 horses & 45 Mules joined 21/10/16. Usual fatigues	E.A.E.
"	23/10/16		Various fatigues. 81 horses & Mules to Brigades	E.A.E.
"	24/10/16		Usual fatigues.	E.A.E.
"	25/10/16		1 Man & 1 horse struck off. Various fatigues.	E.A.E.
"	26/10/16		19 men joined from Base, 1 man to hospital. Usual fatigues	E.A.E.

Instructions regarding War Diaries and Intelligence Summaries are contained in F. S. Regs., Part II. and the Staff Manual respectively. Title pages will be prepared in manuscript.

WAR DIARY
or
INTELLIGENCE SUMMARY.
(Erase heading not required.)

Army Form C. 2118.

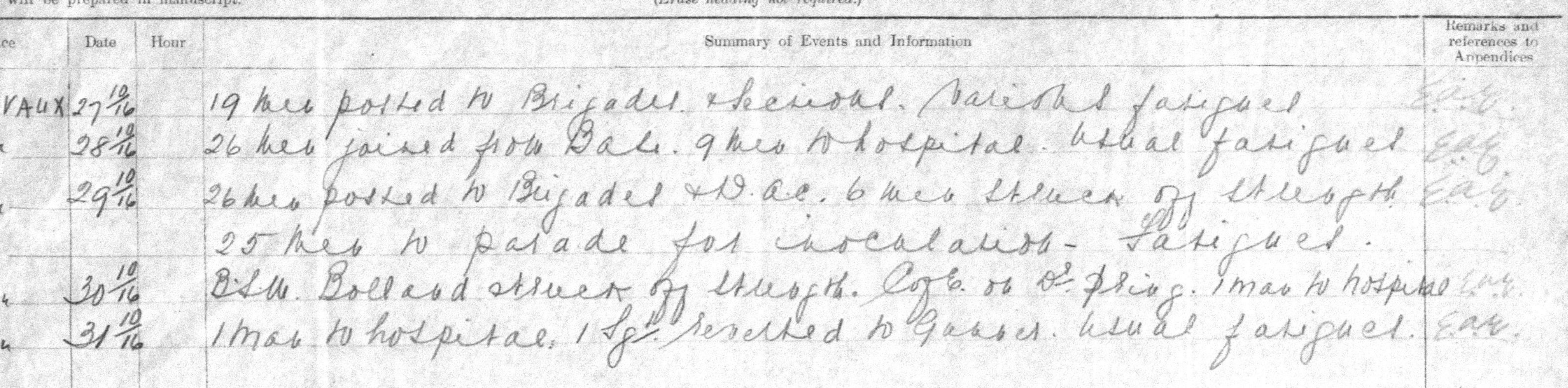

Place	Date	Hour	Summary of Events and Information	Remarks and references to Appendices
MIRVAUX	27/10/16		19 men posted to Brigades & schools. Various fatigues	E.A.E.
"	28/10/16		26 men joined from Base. 9 men to hospital. Usual fatigues	E.A.E.
"	29/10/16		26 men posted to Brigades & D.A.C. 6 men struck off strength. 25 men to parade for inoculation - fatigues.	E.A.E.
"	30/10/16		B.S.M. Bolland struck off strength. Cpl. [illegible] 1 man to hospital	E.A.E.
"	31/10/16		1 man to hospital. 1 Sgt. reverted to Gunner. Usual fatigues.	E.A.E.

2353 Wt. W2544/1454 700,000 5/15 D. D. & L. A.D.S.S./Forms/C. 2118.

23

WAR DIARY
or
INTELLIGENCE SUMMARY.

(Erase heading not required.)

Instructions regarding War Diaries and Intelligence Summaries are contained in F. S. Regs., Part II. and the Staff Manual respectively. Title pages will be prepared in manuscript.

Army Form C. 2118.

Vol 15

Place	Date	Hour	Summary of Events and Information	Remarks and references to Appendices
MIRVAUX	1/11/16		1 Man to hospital. 1 Man struck off. Various fatigues	E.A.E.
—	2/11/16		2 Men struck off strength. 1 Fitter posted to 103 Bde. Fatigues	E.A.E.
—	3/11/16		3 Men struck off. 2 horses struck off. Usual fatigues	E.A.E.
—	4/11/16		1 Sergt & 18 Drivers taken on strength. 3 Men to hospital	E.A.E.
—	5/11/16		3 Men struck off. 1 Sgt & 18 Drivers posted. Fatigues	E.A.E.
—	6/11/16		No 2 Section moved to F.1.b. to relieve No 1 Section	E.A.E.
—	7/11/16		2 Men to hospital. G.O.C. R.A. visited MIRVAUX. Fatigues	E.A.E.
—	8/11/16		2/Lt T.R. KENNEDY to V/23 T.M. Bty. 1 Man to hosp. Usual fatigues	E.A.E.
—	9/11/16		1 N.C.O. & 10 men joined from Base. 1 Man struck off strength	E.A.E.
—	10/11/16		2/Lt J. PALMER struck off strength. 2/Lt N.H. PRING to hospital. Passes to Amiens, Line to leave. G.O.C. R.A. at MIRVAUX	E.A.E.
—	11/11/16		10 N.C.Os & men selected for T.M. Course on 16/10/16. 2/Lt PRING posted to No 1 Section. 2 Men struck off strength.	E.A.E.

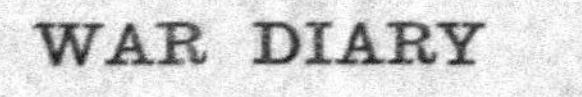

Instructions regarding War Diaries and Intelligence Summaries are contained in F. S. Regs., Part II. and the Staff Manual respectively. Title pages will be prepared in manuscript.

WAR DIARY
or
INTELLIGENCE SUMMARY.
(Erase heading not required.)

Army Form C. 2118.

Place	Date	Hour	Summary of Events and Information	Remarks and references to Appendices
MIRVAUX	12/11/16		1 NCO & 10 men posted to Bdes. 1 Man to hospl. fatigues	E.A.E.
– " –	13/11/16		Route for move of D.A.C. on 14/11/16. 1 Mule struck off strength	E.A.E.
"	14/11/16		D.A.C. marched to FRICOURT & Bivouacked.	E.A.E.
FRICOURT	15/11/16		1 Man taken on strength. 2 men struck off strength. Various fatigues	E.A.E.
"	16/11/16		1 Man to hospital. Ammunition returns called for – fatigues	E.A.E.
"	17/11/16		3 men to hospital. 1 horse to Mobile Vet Section – fatigues	E.A.E.
"	18/11/16		1 Man Killed & 1 Man Wounded. 3 men to hosp. Usual [illegible]	E.A.E.
"	19/11/16		1 Sgt posted to 4 Section. Usual R.E. & Dump fatigues	E.A.E.
"	20/11/16		4 men appd Acting Bombr – Usual fatigues	E.A.E.
"	21/11/16		1 horse to Mobile Vet Section – Usual fatigues	E.A.E.
"	22/11/16		4 men struck off. 10 NCOs & men detailed for T.M. Course	E.A.E.
"	23/11/16		57 men from Bde joined. 5 men struck off	E.A.E.
"	24/11/16		1 Man to hospital. 2 men struck off – Usual fatigues	E.A.E.
"	25/11/16		R.E. & Dump fatigues	E.A.E.

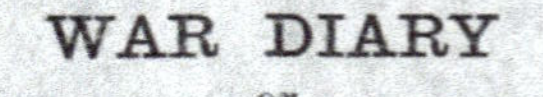

Army Form C. 2118.

Instructions regarding War Diaries and Intelligence Summaries are contained in F. S. Regs., Part II. and the Staff Manual respectively. Title pages will be prepared in manuscript.

WAR DIARY
or
INTELLIGENCE SUMMARY.

(Erase heading not required.)

Place	Date	Hour	Summary of Events and Information	Remarks and references to Appendices
FRICOURT	26/11/16		45 men posted to Bdes. 1 man to hospl. – Usual fatigues	E.A.C.
"	27/11/16		34 men taken on strength. 2 men to hospl. Usual fatigues	E.A.C.
"	28/11/16		28 men posted to Bdes, 3 men to hospl. – fatigues	E.A.C.
"	29/11/16		2 horses struck off. Various fatigues	E.A.C.
"	30/11/16		1 man mustered Gunner. 1 man from hospital. Gol.(?) R. a(?) joined DAC. Usual fatigues	E.A.C.

2353 Wt. W2544/1454 700,000 5/15 D. D. & L. A.D.S.S./Forms/C. 2118.

WAR DIARY
or
INTELLIGENCE SUMMARY.
(Erase heading not required.)

Instructions regarding War Diaries and Intelligence Summaries are contained in F. S. Regs., Part II. and the Staff Manual respectively. Title pages will be prepared in manuscript.

Army Form C. 2118.

23 D Am Col

Vol 16

Place	Date	Hour	Summary of Events and Information	Remarks and references to Appendices
FRICOURT	1/12/16		1 man to hospital. 1 horse struck off. R.E. & Dump fatigues	E.A.E.
"	2/12/16		2 men struck off. 2 N.C.Os promoted. Usual fatigues	E.A.E.
"	3/12/16		12 horses taken on strength. 1 man to hospital. Fatigues	E.A.E.
"	4/12/16		1 man struck off. G.O.C. R.A. visited D.A.C. — "	E.A.E.
"	5/12/16		2 horses struck off. 2/Lt. R. CRUX to 'P' Anti-Aircraft By.	E.A.E.
"	6/12/16		H.Q. & 4 Sections marched to LAVEVILLE, 1.2 & 3 Sections BAZIEUX	E.A.E.
LAVEVILLE	7/12/16		REST.	E.A.E.
"	8/12/16		D.A.C. marched to & billeted at VILLERS BOCAGE.	E.A.E.
VILLERS BOCAGE	9/12/16		D.A.C. marched to & billeted at Occoches.	E.A.E.
OCCOCHES	10/12/16		REST.	E.A.E.
"	11/12/16		D.A.C. marched to & billeted at VACQUERIE-LE-BOUCQ	E.A.E.
VACQUERIE LE-BOUCQ	12/12/16		D.A.C. marched to & billeted at VALHUON.	E.A.E.

2353 Wt. W2544/1454 700,000 5/15 D. D. & L. A.D.S.S./Forms/C. 2118.

Army Form C. 2118.

WAR DIARY
or
INTELLIGENCE SUMMARY.
(Erase heading not required.)

Instructions regarding War Diaries and Intelligence Summaries are contained in F. S. Regs., Part II. and the Staff Manual respectively. Title pages will be prepared in manuscript.

Place	Date	Hour	Summary of Events and Information	Remarks and references to Appendices
VALUHON	13 12/16		REST	E.A.E.
—"—	14 12/16		D.A.C. marched & billeted at LIGNY-LES-AIRE.	E.A.E.
LIGNY-LES AIRE	15 12/16		D.A.C. marched & billeted at BOISEGHEM.	E.A.E.
BOISEGHEM	16 12/16		REST.	E.A.E.
—"—	17 12/16		D.A.C. marched & billeted at REVELD.	E.A.E.
REVELD	18 12/16		4 men to hospital. 1 mule struck off	E.A.E.
—"—	19 12/16		Dr. DEVINE tried by F.G.C.M. Capt WINDOW leave to England	E.A.E.
—"—	20 12/16		4 H.D. horses posted away. Gr. WATKINS died. 2 men [illegible]	E.A.E.
—"—	21 12/16		Order re picture postcards, 2 men to hosp.	E.A.E.
—"—	22 12/16		3 men to hospital 1 man from hosp.	E.A.E.
—"—	23 12/16		2 men to hospital	E.A.E.

Army Form C. 2118.

WAR DIARY
or
INTELLIGENCE SUMMARY.

(Erase heading not required.)

[Instr]uctions regarding War Diaries and Intelligence Summaries are contained in F. S. Regs., Part II. and the Staff Manual respectively. Title pages will be prepared in manuscript.

Place	Date	Hour	Summary of Events and Information	Remarks and references to Appendices
REVELD	24/12/16		General fatigues	E.A.C.
—	25/12/16		4 men to hospital	E.A.C.
—	26/12/16		HQ D Co marched & bivouaced at X.13.c. Map 28	E.A.C.
			about 4 kilometres SW of DENNAGHELST	
	27/12/16		15 men detailed for T.M. Coy. 6 NCOs & men struck off & 10 hospital	E.A.C.
	28/12/16		4 Mules struck off strength	E.A.C.
	29/12/16		8 men struck off strength. 3 men to hospital. 5 men wounded	E.A.C.
	30/12/16		2/Lt A LINES & W. K. MISES taken on strength. 2 NCOs reverted	E.A.C.
			1 man to hospital. 3 men tried by F.G.C.M.	
	31/12/16		4 men struck off. Pte Mc released [illegible] Suspension Act	E.A.C.
			27/12/16. 3 men to hospital	

2353 Wt. W2544/1454 700,000 5/15 D. D. & L. A.D.S.S./Forms/C. 2118.

Instructions regarding War Diaries and Intelligence Summaries are contained in F. S. Regs., Part II. and the Staff Manual respectively. Title pages will be prepared in manuscript.

WAR DIARY
or
INTELLIGENCE SUMMARY.
(Erase heading not required.)

23 D. Amm Col

Vol 11

Army Form C. 2118.

Place	Date	Hour	Summary of Events and Information	Remarks and references to Appendices
A 13 C	1/1/17		66 men posted to Bdes. 3 men struck off. Cpl Murray killed in A	EAE
Sheet 28	2/1/17		3 men & 5 horses struck off. 2 men to hospital.	EAE
BELGIUM	3/1/17		4 men struck off. 3 men to hospital.	EAE
"	4/1/17		3 men struck off. 3 men to hospital. H.Q. D.A.C. moved to POPERINGHE.	EAE
POPERINGHE	5/1/17		4 Drivers mustered "Gunners". 2 men to hospital.	EAE
"	6/1/17		8 men struck off strength. 8 horses posted 2 Section	EAE
"	7/1/17		2/Lieuts L.K. MOSES & LOCK joined. Dr Cook 3 Section injured	EAE
"	8/1/17		31 NCOs & men posted to Bdes. 3 men struck off.	EAE
"	9/1/17		8 men detailed for Signalling Course. Lt EWART appd Adjutant 23 D.A.C. of 27-12-16. 3 men to hospl	EAE
"	10/1/17		2 NCOs & 8 men detailed for T.M. Course. 6 Sgts posted to Bdes.	EAE

Army Form C. 2118.

Instructions regarding War Diaries and Intelligence Summaries are contained in F. S. Regs., Part II. and the Staff Manual respectively. Title pages will be prepared in manuscript.

WAR DIARY
or
INTELLIGENCE SUMMARY.
(Erase heading not required.)

Place	Date	Hour	Summary of Events and Information	Remarks and references to Appendices
POPERINGHE	11/1/17		Order re men on Parades being fully equipped. 1 man to hosp	E.A.E.
"	12/1/17		17 Drivers posted to 2 Section from Base. 4 men struck off.	E.A.E.
"	13/1/17		7 men posted from Sections to H.Q. Order re Gum Boots	E.A.E.
"	14/1/17		2 men to hospital – Reorganisation of D.A.C. 23/1/17	E.A.E.
"	15/1/17		2 men struck off. 1 man wounded – 1 man from hosp.	E.A.E.
"	16/1/17		2 men to prison. 4 men from hospital. 1 man to hosp. [illegible]	E.A.E.
"	17/1/17		2 men wounded. 2 men to hosp. 4 men struck off	E.A.E.
"	18/1/17		4 horses struck off. Order re Poperinghe out of bounds.	E.A.E.
"	19/1/17		19 NCOs & men posted to T.M. Btys. 6 Drivers mustered Gunners	E.A.E.
"	20/1/17		7 NCOs & men posted to T.M. Btys. 60 Mules taken on strength	E.A.E.
"	21/1/17		3 men struck off. 5 Drivers mustered Gunners. 1 man to hosp	E.A.E.

2353 Wt. W2544/1454 700,000 5/15 D. D. & L. A.D.S.S./Forms/C. 2118.

WAR DIARY
or
INTELLIGENCE SUMMARY.
(Erase heading not required.)

Army Form C. 2118.

Instructions regarding War Diaries and Intelligence Summaries are contained in F. S. Regs., Part II. and the Staff Manual respectively. Title pages will be prepared in manuscript.

Place	Date	Hour	Summary of Events and Information	Remarks and references to Appendices
POPERINGHE	22/1/17		3 men to hospital, 2 men from hosp. 11 NCOs & men posted to Bdes	E.A.G.
"	23/1/17		2 men struck off strength, 2 men to hospital.	E.A.G.
"	24/1/17		Capt. E.S. JAMES & 2/Lieut J. CASHIN joined D.A.C. 2/Lieut J. CASHIN posted to C/103 Bde 27/1/17	E.A.G.
"	25/1/17		Various promotions in D.A.C. Cpl Clayton to B/102 Bde	E.A.G.
"	26/1/17		10 N.C.Os. detailed for T.M. Course 1/2/17 & 9 men to Bdes	E.A.G.
"	27/1/17		2/Lt. E.R. CHEESMAN joined from Base. 9 animals struck off.	E.A.G.
"			50 Gunners & 10 Drivers posted to D.A.C. from Base.	
"	28/1/17		11 men posted to Bdes. 12 men posted to T.M. Btys 28/1/17	E.A.G.
"	29/1/17		2 men to hospital. 2 men from hospital. 2 NCOs posted	E.A.G.
"	30/1/17		2 men struck off strength. Usual fatigues	E.A.G.
"	31/1/17		T.M. Course to proceed to Course from Reninghelst.	E.A.G.

2353 Wt. W2544/1454 700,000 5/15 D. D. & L. A.D.S.S./Forms/C. 2118.

Instructions regarding War Diaries and Intelligence Summaries are contained in F. S. Regs., Part II. and the Staff Manual respectively. Title pages will be prepared in manuscript.

WAR DIARY
or
INTELLIGENCE SUMMARY.
(Erase heading not required.)

Army Form C. 2118.

Place	Date	Hour	Summary of Events and Information	Remarks and references to Appendices
POPERINGHE	1/2/17		5 men posted - 1 man to hosp - various returns called for.	DWSH
	2/2/17		Calling for names for T.M. Course. 3 men to hosp. 10 men	DWSH
"			to be detailed daily for inoculation. Various fatigues	DWSH
"	3/2/17		10 men posted to T.M. Bys. 2 men from T.M. Bys to D.A.C.	DWSH
"	4/2/17		4 men struck off. 1 man from T.M. Bys. 1 man to hospital	DWSH
"	5/2/17		Men not to go on Courses unless medically fit. 1 man to Hosp.	DWSH
"	6/2/17		2 men to hosp - 1 man from hosp. Field Dressing Class	DWSH
"			to commence 7/2/17 - Various fatigues	DWSH
"	7/2/17		16 N.C.Os & men posted to Bdes. 6 to D.A.C. from Base.	DWSH
"	8/2/17		5 men posted to Bdes, 5 to D.A.C. from Base, R.E. & Dump fatigues	DWSH
"	9/2/17		2 men struck off strength. R.E. & Dump fatigues	DWSH

Instructions regarding War Diaries and Intelligence Summaries are contained in F. S. Regs., Part II. and the Staff Manual respectively. Title pages will be prepared in manuscript.

WAR DIARY
or
INTELLIGENCE SUMMARY.
(Erase heading not required.)

Army Form C. 2118.

Place	Date	Hour	Summary of Events and Information	Remarks and references to Appendices
POPERINGHE	10 2/17		Corps Order re published, re Drafts arriving at front not equipped	DWSH
"	11 2/17		Return of Gum Boots, Thigh, to be rendered. Various fatigues	DWSH
"	12 2/17		Lecture at TALBOT HOUSE. 1 man from hospital. Fatigues	DWSH
"	13 2/17		5 horses struck off. 5 men to hosp. 2 men to T.M. Bty.	DWSH
"	14 2/17		3 men struck off. Corps Order of 7/2/17 published re Mange	DWSH
"	15 2/17		Order re wearing discs. 1 NCO struck off. Various fatigues	DWSH
"	16 2/17		2 men struck off strength. 2 men to hospl. Fatigues	DWSH
"	17 2/17		26 mules & 1 horse taken on strength. 1 NCO reverted	DWSH
"	18 2/17		134 NCOs & men joined from Base. 1 man struck off.	DWSH
"	19 2/17		2/Lt. BLOMFIELD joined D.A.C. from Base. 96 posted to Btties	DWSH
"	20 2/17		37 men posted to Sections. 5 L.D. to Mobile V.S. 3 men to Hosp.	DWSH
"	21 2/17		Capt. DALGLEISH struck off. 3 men struck off. Various fatigues	DWSH

2353 Wt. W2544/1454 700,000 5/15 D. D. & L. A.D.S.S./Forms/C. 2118.

Instructions regarding War Diaries and Intelligence Summaries are contained in F. S. Regs., Part II. and the Staff Manual respectively. Title pages will be prepared in manuscript.

WAR DIARY
or
INTELLIGENCE SUMMARY.

(Erase heading not required.)

Army Form C. 2118.

23 D Am Col
Vol 18

Place	Date	Hour	Summary of Events and Information	Remarks and references to Appendices
POPERINGHE	22 2/17		1 man to hospital, 1 man from hospital. Various fatigues	DWSH
"	23 2/17		22 Mules taken on strength. 2/Lt CHEESMAN posted to 1 Section	DWSH
"	24 2/17		3 men to hospital. 2/Lt LOCK posted to 1 Section. Fatigues	DWSH
"	25 2/17		D.A.C. marched to & billeted at HERZEELE.	DWSH
HERZEELE	26 2/17		D.A.C. marched to & billeted at BOLIZEEL	DWSH
BOLIZEELE	27 2/17		D.A.C. marched to & billeted at RUMINGHEN.	DWSH
"	28 2/17		Lieut D.W.S. HACKER took over Adjutancy of D.A.C. from Lieut E.A. EWART. 3 L.D. horses struck off	DWSH

2353 Wt. W2544/1454 700,000 5/15 D. D. & L. A.D.S.S./Forms/C. 2118.

Instructions regarding War Diaries and Intelligence Summaries are contained in F. S. Regs., Part II. and the Staff Manual respectively. Title pages will be prepared in manuscript.

WAR DIARY
or
INTELLIGENCE SUMMARY.
(Erase heading not required.)

Army Form C. 2118.

Place	Date	Hour	Summary of Events and Information	Remarks and references to Appendices
RUMINGHEM	1/3/17		2 men struck off. 1 N.C.O. promoted. Order re [illegible]	DWSH
"	2/3/17		1 horse destroyed. Wagons to Lederzeele for rations	DWSH
			at MUNCQ-NIEURLET to draw supplies–	Do
"	3/3/17		7 horses transferred. Various promotions. G.O.C. D.A. visited D.A.C.	DWSH
"	4/3/17		Refilling point J.15.b.6.1. Various promotions & appointments	DWSH
"	5/3/17		17 mules taken on strength. G.O.C. visited D.A.C.	DWSH
"	6/3/17		1 man to hospital. G.O.C. D.A. visited D.A.C.	DWSH.
"	7/3/17		2 men for F.G.C.M. Various promotions.	DWSH
"	8/3/17		1 man to Z/23 T.M. Bty. G.O.C. D.A. visited D.A.C.	DWSH
"	9/3/17		5 horses evacuated to Mob Vet Sect. 2nd Lt T.R. HAWKINS to hosp.	DWSH.
"	10/3/17		4 horses to Mob Vet Sect. 2 men to hospital.	DWSH
"	11/3/17		Empty petrol tins &c to be sent to Base. 1 man joined.	DWSH

Army Form C. 2118.

Instructions regarding War Diaries and Intelligence Summaries are contained in F. S. Regs., Part II. and the Staff Manual respectively. Title pages will be prepared in manuscript.

WAR DIARY
or
INTELLIGENCE SUMMARY.
(Erase heading not required.)

Place	Date	Hour	Summary of Events and Information	Remarks and references to Appendices
RUMINGHEM	12/3/17		2/Lieut MANN joined from Base. Lecture on Water Cart.	DWSH
"	13/3/17		2/Lieut MANN posted to 102 Bde. 26 Mules taken on strength.	DWSH.
"	14/3/17		3 Sergts attached to 103 Bde from D.A.C. ZENITH fuses to be dispatched to Base as per orders –	DWSH DWSH
"	15/3/17		6 NCOs & men from Base to 103 Bde. 2 men struck off.	DWSH
"	16/3/17		Order published re outbreak of measles in England	DWSH
"	17/3/17		1 man from hospital. Return called for re leave.	DWSH.
"	18/3/17		Demonstration in cooking. 5 horses to Mob Vet Section.	DWSH
"	19/3/17		Orders received to be ready to move at short notice.	DWSH
"	20/3/17		Cleaning up – General fatigues.	DWSH
"	21/3/17		D.A.C. marched & billeted at LEDERZEELE.	DWSH
LEDERZEELE	22/3/17		D.A.C. marched to HERZELE and billeted there.	DWSH

Instructions regarding War Diaries and Intelligence Summaries are contained in F. S. Regs., Part II. and the Staff Manual respectively. Title pages will be prepared in manuscript.

WAR DIARY
or
INTELLIGENCE SUMMARY.
(Erase heading not required.)

Army Form C. 2118.

23 D Am Col
Vol 19

Place	Date	Hour	Summary of Events and Information	Remarks and references to Appendices
HERZEELE	23 3/17		2 men to hospital, various promotions. fatigues.	DWSH
"	24 3/17		2 men committed to prison. 2 men to hospital.	DWSH
"	25 3/17		2 men from hospital. Capt. T. W. RICE. Lieut. A. ANDREWS joined.	DWSH
"	26 3/17		2/Lt. E. R. CHEESMAN to T. M. Bty. 2 men for F.G.C.M. 5 horses to M.V.S.	DWSH
"	27 3/17		Clean clothing to be drawn. 2 men to hospital. B 77 called for.	DWSH
"	28 3/17		G.O.C. 2nd Army inspected 2 Section in Drill order.	DWSH
"	29 3/17		2 men struck off. 1 man to hospital. Baths allotted to D.A.C.	DWSH
"	30 3/17		3 Sgts. posted to 103 Bde. Dripping returns called for.	DWSH
"	31 3/17		4 men struck off. Ct. of inquiry to Gr. Deacon – 2 men to hospital	DWSH

WAR DIARY
or
INTELLIGENCE SUMMARY.
(Erase heading not required.)

Instructions regarding War Diaries and Intelligence Summaries are contained in F. S. Regs., Part II. and the Staff Manual respectively. Title pages will be prepared in manuscript.

Army Form C. 2118.

23 D Arm Col
Vol 20

Place	Date	Hour	Summary of Events and Information	Remarks and references to Appendices
HERZEELE	1/4/17		Cpl Paterson died from injuries - Fatigues for Town Major	[illegible]
"	2/4/17		2/Lieuts F.G. PORSER, J.A. DIX & H. ARNOLL joined from Base.	[illegible]
			2 NCOs & 6 men posted to 103 Bde. 3 men to hospital. [illegible]	
"	3/4/17		5 horses struck off. Various [illegible]. Fatigues	[illegible]
"	4/4/17		Baths allotted to DAC. 1 Man to hospital. Fatigues	[illegible]
"	5/4/17		1 Man from hospital, fatigues at WORMHOUDT.	[illegible]
"	6/4/17		Divine Service. Lieut DIX to V/23 T.M. By. 1 Man to Base	[illegible]
"	7/4/17		G.O.C. R.A. visited DAC. Fatigues	[illegible]
"	8/4/17		1 Man struck off. Various fatigues	[illegible]
"	9/4/17		B. Echelon marched to forward area. G.14.d.0.5. Several	[illegible]
			promotions & appointments. Board detailed to examine	
			Cold Shoers for Shoeing Smiths	

Instructions regarding War Diaries and Intelligence Summaries are contained in F. S. Regs., Part II. and the Staff Manual respectively. Title pages will be prepared in manuscript.

WAR DIARY
or
INTELLIGENCE SUMMARY.
(Erase heading not required.)

Army Form C. 2118.

Place	Date	Hour	Summary of Events and Information	Remarks and references to Appendices
HERZEELE	10/4/17		3 men to hospital. 1 Mule struck off. Various fatigues.	DSH
"	11/4/17		4 men to hospital. 1 Mule died. Several promotions. Fatigues	DSH
"	12/4/17		1 Driver mustered Gunner, 1 Gunner mustered Driver. Fatigues	DSH
"	13/4/17		2/Lt JACKSON joined from Base. 2 men to hospital. 1 man from hosp.	DSH
"	14/4/17		No 5 Mills Grenades to be returned to Munitions Railhead	DSH
			6 Cold Shoers qualified as Shoeing Smiths. Fatigues	DSH
"	15/4/17		4 horses struck off 1 man to hospital. Fatigues	DSH
"	16/4/17		Lt ANDREWS posted to 2 Sections. 1 Sitter & 15 men to be posted to T.M.	DSH
"	17/4/17		3 men struck off. 2 men to hosp. 2 men discharged from hosp	DSH
"	18/4/17		3 men to hosp. 1 man from hosp. 2 Drivers mustered Gunners	DSH
"	19/4/17		H.Q. & D.A.C. (1&2 Sections) marched & billeted at Poperinghe	DSH.
POPERINGHE	20/4/17		6 men struck off strength. Sgt SAWYER & Q.M.S. LATTO to Base	DSH.

Instructions regarding War Diaries and Intelligence Summaries are contained in F. S. Regs., Part II. and the Staff Manual respectively. Title pages will be prepared in manuscript.

WAR DIARY
or
INTELLIGENCE SUMMARY.
(Erase heading not required.)

Army Form C. 2118.

Place	Date	Hour	Summary of Events and Information	Remarks and references to Appendices
POPERINGHE	21/4/17		34 details from Base. 18 Pr. Cartridges filled N.C.T. 14 to be returned to Dump – 5 men from hospital. Various fatigues.	D.W.S.H.
"	22/4/17		23 men posted to Bdes. 1 man to Sanitary Class. Fatigues	D.W.S.H.
"	23/4/17		Board of Officers on Cold Shoes – Baths allotted to D.A.C.	D.W.S.H.
"	24/4/17		Poperinghe Town Orders republished. 2 horses struck off – Fatigues	D.W.S.H.
"	25/4/17		1 man from D/103 posted. Mail Wagon detailed. Various fatigues	D.W.S.H.
"	26/4/17		Cpl. E. of Sgt Crawford injured – 4 C.S. qualified as Shoeing Smiths	D.W.S.H.
"	27/4/17		3 men from hospital, 1 horse to M.V. Section – Fatigues	D.W.S.H.
"	28/4/17		R.E. & Dump fatigues –	D.W.S.H.
"	29/4/17		2 men to hospital. G.O.C. R.A. visited D.A.C. – Fatigues	D.W.S.H.
"	30/4/17		2/Lieuts CLARK, LAMBERT & LOCK joined from Base & posted to Bdes, R.E. & Dump fatigues.	D.W.S.H.

2353 Wt. W2544/1454 700,000 5/15 D. D. & L. A.D.S.S./Forms/C. 2118.

Instructions regarding War Diaries and Intelligence Summaries are contained in F. S. Regs., Part II. and the Staff Manual respectively. Title pages will be prepared in manuscript.

WAR DIARY
or
INTELLIGENCE SUMMARY.
(Erase heading not required.)

Army Form C. 2118.

23 D Am Col

Vol 21

Place	Date	Hour	Summary of Events and Information	Remarks and references to Appendices
Poperinghe	1/5/17		4 men to hospital. 1 man to Cold Shoeing Course.	[illegible]
"	2/5/17		D.A.C. marched to & billeted at REVELD. No 1 Section at J.33.b.6.6. No 2 Section J.34.a.4.9. No 3 Section + H.Q. at J.27.d.2.8	[illegible]
REVELD	3/5/17		2 men to hospital. Lt ARNALL to 1 Section from 2 Section	[illegible]
"	4/5/17		G.O.C. 23 Division inspected whole D.A.C. horses &c	[illegible]
"	5/5/17		Coy parade. Orders published re Sanitation, also re water supply	[illegible]
"	6/5/17		1 man to hosp. 2 L.D. evacuated. 1 man struck off	[illegible]
"	7/5/17		Several promotions & appointments. 1 man struck off	[illegible]
"	8/5/17		Orders re move to forward area received. Clean clothes drawn from Steenvoorde for D.A.C. Lt HADDOCK, from Base	[illegible]
"	9/5/17		Establishment for Box Respirators issued. 1 man to hospital. Various promotions.	[illegible]

Instructions regarding War Diaries and Intelligence Summaries are contained in F. S. Regs., Part II. and the Staff Manual respectively. Title pages will be prepared in manuscript.

WAR DIARY
or
INTELLIGENCE SUMMARY.
(Erase heading not required.)

Army Form C. 2118.

Place	Date	Hour	Summary of Events and Information	Remarks and references to Appendices
REVELD	10/5/17		2/Lt MOSES posted to T.M. Bty. Order re green envelopes.	DWH
"	11/5/17		D.A.C. marched to & billeted & bivouaced at G.19.b.9.8.	DWH
			G.15.c.5.6. & G.14.d.0.5. 2/Lt F. SHEARBURN joined from 57 Div.	DWH
Poperinghe	12/5/17		H.Q. moved & bivouaced at G.14.a.8.2	DWH
	13/5/17		20 N.C.O.s & men posted to Bdes & Sections. Fatigues	DWH
	14/5/17		2/Lt CORSER to Bombing Course. Baths allotted for 15/5/17.	DWH
	15/5/17		Report called for re Box Respirators – Various fatigues.	DWH
"	16/5/17		11 men posted to T.M. Bty. Capt. WINDOW evacuated.	DWH
"	17/5/17		B.S.M. Pitman to R.S.M. Baths allotted H.Q. D.A.C.	DWH
			Moved to G.20.b.3.1 Fatigues	DWH
"	18/5/17		2 men to hospital. Various fatigues.	DWH

2353 Wt. W2544/1454 700,000 5/15 D. D. & L. A.D.S.S./Forms/C. 2118.

Army Form C. 2118.

Instructions regarding War Diaries and Intelligence Summaries are contained in F. S. Regs., Part II. and the Staff Manual respectively. Title pages will be prepared in manuscript.

WAR DIARY
or
INTELLIGENCE SUMMARY.
(Erase heading not required.)

Place	Date	Hour	Summary of Events and Information	Remarks and references to Appendices
POPERINGHE	19/5/17		Bn. Ws posted to 3 Section. 1 Man struck off - 2 men to hospital	DWSH
"	20/5/17		Order re upkeep of spare parts. 1 Man to hosp. Fatigues	DWSH
"	21/5/17		Baths allotted as follows. 3 men to hosp. Fatigues	DWSH
"	22/5/17		Various Ammunition & D.C. fatigues.	DWSH
"	23/5/17		4 men struck off 3 men from [illegible] - fatigues	DWSH
"	24/5/17		40 horses to be dipped. Baths allotted - fatigues	DWSH
"	25/5/17		Various Ammunition, D.C. & Dump fatigues	DWSH
"	26/5/17		3 men to hospital 3 men from hospital. Fatigues.	DWSH
"	27/5/17		1 Man joined from prison. D.C. & Dump fatigues.	DWSH
"	28/5/17		6 men struck off strength. 1 Man to hospital - Fatigues.	DWSH

2353 Wt. W2544/1454 700,000 5/15 D. D. & L. A.D.S.S./Forms/C. 2118.

Instructions regarding War Diaries and Intelligence Summaries are contained in F. S. Regs., Part II. and the Staff Manual respectively. Title pages will be prepared in manuscript.

WAR DIARY
or
INTELLIGENCE SUMMARY.
(Erase heading not required.)

Army Form C. 2118.

Place	Date	Hour	Summary of Events and Information	Remarks and references to Appendices
POPERINGHE	29/5/17		Lieut ANDREWS killed. 1 O.R. killed, 2/Lt CORSER + 4 O.R. wounded	WSH
"	30/5/17		4 men to hosp, 2 men from hosp. 6 horses struck off.	WSH
"	31/5/17		4 horses struck off. 2/Lt HAWKINS from hosp. Fatigues	WSH.

2353 Wt. W2544/1454 700,000 5/15 D. D. & L. A.D.S.S./Forms/C. 2118.

Instructions regarding War Diaries and Intelligence Summaries are contained in F. S. Regs., Part II. and the Staff Manual respectively. Title pages will be prepared in manuscript.

WAR DIARY
or
INTELLIGENCE SUMMARY.
(Erase heading not required.)

Army Form C. 2118.

23 D Am Col
Vol 22

Place	Date	Hour	Summary of Events and Information	Remarks and references to Appendices
DOZERINGHE	1/6/17		St ANDREWS & CORSER struck off. Order re Traffic	DWSH
"	2/6/17		1 man Killed 5 Wounded Lt. Raff from [illegible] joined.	DWSH
"	3/6/17		R.E. & Dump fatigues.	DWSH
"	4/6/17		6 men struck off 6 men to hospital. 1 man to Base. fatigues	DWSH
"	5/6/17		Cpl. on injuries. R.E. and Dump fatigues	DWSH
"	6/6/17		22 Mules taken on strength Fatigues.	DWSH
"	7/6/17		1 man Killed in action. 2 men from hospital.	DWSH
"	8/6/17		24 men posted to 103 Bde 4 men Wounded in action	DWSH
"	9/6/17		R.E. & Dump fatigues.	DWSH
"	10/6/17		30 horses taken on strength 2 men to hosp. Fatigues	DWSH
"	11/6/17		2 men to hospital. 100 men to Baths. Fatigues	DWSH

2353 Wt. W2544/1454 700,000 5/15 D. D. & L. A.D.S.S./Forms/C. 2118.

Instructions regarding War Diaries and Intelligence Summaries are contained in F. S. Regs., Part II. and the Staff Manual respectively. Title pages will be prepared in manuscript.

WAR DIARY
or
INTELLIGENCE SUMMARY.
(Erase heading not required.)

Army Form C. 2118.

Place	Date	Hour	Summary of Events and Information	Remarks and references to Appendices
POPERINGHE	12/6/17		R. E. & Dump fatigues	DWSH
"	13/6/17		D.A.C. moved and marched to H.31.c.5.0 Sheet 28.	DWSH
H.31.c.5.0	14/6/17		2/Lt Coad joined from Base. 4 men from hospital. One man joined from prison. Fatigues	DWSH
"	15/6/17		2 men posted - various wagon fatigues	DWSH
"	16/6/17		22 horses taken on strength. 1 man to hospital	DWSH
"	17/6/17		Various wagon fatigues -	DWSH
"	18/6/17		Various wagon fatigues.	DWSH
"	19/6/17		2 men struck off - 4 men to hospital. Fatigues	DWSH
"	20/6/17		2 men from hospital. Various fatigues	DWSH
"	21/6/17		14 NCOs from Base arrived. 2 men from hospital	DWSH
"	22/6/17		DAC received orders at 11 am & marched at 3 pm to (Sheet 27) HQ & No 1 at Q.23.c.8.5. No 2 Sect Q.23.a.3.3. No 3 Section at Q.28.b.9.9.	DWSH

2353 Wt. W3544/1454 700,000 5/15 D. D. & L. A.D.S.S./Forms/C. 2118.

Instructions regarding War Diaries and Intelligence Summaries are contained in F. S. Regs., Part II. and the Staff Manual respectively. Title pages will be prepared in manuscript.

WAR DIARY
or
INTELLIGENCE SUMMARY.

(Erase heading not required.)

Army Form C. 2118.

Place	Date	Hour	Summary of Events and Information	Remarks and references to Appendices
Q.23.c.8.5	23/6/17		14 NCOs posted to Bdes. 2 men to hospital. 4 men to T.M. Coys	[illegible]
"	24/6/17		Bands allotted to Bdes. 3 Lorries struck off. Div. Horse Show held	[illegible]
"	25/6/17		2 & 3 Sections warned to be ready to move to new lines.	[illegible]
"	26/6/17		2 & 3 Sections moved to Q.24.a.2.5 & Q.29.b.5.6. 2 men from hospital	[illegible]
"	27/6/17		1 NCO wounded. 2/Lieut Corser rejoined from Hospital	[illegible]
"	28/6/17		1 NCO & 6 men from Base. 2 S/Smiths joined. 1 man to hosp.	[illegible]
"	29/6/17		1 NCO & 5 men posted to Bdes. 1 man to hospital	[illegible]
"	30/6/17		2 men to hospital, 1 Sergt. & 1 Driver tried by F.G.C.M.	[illegible]

Instructions regarding War Diaries and Intelligence Summaries are contained in F. S. Regs., Part II. and the Staff Manual respectively. Title pages will be prepared in manuscript.

WAR DIARY
or
INTELLIGENCE SUMMARY.
(Erase heading not required.)

Army Form C. 2118.

23 D Am Col

Jul 23

Place	Date	Hour	Summary of Events and Information	Remarks and references to Appendices
G. 23. c. 5. 8	1/7/17		2 F.G. C.M. promulgated. B.S.M. Tayler posted to 102 Bde	[initials]
"	2/7/17		2 men to hospital 1 man from hospital. 1 A.V.C. Sgt joined	[initials]
"	3/7/17		2/Lt SHEARBURN to 102 Bde. 1 Cpl reverted to Gunner.	[initials]
"	4/7/17		D.A.C. marched & camped at H.Q. N.3.b.2.9	
			No. 1 Section H.31.c.3.7. 2 Sect N.2.b.6.9. 3 Sect. K.33.d.5.5	[initials]
N.3.b.2.9 Sheet 28	5/7/17		Various fatigues.	[initials]
"	6/7/17		51 men joined from Base. 2 men to hospital. Fatigues.	[initials]
"	7/7/17		48 men posted to 102 & 3 Bdes. 2/Lt HAWKINS to hospital	[initials]
"	8/7/17		R.E. & Dump fatigues. Dr Besford to prison	[initials]
"	9/7/17		4 men struck off strength. 2 men wounded. Fatigues	
			No. 3 Section moved to G.35.c.8.6.	[initials]

2353 Wt. W2544/1454 700,000 5/15 D. D. & L. A.D.S.S./Forms/C. 2118.

Instructions regarding War Diaries and Intelligence Summaries are contained in F. S. Regs., Part II. and the Staff Manual respectively. Title pages will be prepared in manuscript.

WAR DIARY
or
INTELLIGENCE SUMMARY.
(Erase heading not required.)

Army Form C. 2118.

Place	Date	Hour	Summary of Events and Information	Remarks and references to Appendices
N.36.2.9	10/7/17		2 men to hospital. 2 men died. H.Q. DAC moved to N.1. Central Sheet 28 opposite A.R.P.	FWSH
N.I.Central	11/7/17		Baths allotted to DAC. R.E. & Dump fatigues	FWSH
"	12/7/17		Sgt Taylor to England for Cadet Course. 4 men struck off.	FWSH
"	13/7/17		27 N.C.O.s & men joined from Base & posted to Bdes.	FWSH
"	14/7/17		4 men to hospital. 2 men wounded. 18 N.C.O.s & men joined from Base & posted to Brigades. Fatigues.	FWSH
"	15/7/17		2/Lt. JACKSON to T.M. Bty. 4 men to hospital. Fatigues	FWSH
"	16/7/17		Order published re handling Gas Shells. 2 men wounded.	FWSH
"	17/7/17		2 men to hospital 2 men from hospital. Various fatigues	FWSH
"	18/7/17		3 N.C.O.s to Gas Course. 3 men struck off. Fatigues Dump at N.1 Central handed over to 24th Division	FWSH

2353 Wt. W2544/1454 700,000 5/15 D. D. & L. A.D.S.S./Forms/C. 2118.

Instructions regarding War Diaries and Intelligence Summaries are contained in F. S. Regs., Part II. and the Staff Manual respectively. Title pages will be prepared in manuscript.

WAR DIARY
or
INTELLIGENCE SUMMARY.
(Erase heading not required.)

Army Form C. 2118.

Place	Date	Hour	Summary of Events and Information	Remarks and references to Appendices
N. 1. Canal	19 7/17		26 men joined from Base. 2 men from hospital. Fatigues.	FWSH
"	20 7/17		25 men posted to Bdes. 14 L.D. horses posted to DAC.	FWSH
"	21 7/17		Return of leave allotment. 3 men to hosp. Fatigues	FWSH
"	22 7/17		2 men from hospital. 3 Acting Bdrs appd. - Fatigues	FWSH
"	23 7/17		Darts allotted to DAC. 23 Div attached to 24 Division for Ordnance Services. 4 men to hospital. Fatigues	FWSH
"	24 7/17		R.E. and Ammunition fatigues.	FWSH
"	25 7/17		2 men wounded. Return of Skilled Tradesmen called for. 1 man to hospital. 1 man from hospital.	FWSH

2353 Wt. W2544/1454 700,000 5/15 D. D. & L. A.D.S.S./Forms/C. 2118.

Instructions regarding War Diaries and Intelligence Summaries are contained in F. S. Regs., Part II. and the Staff Manual respectively. Title pages will be prepared in manuscript.

WAR DIARY
or
INTELLIGENCE SUMMARY.
(Erase heading not required.)

Army Form C. 2118.

Place	Date	Hour	Summary of Events and Information	Remarks and references to Appendices
N.1. Central	26/7/17		3 N.C.Os from Gas Course. Orders re Camelcar.	[illegible]
"	27/7/17		2nd Lt A.H. PARKER joined from 103 Bde. 3 N.C.Os for Gas Course.	[illegible]
"	28/7/17		D.E. Dump & wagon fatigues.	[illegible]
"	29/7/17		1 officer & 70 men to forward area on road making fatigues	[illegible]
"	30/7/17		7 men to hospital. 2 men of Road making party killed. 2 men from hospital. 1 man wounded. Fatigues.	[illegible]
"	31/7/17		2 Mules struck off. 2 men to hospital. 2 men killed in action	[illegible]

Instructions regarding War Diaries and Intelligence Summaries are contained in F. S. Regs., Part II. and the Staff Manual respectively. Title pages will be prepared in manuscript.

WAR DIARY
or
INTELLIGENCE SUMMARY.
(Erase heading not required.)

Army Form C. 2118.

Vol 24

Place	Date	Hour	Summary of Events and Information	Remarks and references to Appendices
N. 1. Central	1/8/17		Ammunition R.E. & Wagon fatigues	[initials]
"	2/8/17		2 N.C.Os. to Gas Course. 6 men struck off	[initials]
"	3/8/17		3 N.C.Os. from Gas School. 2 men to hospital. Div. Fatigues	[initials]
"	4/8/17		2 men to hospital. Return of Tradesmen called for.	[initials]
"	5/8/17		4 men struck off. 27 men from Base posted to	[initials]
	"		Ddes. 4 men admitted to hospital. Div. Fatigues.	[initials]
"	6/8/17		R.E. & Ammunition fatigues	[initials]
"	7/8/17		8 men (6 wounded) to hospital. 2 O.R. struck off	[initials]
"	8/8/17		11 men struck off strength. 4 horses posted to Ddes	[initials]
"	9/8/17		R.E. Dump & Ammunition fatigues	[initials]

Instructions regarding War Diaries and Intelligence Summaries are contained in F. S. Regs., Part II. and the Staff Manual respectively. Title pages will be prepared in manuscript.

WAR DIARY
or
INTELLIGENCE SUMMARY.

(Erase heading not required.)

Army Form C. 2118.

Place	Date	Hour	Summary of Events and Information	Remarks and references to Appendices
N.1 Canal	10/8/17		49 men from Base posted to Brigades. 2 men to hosp.	RWH
"	11/8/17		51 men from Base posted to Bdes & D.A.C. Fatigues	RWH
"	12/8/17		29 men from Base posted to Bdes. Various fatigues	RWH
"	13/8/17		25 men from Base posted to Bdes & Sections. Fatigues	RWH
"	14/8/17		G.O.C. R.A. presented medal to Cpl. Tait. Fatigues	RWH
"	15/8/17		D.A.C. marched & bivouaced at F.24.a.5.5 (Sheet 27)	RWH
F.24.a.5.5	16/8/17		2 Off. 100 men & 200 horses with pack saddlery employed with 4 & D.A.C. 12 men from Base posted to Bdes	RWH
"	17/8/17		G.O.C. R.A. visited D.A.C. Fatigues	RWH
"	18/8/17		2 fitters posted to 102 Bde. 1 man to hospital.	RWH
"	19/8/17		3 men tried by F.G.C.M. Various fatigues	RWH
"	20/8/17		3 men struck off - 4 men to hospital. 2 L.D. struck off	RWH

Instructions regarding War Diaries and Intelligence Summaries are contained in F. S. Regs., Part II. and the Staff Manual respectively. Title pages will be prepared in manuscript.

WAR DIARY
or
INTELLIGENCE SUMMARY.
(Erase heading not required.)

Army Form C. 2118.

Place	Date	Hour	Summary of Events and Information	Remarks and references to Appendices
F.24.a.5.5	21/8/17		New A.R.P. taken over by Lieut Kidd – H.2.d.8.5	[illegible]
"	22/8/17		H.Q. & 'A' Echelon moved to A.30.b.9.7 (Sheet 28)	[illegible]
A30.b.9.7	23/8/17		3 men to hospital, 4 men from hospital. 1 man wounded.	[illegible]
"	24/8/17		10 men struck off – F.G.C.M. at H.Q. D.A.C. 3 Sections moved to B.26.c.6.0	[illegible]
"	25/8/17		107 men joined from Base. Ammunition fatigues.	[illegible]
"	26/8/17		107 men posted to Btns & Sections. Various fatigues	[illegible]
"	27/8/17		10 men of T.F. allotted fresh numbers. fatigues.	[illegible]
"	28/8/17		R.S.M. Ransome to hospital. Various fatigues.	[illegible]
"	29/8/17		2 horses struck off. Sentence of Dr Stowell suspended.	[illegible]
"	30/8/17		6 men wanted for T.M. Course – various promotions.	[illegible]
"	31/8/17		2 Cpls from Base posted to Btns. Dr Ogden tried by F.G.C.M.	[illegible]

2353 Wt. W2544/1454 700,000 5/15 D. D. & L. A.D.S.S./Forms/C. 2118.

Instructions regarding War Diaries and Intelligence Summaries are contained in F. S. Regs., Part II. and the Staff Manual respectively. Title pages will be prepared in manuscript.

WAR DIARY
or
INTELLIGENCE SUMMARY.
(Erase heading not required.)

Army Form C. 2118.

Vol 25

Place	Date	Hour	Summary of Events and Information	Remarks and references to Appendices
Sheet 28 A30.b.9.7	1/9/17		4 Gunners posted to 102 Bde. R.E. & Dump fatigues	DWSH
"	2/9/17		2/Lt. TULLOCH-GAIR joined from 103 Bde, 3 men to hospital	
"			4 men from hospital, 2 men 2 Section killed in action	DWSH
"	3/9/17		2 men struck off. R.E. & Ammunition fatigues.	DWSH.
"	4/9/17		3 men from Base posted to 103 Bde. 3 men to hospital.	DWSH
"	5/9/17		9 L.D. taken on strength. Various fatigues.	DWSH.
"	6/9/17		Orders received to move to back area – fatigues	DWSH.
"	7/9/17		D.A.C. marched to & bivouaced at HAMHOEK.	DWSH
HAMHOEK	8/9/17		D.A.C. marched to – H.Q. The Square, BOESCHEPE. No 1 & 2 Section R.8.d.8.6 (Sheet 27) No 3 Section at M.8.a.3.4 (Sheet 28)	DWSH
BOESCHEPE	9/9/17		R.S.M. Ransome & B.S.M. Smith struck off. Sent to T.M. Course	DWSH

2353 Wt. W2544/1454 700,000 5/15 D. D. & L. A.D.S.S./Forms/C. 2118.

Instructions regarding War Diaries and Intelligence Summaries are contained in F. S. Regs., Part II. and the Staff Manual respectively. Title pages will be prepared in manuscript.

WAR DIARY
or
INTELLIGENCE SUMMARY.
(Erase heading not required.)

Army Form C. 2118.

Place	Date	Hour	Summary of Events and Information	Remarks and references to Appendices
BOESCHOPE	10/9/17		2 men from Base posted to 103 Bde. 3 men to T.M's. Fatigues	DWH
"	11/9/17		9 men from Base posted to 103 Bde. 1 man evacuated.	DWH
"	12/9/17		No. 2 Section moved to forward area N.8.b.5.6 (Sheet 28)	DWH
"	13/9/17		Took over A.R.P. at N.1. central, Sheet 27. 5 men from Base	DWH
"	14/9/17		11 Water Carts & harness drawn from ABEELE & taken to HQ D.A. No 1 Section moved to R.17.a.0.3 (Sheet 27)	DWH
"	15/9/17		43 N.C.O's & men from Base. B.S.M. Alexander Commissioned	DWH
"	16/9/17		Draft from Base posted to Bdes & D.A.C. 2 men wounded.	DWH
"	17/9/17		1 Man to Base (released for mining) Fatigues	DWH
"	18/9/17		29 men from Base posted. 2 men committed to prison.	DWH

2353 Wt. W2544/1454 700,000 5/15 D. D. & L. A.D.S.S./Forms/C. 2118.

WAR DIARY

or

INTELLIGENCE SUMMARY.

(Erase heading not required.)

Army Form C. 2118.

Instructions regarding War Diaries and Intelligence Summaries are contained in F. S. Regs., Part II. and the Staff Manual respectively. Title pages will be prepared in manuscript.

Place	Date	Hour	Summary of Events and Information	Remarks and references to Appendices
BOESCHEPPE	19/9/17		9 men attached N.T.M. 5 Drivers marked Class. 1 man to Base (under age). Various fatigues.	DWH
"	20/9/17		Leave via Boulogne suspended. 2/Lt Gibb N.F. attached to 23rd A.R.P. for instructions. Fatigues	DWH
"	21/9/17		2 men struck off. 1 man to hospital. [illegible] awarded Mil. Medal	DWH
"	22/9/17		Usual Ammunition supply – Various fatigues	DWH
"	23/9/17		1 man to hospital. No 1 Section moved into H. 34 c. 5.5 (Sheet 27)	DWH
"	24/9/17		1 A.V.C. Sergeant invalided – Usual fatigues.	DWH
"	25/9/17		1 man to hospital. Sailings via Calais resumed. Fatigues.	DWH
"	26/9/17		9 men joined from Base. 1 Sergt wounded. Fatigues.	DWH
"	27/9/17		7 men posted to Bdes, 6 men from T.M. Course – 1 man to hosp.	DWH
"	28/9/17		1 Sergt to hospital. Usual Ammunition Supply	DWH
"	29/9/17		26 men posted to Bdes from Base. 2 men to hospital –	DWH
"	30/9/17		4 horses killed & 4 wounded, shell fire. Fatigues.	DWH

Instructions regarding War Diaries and Intelligence Summaries are contained in F. S. Regs., Part II. and the Staff Manual respectively. Title pages will be prepared in manuscript.

WAR DIARY
or
INTELLIGENCE SUMMARY.
(Erase heading not required.)

Army Form C. 2118.

Place	Date	Hour	Summary of Events and Information	Remarks and references to Appendices
BOESCHEPE	1/10/17		71 horses arrived from Calais. 1 Cpl. from Base. 6 L.D. Killed	M
"	2/10/17		4 men to hospital. 3 men wounded in action. Fatigues.	M
"	3/10/17		43 men from Base posted to Bdes. Fatigues.	M
"	4/10/17		1 man killed & 3 wounded in action. 1 man died from wounds.	M
"	5/10/17		11 N.C.Os from Base. 1 man to hospital. Fatigues	M
"	6/10/17		1 S.S. Corpl to Base. 11 N.C.Os. posted to Brigades.	M
"	7/10/17		Winter time came into use. 6 Gunners sent to 103 Bde	M
"	8/10/17		12 N.C.Os from Base. 2 men wounded. 3 men to hospital	M
"	9/10/17		24 NCOs & men posted to Bdes. Usual Ammunition supply	M
"	10/10/17		2Lt HAWKINS to 102 Bde. Order re protection of horse lines from Bombs. 6 G.S. Wagons attached Bomb store	M
"	11/10/17		16 men from Base posted to Bdes. 6 men from D.A.C. to 103 Bde. B.S.M. HARMAN & BOWDEN posted to D.A.C. Fatigues	M
"	12/10/17		72 men joined from Base. 1 man killed in action. Fatigues	M
"	13/10/17		72 men posted to Bdes. 1 man to hospital. Fatigues	M

T2134. Wt. W708—776. 500000. 4/15. Sir J. C. & S.

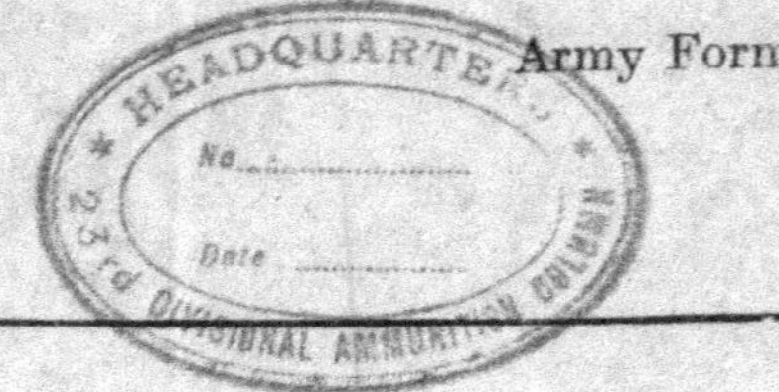

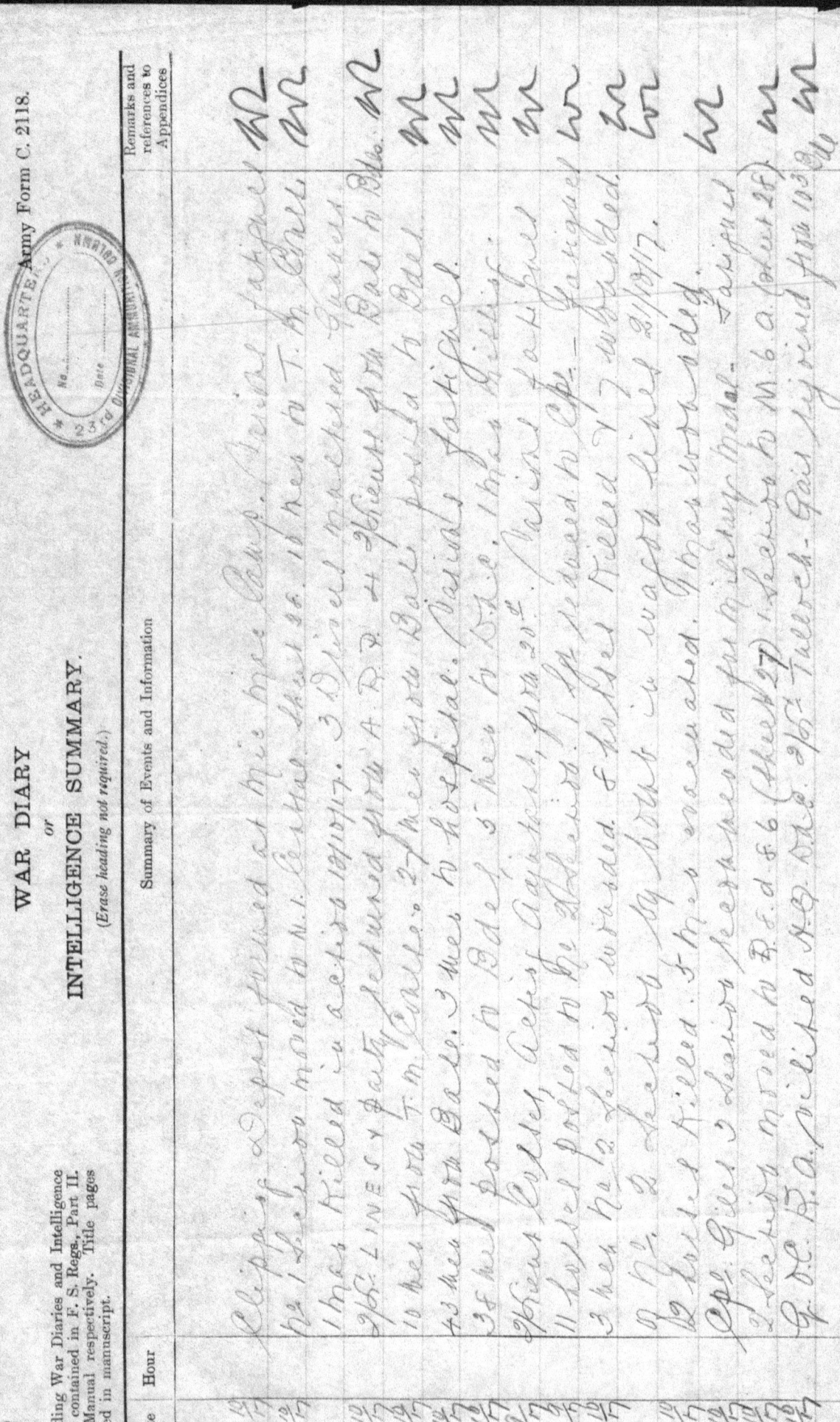

Army Form C. 2118.

Instructions regarding War Diaries and Intelligence Summaries are contained in F. S. Regs., Part II. and the Staff Manual respectively. Title pages will be prepared in manuscript.

WAR DIARY
or
INTELLIGENCE SUMMARY.
(Erase heading not required.)

Place	Date	Hour	Summary of Events and Information	Remarks and references to Appendices
BOESCHEPE	14/10/17		Clipping Depot formed at Mic Mac Camp. Various fatigues	WR
"	15/10/17		No 1 Section moved to N.1. Central Sheet 28. 10 men to T.M. Course	WR
			1 man killed in action 13/10/17. 3 Drivers attached Guards.	
"	16/10/17		2/Lt LINES & party returned from A.R.P. 4 2/Lieuts from Base to Bdes.	WR
"	17/10/17		10 men from T.M. Course. 27 men from Base posted to Bdes.	WR
"	18/10/17		43 men from Base. 3 men to hospital. Various fatigues.	WR
"	19/10/17		38 men posted to Bdes, 5 men to D.A.C. 1 man missing.	WR
"	20/10/17		2/Lieut Coles, Acting Adjutant, from 20th. Various fatigues	WR
"	21/10/17		11 horses posted to No 2 Section. 1 Sgt reduced to Cpl. — Fatigues	WR
"	22/10/17		3 men No 2 Section wounded. 8 horses killed & 7 wounded.	WR
			of No. 2 Section by bomb in wagon lines 21/10/17.	WR
"	23/10/17		2 horses killed. 5 men evacuated. 1 man wounded.	WR
"	24/10/17		Cpl. Giles 3 Section recommended for Military Medal — Fatigues	WR
"	25/10/17		2 Sections moved to R.8.d.8.6 (Sheet 27) 1 Section to M.6.a. (Sheet 28)	WR
"	26/10/17		G.O.C. R.A. visited H.Q. D.A.C. 2/Lt Tulloch-Gair rejoined from 103 Bde	WR

T2134. Wt. W708—776. 500000. 4/15. Sir J. C. & S.

Instructions regarding War Diaries and Intelligence Summaries are contained in F. S. Regs., Part II. and the Staff Manual respectively. Title pages will be prepared in manuscript.

WAR DIARY
or
INTELLIGENCE SUMMARY.
(Erase heading not required.)

Army Form C. 2118.

Vol 26

Place	Date	Hour	Summary of Events and Information	Remarks and references to Appendices
BOESCHEPE	27/10/17		No. 1 Section moved to R.C. 2 9. 2 (Sheet 27) 2 men to hospital. Various promotions made.	WL
"	28/10/17		22 men from Base posted to Bdes. 2 Drivers [illegible] [illegible]. Orders to march out received.	WL
"	29/10/17		2 men to hospital. 64 Remounts issued. G.O.C. R.A. visited H.Q. D.A.C. All men recalled from leave.	WL
"	30/10/17		10 men from Base posted to Bde. 3 men to hospital. Fatigues.	WL
"	31/10/17		3 men struck off. 8 men from T.M. Course. Fatigues.	WL

T2134. Wt. W708—776. 500000. 4/15. Sir J. C. & S.

www.ingramcontent.com/pod-product-compliance
Lightning Source LLC
Chambersburg PA
CBHW081427300426
44108CB00016BA/2318
* 9 7 8 1 4 7 4 5 1 2 5 1 0 *